結界師

KEKKAISHI

31

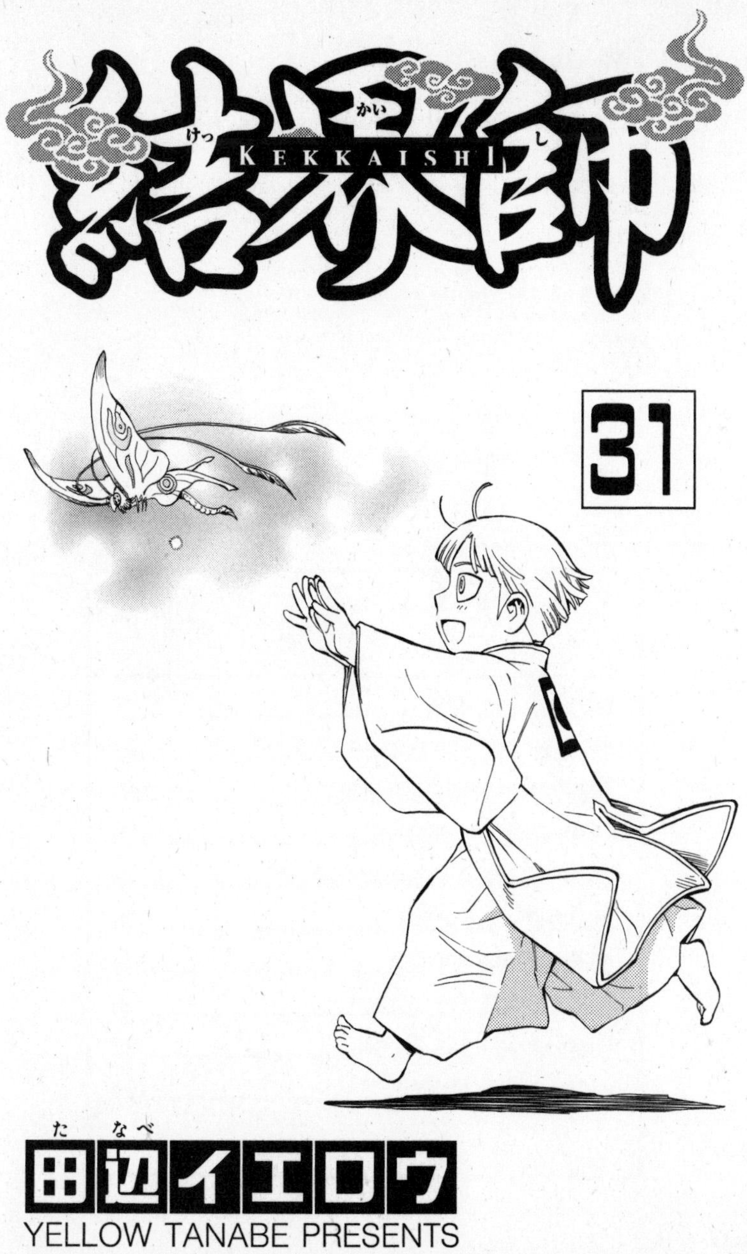

田辺イエロウ

YELLOW TANABE PRESENTS

THE STORY THUS FAR

Yoshimori enters the mysterious black castle that has arisen from the Karasumori Site. When he at last meets Karasumori's guardian face-to-face, he is confronted by...a little child with an innocent smile.

Guided by the shikigami who is the spitting image of his mother, Sumiko, Yoshimori sets out on a journey to transport Lord Chushinmaru from Karasumori to a new home.

The two reach an abandoned house in the mountains where Yoshimori hopes to train to seal the Lord of Karasumori once and for all. But the two are confronted by a mysterious man who controls an ayakashi named Kumon..and Yoshimori is easily lured into a trap!

KEKKAISHI VOL. 31

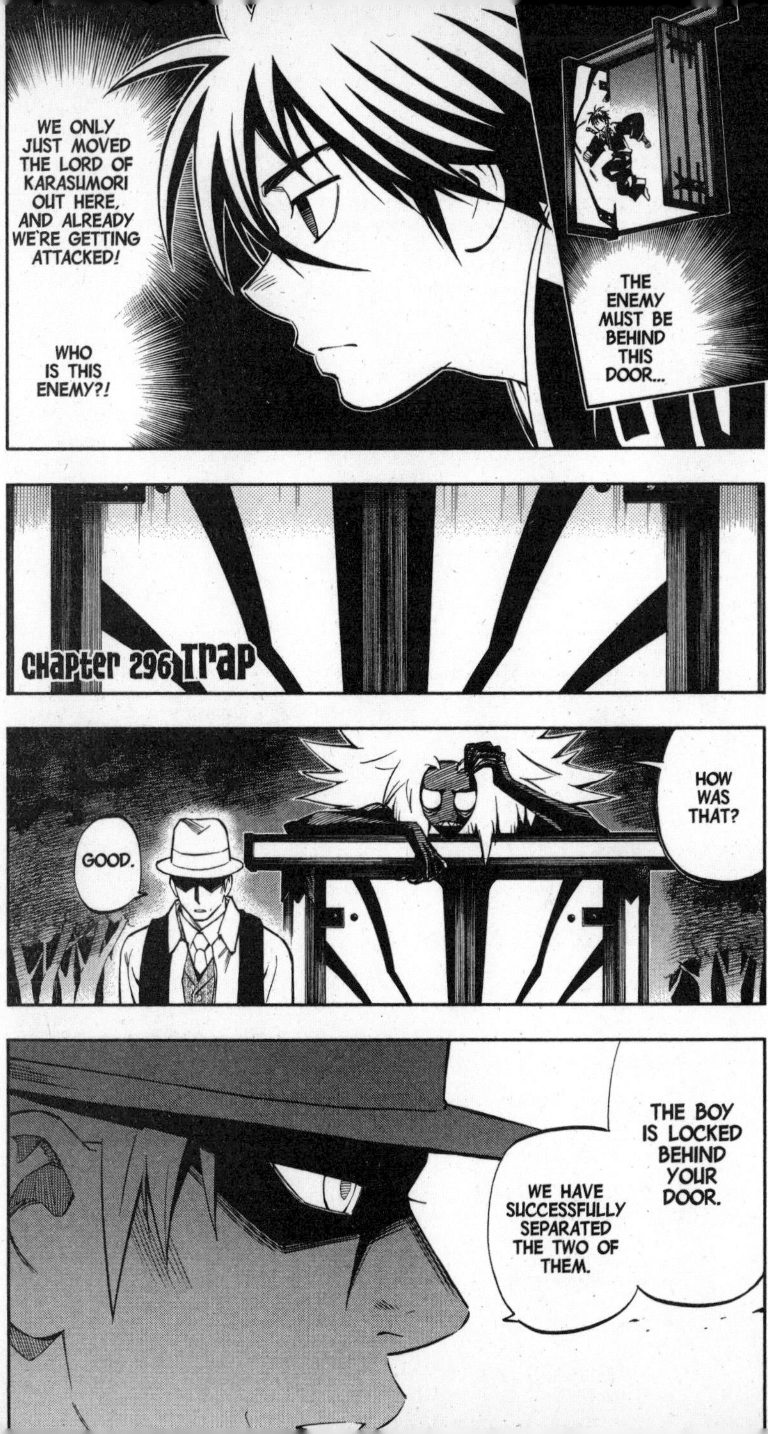
THE ENEMY MUST BE BEHIND THIS DOOR...
WE ONLY JUST MOVED THE LORD OF KARASUMORI OUT HERE, AND ALREADY WE'RE GETTING ATTACKED!
WHO IS THIS ENEMY?!
Chapter 296 Trap
HOW WAS THAT?
GOOD.
THE BOY IS LOCKED BEHIND YOUR DOOR.
WE HAVE SUCCESSFULLY SEPARATED THE TWO OF THEM.

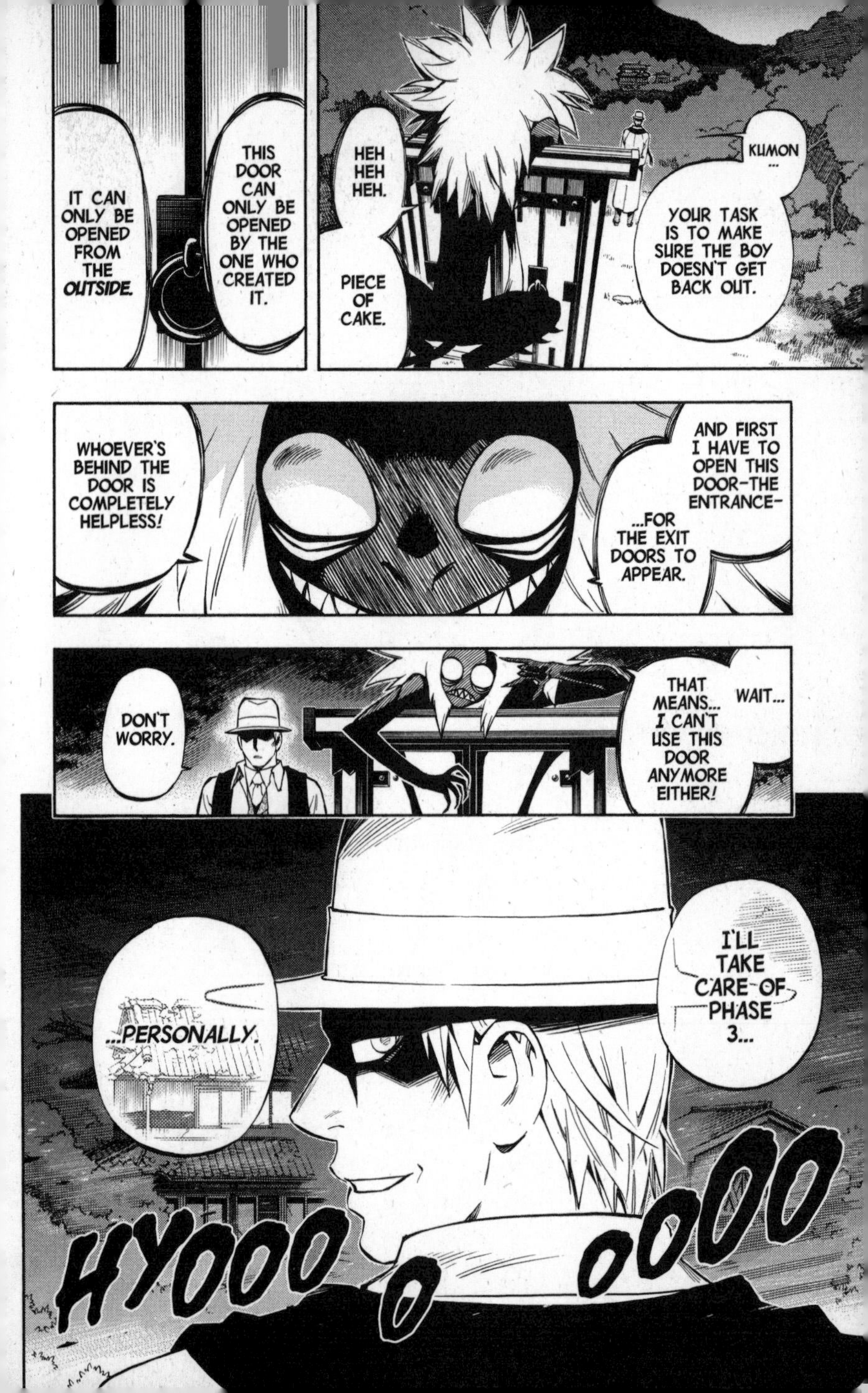
KUMON ...
YOUR TASK IS TO MAKE SURE THE BOY DOESN'T GET BACK OUT.
HEH HEH HEH.
PIECE OF CAKE.
THIS DOOR CAN ONLY BE OPENED BY THE ONE WHO CREATED IT.
IT CAN ONLY BE OPENED FROM THE *OUTSIDE.*
AND FIRST I HAVE TO OPEN THIS DOOR–THE ENTRANCE–
...FOR THE EXIT DOORS TO APPEAR.
WHOEVER'S BEHIND THE DOOR IS COMPLETELY HELPLESS!
WAIT...
THAT MEANS... *I* CAN'T USE THIS DOOR ANYMORE EITHER!
DON'T WORRY.
I'LL TAKE CARE OF PHASE 3...
...PERSONALLY.
HYOOO O OOOO

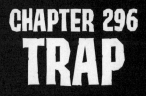

CHAPTER 296
TRAP

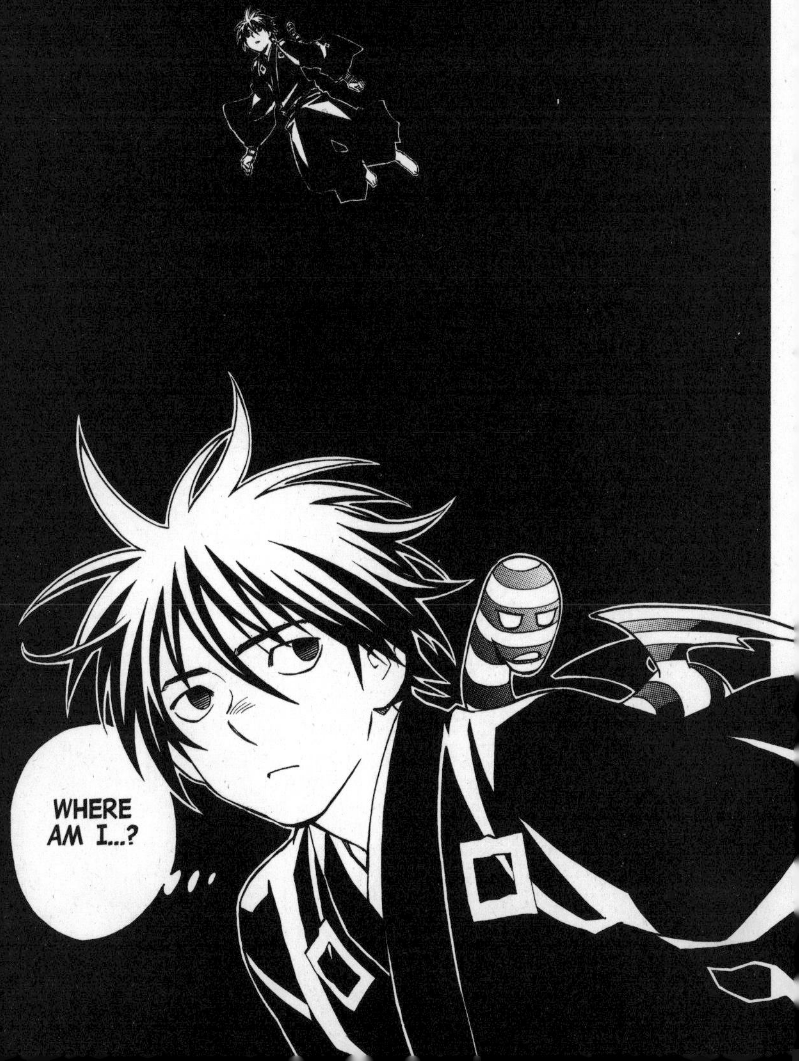
WHERE AM I...?

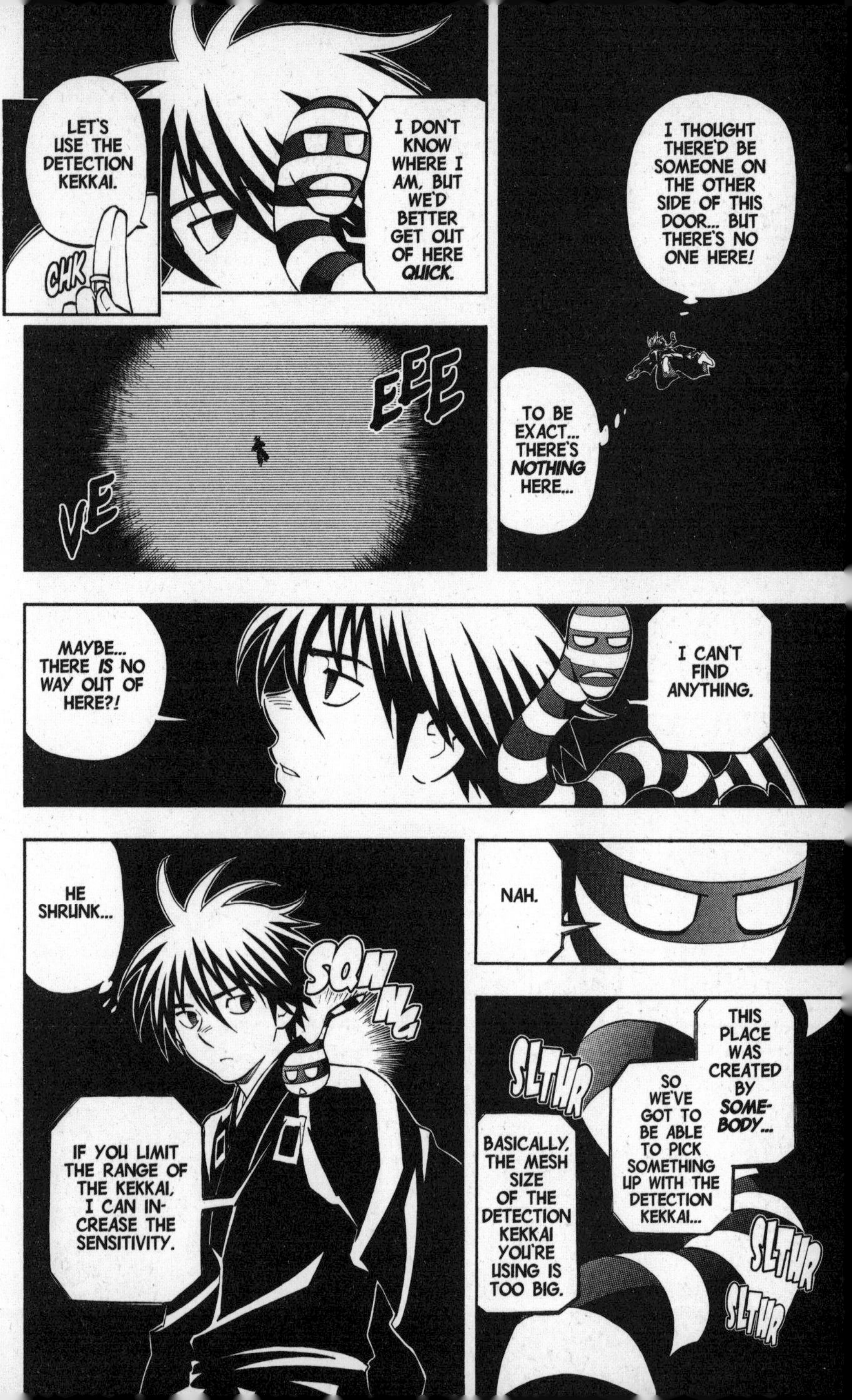
I THOUGHT THERE'D BE SOMEONE ON THE OTHER SIDE OF THIS DOOR... BUT THERE'S NO ONE HERE!
TO BE EXACT... THERE'S *NOTHING* HERE...
I DON'T KNOW WHERE I AM, BUT WE'D BETTER GET OUT OF HERE *QUICK*.
LET'S USE THE DETECTION KEKKAI.
CHK
EEE
VE
I CAN'T FIND ANYTHING.
MAYBE... THERE *IS* NO WAY OUT OF HERE?!
NAH.
THIS PLACE WAS CREATED BY *SOMEBODY*...
SO WE'VE GOT TO BE ABLE TO PICK SOMETHING UP WITH THE DETECTION KEKKAI...
SLTHR
BASICALLY, THE MESH SIZE OF THE DETECTION KEKKAI YOU'RE USING IS TOO BIG.
SLTHR
SLTHR
HE SHRUNK...
SQNNG
IF YOU LIMIT THE RANGE OF THE KEKKAI, I CAN IN-CREASE THE SENSITIVITY.

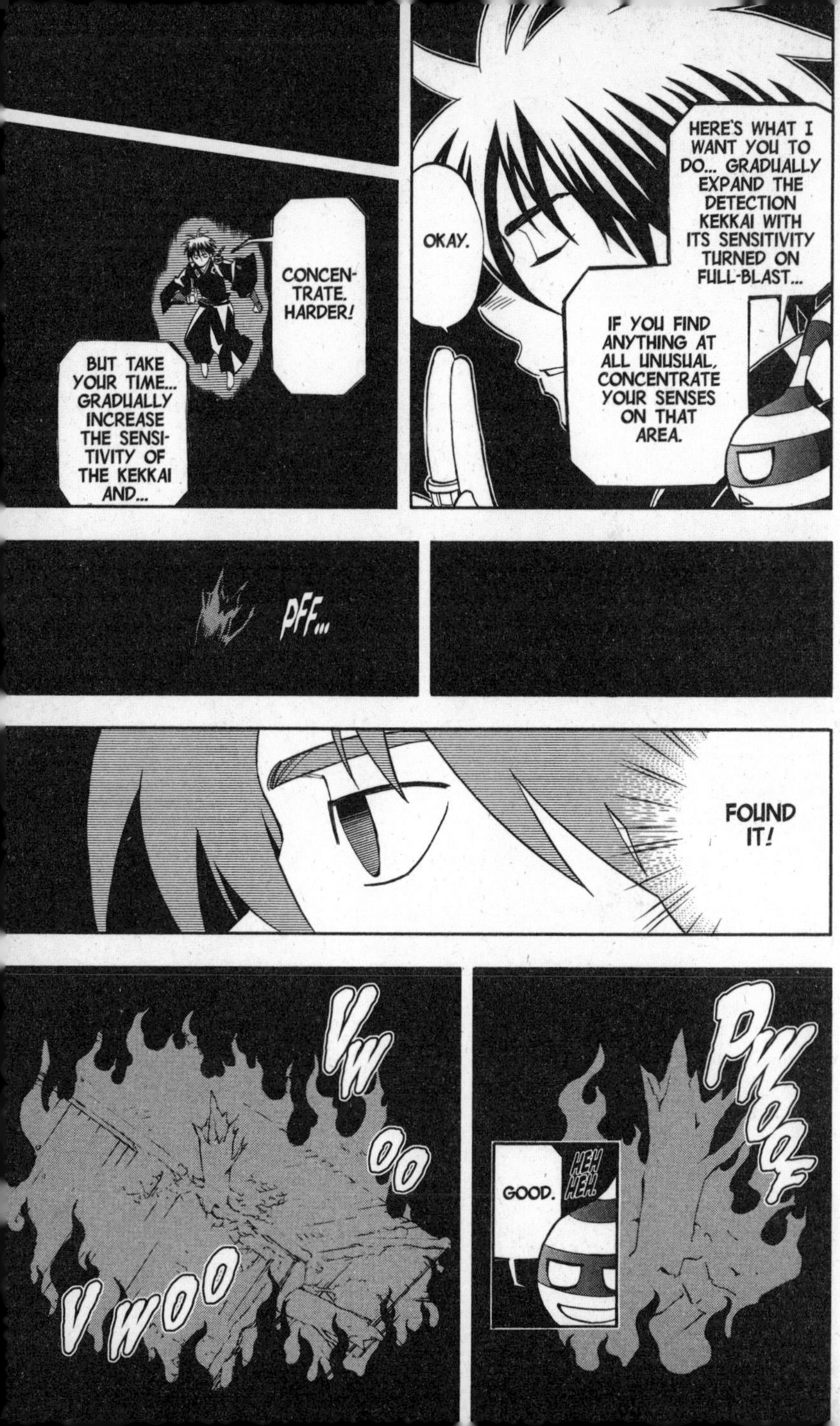
HERE'S WHAT I WANT YOU TO DO... GRADUALLY EXPAND THE DETECTION KEKKAI WITH ITS SENSITIVITY TURNED ON FULL-BLAST...
OKAY.
IF YOU FIND ANYTHING AT ALL UNUSUAL, CONCENTRATE YOUR SENSES ON THAT AREA.
CONCEN-TRATE. HARDER!
BUT TAKE YOUR TIME... GRADUALLY INCREASE THE SENSI-TIVITY OF THE KEKKAI AND...
PFF...
FOUND IT!
PWOOF
HEH HEH.
GOOD.
VWOO
VWOO

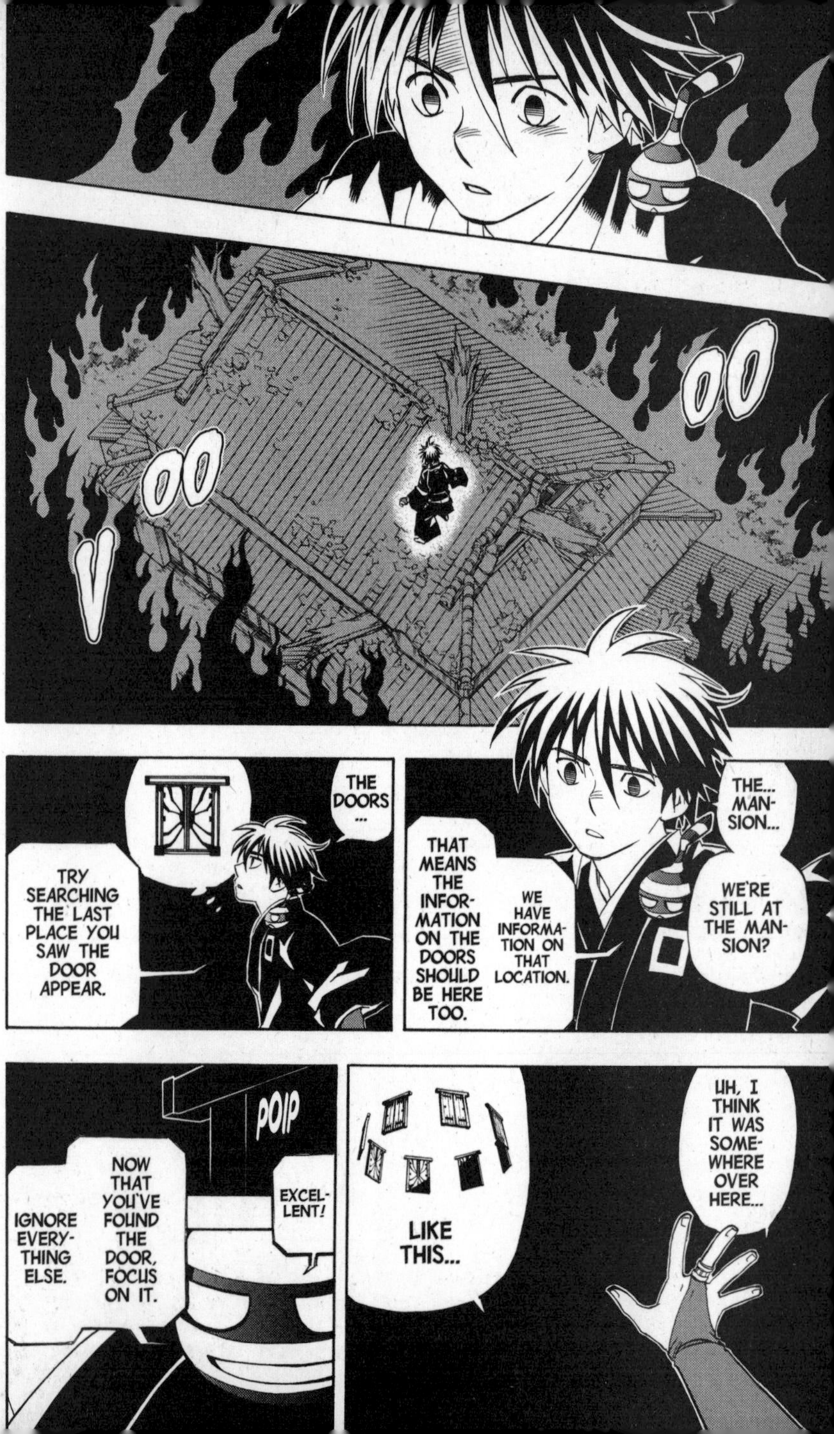
VOOOO
THE... MANSION...
WE'RE STILL AT THE MANSION?
WE HAVE INFORMATION ON THAT LOCATION.
THAT MEANS THE INFORMATION ON THE DOORS SHOULD BE HERE TOO.
THE DOORS...
TRY SEARCHING THE LAST PLACE YOU SAW THE DOOR APPEAR.
UH, I THINK IT WAS SOMEWHERE OVER HERE...
LIKE THIS...
POIP
EXCELLENT!
NOW THAT YOU'VE FOUND THE DOOR, FOCUS ON IT.
IGNORE EVERYTHING ELSE.

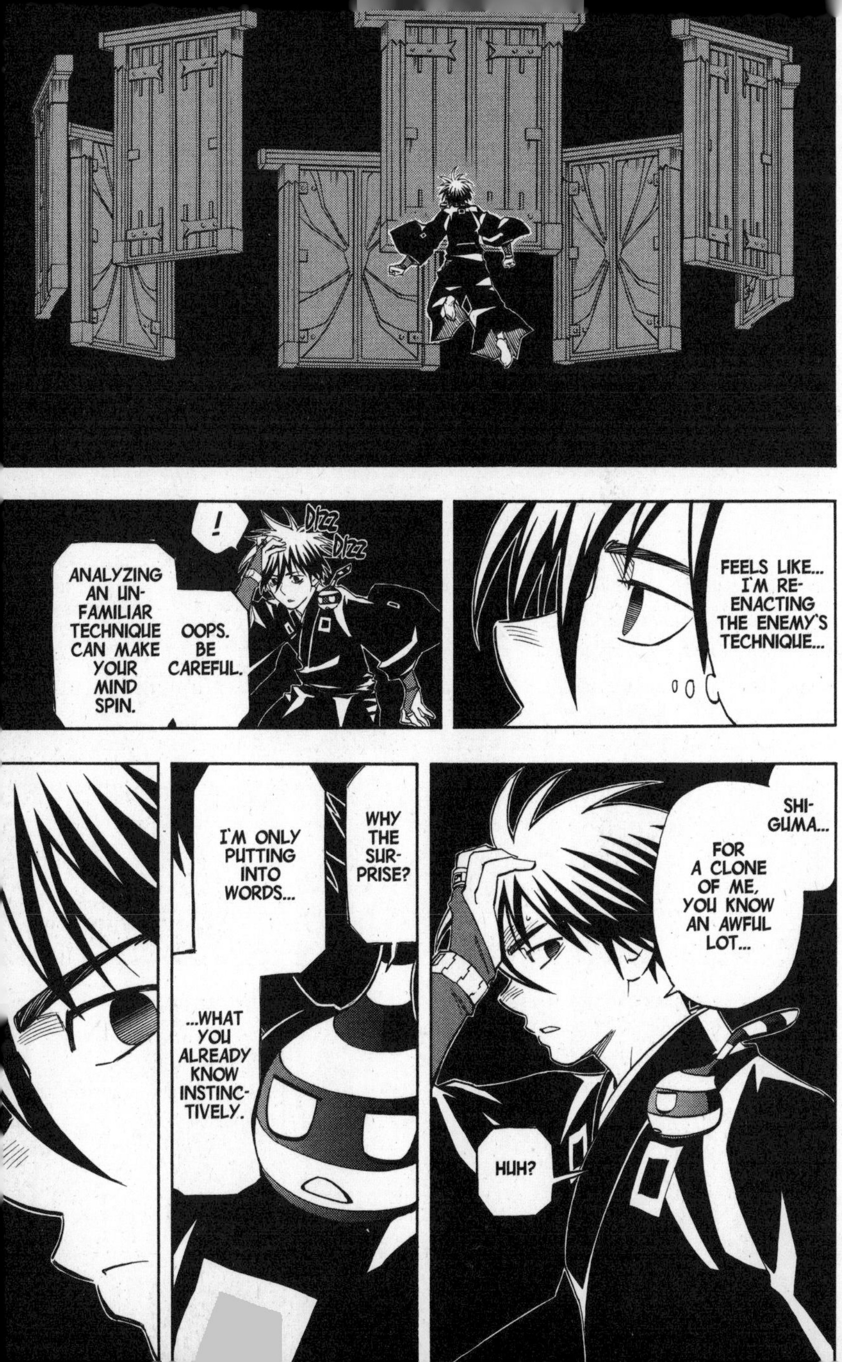
FEELS LIKE... I'M RE-ENACTING THE ENEMY'S TECHNIQUE...
!
DIZZ DIZZ
OOPS. BE CAREFUL.
ANALYZING AN UN-FAMILIAR TECHNIQUE CAN MAKE YOUR MIND SPIN.
SHI-GUMA...
FOR A CLONE OF ME, YOU KNOW AN AWFUL LOT...
HUH?
WHY THE SUR-PRISE?
I'M ONLY PUTTING INTO WORDS...
...WHAT YOU ALREADY KNOW INSTINCTIVELY.

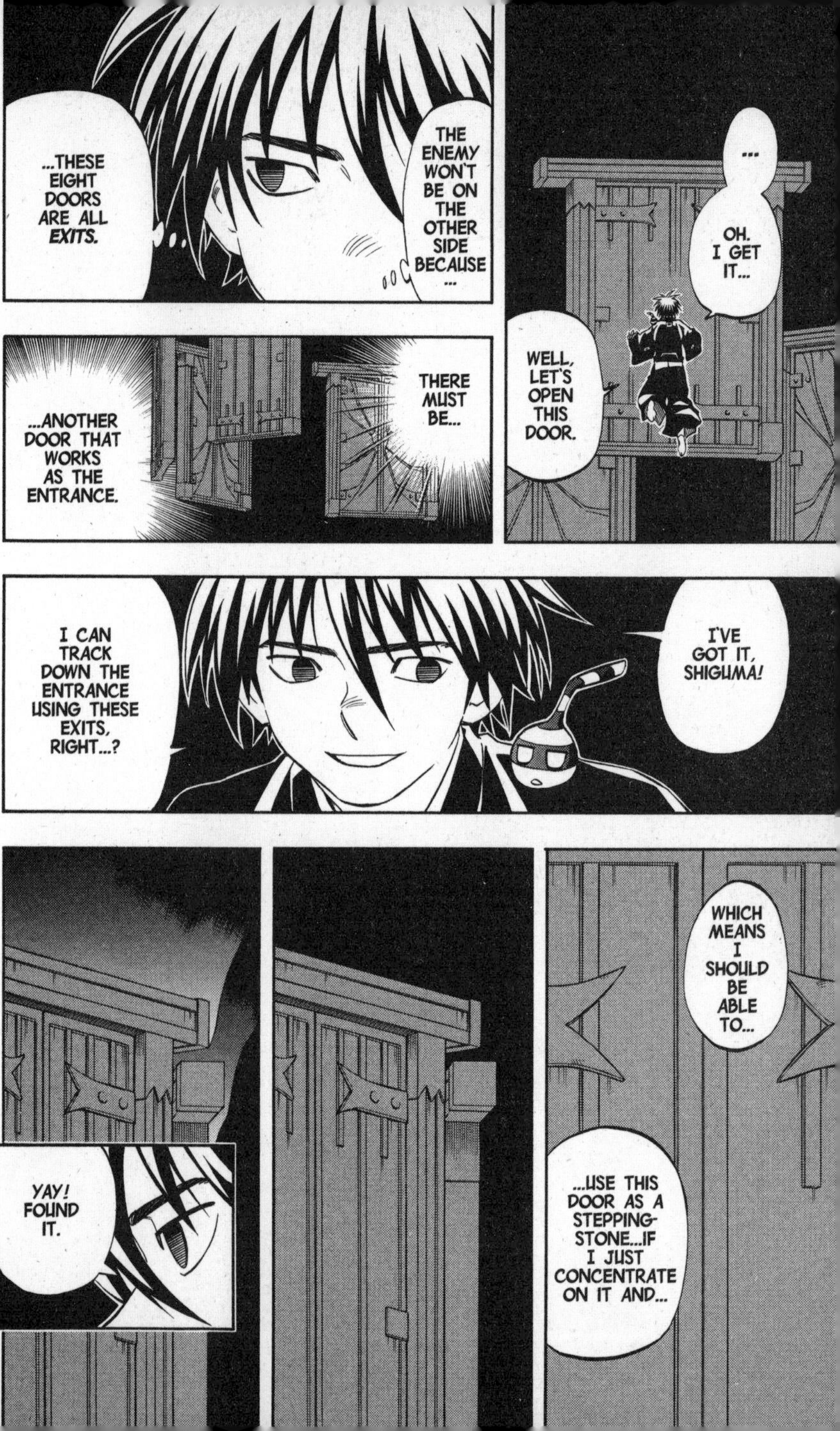
...
OH. I GET IT...
WELL, LET'S OPEN THIS DOOR.
THE ENEMY WON'T BE ON THE OTHER SIDE BECAUSE...
...THESE EIGHT DOORS ARE ALL *EXITS.*
THERE MUST BE...
...ANOTHER DOOR THAT WORKS AS THE ENTRANCE.
I'VE GOT IT, SHIGUMA!
I CAN TRACK DOWN THE ENTRANCE USING THESE EXITS, RIGHT...?
WHICH MEANS I SHOULD BE ABLE TO...
...USE THIS DOOR AS A STEPPING-STONE...IF I JUST CONCENTRATE ON IT AND...
YAY! FOUND IT.

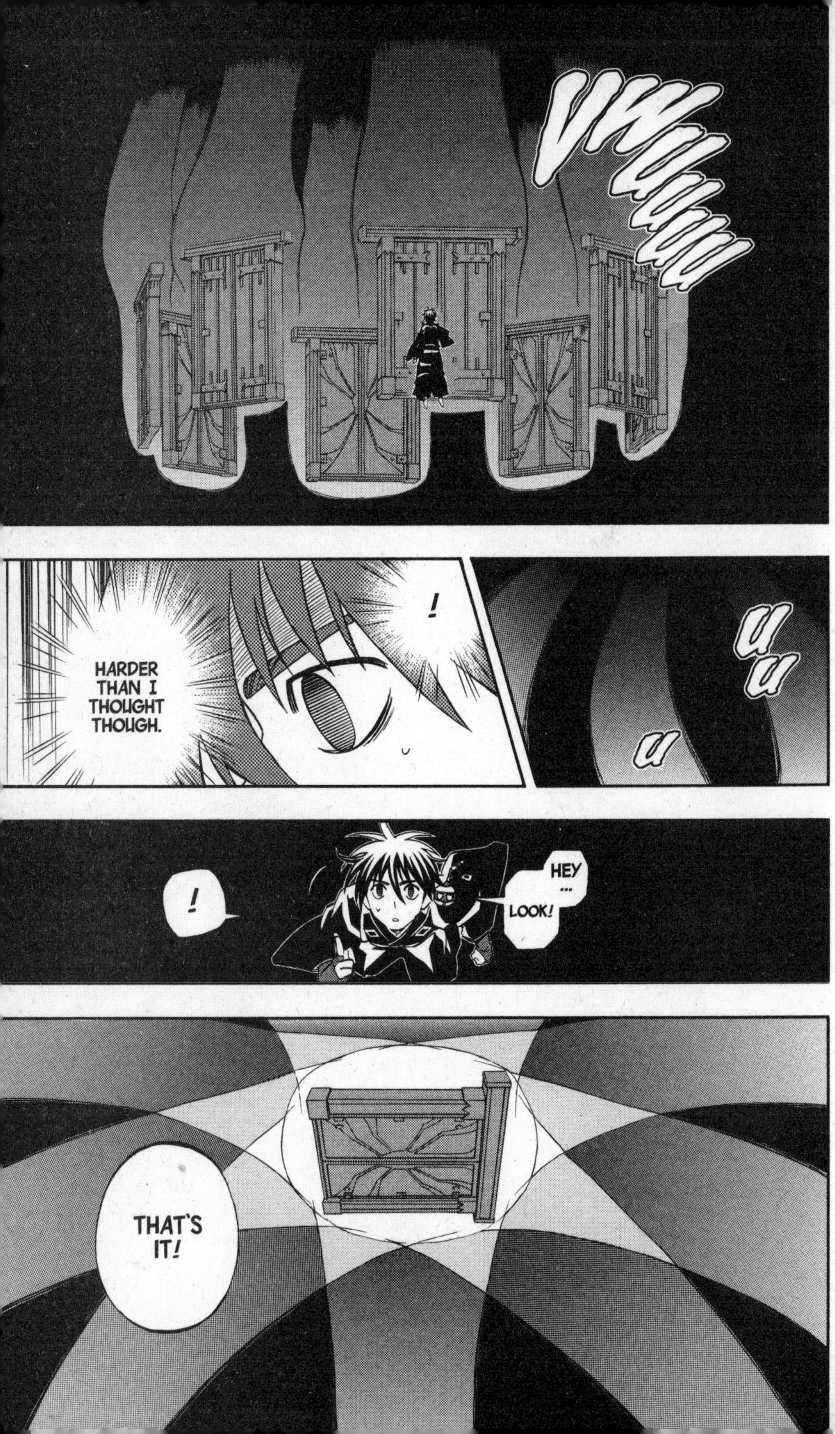
VWUUUU
u u u
!
HARDER THAN I THOUGHT THOUGH.
HEY ... LOOK!
!
THAT'S IT!

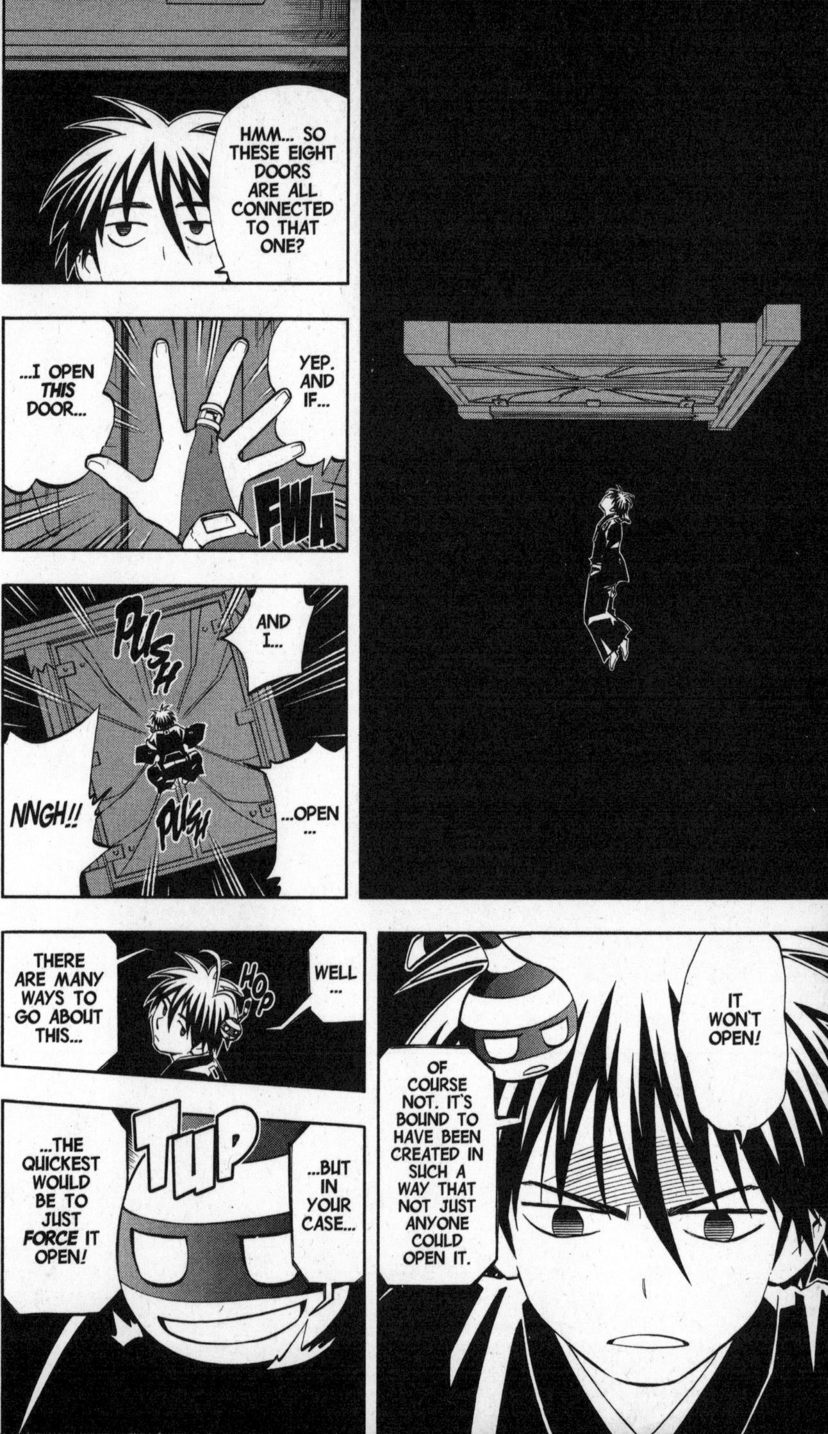
HMM... SO THESE EIGHT DOORS ARE ALL CONNECTED TO THAT ONE?
YEP. AND IF...
...I OPEN THIS DOOR...
FWA
AND I...
PUSH
...OPEN...
PUSH
NNGH!!
IT WON'T OPEN!
OF COURSE NOT. IT'S BOUND TO HAVE BEEN CREATED IN SUCH A WAY THAT NOT JUST ANYONE COULD OPEN IT.
WELL...
HOP
THERE ARE MANY WAYS TO GO ABOUT THIS...
...BUT IN YOUR CASE...
TUP
...THE QUICKEST WOULD BE TO JUST FORCE IT OPEN!

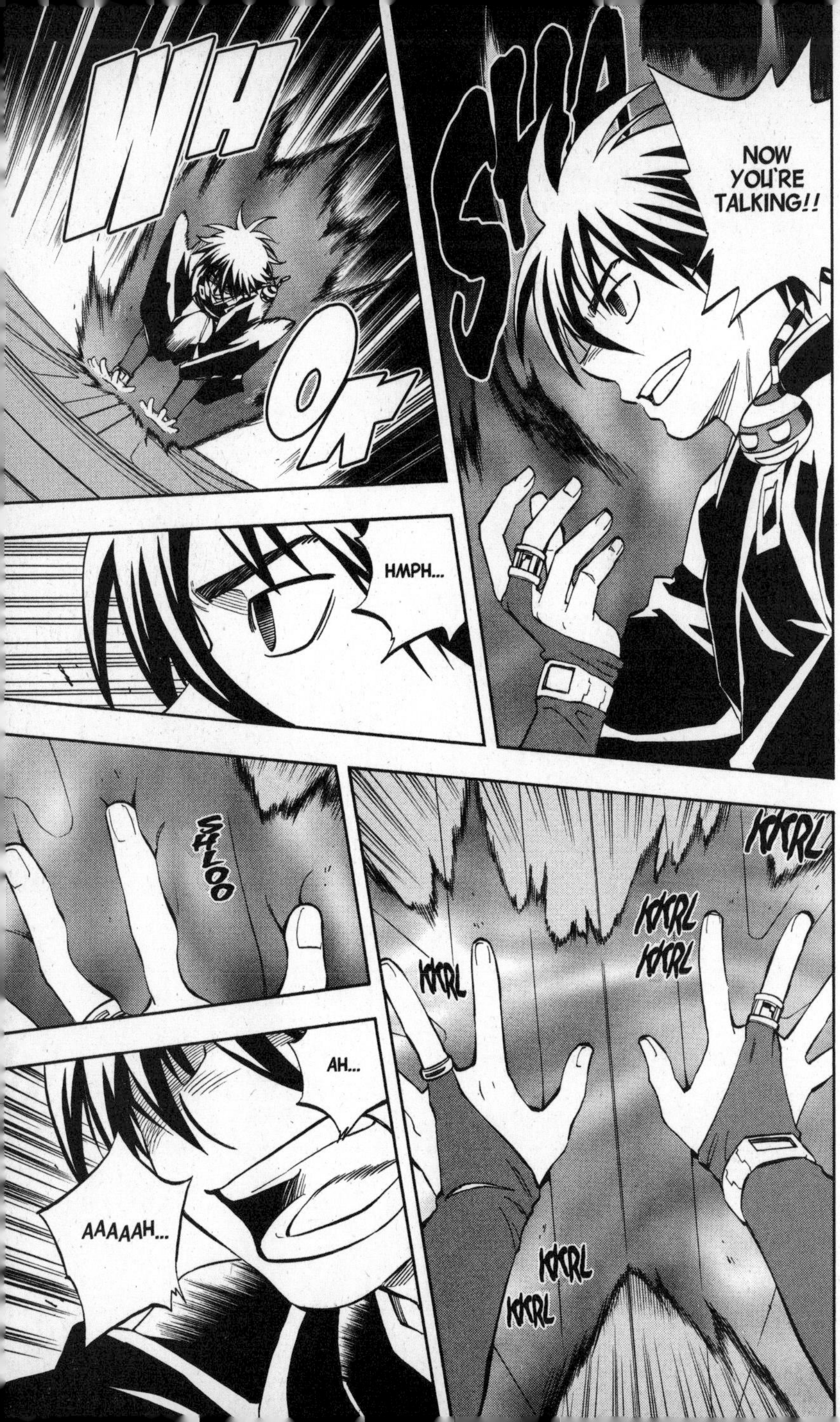
SHA
NOW YOU'RE TALKING!!
WHA
OM
HMPH...
KKRL
KKRL
KKRL
KKRL
KKRL
KKRL
SHLOO
AH...
AAAAAH...

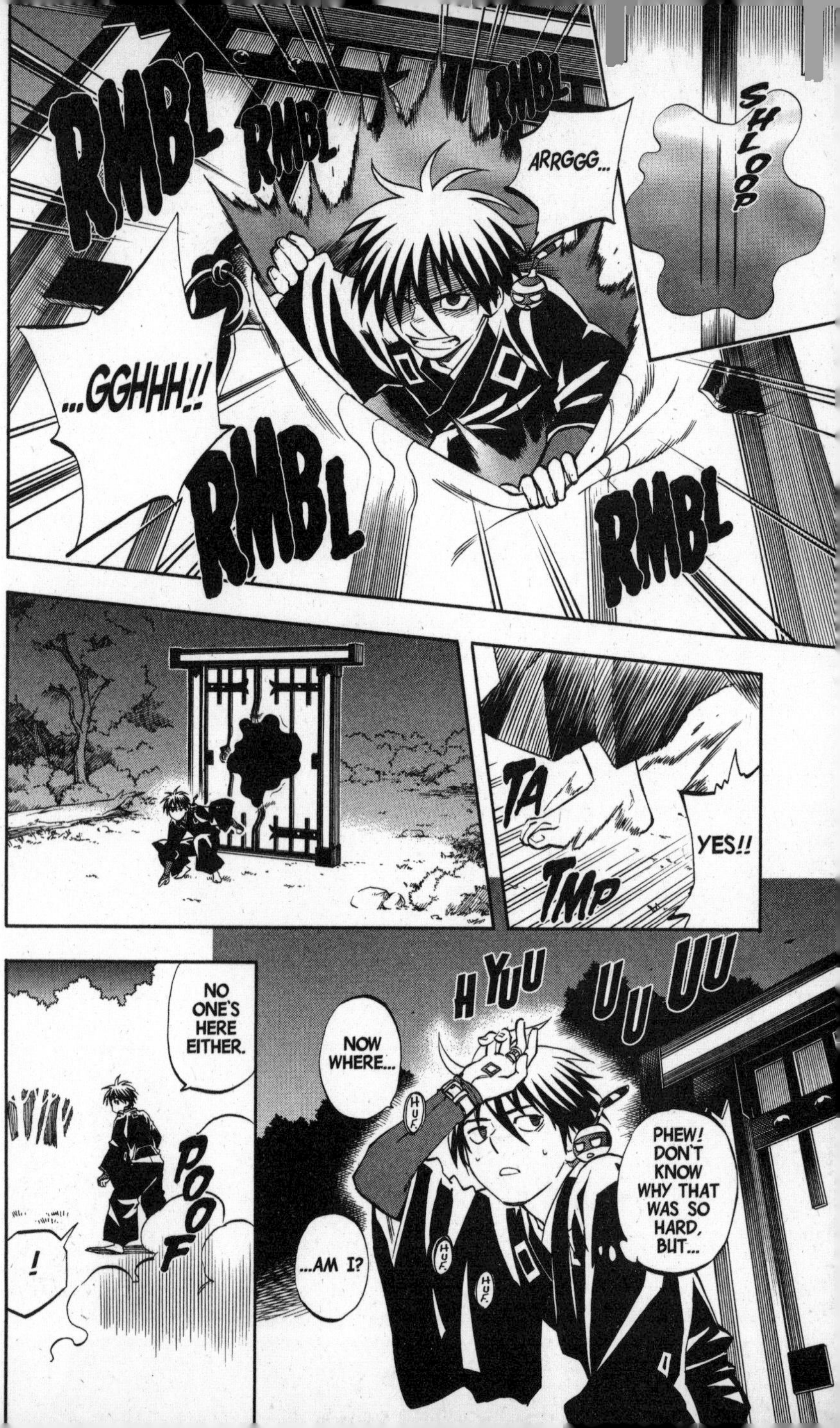
SHLOOP
ARRGGG...
RMBL
RMBL
RMBL
...GGHHH!!
RMBL
RMBL
YES!!
TA
TMP
HYUUUUUU
PHEW! DON'T KNOW WHY THAT WAS SO HARD, BUT...
NOW WHERE...
HUF
HUF
HUF
...AM I?
NO ONE'S HERE EITHER.
POOOF
!

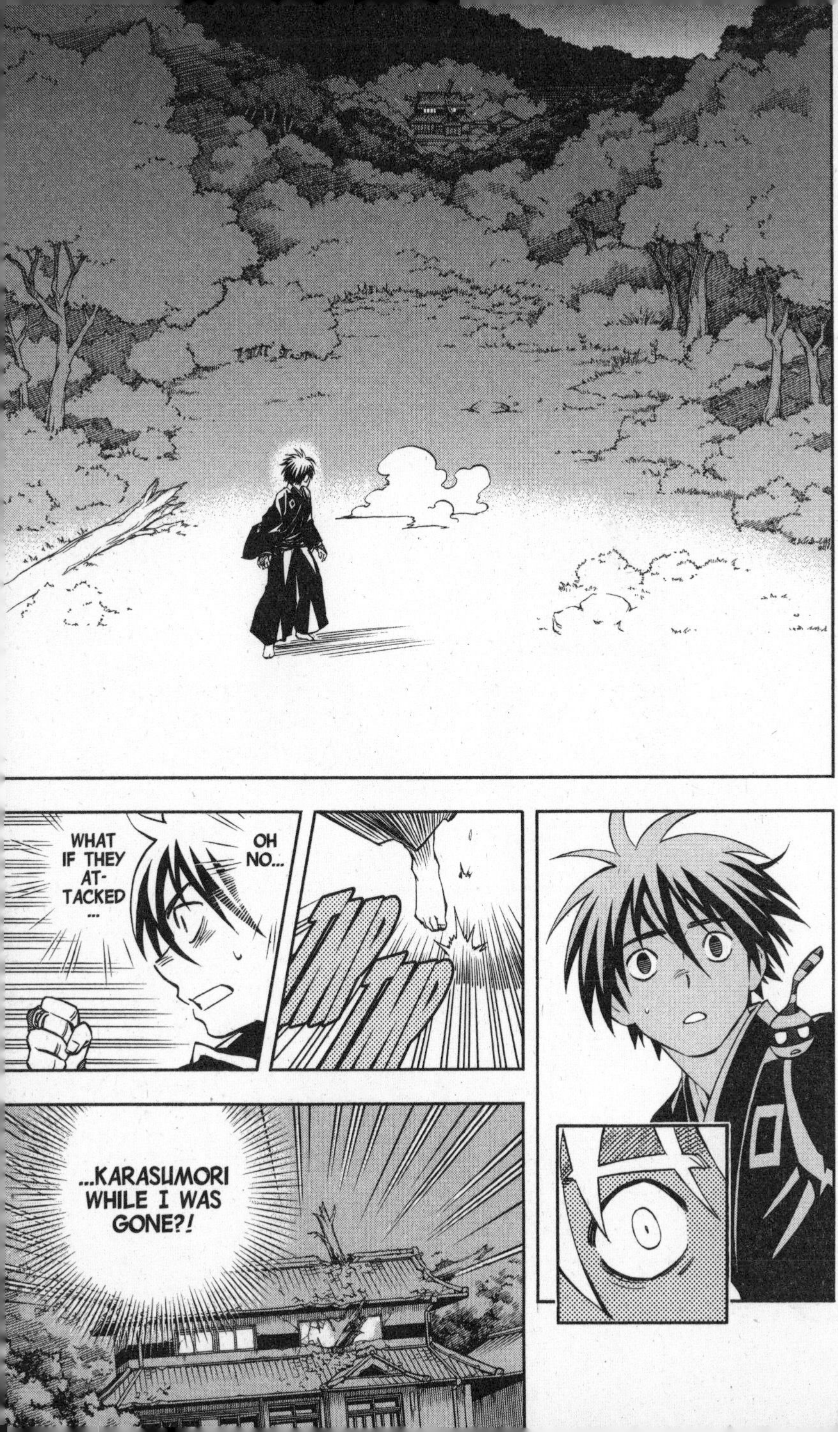
OH NO...
WHAT IF THEY AT-TACKED...
...KARASUMORI WHILE I WAS GONE?!

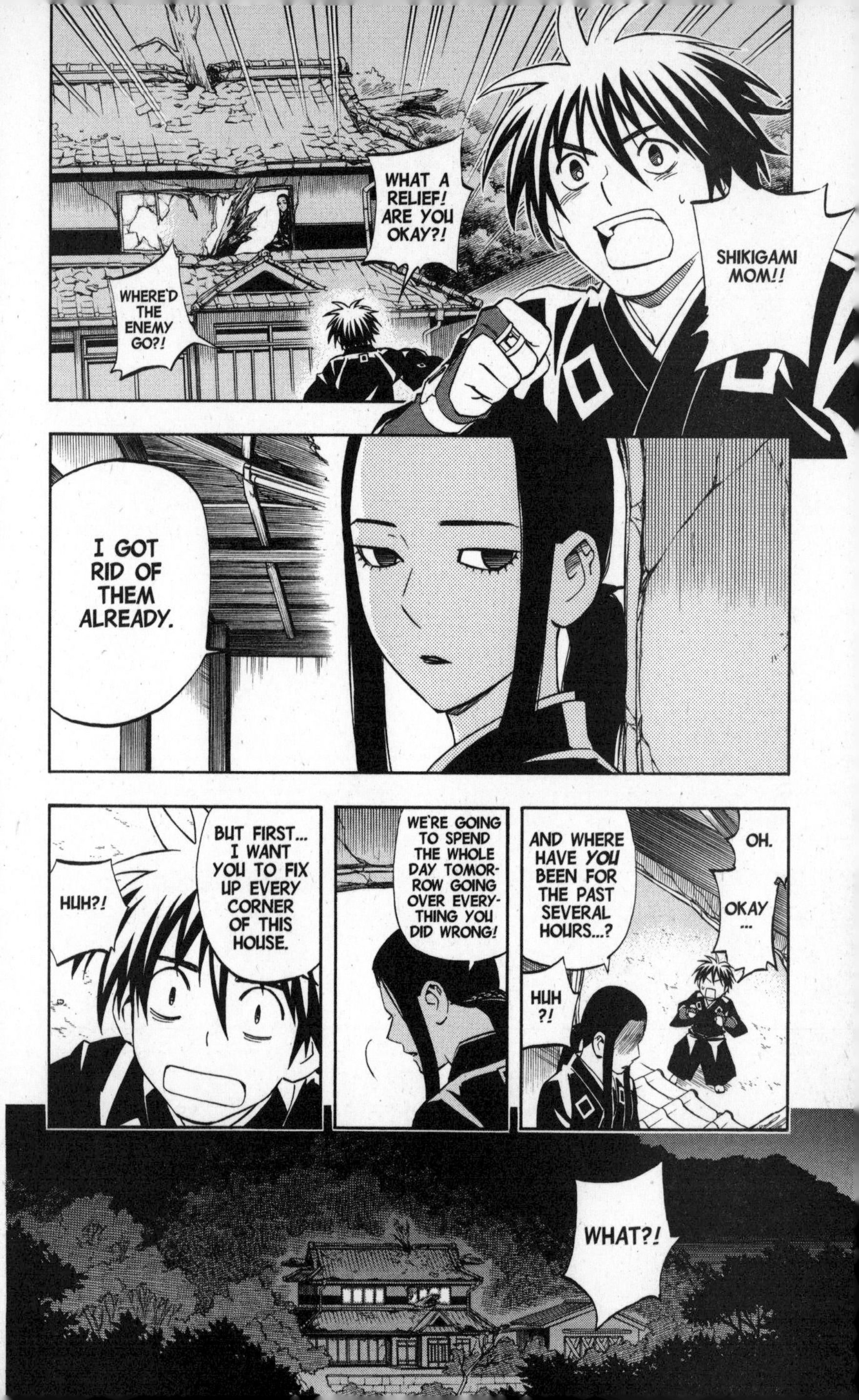
SHIKIGAMI MOM!!
WHAT A RELIEF! ARE YOU OKAY?!
WHERE'D THE ENEMY GO?!
I GOT RID OF THEM ALREADY.
OH.
OKAY ...
AND WHERE HAVE YOU BEEN FOR THE PAST SEVERAL HOURS...?
HUH ?!
WE'RE GOING TO SPEND THE WHOLE DAY TOMORROW GOING OVER EVERYTHING YOU DID WRONG!
BUT FIRST... I WANT YOU TO FIX UP EVERY CORNER OF THIS HOUSE.
HUH?!
WHAT?!

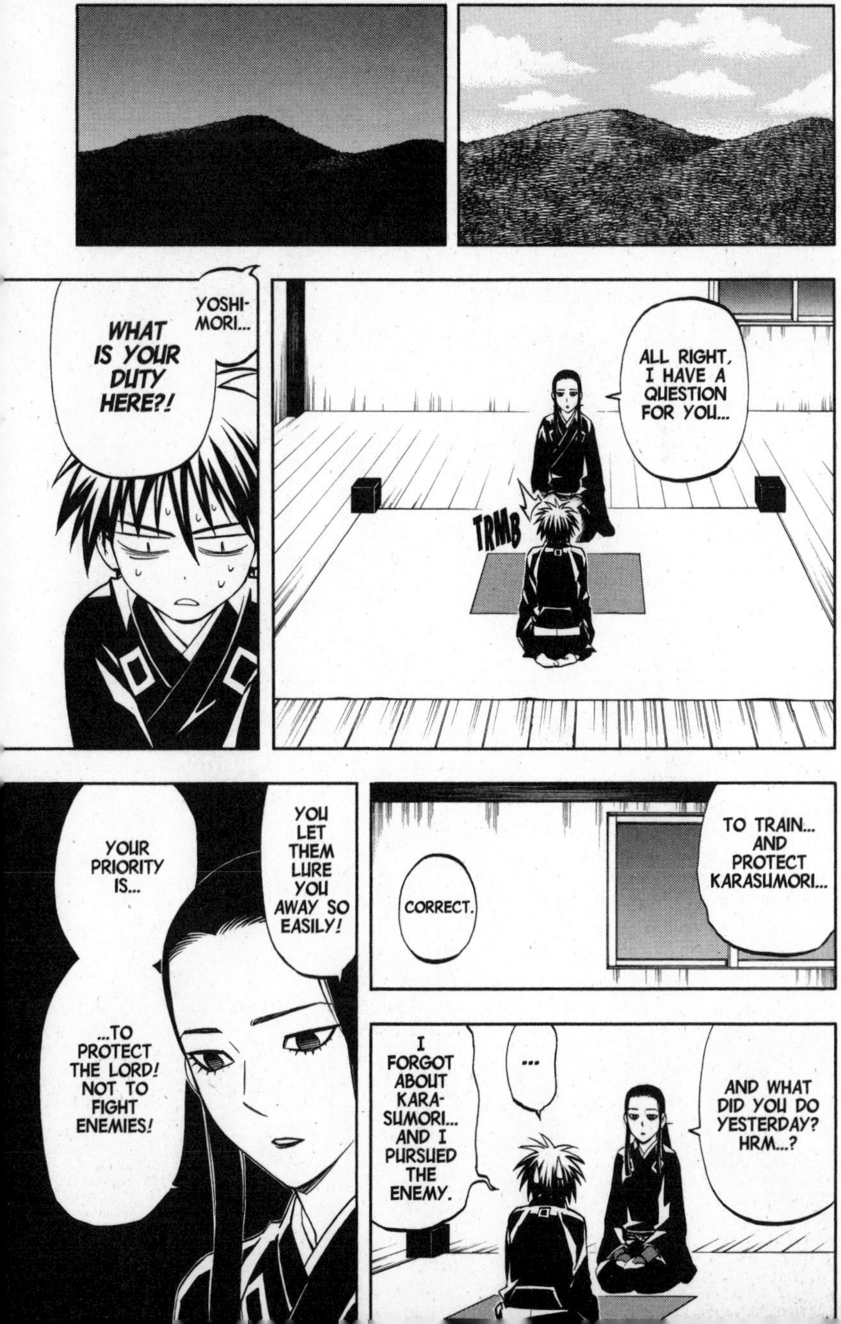
ALL RIGHT, I HAVE A QUESTION FOR YOU...
TRMB
YOSHIMORI...
WHAT IS YOUR DUTY HERE?!
TO TRAIN... AND PROTECT KARASUMORI...
CORRECT.
AND WHAT DID YOU DO YESTERDAY? HRM...?
...
I FORGOT ABOUT KARASUMORI... AND I PURSUED THE ENEMY.
YOU LET THEM LURE YOU AWAY SO EASILY!
YOUR PRIORITY IS...
...TO PROTECT THE LORD! NOT TO FIGHT ENEMIES!

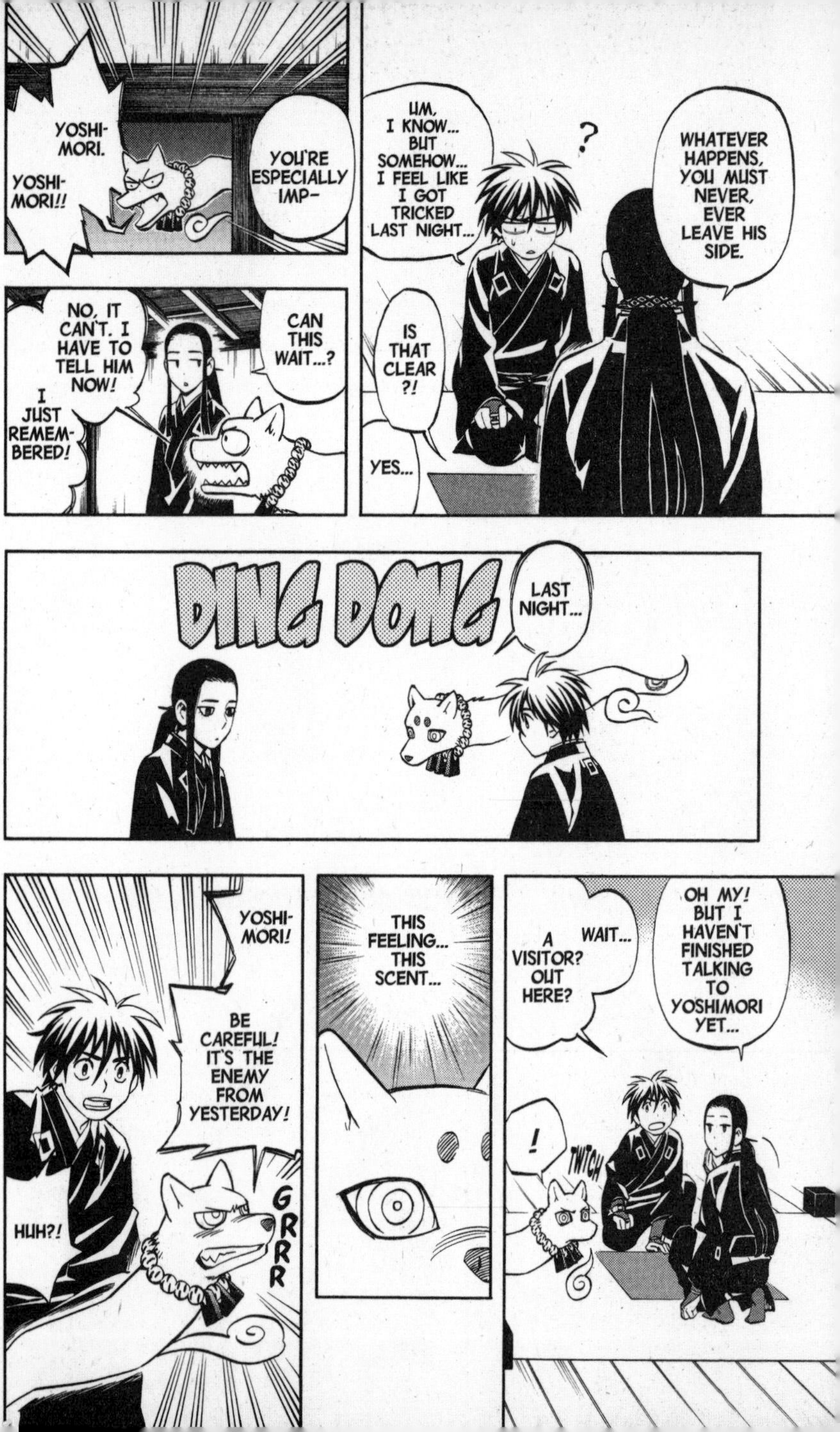
WHATEVER HAPPENS, YOU MUST NEVER, EVER LEAVE HIS SIDE.
?
UM, I KNOW... BUT SOMEHOW... I FEEL LIKE I GOT TRICKED LAST NIGHT...
IS THAT CLEAR ?!
YES...
YOU'RE ESPECIALLY IMP-
YOSHI-MORI.
YOSHI-MORI!!
CAN THIS WAIT...?
NO, IT CAN'T. I HAVE TO TELL HIM NOW!
I JUST REMEM-BERED!
LAST NIGHT...
DING DONG
OH MY! BUT I HAVEN'T FINISHED TALKING TO YOSHIMORI YET...
WAIT...
A VISITOR? OUT HERE?
!
TWITCH
THIS FEELING... THIS SCENT...
YOSHI-MORI!
BE CAREFUL! IT'S THE ENEMY FROM YESTERDAY!
GRRR
HUH?!

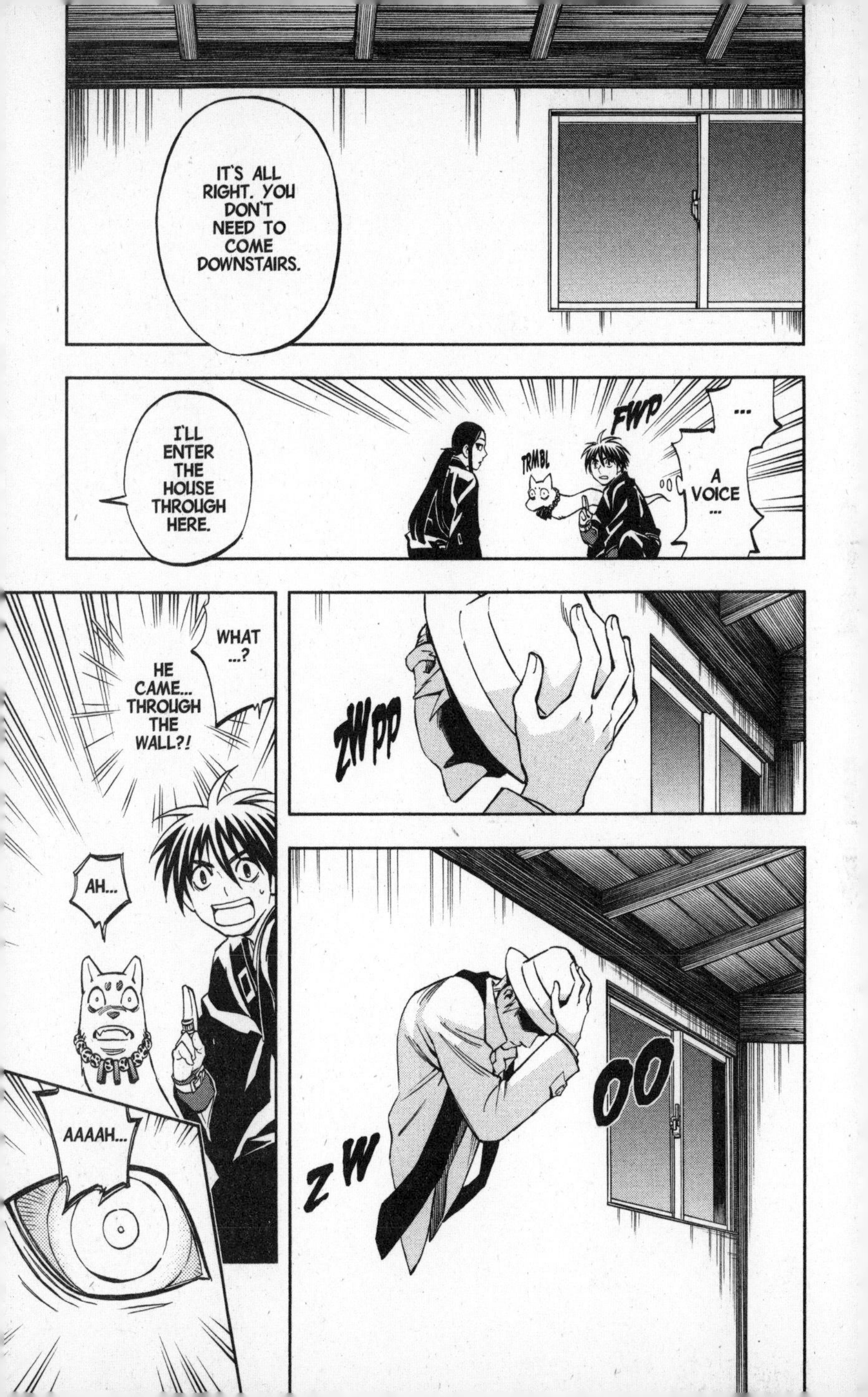

IT'S ALL RIGHT. YOU DON'T NEED TO COME DOWNSTAIRS.
...
FWP
A VOICE ...
TRMBL
I'LL ENTER THE HOUSE THROUGH HERE.
ZWPP
OO
ZW
WHAT ...?
HE CAME... THROUGH THE WALL?!
AH...
AAAAH...

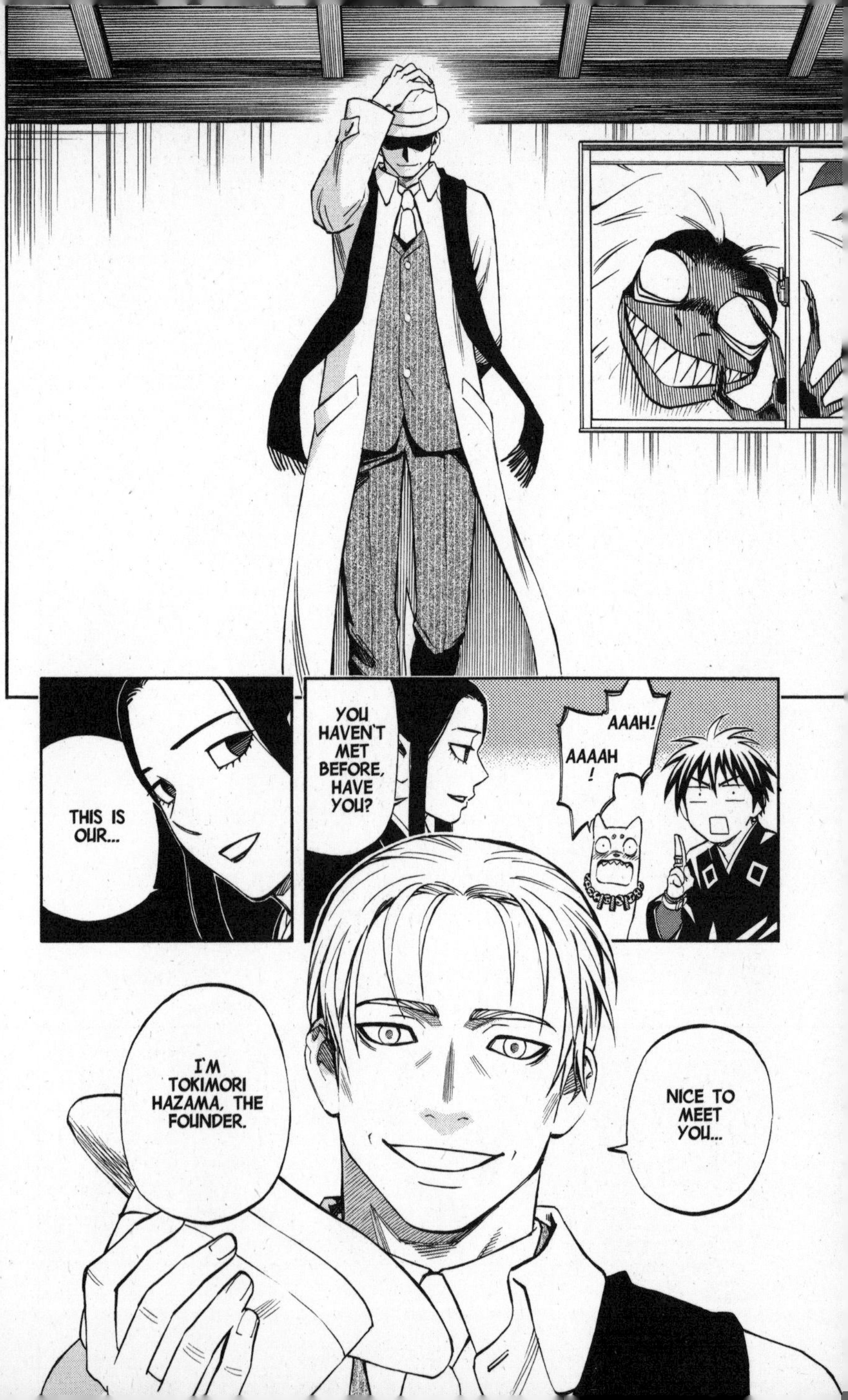
AAAH!
AAAAH!
YOU HAVEN'T MET BEFORE, HAVE YOU?
THIS IS OUR...
NICE TO MEET YOU...
I'M TOKIMORI HAZAMA, THE FOUNDER.

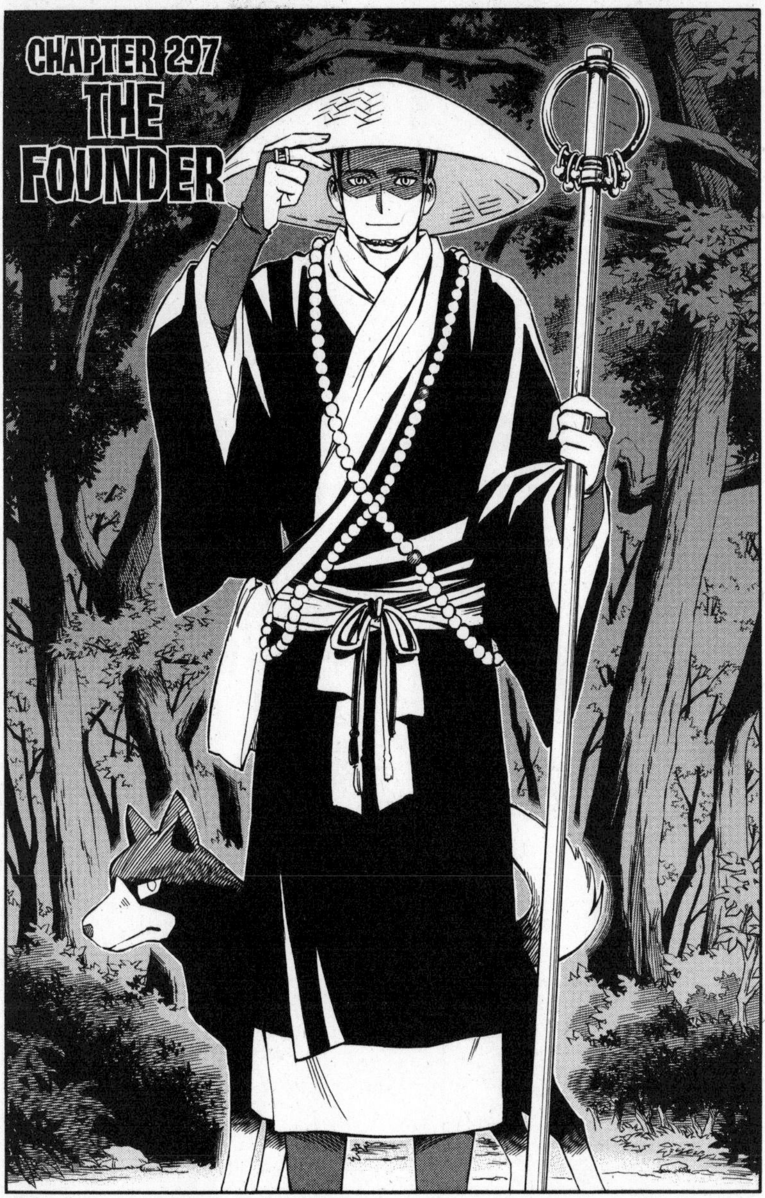
CHAPTER 297
THE FOUNDER

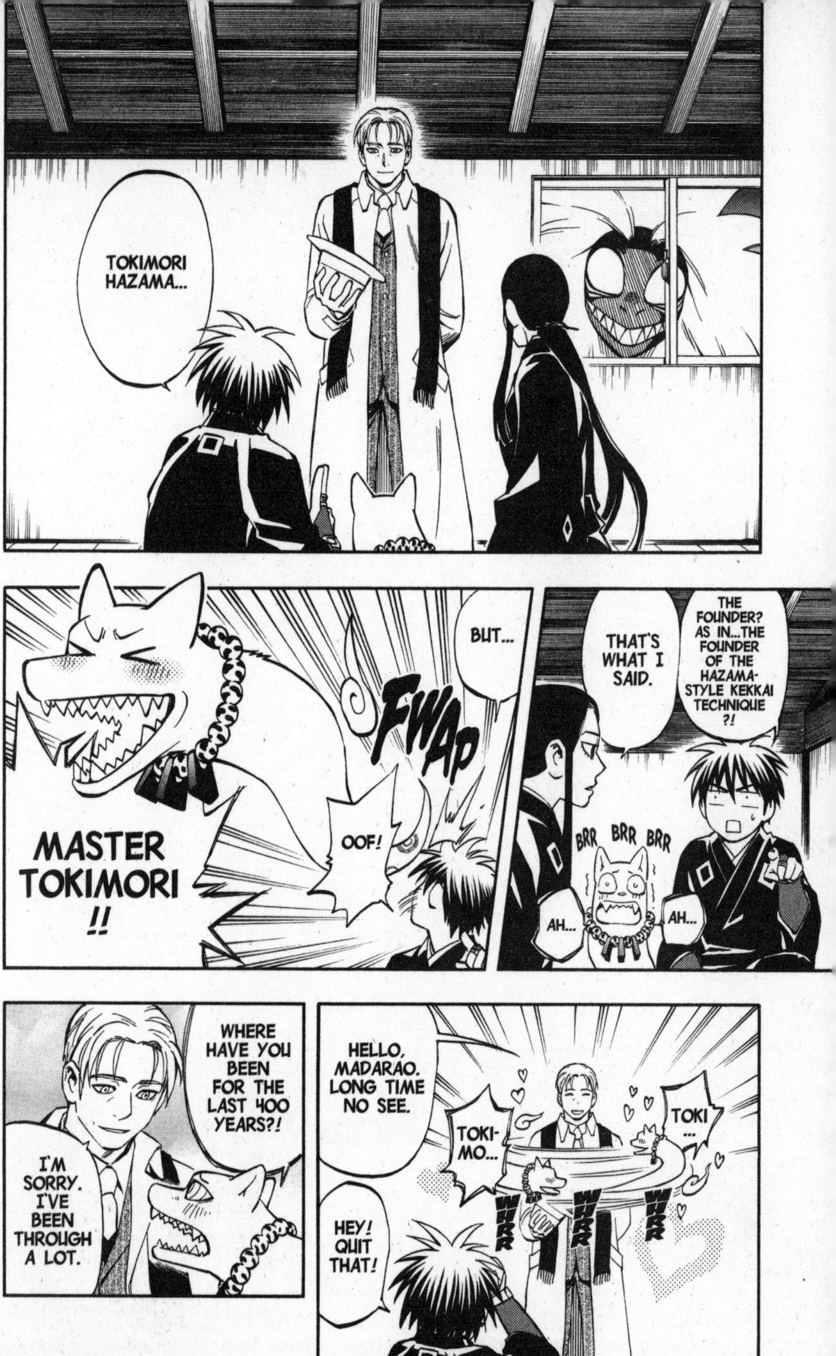
TOKIMORI HAZAMA...
THE FOUNDER? AS IN...THE FOUNDER OF THE HAZAMA-STYLE KEKKAI TECHNIQUE?!
THAT'S WHAT I SAID.
BRR BRR BRR
AH...
AH...
BUT...
FWAP
OOF!
MASTER TOKIMORI!!
HELLO, MADARAO. LONG TIME NO SEE.
TOKI...
TOKI-MO...
WURR
WURR
WURR
HEY! QUIT THAT!
WHERE HAVE YOU BEEN FOR THE LAST 400 YEARS?!
I'M SORRY. I'VE BEEN THROUGH A LOT.

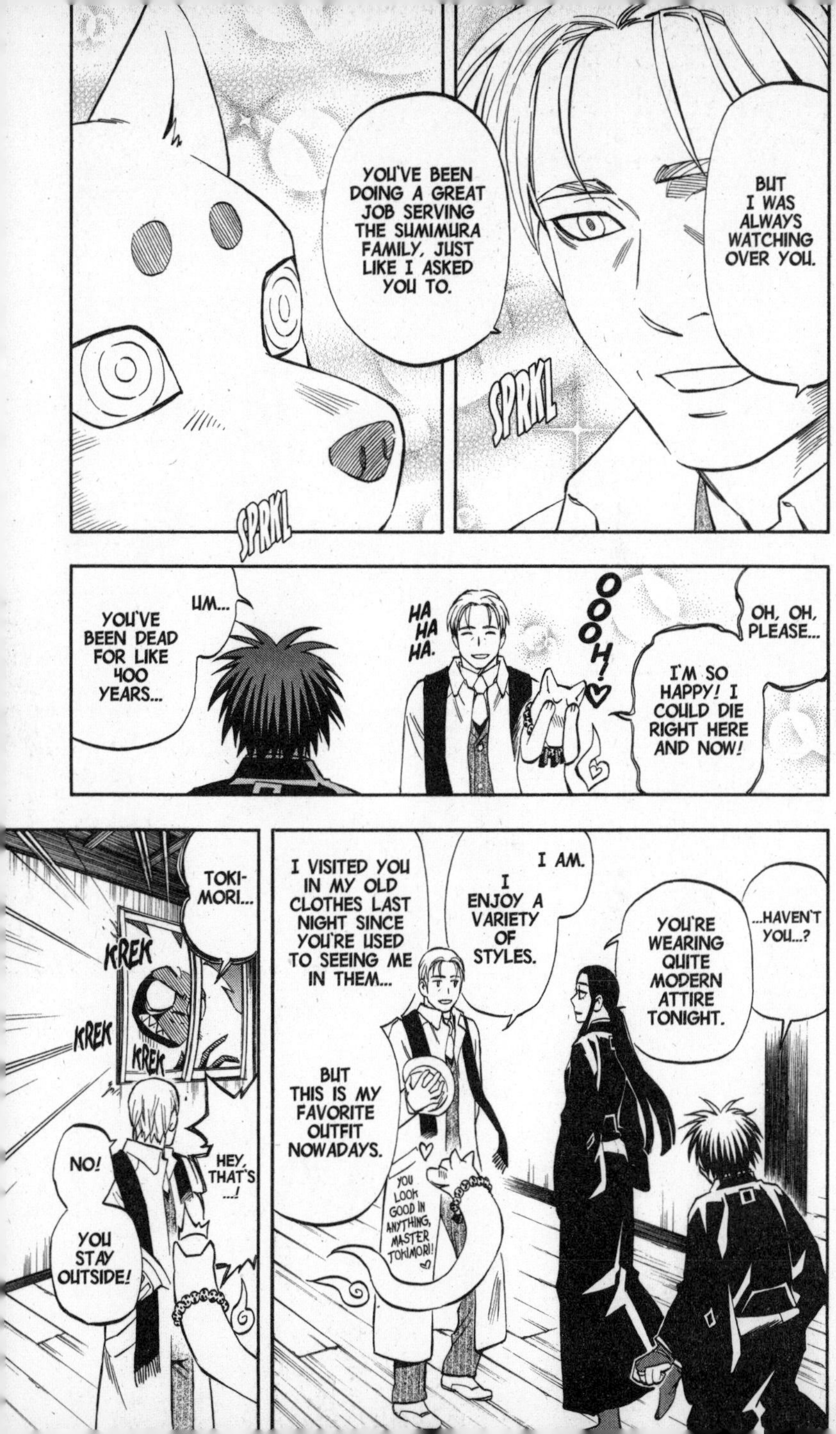
BUT I WAS ALWAYS WATCHING OVER YOU.
SPRKL
YOU'VE BEEN DOING A GREAT JOB SERVING THE SUMIMURA FAMILY, JUST LIKE I ASKED YOU TO.
SPRKL
OH, OH, PLEASE...
I'M SO HAPPY! I COULD DIE RIGHT HERE AND NOW!
OOOOH!♥
HA HA HA.
UM...
YOU'VE BEEN DEAD FOR LIKE 400 YEARS...
YOU'RE WEARING QUITE MODERN ATTIRE TONIGHT.
...HAVEN'T YOU...?
I AM.
I ENJOY A VARIETY OF STYLES.
I VISITED YOU IN MY OLD CLOTHES LAST NIGHT SINCE YOU'RE USED TO SEEING ME IN THEM...
BUT THIS IS MY FAVORITE OUTFIT NOWADAYS.
YOU LOOK GOOD IN ANYTHING, MASTER TOKIMORI! ♥
TOKI-MORI...
KREK
KREK
KREK
HEY, THAT'S ...!
NO!
YOU STAY OUTSIDE!

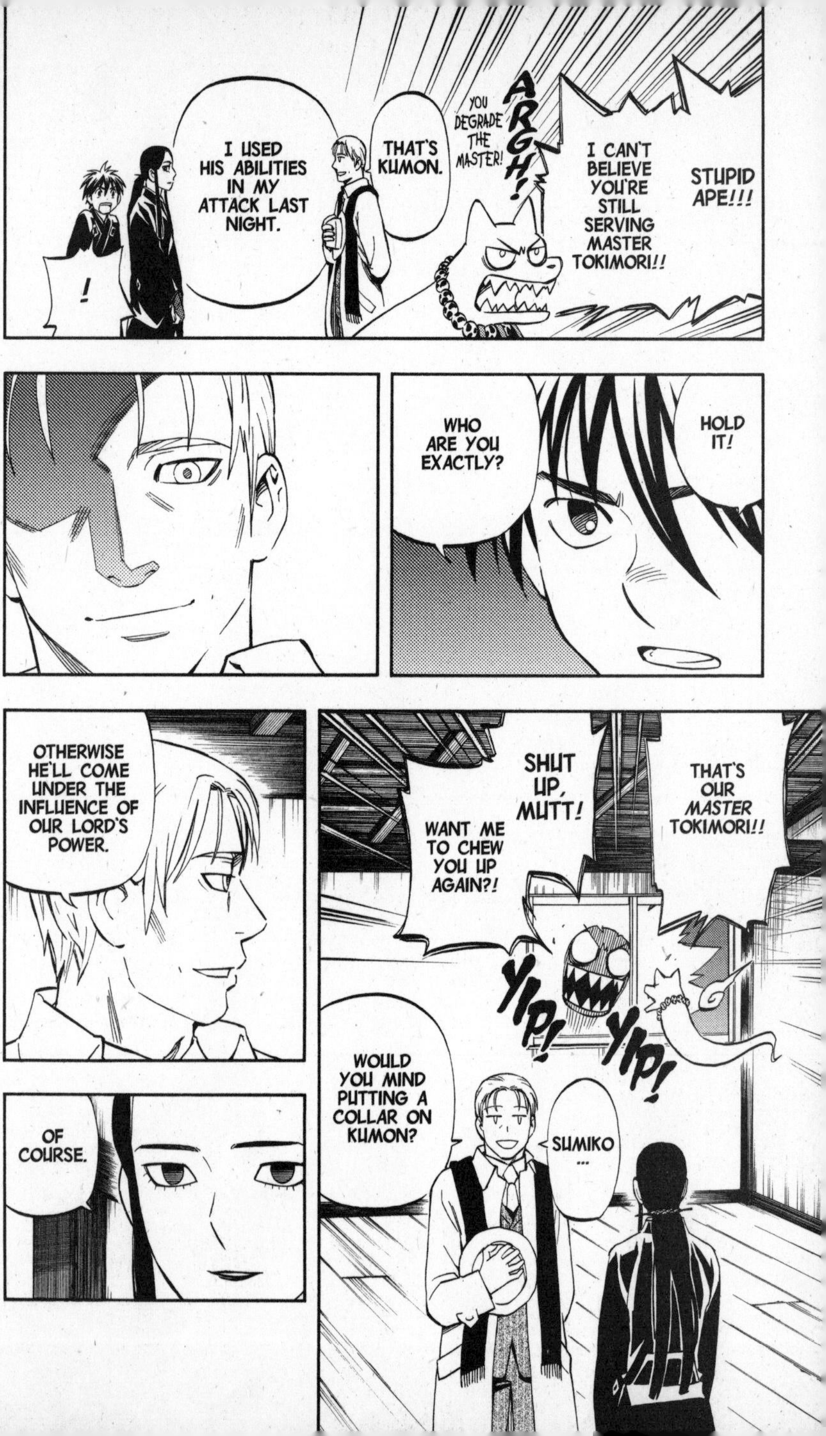
STUPID APE!!!
I CAN'T BELIEVE YOU'RE STILL SERVING MASTER TOKIMORI!!
ARGH!
YOU DEGRADE THE MASTER!
THAT'S KUMON.
I USED HIS ABILITIES IN MY ATTACK LAST NIGHT.
!
HOLD IT!
WHO ARE YOU EXACTLY?
THAT'S OUR MASTER TOKIMORI!!
SHUT UP, MUTT!
WANT ME TO CHEW YOU UP AGAIN?!
YIP!
YIP!
SUMIKO...
WOULD YOU MIND PUTTING A COLLAR ON KUMON?
OTHERWISE HE'LL COME UNDER THE INFLUENCE OF OUR LORD'S POWER.
OF COURSE.

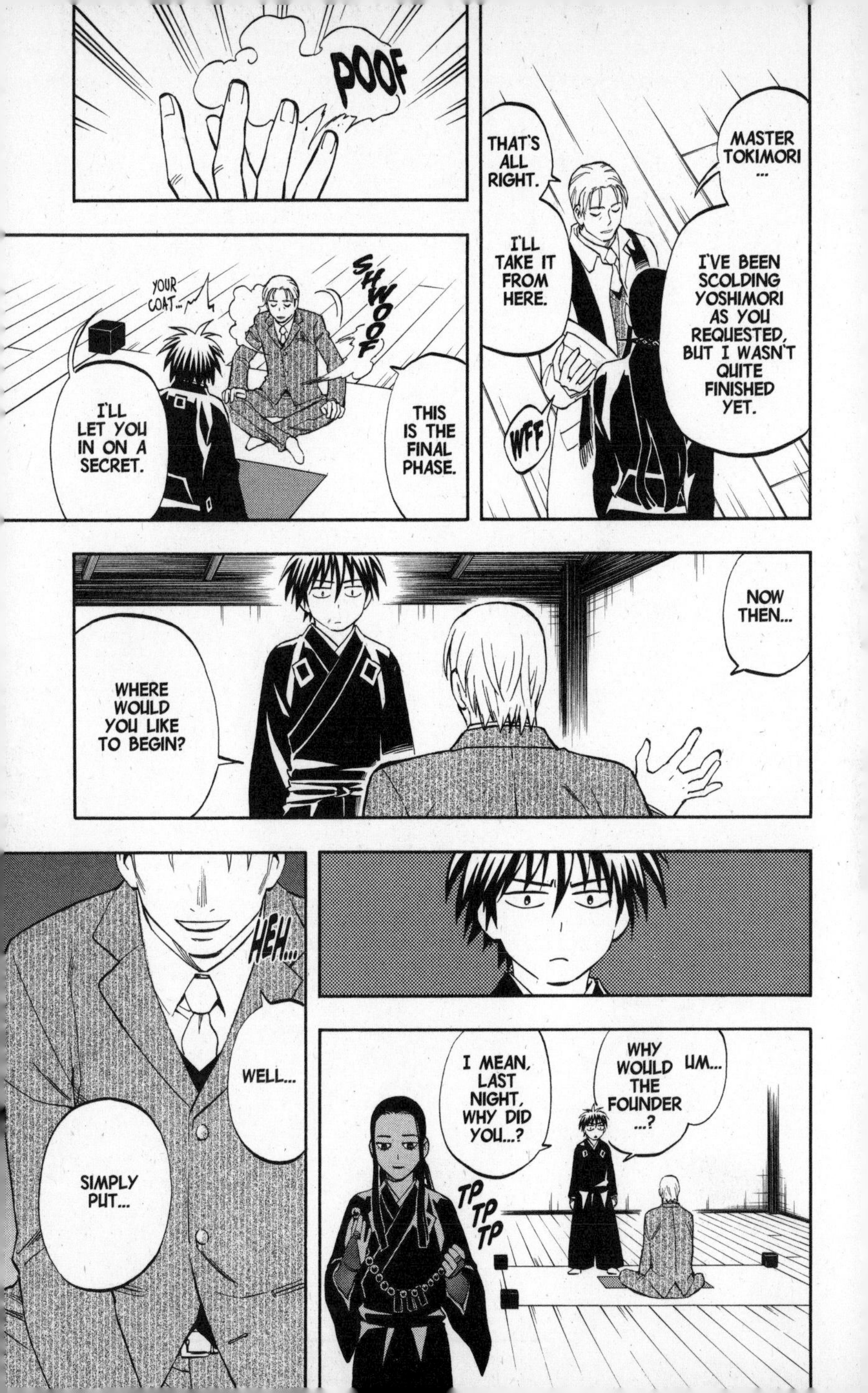
MASTER TOKIMORI...
I'VE BEEN SCOLDING YOSHIMORI AS YOU REQUESTED, BUT I WASN'T QUITE FINISHED YET.
THAT'S ALL RIGHT.
I'LL TAKE IT FROM HERE.
WFF
POOF
SHWOOOF
THIS IS THE FINAL PHASE.
YOUR COAT...
I'LL LET YOU IN ON A SECRET.
NOW THEN...
WHERE WOULD YOU LIKE TO BEGIN?
UM...
WHY WOULD THE FOUNDER...?
I MEAN, LAST NIGHT, WHY DID YOU...?
TP TP TP
HEH...
WELL...
SIMPLY PUT...

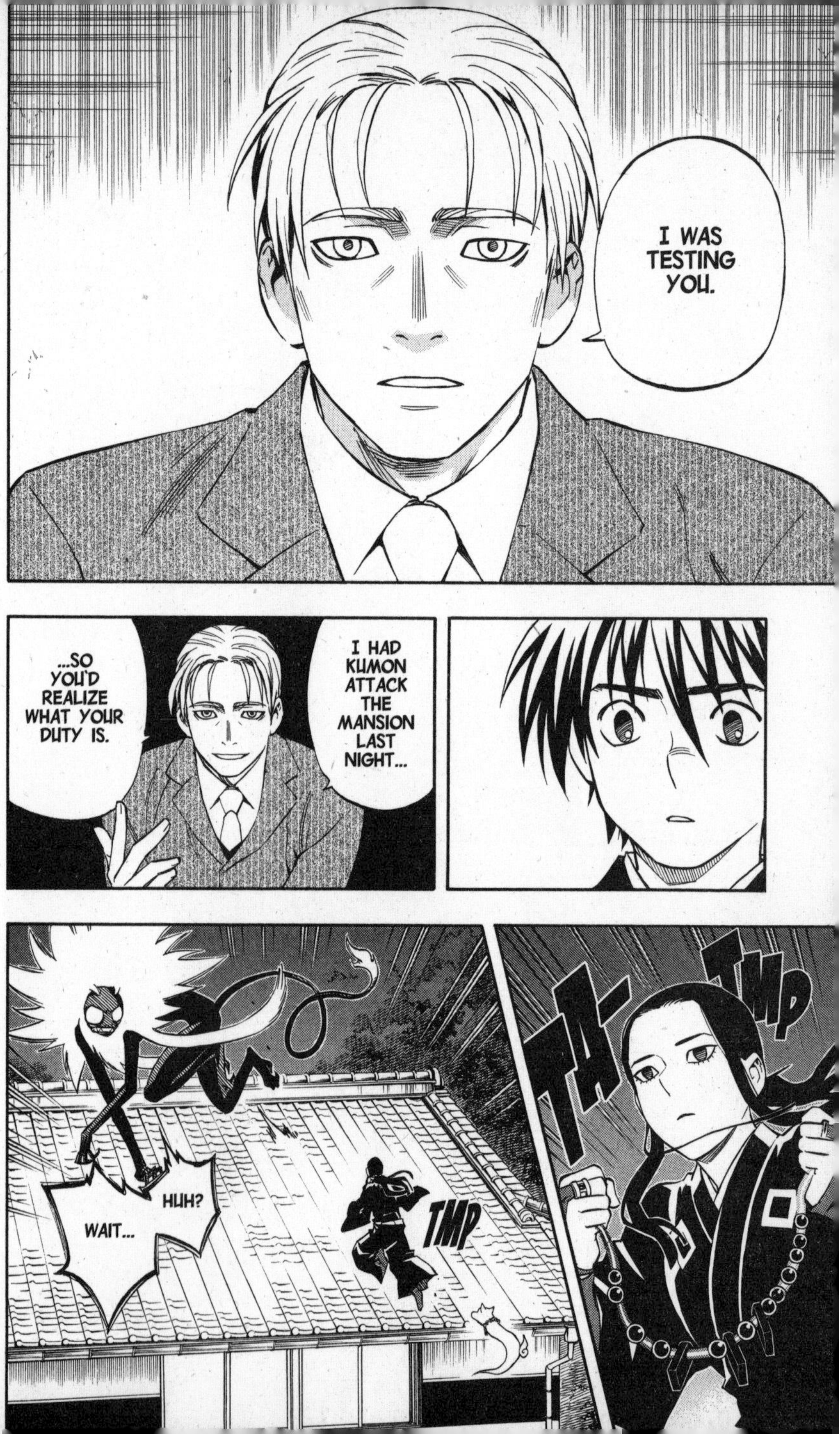
I WAS TESTING YOU.
I HAD KUMON ATTACK THE MANSION LAST NIGHT...
...SO YOU'D REALIZE WHAT YOUR DUTY IS.
TA-
TMP
TMP
HUH?
WAIT...

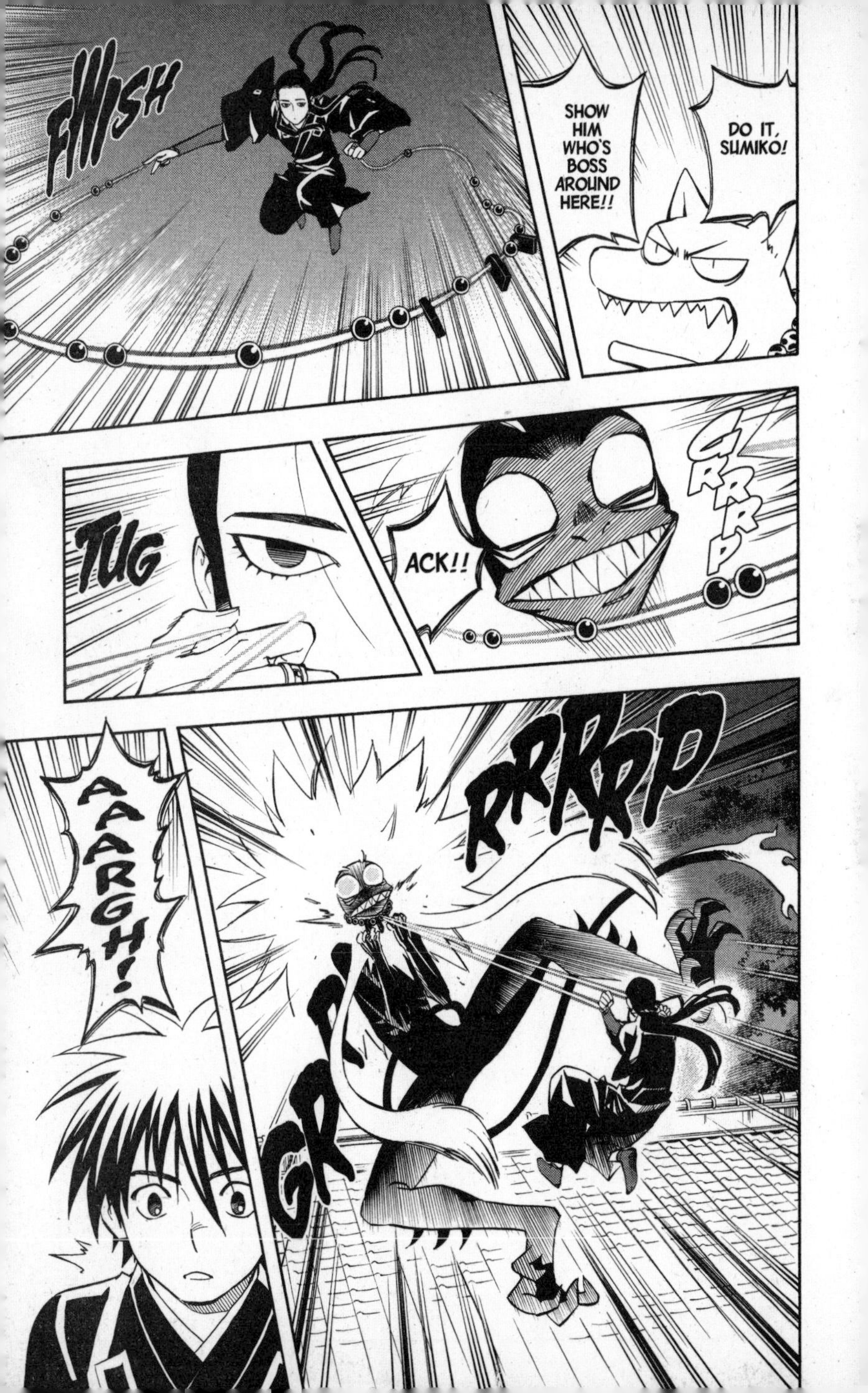
DO IT, SUMIKO!
SHOW HIM WHO'S BOSS AROUND HERE!!
FWISH
GRRRP
ACK!!
TUG
RRRRP
GR
AAARGH!

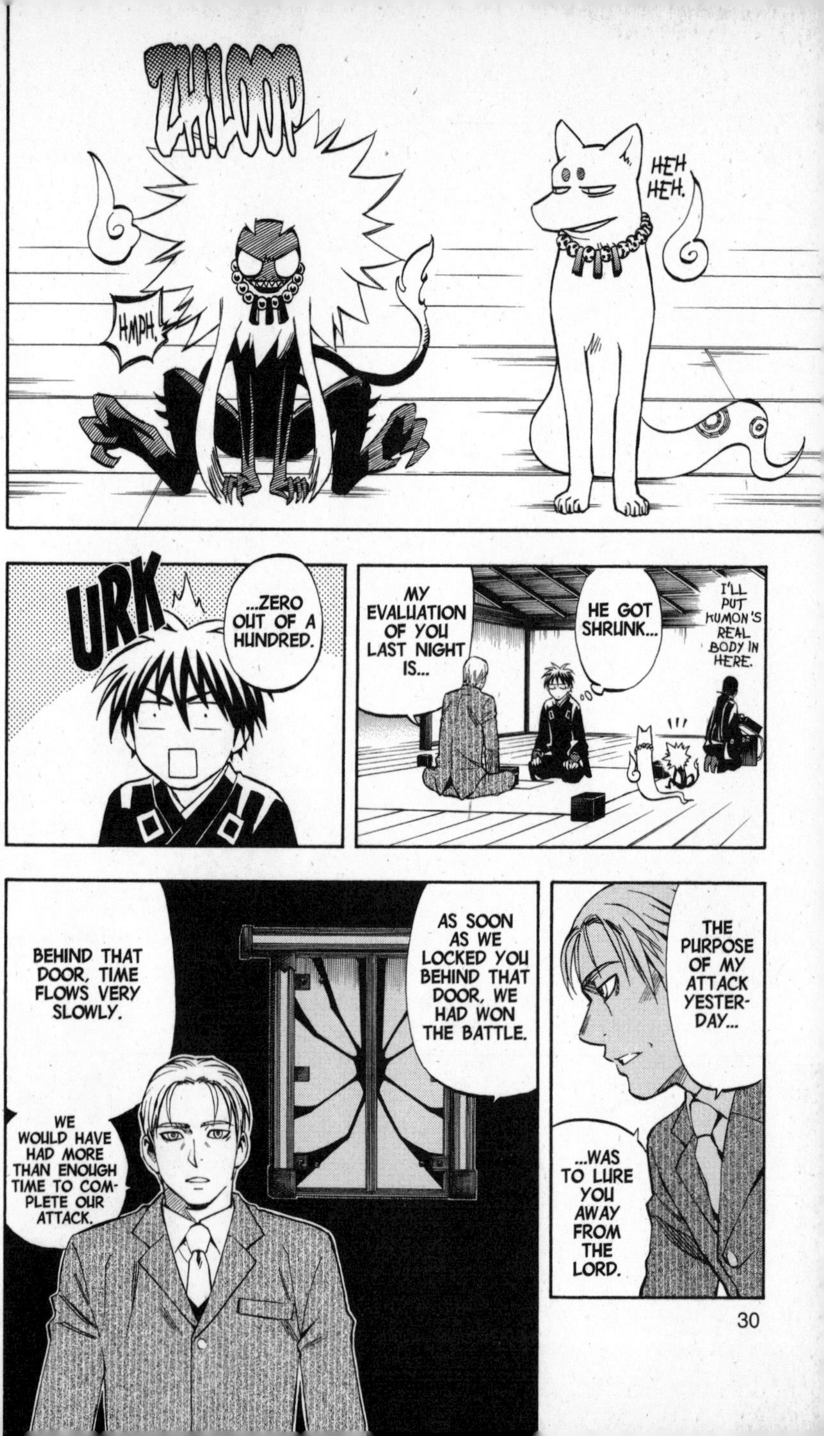
ZHLOOP
HEH HEH.
HMPH.
I'LL PUT KUMON'S REAL BODY IN HERE.
HE GOT SHRUNK...
MY EVALUATION OF YOU LAST NIGHT IS...
...ZERO OUT OF A HUNDRED.
URK
THE PURPOSE OF MY ATTACK YESTER-DAY...
...WAS TO LURE YOU AWAY FROM THE LORD.
AS SOON AS WE LOCKED YOU BEHIND THAT DOOR, WE HAD WON THE BATTLE.
BEHIND THAT DOOR, TIME FLOWS VERY SLOWLY.
WE WOULD HAVE HAD MORE THAN ENOUGH TIME TO COM-PLETE OUR ATTACK.

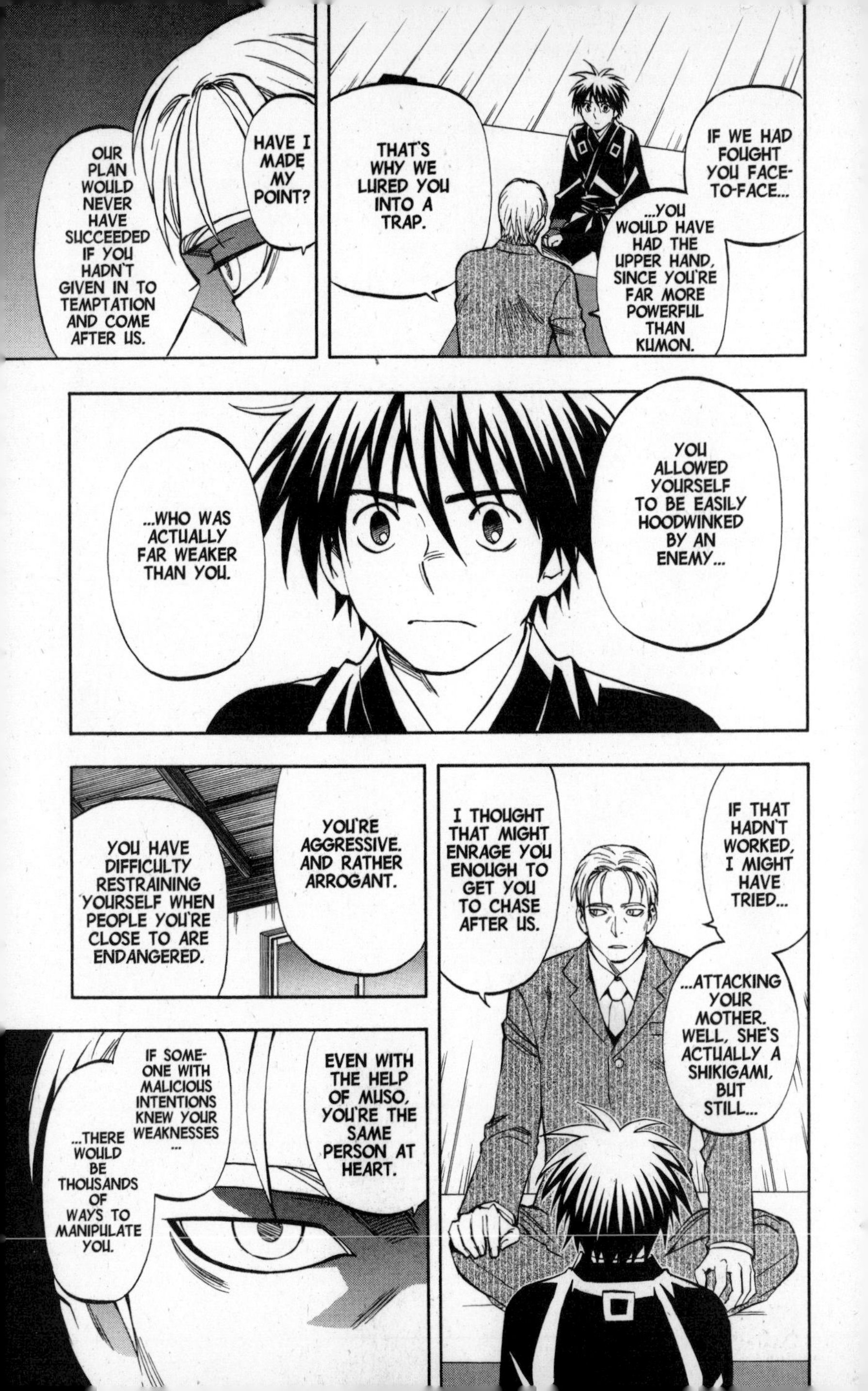
IF WE HAD FOUGHT YOU FACE-TO-FACE...
...YOU WOULD HAVE HAD THE UPPER HAND, SINCE YOU'RE FAR MORE POWERFUL THAN KUMON.
THAT'S WHY WE LURED YOU INTO A TRAP.
HAVE I MADE MY POINT?
OUR PLAN WOULD NEVER HAVE SUCCEEDED IF YOU HADN'T GIVEN IN TO TEMPTATION AND COME AFTER US.
YOU ALLOWED YOURSELF TO BE EASILY HOODWINKED BY AN ENEMY...
...WHO WAS ACTUALLY FAR WEAKER THAN YOU.
IF THAT HADN'T WORKED, I MIGHT HAVE TRIED...
...ATTACKING YOUR MOTHER. WELL, SHE'S ACTUALLY A SHIKIGAMI, BUT STILL...
I THOUGHT THAT MIGHT ENRAGE YOU ENOUGH TO GET YOU TO CHASE AFTER US.
YOU'RE AGGRESSIVE. AND RATHER ARROGANT.
YOU HAVE DIFFICULTY RESTRAINING YOURSELF WHEN PEOPLE YOU'RE CLOSE TO ARE ENDANGERED.
EVEN WITH THE HELP OF MUSO, YOU'RE THE SAME PERSON AT HEART.
IF SOME-ONE WITH MALICIOUS INTENTIONS KNEW YOUR WEAKNESSES...
...THERE WOULD BE THOUSANDS OF WAYS TO MANIPULATE YOU.

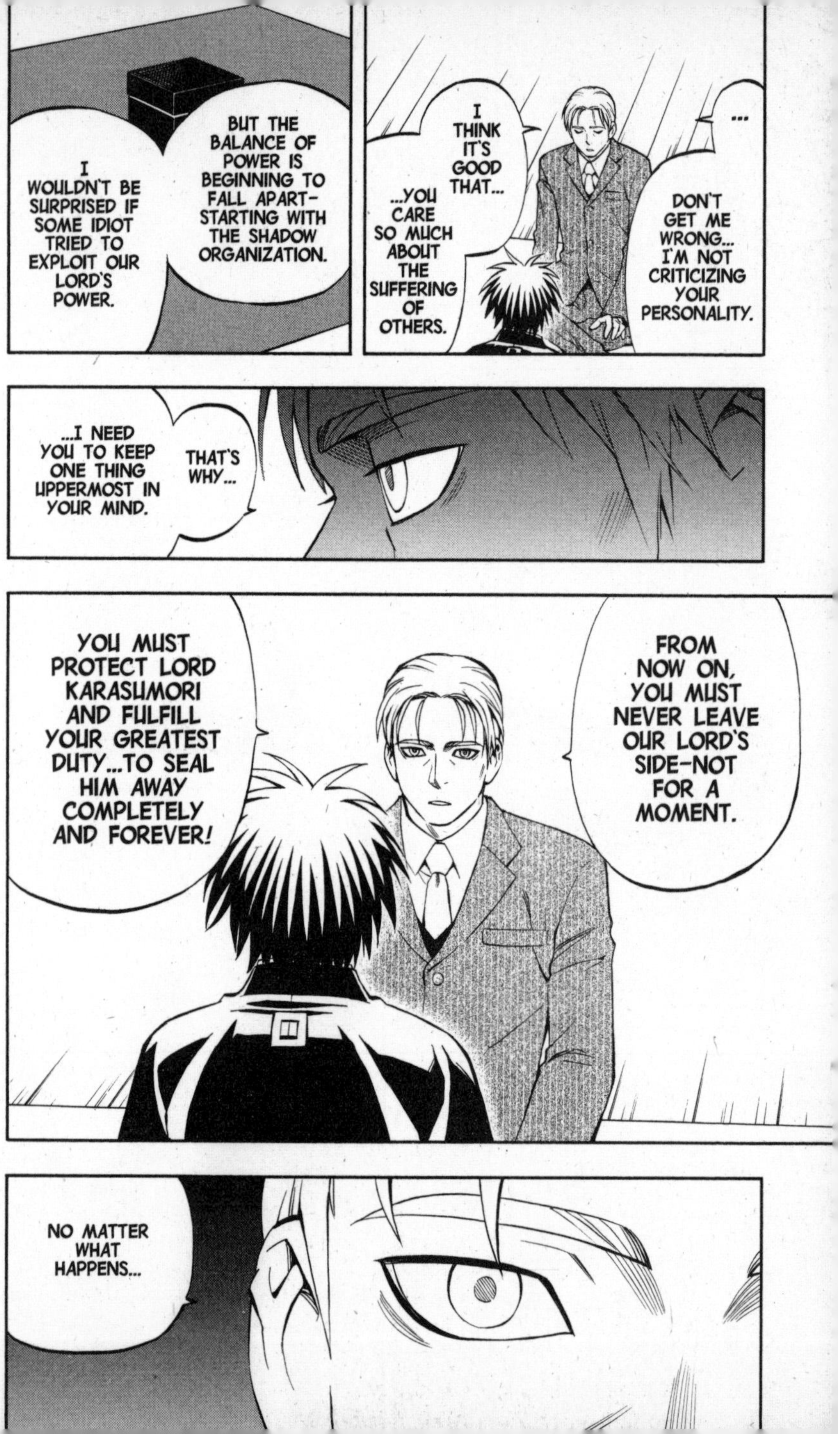
...
DON'T GET ME WRONG... I'M NOT CRITICIZING YOUR PERSONALITY.
I THINK IT'S GOOD THAT...
...YOU CARE SO MUCH ABOUT THE SUFFERING OF OTHERS.
BUT THE BALANCE OF POWER IS BEGINNING TO FALL APART–STARTING WITH THE SHADOW ORGANIZATION.
I WOULDN'T BE SURPRISED IF SOME IDIOT TRIED TO EXPLOIT OUR LORD'S POWER.
THAT'S WHY...
...I NEED YOU TO KEEP ONE THING UPPERMOST IN YOUR MIND.
FROM NOW ON, YOU MUST NEVER LEAVE OUR LORD'S SIDE–NOT FOR A MOMENT.
YOU MUST PROTECT LORD KARASUMORI AND FULFILL YOUR GREATEST DUTY...TO SEAL HIM AWAY COMPLETELY AND FOREVER!
NO MATTER WHAT HAPPENS...

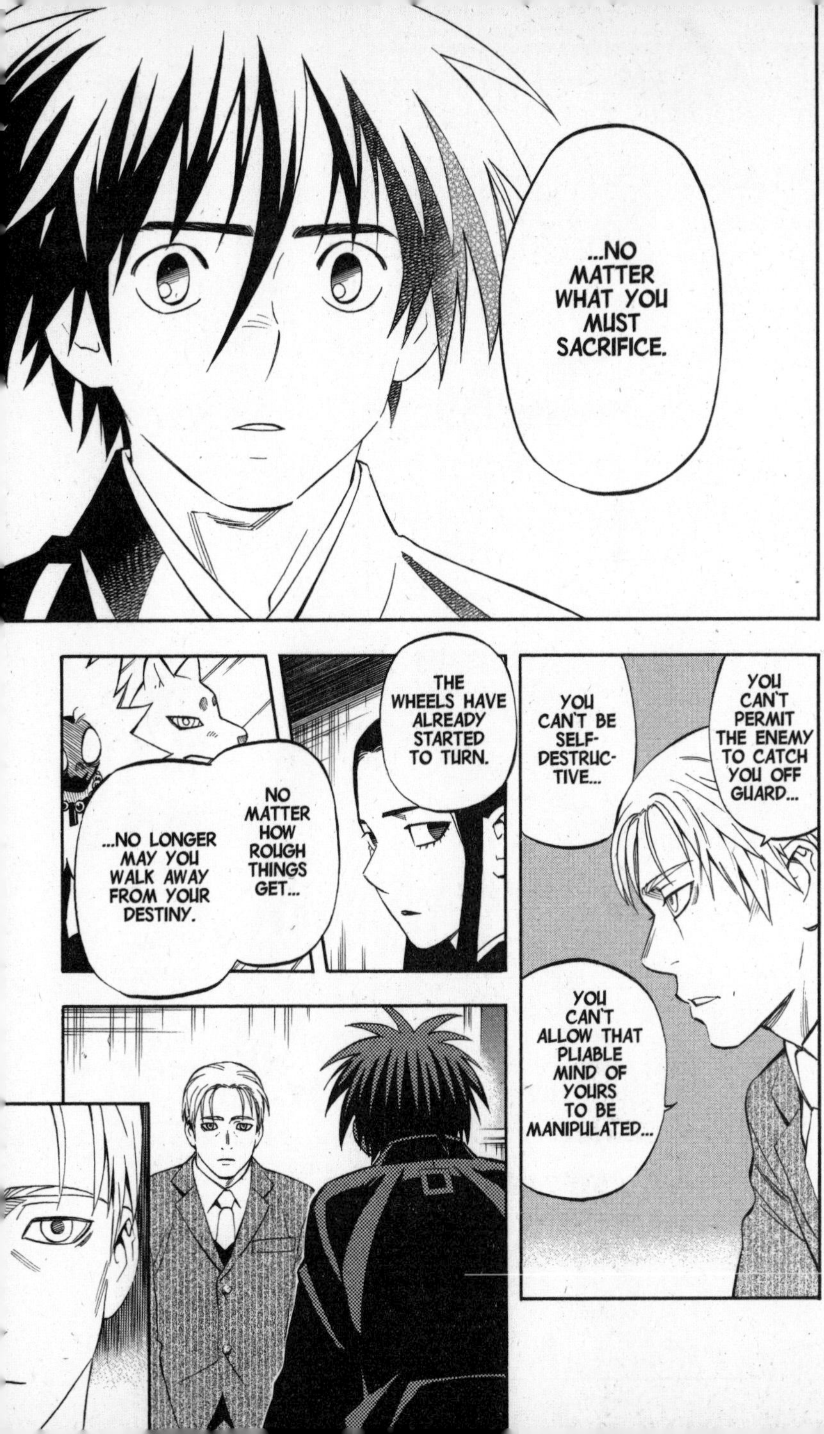
...NO MATTER WHAT YOU MUST SACRIFICE.
YOU CAN'T PERMIT THE ENEMY TO CATCH YOU OFF GUARD...
YOU CAN'T BE SELF-DESTRUCTIVE...
YOU CAN'T ALLOW THAT PLIABLE MIND OF YOURS TO BE MANIPULATED...
THE WHEELS HAVE ALREADY STARTED TO TURN.
NO MATTER HOW ROUGH THINGS GET...
...NO LONGER MAY YOU WALK AWAY FROM YOUR DESTINY.

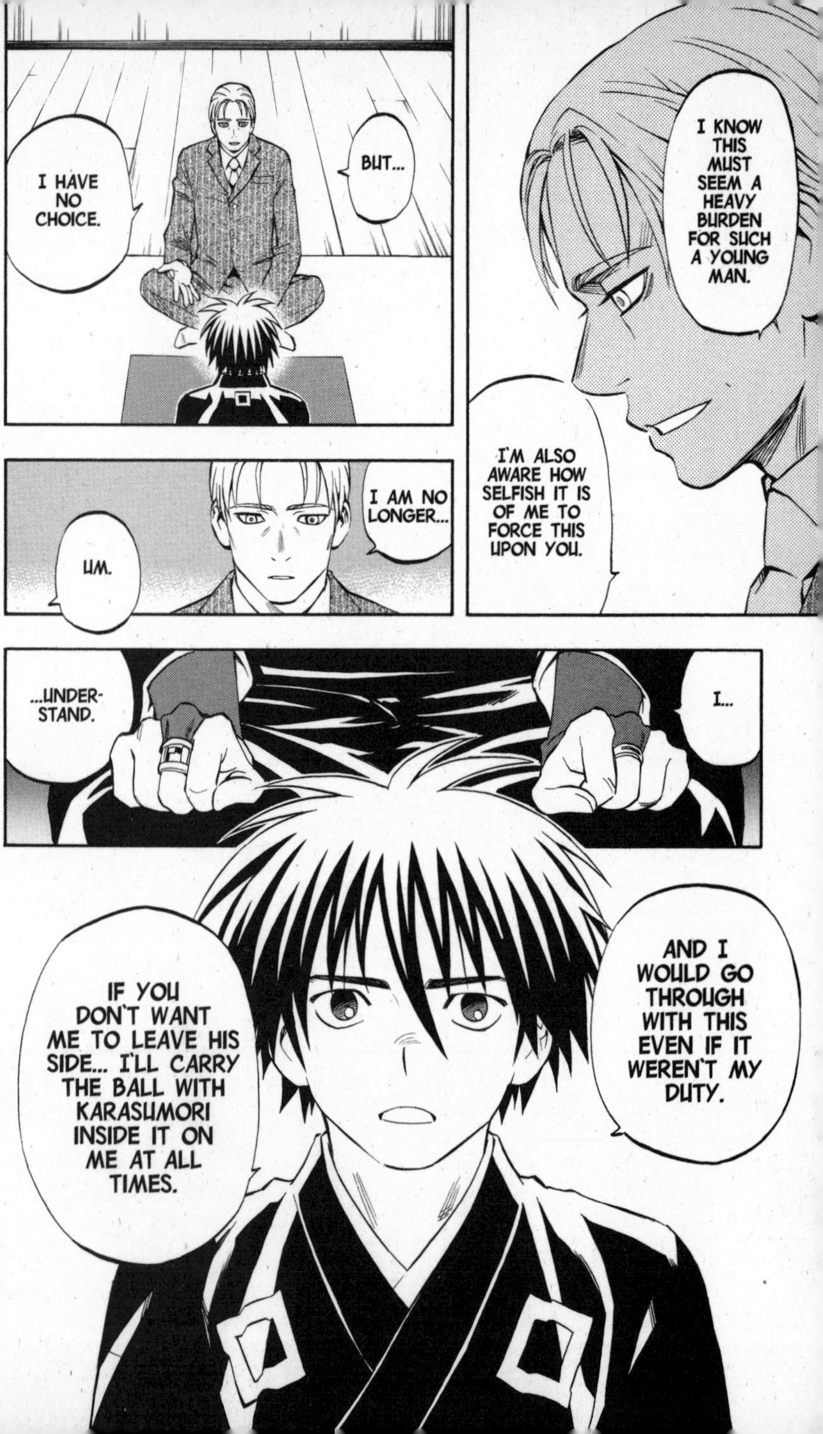
I KNOW THIS MUST SEEM A HEAVY BURDEN FOR SUCH A YOUNG MAN.
I'M ALSO AWARE HOW SELFISH IT IS OF ME TO FORCE THIS UPON YOU.
BUT...
I HAVE NO CHOICE.
I AM NO LONGER...
UM.
I...
...UNDER-STAND.
AND I WOULD GO THROUGH WITH THIS EVEN IF IT WEREN'T MY DUTY.
IF YOU DON'T WANT ME TO LEAVE HIS SIDE... I'LL CARRY THE BALL WITH KARASUMORI INSIDE IT ON ME AT ALL TIMES.

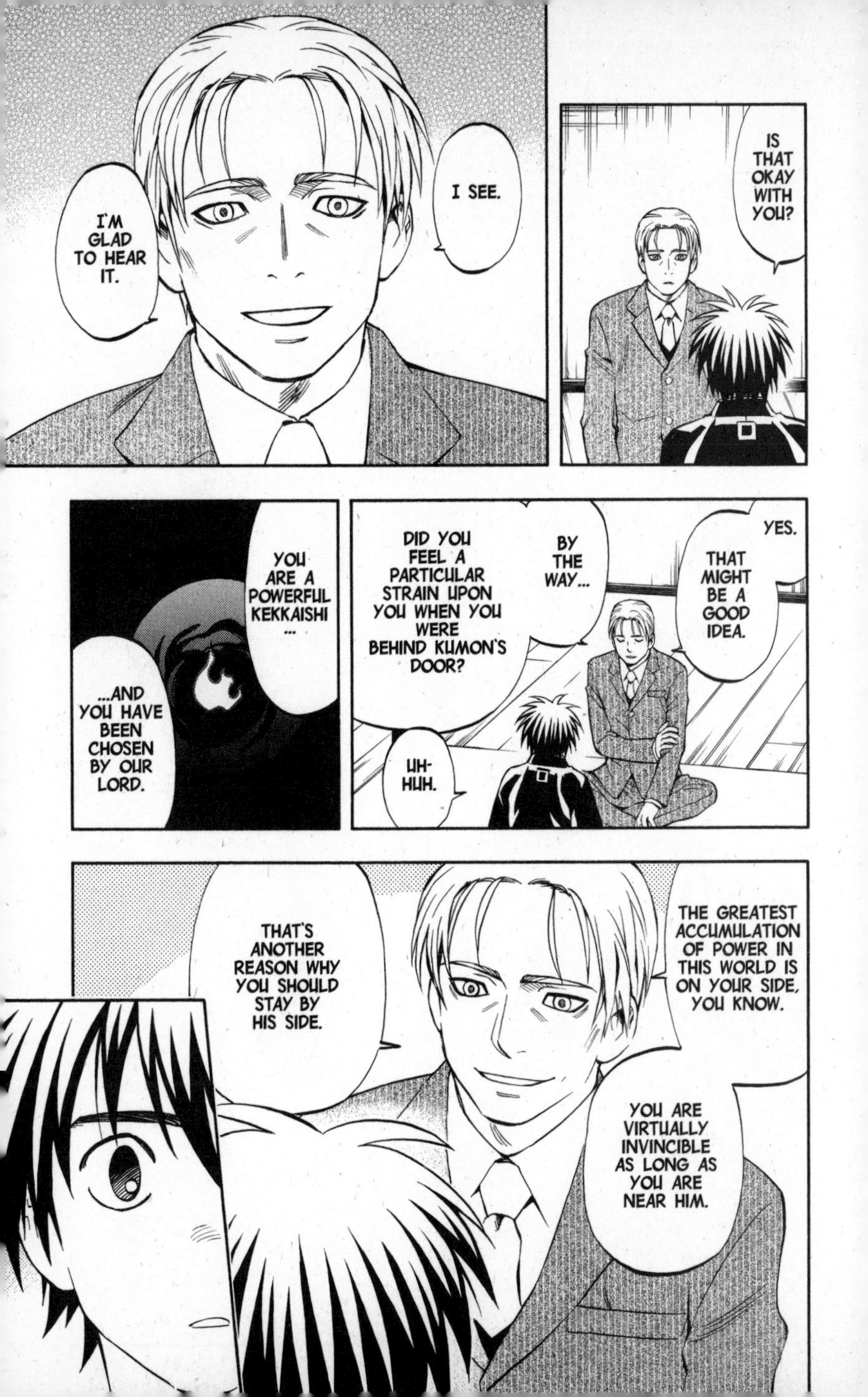
IS THAT OKAY WITH YOU?
I SEE.
I'M GLAD TO HEAR IT.
YES.
THAT MIGHT BE A GOOD IDEA.
BY THE WAY...
DID YOU FEEL A PARTICULAR STRAIN UPON YOU WHEN YOU WERE BEHIND KUMON'S DOOR?
UH-HUH.
YOU ARE A POWERFUL KEKKAISHI ...
...AND YOU HAVE BEEN CHOSEN BY OUR LORD.
THE GREATEST ACCUMULATION OF POWER IN THIS WORLD IS ON YOUR SIDE, YOU KNOW.
YOU ARE VIRTUALLY INVINCIBLE AS LONG AS YOU ARE NEAR HIM.
THAT'S ANOTHER REASON WHY YOU SHOULD STAY BY HIS SIDE.

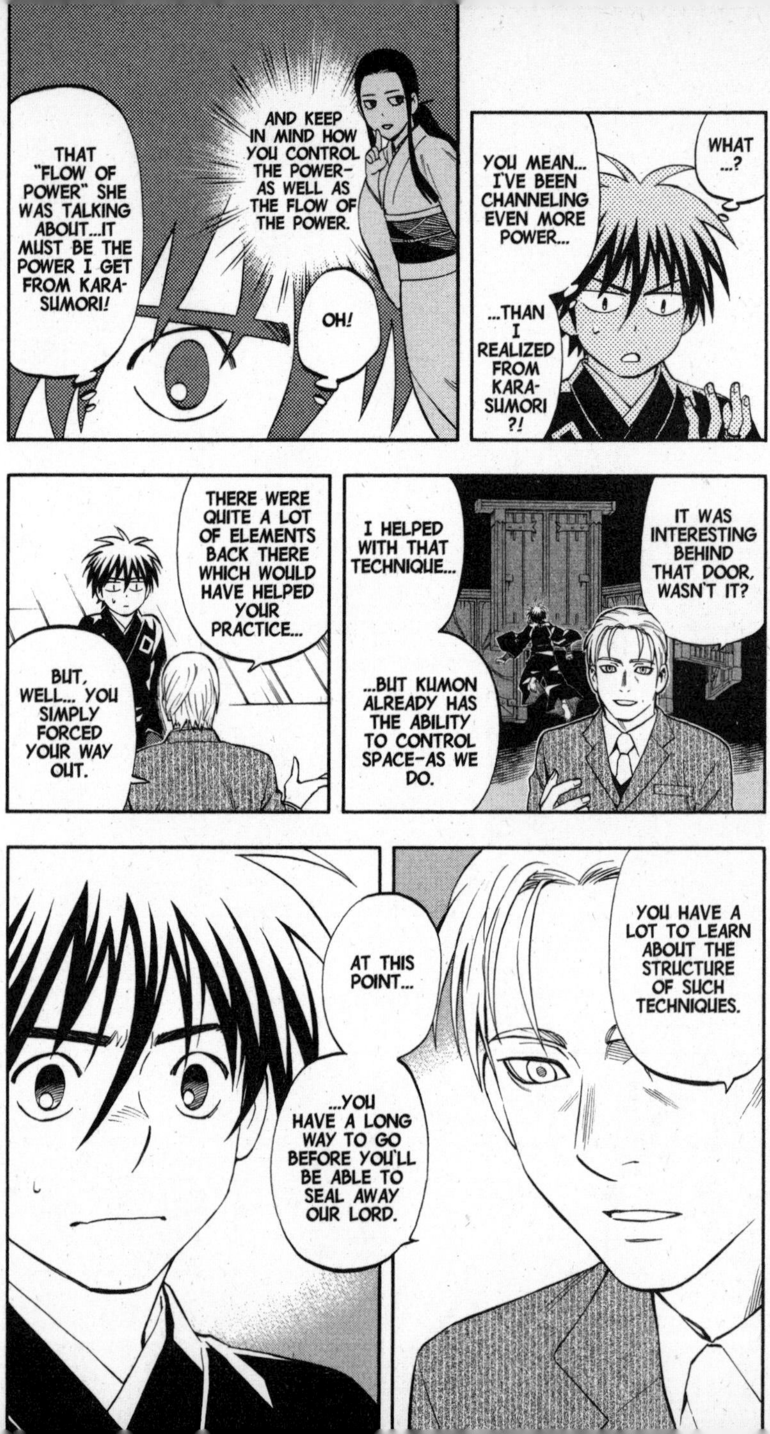
WHAT ...?
YOU MEAN... I'VE BEEN CHANNELING EVEN MORE POWER...
...THAN I REALIZED FROM KARA-SUMORI ?!
AND KEEP IN MIND HOW YOU CONTROL THE POWER– AS WELL AS THE FLOW OF THE POWER.
THAT "FLOW OF POWER" SHE WAS TALKING ABOUT...IT MUST BE THE POWER I GET FROM KARA-SUMORI!
OH!
IT WAS INTERESTING BEHIND THAT DOOR, WASN'T IT?
I HELPED WITH THAT TECHNIQUE...
...BUT KUMON ALREADY HAS THE ABILITY TO CONTROL SPACE–AS WE DO.
THERE WERE QUITE A LOT OF ELEMENTS BACK THERE WHICH WOULD HAVE HELPED YOUR PRACTICE...
BUT, WELL... YOU SIMPLY FORCED YOUR WAY OUT.
YOU HAVE A LOT TO LEARN ABOUT THE STRUCTURE OF SUCH TECHNIQUES.
AT THIS POINT...
...YOU HAVE A LONG WAY TO GO BEFORE YOU'LL BE ABLE TO SEAL AWAY OUR LORD.

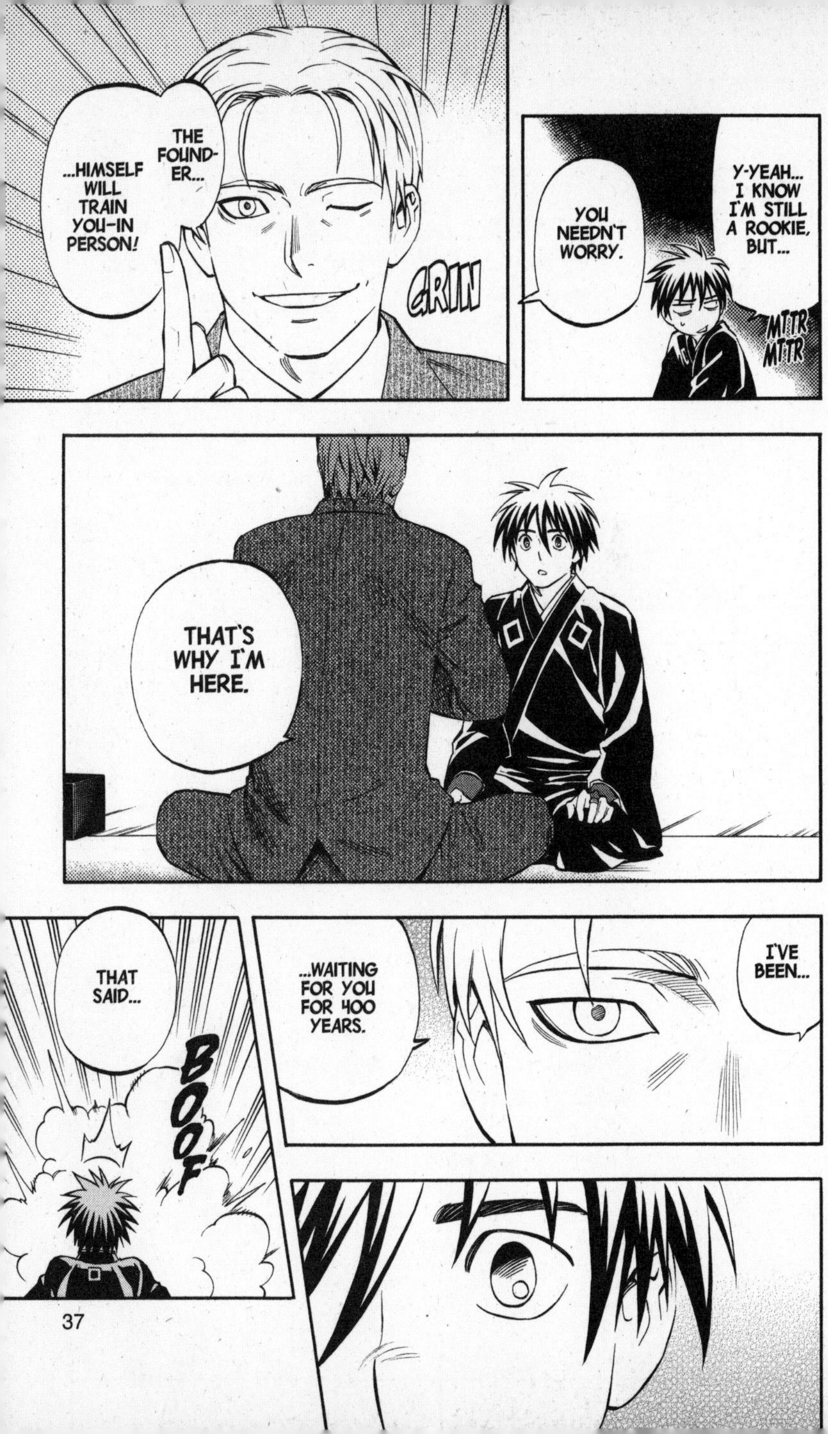
Y-YEAH... I KNOW I'M STILL A ROOKIE, BUT...
MTTR MTTR
YOU NEEDN'T WORRY.
THE FOUNDER-ER...
...HIMSELF WILL TRAIN YOU-IN PERSON!
GRIN
THAT'S WHY I'M HERE.
I'VE BEEN...
...WAITING FOR YOU FOR 400 YEARS.
THAT SAID...
BOOOF

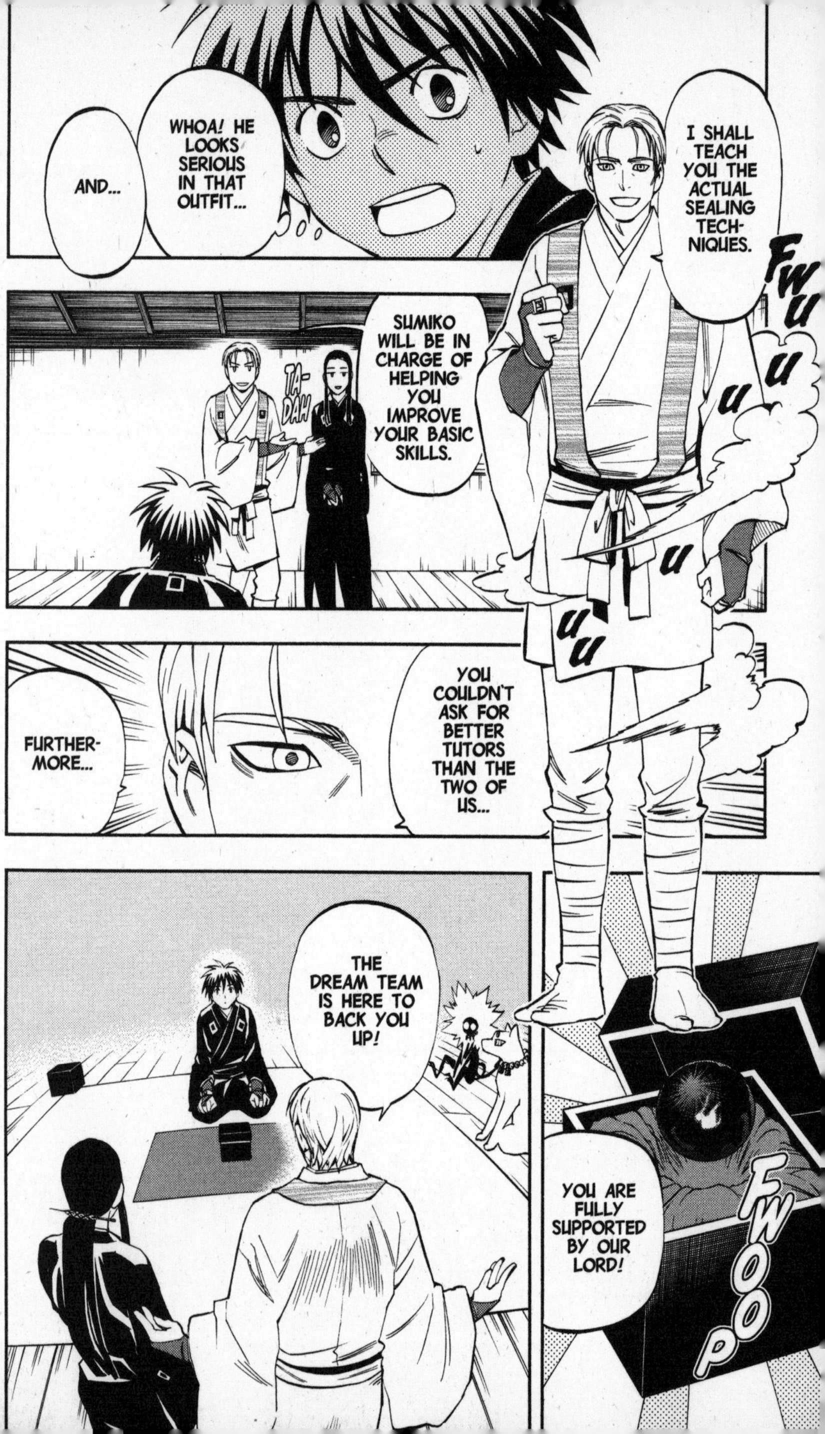
I SHALL TEACH YOU THE ACTUAL SEALING TECH-NIQUES.
FWUUUUUUU
WHOA! HE LOOKS SERIOUS IN THAT OUTFIT...
AND...
SUMIKO WILL BE IN CHARGE OF HELPING YOU IMPROVE YOUR BASIC SKILLS.
TA-DAH
YOU COULDN'T ASK FOR BETTER TUTORS THAN THE TWO OF US...
FURTHER-MORE...
YOU ARE FULLY SUPPORTED BY OUR LORD!
FWOOP
THE DREAM TEAM IS HERE TO BACK YOU UP!

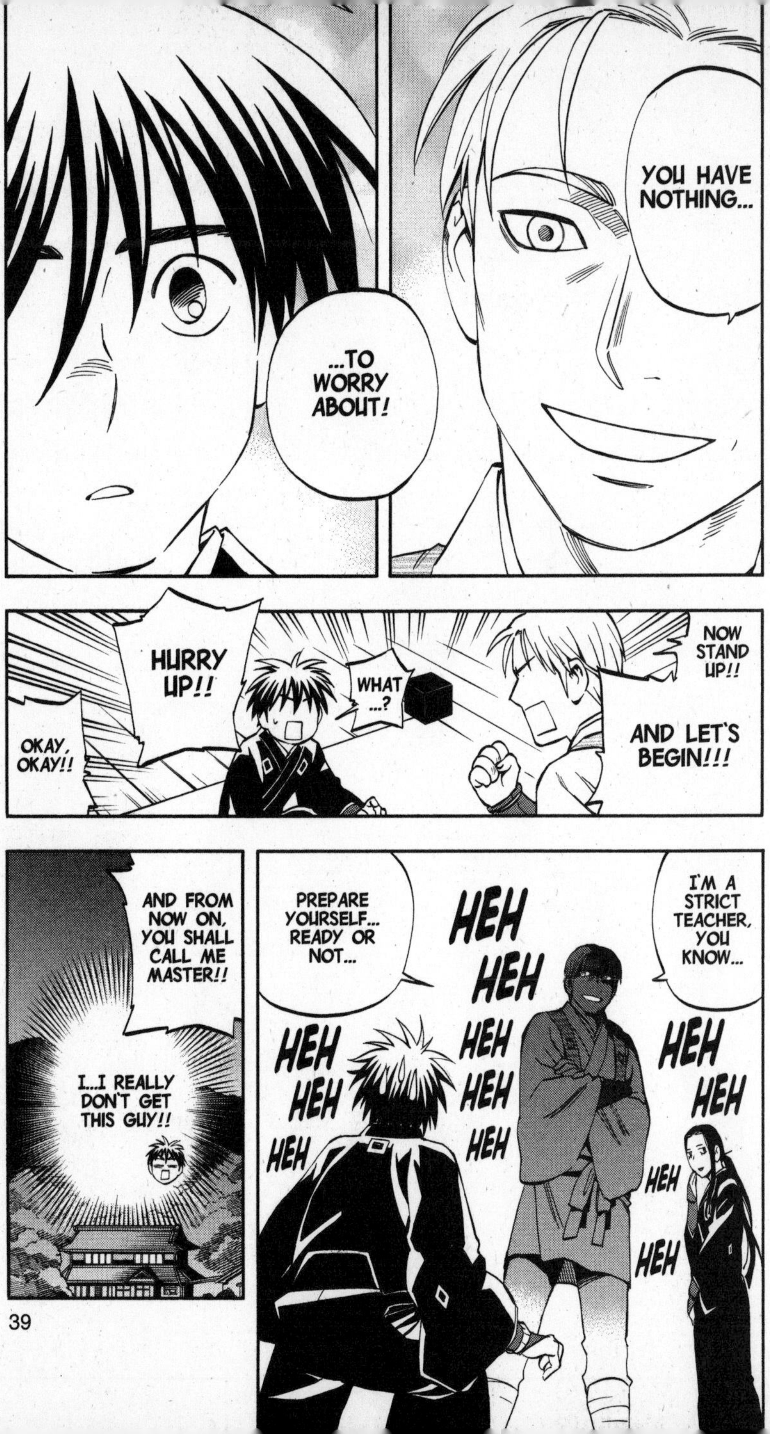
YOU HAVE NOTHING...
...TO WORRY ABOUT!
NOW STAND UP!!
AND LET'S BEGIN!!!
WHAT ...?
HURRY UP!!
OKAY, OKAY!!
I'M A STRICT TEACHER, YOU KNOW...
HEH HEH
HEH HEH
HEH HEH HEH HEH HEH
PREPARE YOURSELF... READY OR NOT...
HEH HEH HEH
AND FROM NOW ON, YOU SHALL CALL ME MASTER!!
I...I REALLY DON'T GET THIS GUY!!

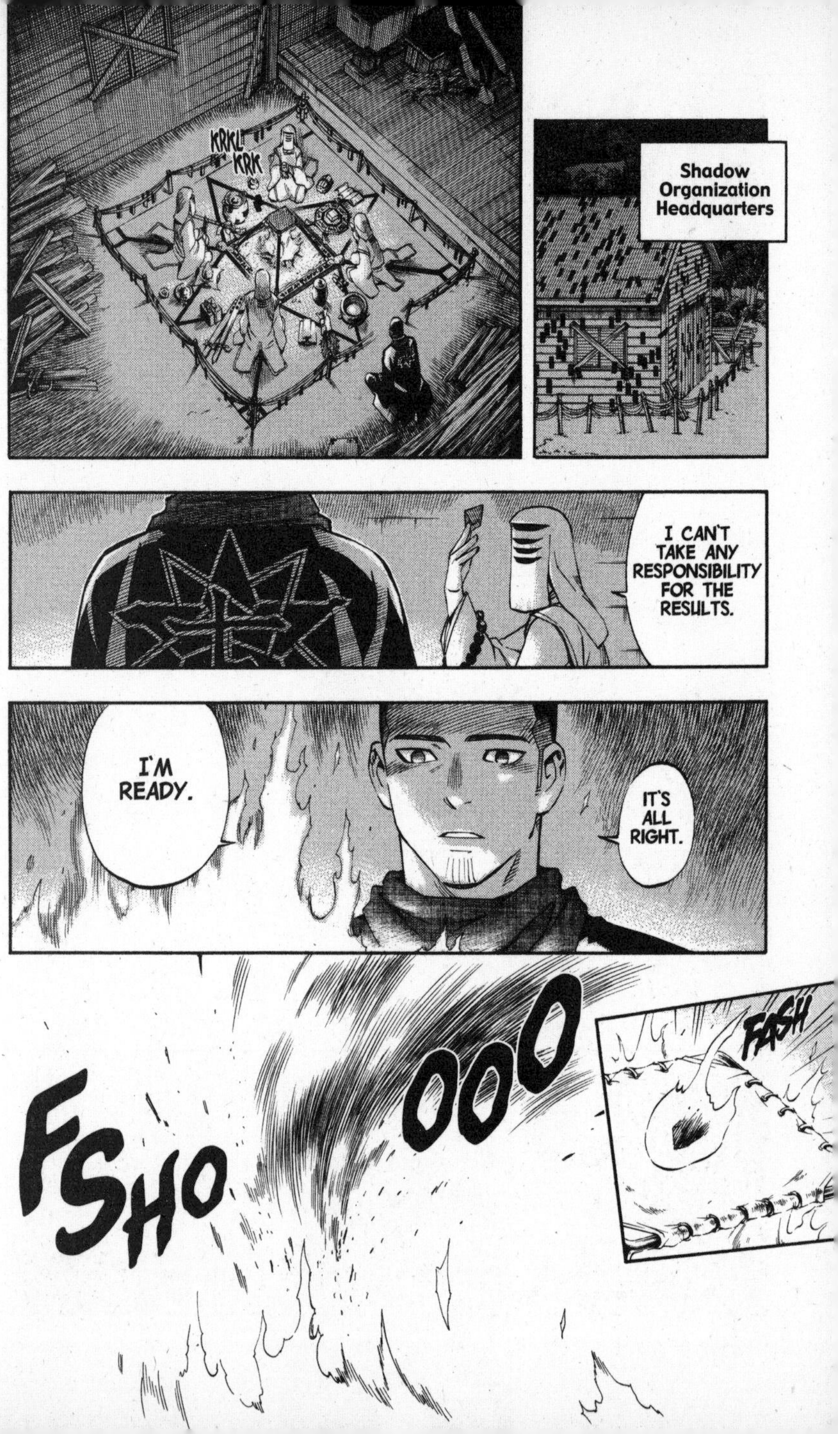
Shadow Organization Headquarters
KRKL KRK
I CAN'T TAKE ANY RESPONSIBILITY FOR THE RESULTS.
IT'S ALL RIGHT.
I'M READY.
FASH
FSHOOOO

CHAPTER 298
RESURRECTION

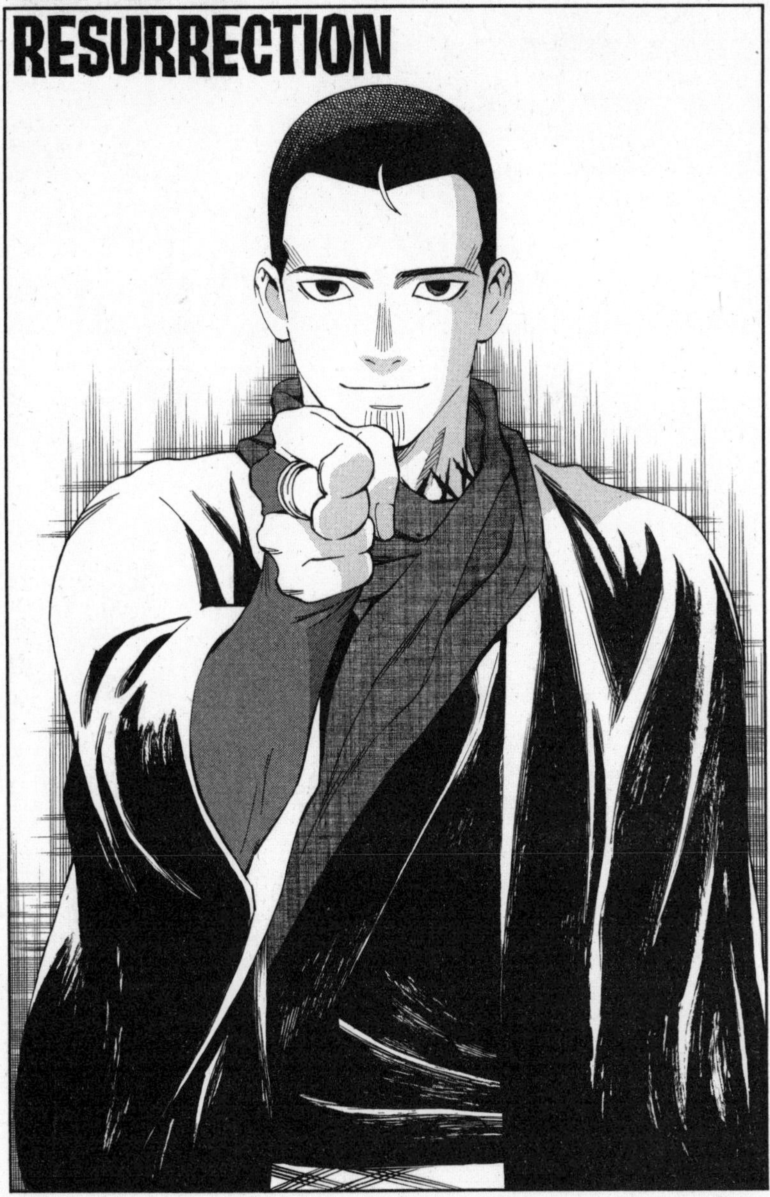

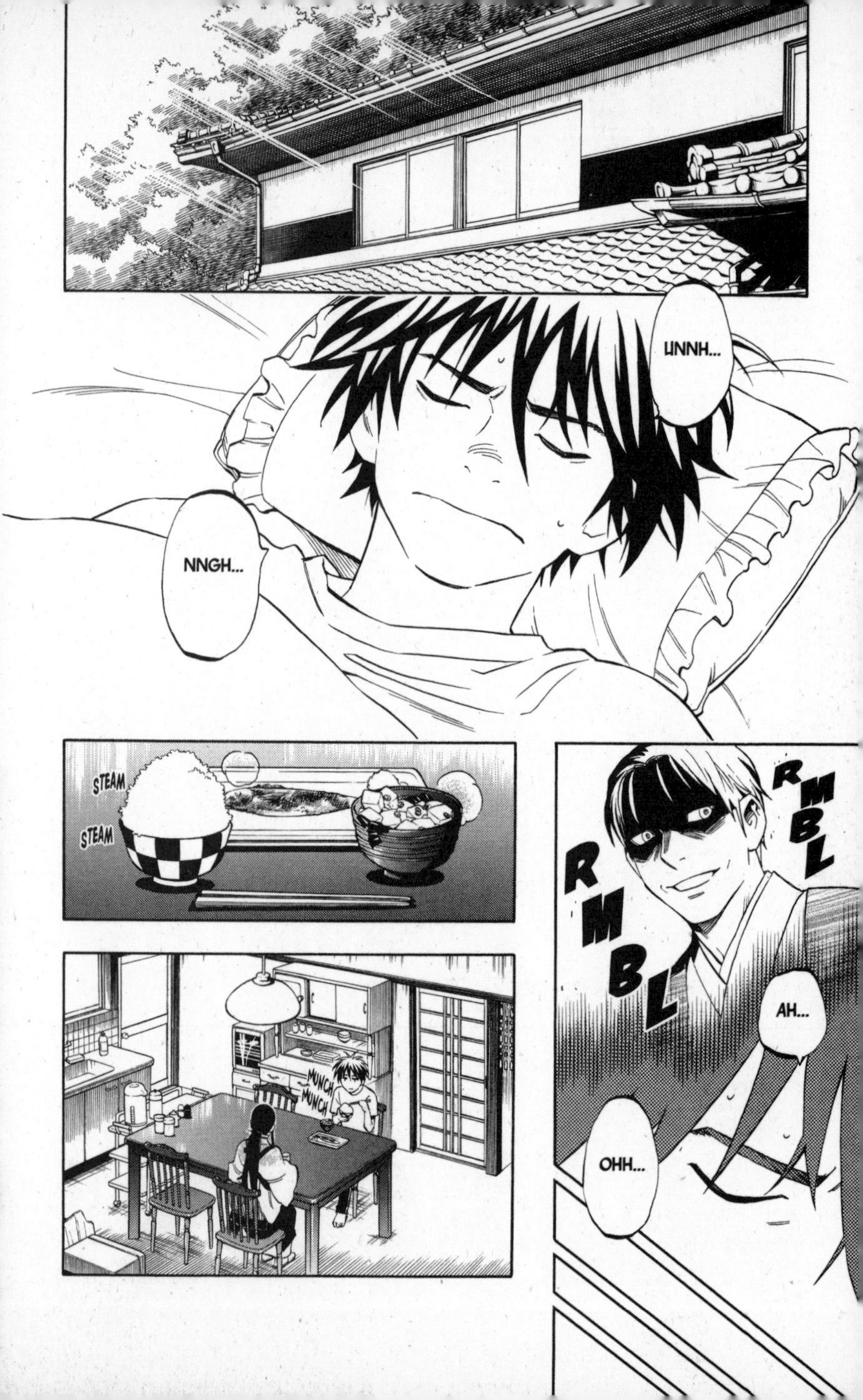
UNNH...
NNGH...
RMBL
RMBL
AH...
OHH...
STEAM
STEAM
MUNCH
MUNCH

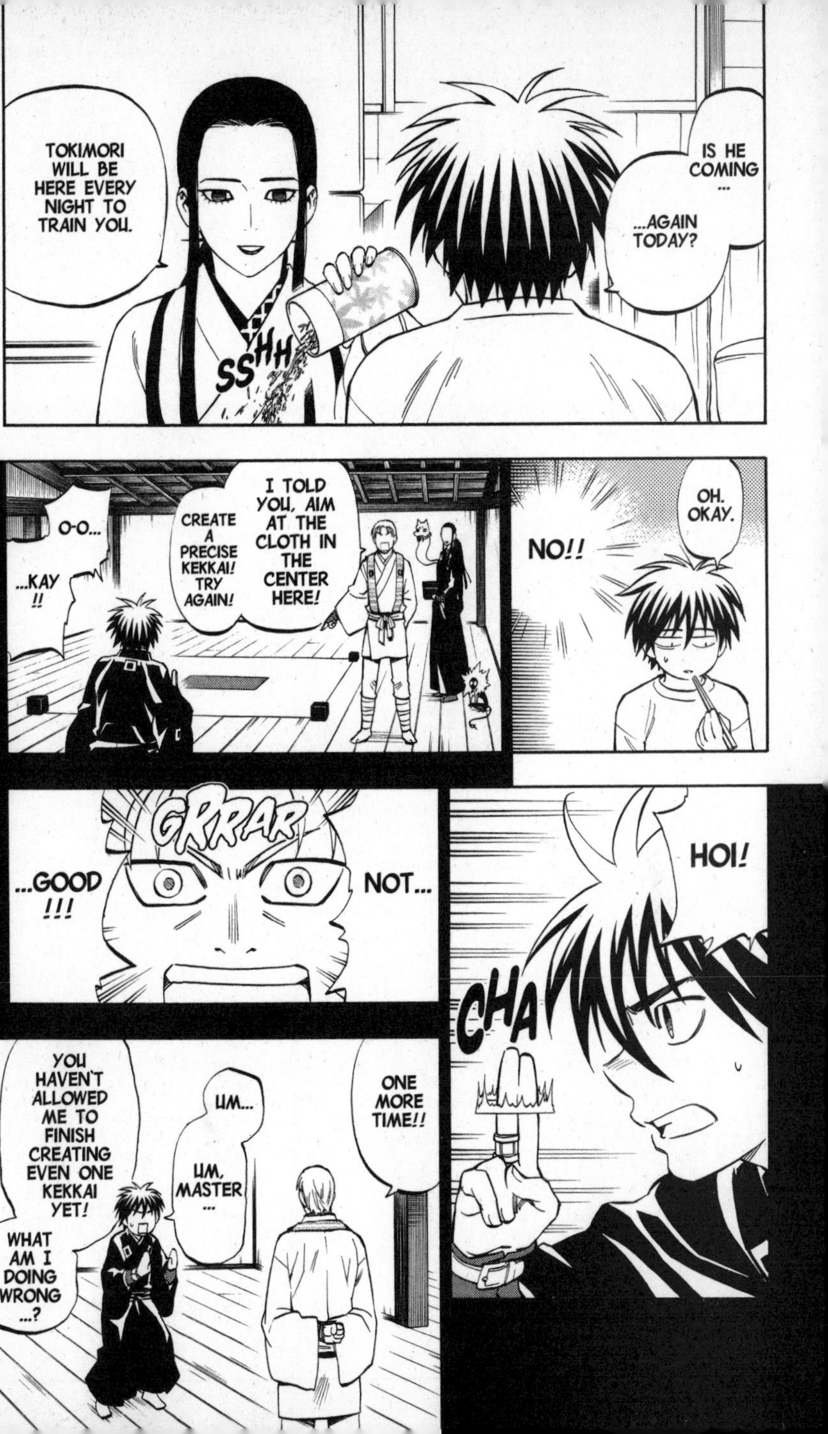
IS HE COMING ...
...AGAIN TODAY?
TOKIMORI WILL BE HERE EVERY NIGHT TO TRAIN YOU.
SSHH
OH. OKAY.
NO!!
I TOLD YOU, AIM AT THE CLOTH IN THE CENTER HERE!
CREATE A PRECISE KEKKAI! TRY AGAIN!
O-O...
...KAY !!
HOI!
CHA
NOT...
GRRAR
...GOOD !!!
ONE MORE TIME!!
UM...
UM, MASTER ...
YOU HAVEN'T ALLOWED ME TO FINISH CREATING EVEN ONE KEKKAI YET!
WHAT AM I DOING WRONG ...?

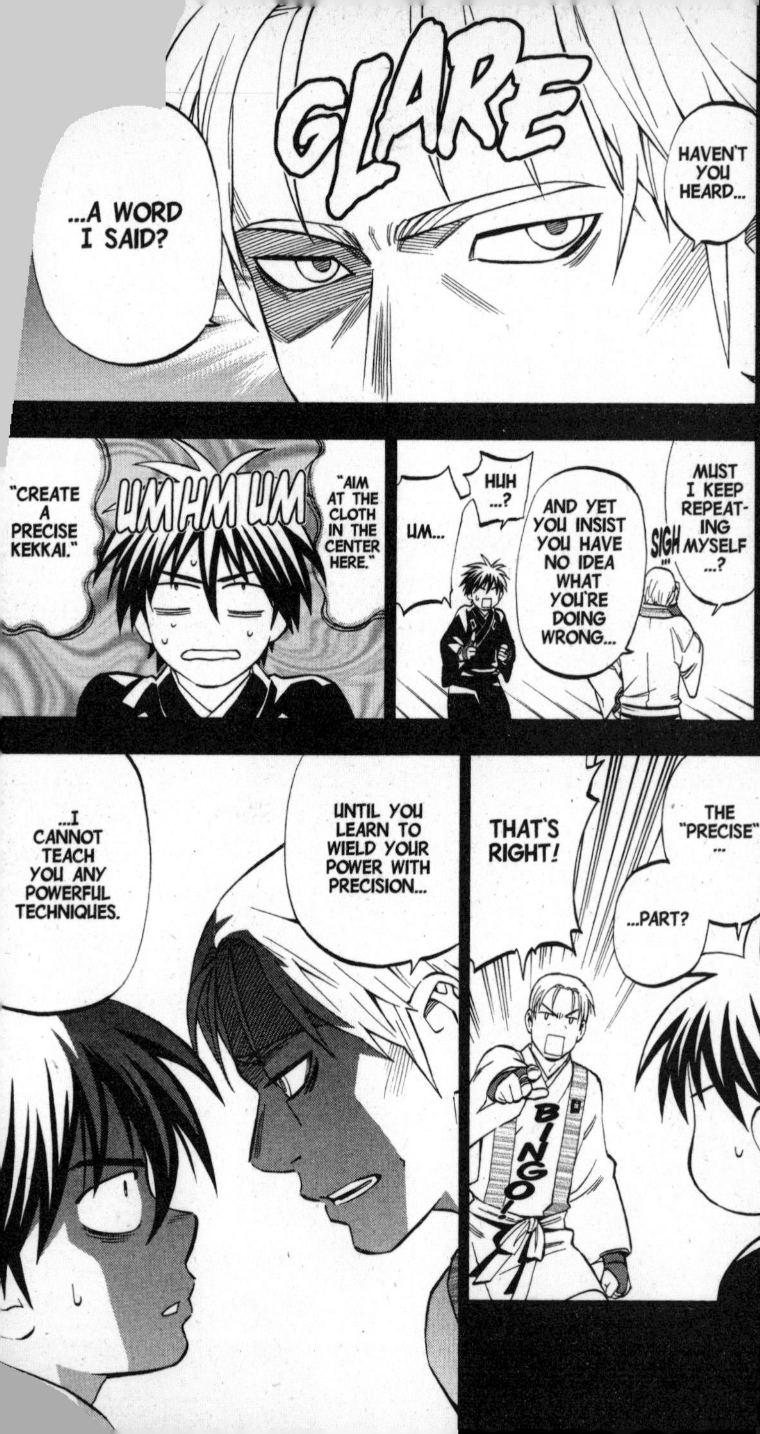
HAVEN'T YOU HEARD...
GLARE
...A WORD I SAID?
MUST I KEEP REPEAT-ING MYSELF...?
SIGH
AND YET YOU INSIST YOU HAVE NO IDEA WHAT YOU'RE DOING WRONG...
HUH...?
UM...
"AIM AT THE CLOTH IN THE CENTER HERE."
UM HM UM
"CREATE A PRECISE KEKKAI."
THE "PRECISE"...
...PART?
THAT'S RIGHT!
BINGO!
UNTIL YOU LEARN TO WIELD YOUR POWER WITH PRECISION...
...I CANNOT TEACH YOU ANY POWERFUL TECHNIQUES.

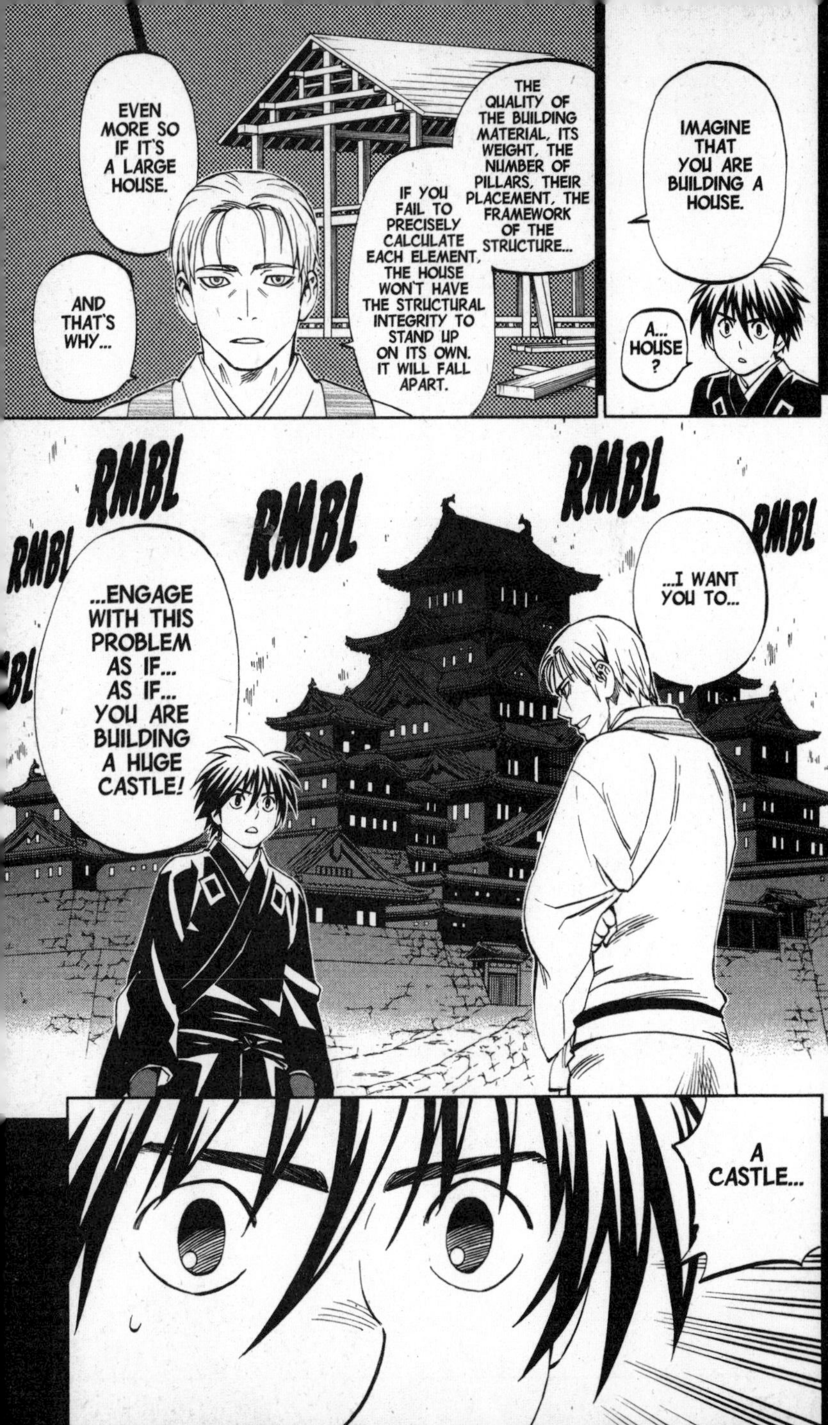
IMAGINE THAT YOU ARE BUILDING A HOUSE.
A... HOUSE?
THE QUALITY OF THE BUILDING MATERIAL, ITS WEIGHT, THE NUMBER OF PILLARS, THEIR PLACEMENT, THE FRAMEWORK OF THE STRUCTURE...
IF YOU FAIL TO PRECISELY CALCULATE EACH ELEMENT, THE HOUSE WON'T HAVE THE STRUCTURAL INTEGRITY TO STAND UP ON ITS OWN. IT WILL FALL APART.
EVEN MORE SO IF IT'S A LARGE HOUSE.
AND THAT'S WHY...
RMBL
RMBL
RMBL
RMBL
RMBL
...I WANT YOU TO...
...ENGAGE WITH THIS PROBLEM AS IF... AS IF... YOU ARE BUILDING A HUGE CASTLE!
A CASTLE...

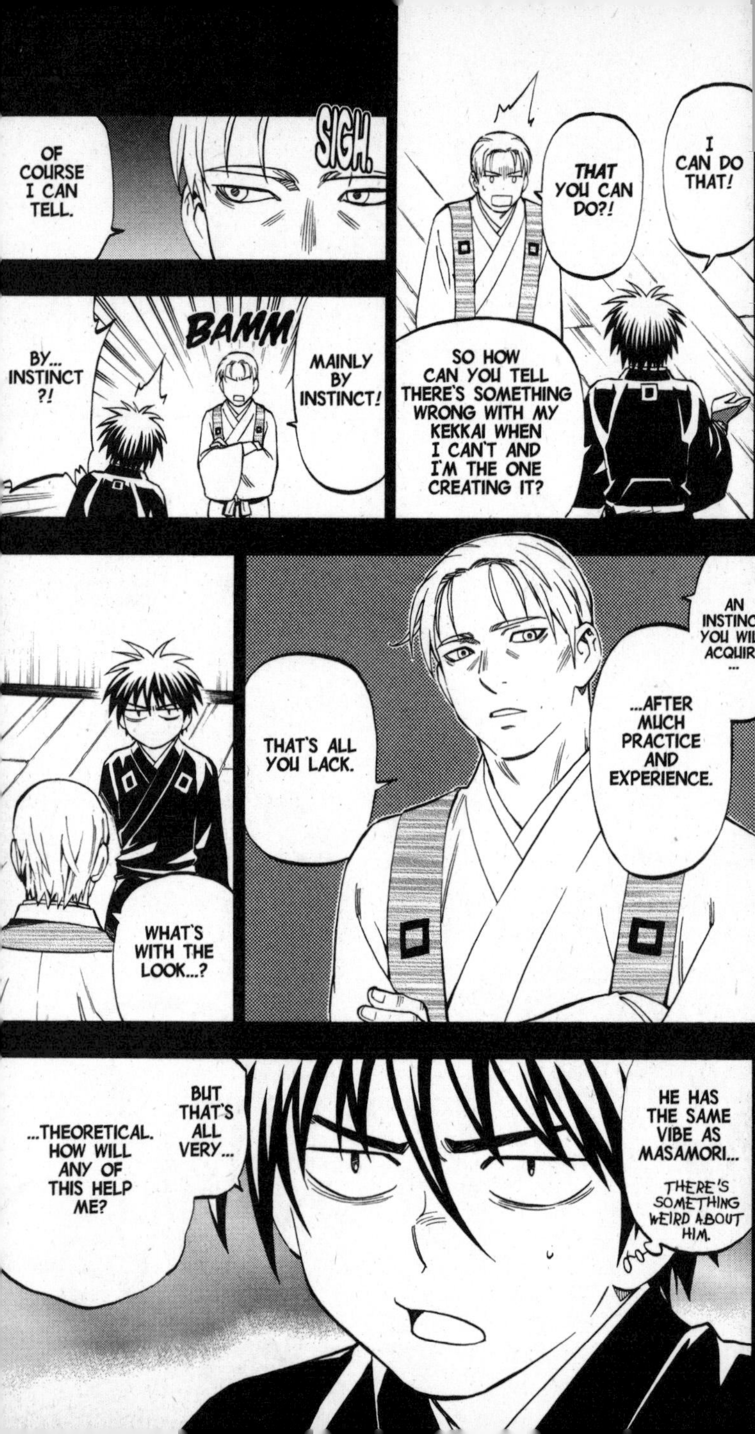
I CAN DO THAT!
THAT YOU CAN DO?!
SO HOW CAN YOU TELL THERE'S SOMETHING WRONG WITH MY KEKKAI WHEN I CAN'T AND I'M THE ONE CREATING IT?
SIGH.
OF COURSE I CAN TELL.
BAMM
MAINLY BY INSTINCT!
BY... INSTINCT?!
AN INSTINC YOU WIL ACQUIRE ...
...AFTER MUCH PRACTICE AND EXPERIENCE.
THAT'S ALL YOU LACK.
WHAT'S WITH THE LOOK...?
HE HAS THE SAME VIBE AS MASAMORI...
THERE'S SOMETHING WEIRD ABOUT HIM.
BUT THAT'S ALL VERY...
...THEORETICAL. HOW WILL ANY OF THIS HELP ME?

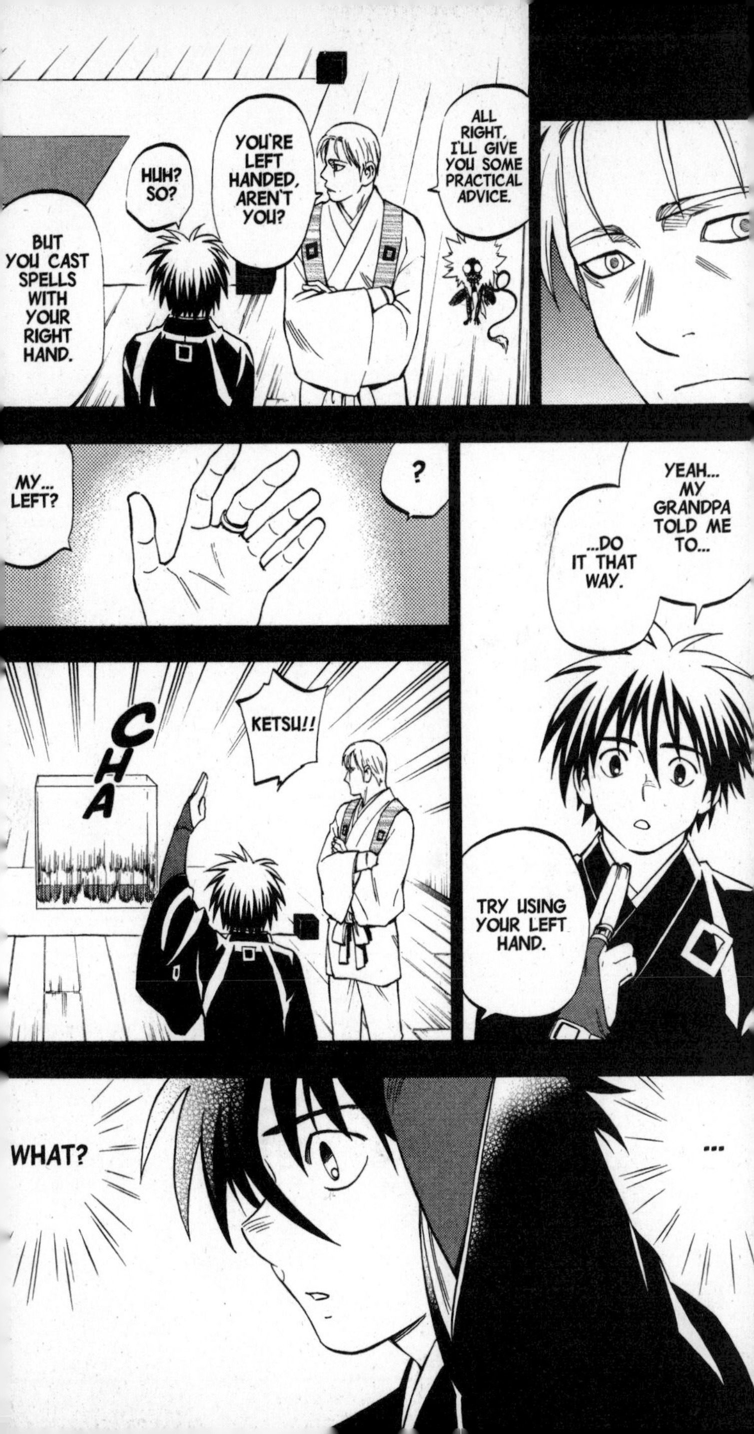
ALL RIGHT, I'LL GIVE YOU SOME PRACTICAL ADVICE.
YOU'RE LEFT HANDED, AREN'T YOU?
HUH? SO?
BUT YOU CAST SPELLS WITH YOUR RIGHT HAND.
YEAH... MY GRANDPA TOLD ME TO...
...DO IT THAT WAY.
TRY USING YOUR LEFT HAND.
?
MY... LEFT?
KETSU!!
CHA
...
WHAT?

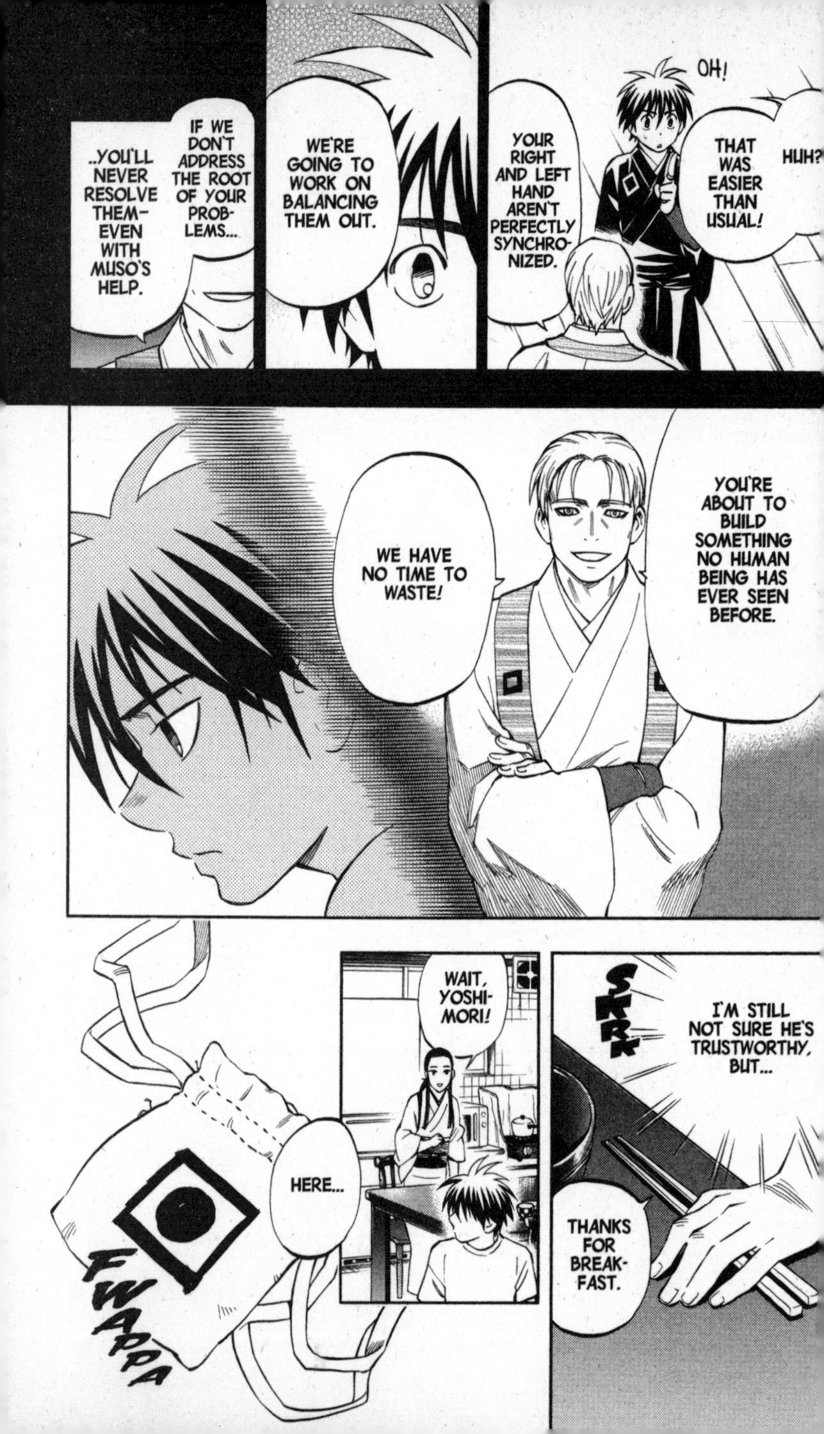
OH!
HUH?
THAT WAS EASIER THAN USUAL!
YOUR RIGHT AND LEFT HAND AREN'T PERFECTLY SYNCHRONIZED.
WE'RE GOING TO WORK ON BALANCING THEM OUT.
IF WE DON'T ADDRESS THE ROOT OF YOUR PROBLEMS...
..YOU'LL NEVER RESOLVE THEM—EVEN WITH MUSO'S HELP.
YOU'RE ABOUT TO BUILD SOMETHING NO HUMAN BEING HAS EVER SEEN BEFORE.
WE HAVE NO TIME TO WASTE!
SKRK
I'M STILL NOT SURE HE'S TRUSTWORTHY, BUT...
THANKS FOR BREAKFAST.
WAIT, YOSHIMORI!
HERE...
FWAPPA

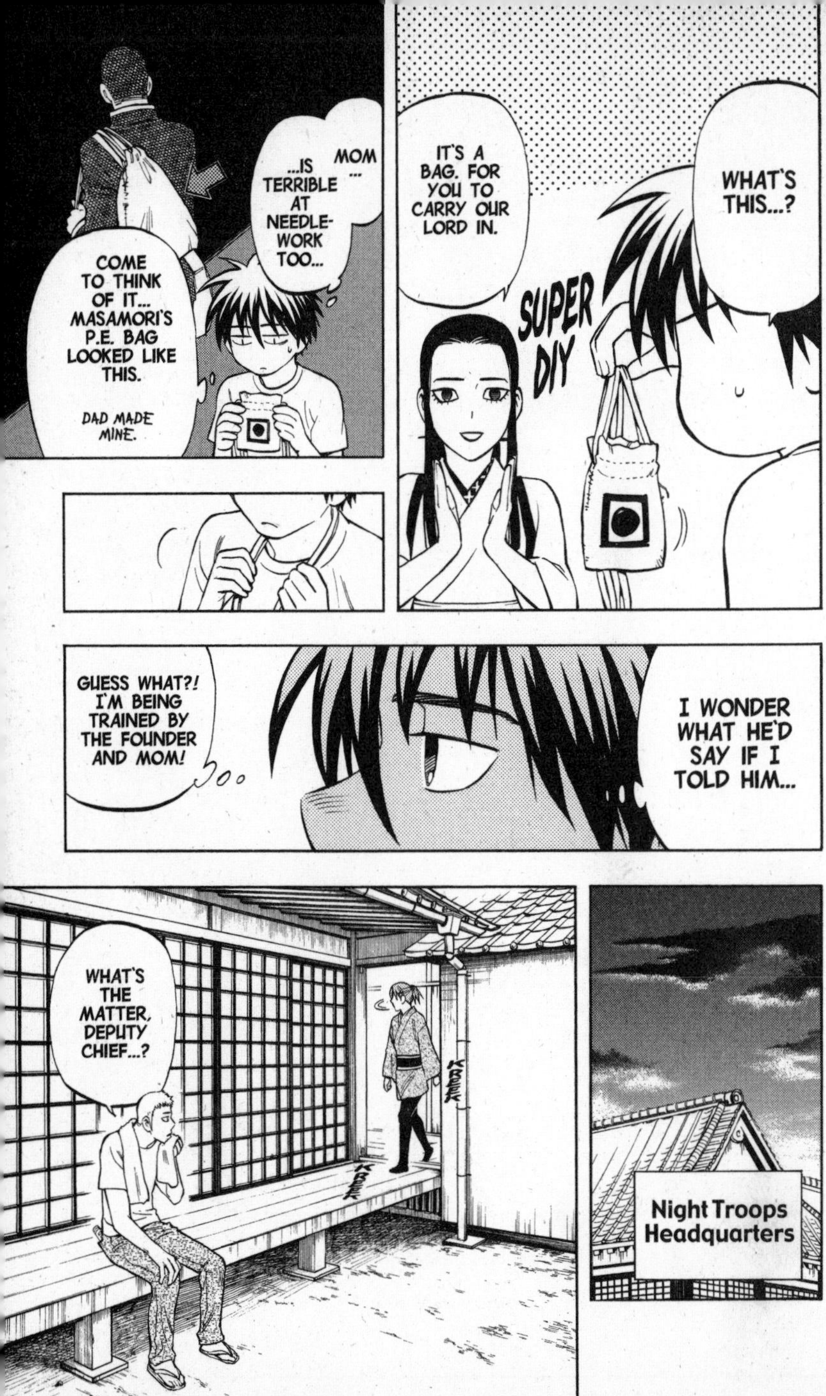
WHAT'S THIS...?
IT'S A BAG. FOR YOU TO CARRY OUR LORD IN.
SUPER DIY
MOM ... ...IS TERRIBLE AT NEEDLE-WORK TOO...
COME TO THINK OF IT... MASAMORI'S P.E. BAG LOOKED LIKE THIS.
DAD MADE MINE.
I WONDER WHAT HE'D SAY IF I TOLD HIM...
GUESS WHAT?! I'M BEING TRAINED BY THE FOUNDER AND MOM!
Night Troops Headquarters
KREEK
KREEK
WHAT'S THE MATTER, DEPUTY CHIEF...?

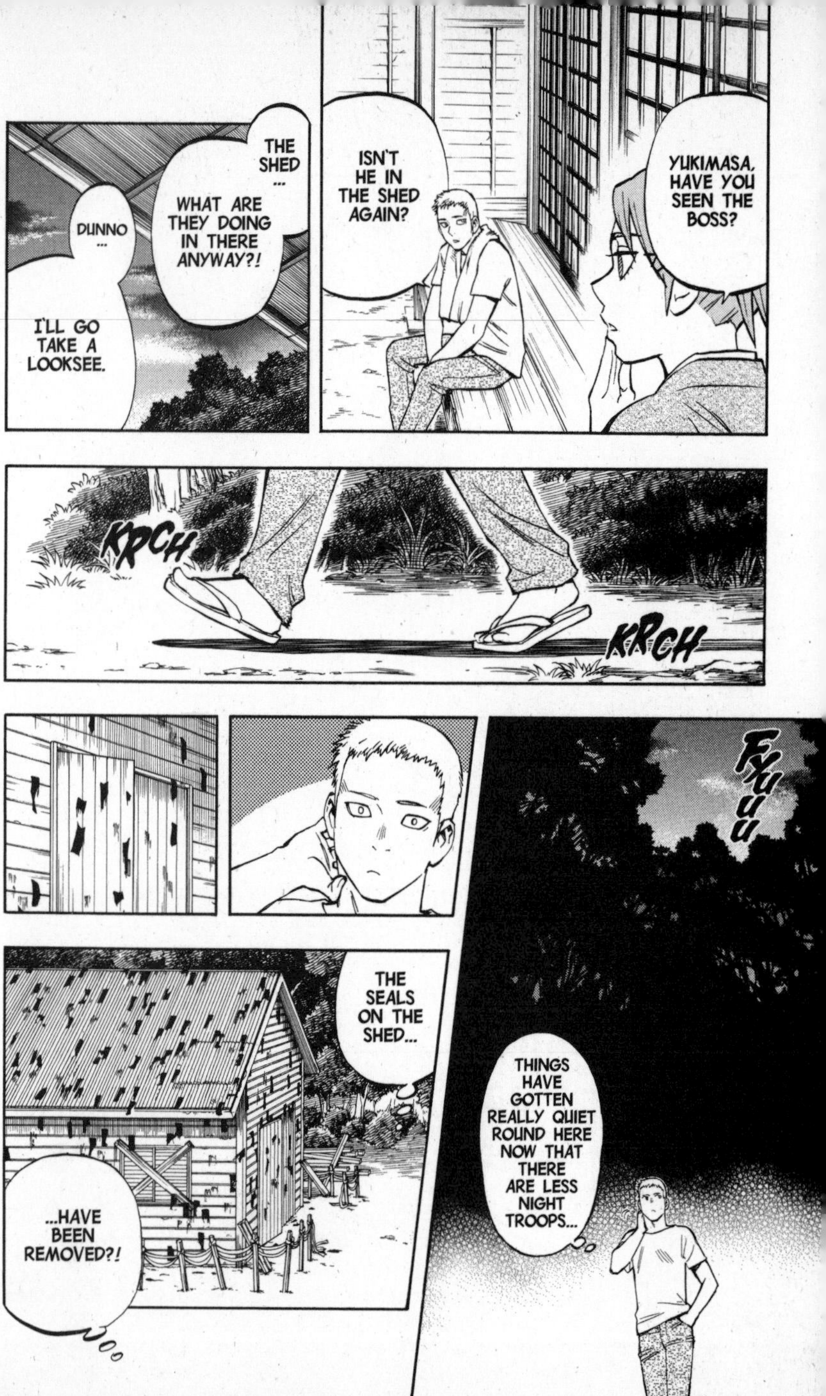
YUKIMASA, HAVE YOU SEEN THE BOSS?
ISN'T HE IN THE SHED AGAIN?
THE SHED ...
WHAT ARE THEY DOING IN THERE ANYWAY?!
DUNNO ...
I'LL GO TAKE A LOOKSEE.
KRCH
KRCH
FYUUU
THINGS HAVE GOTTEN REALLY QUIET ROUND HERE NOW THAT THERE ARE LESS NIGHT TROOPS...
THE SEALS ON THE SHED...
...HAVE BEEN REMOVED?!

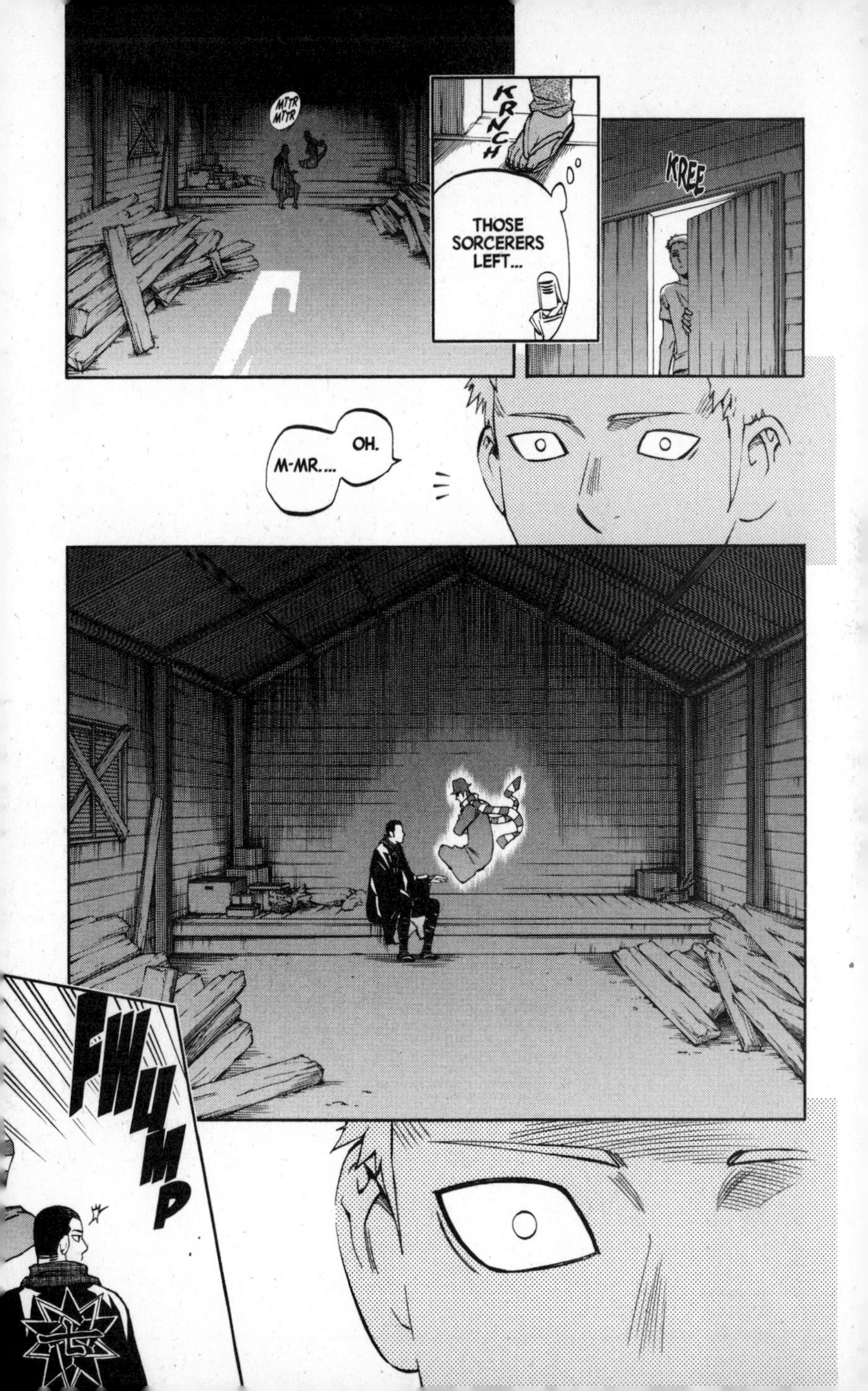
KREE
KRNCH
THOSE SORCERERS LEFT...
MTTR MTTR
OH.
M-MR....
FWUMP

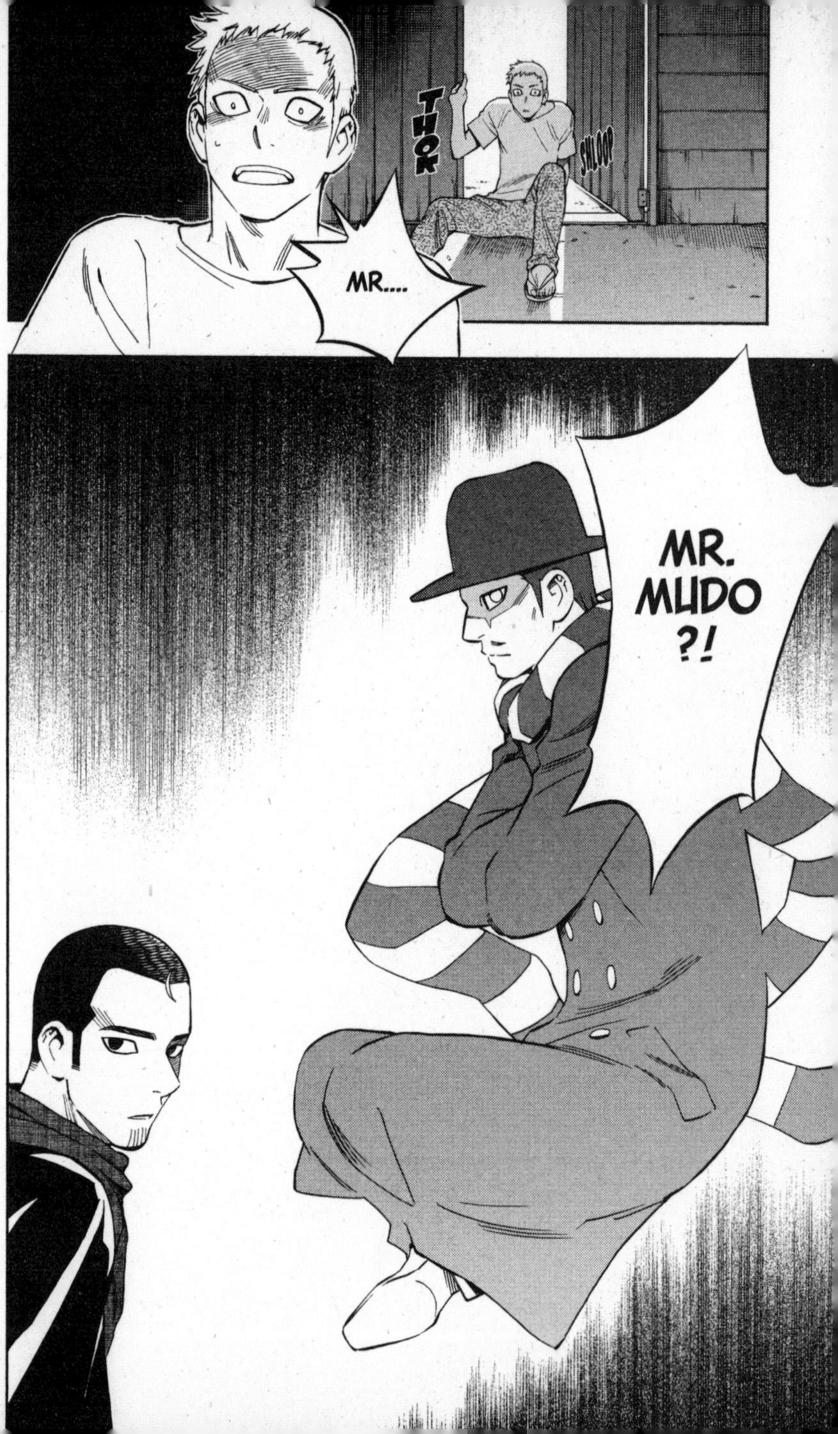
THOK
SHLOOP
MR....
MR. MUDO ?!

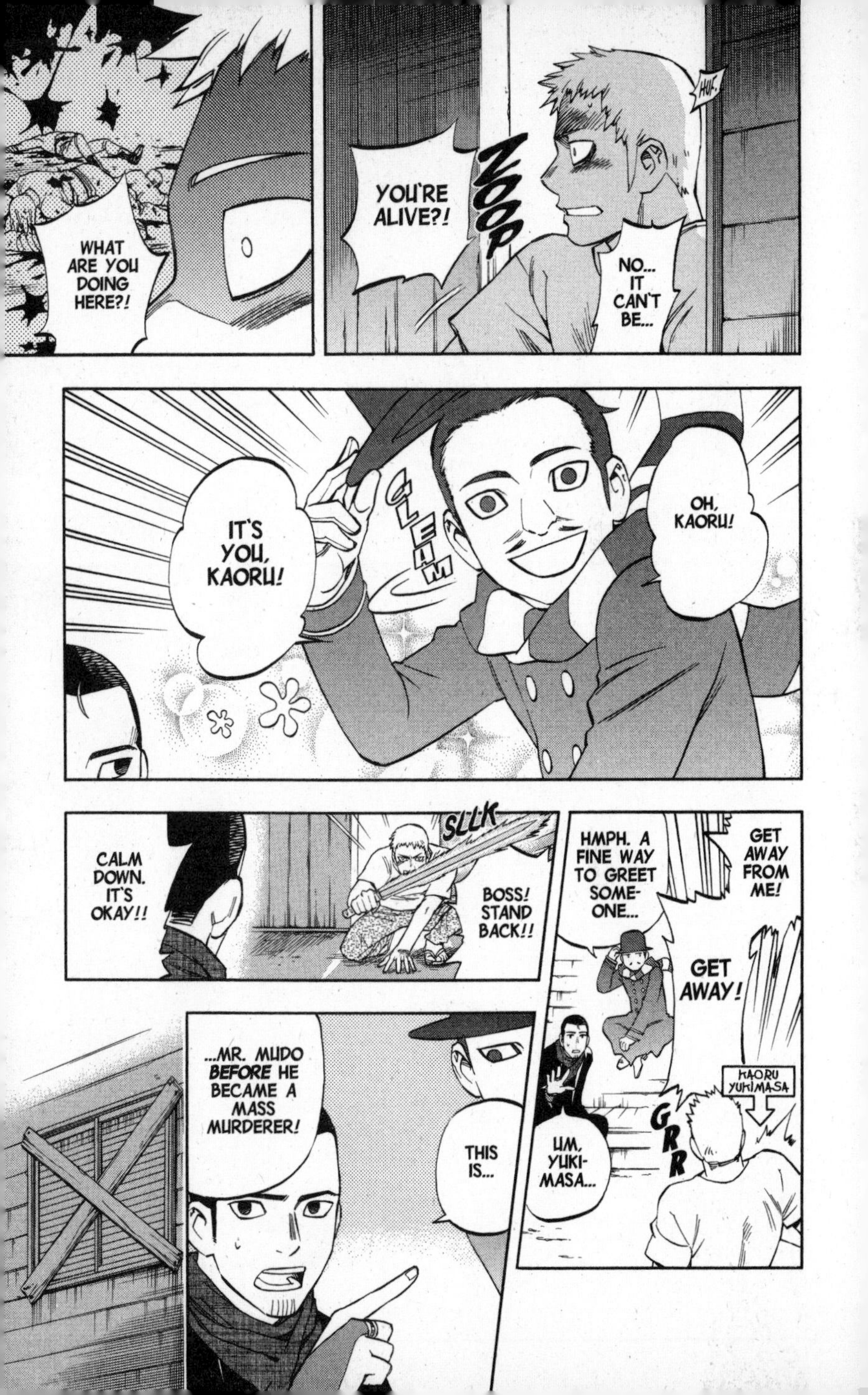
HUF
NO... IT CAN'T BE...
ZOOP
YOU'RE ALIVE?!
WHAT ARE YOU DOING HERE?!
OH, KAORU!
GLEAM
IT'S YOU, KAORU!
GET AWAY FROM ME!
HMPH. A FINE WAY TO GREET SOME-ONE...
GET AWAY!
KAORU YUKIMASA
GRR
UM, YUKI-MASA...
SLLK
BOSS! STAND BACK!!
CALM DOWN. IT'S OKAY!!
THIS IS...
...MR. MUDO *BEFORE* HE BECAME A MASS MURDERER!

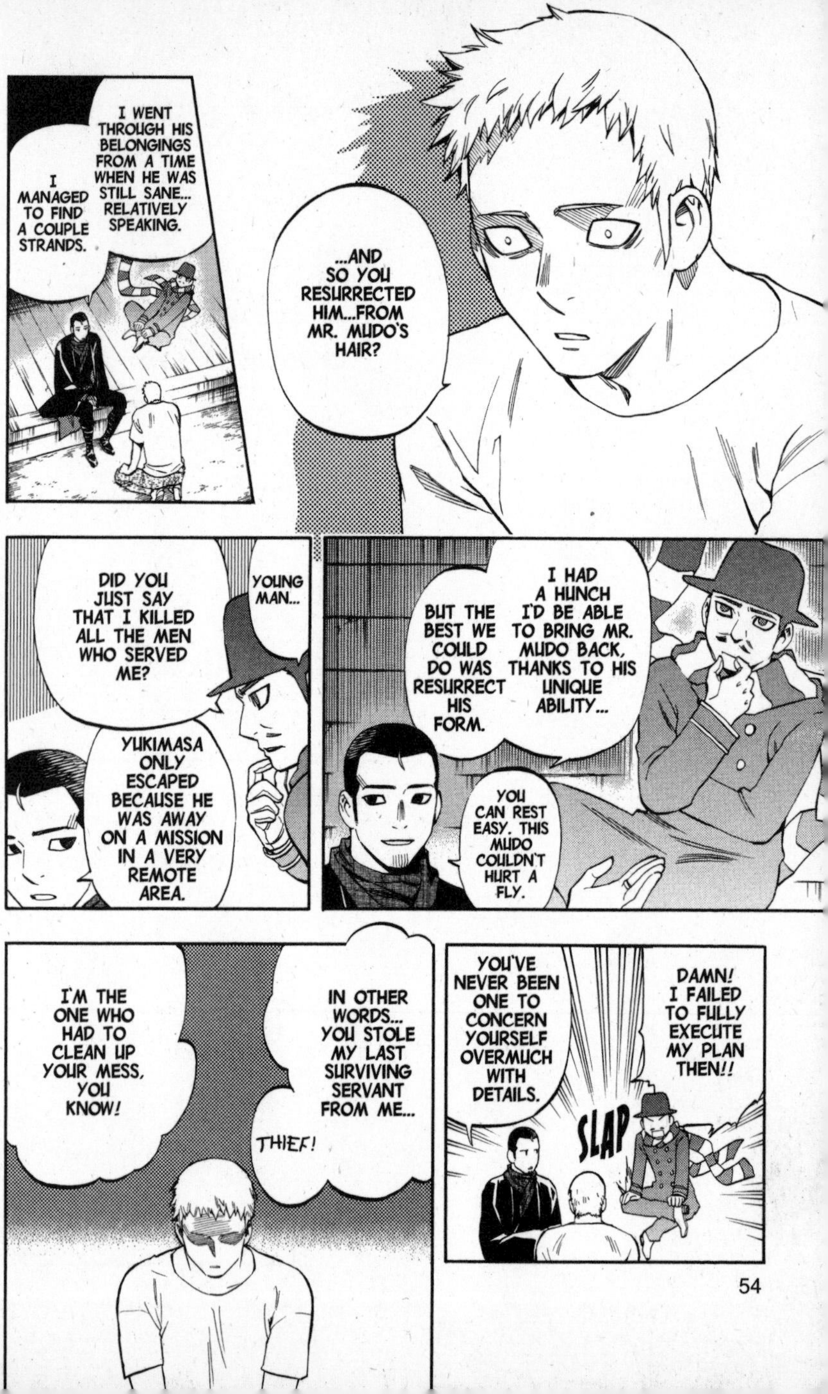
...AND SO YOU RESURRECTED HIM...FROM MR. MUDO'S HAIR?
I WENT THROUGH HIS BELONGINGS FROM A TIME WHEN HE WAS STILL SANE... RELATIVELY SPEAKING.
I MANAGED TO FIND A COUPLE STRANDS.
I HAD A HUNCH I'D BE ABLE TO BRING MR. MUDO BACK, THANKS TO HIS UNIQUE ABILITY...
BUT THE BEST WE COULD DO WAS RESURRECT HIS FORM.
YOU CAN REST EASY. THIS MUDO COULDN'T HURT A FLY.
YOUNG MAN...
DID YOU JUST SAY THAT I KILLED ALL THE MEN WHO SERVED ME?
YUKIMASA ONLY ESCAPED BECAUSE HE WAS AWAY ON A MISSION IN A VERY REMOTE AREA.
DAMN! I FAILED TO FULLY EXECUTE MY PLAN THEN!!
YOU'VE NEVER BEEN ONE TO CONCERN YOURSELF OVERMUCH WITH DETAILS.
SLAP
IN OTHER WORDS... YOU STOLE MY LAST SURVIVING SERVANT FROM ME...
THIEF!
I'M THE ONE WHO HAD TO CLEAN UP YOUR MESS, YOU KNOW!

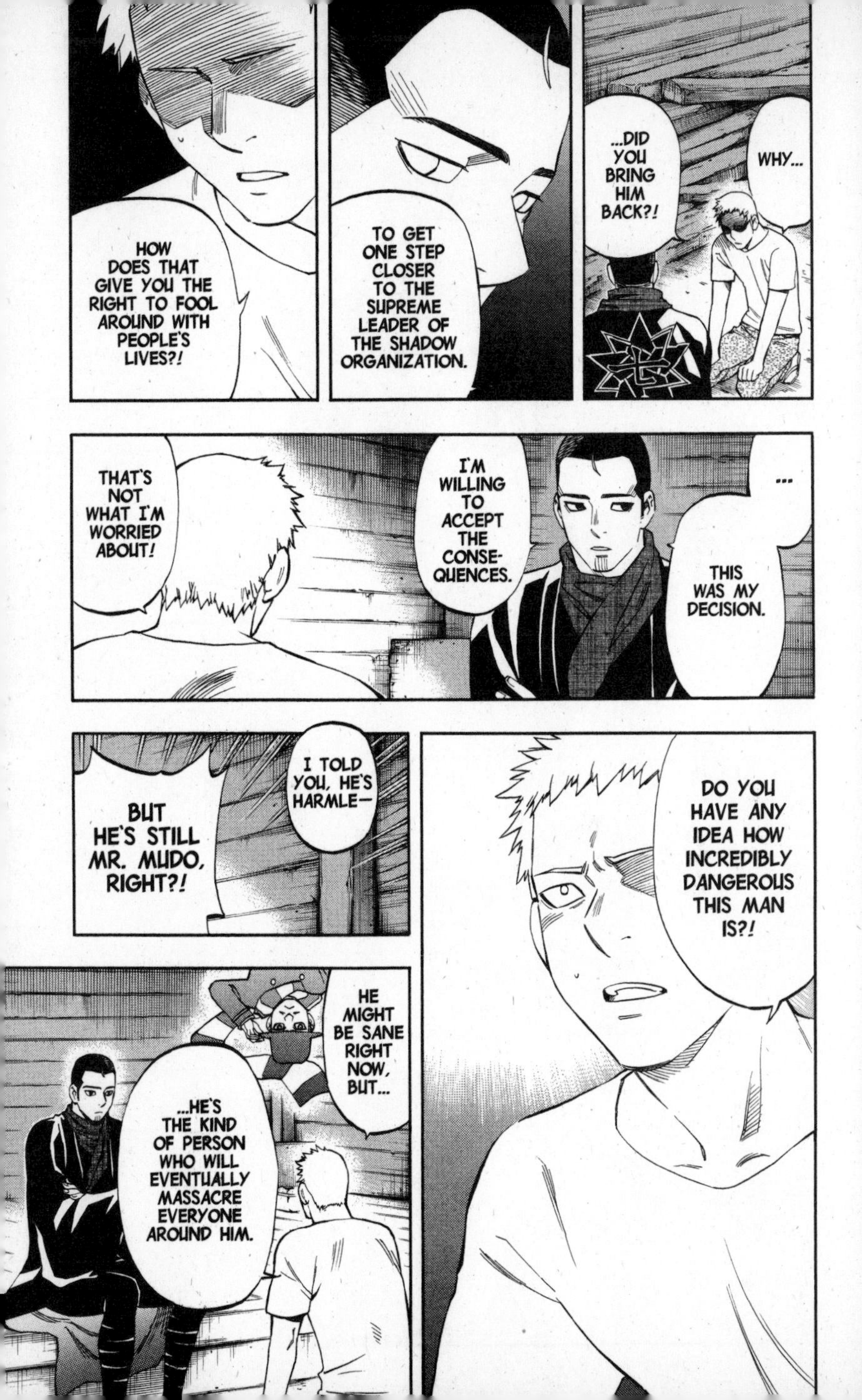
WHY...
...DID YOU BRING HIM BACK?!
TO GET ONE STEP CLOSER TO THE SUPREME LEADER OF THE SHADOW ORGANIZATION.
HOW DOES THAT GIVE YOU THE RIGHT TO FOOL AROUND WITH PEOPLE'S LIVES?!
...
THIS WAS MY DECISION.
I'M WILLING TO ACCEPT THE CONSE-QUENCES.
THAT'S NOT WHAT I'M WORRIED ABOUT!
DO YOU HAVE ANY IDEA HOW INCREDIBLY DANGEROUS THIS MAN IS?!
I TOLD YOU, HE'S HARMLE—
BUT HE'S STILL MR. MUDO, RIGHT?!
HE MIGHT BE SANE RIGHT NOW, BUT...
...HE'S THE KIND OF PERSON WHO WILL EVENTUALLY MASSACRE EVERYONE AROUND HIM.

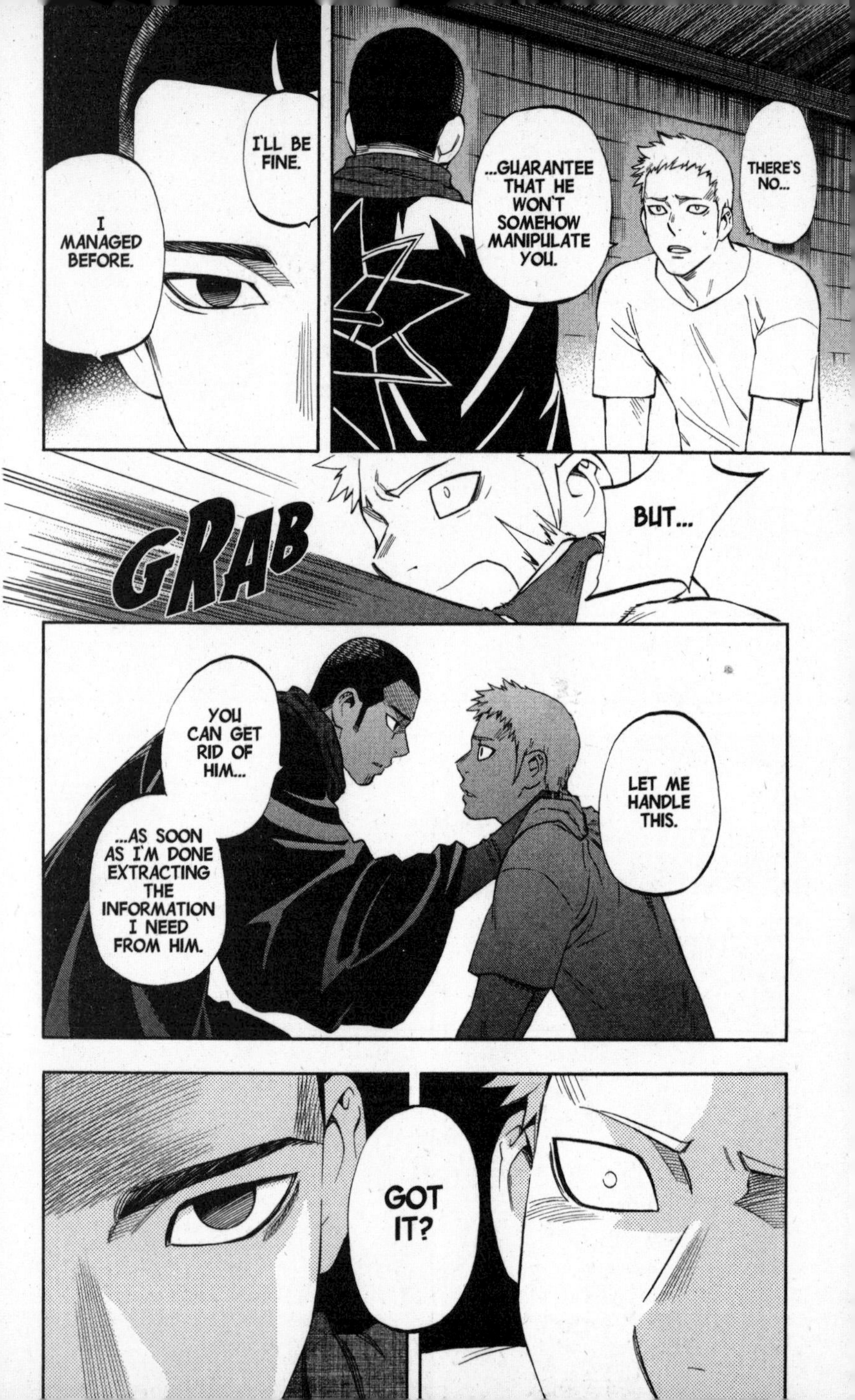
THERE'S NO...
...GUARANTEE THAT HE WON'T SOMEHOW MANIPULATE YOU.
I'LL BE FINE.
I MANAGED BEFORE.
BUT...
GRAB
LET ME HANDLE THIS.
YOU CAN GET RID OF HIM...
...AS SOON AS I'M DONE EXTRACTING THE INFORMATION I NEED FROM HIM.
GOT IT?

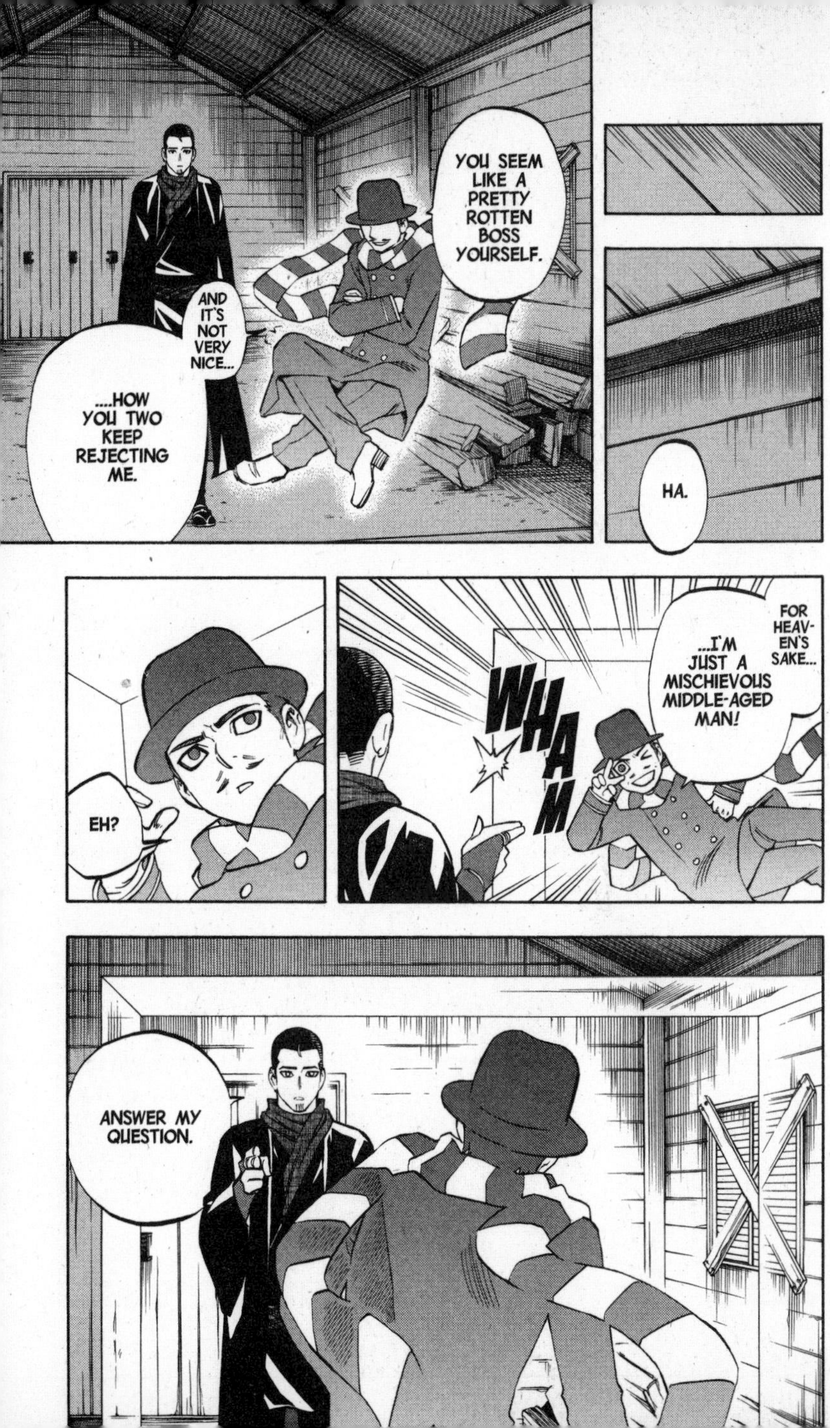
HA.
YOU SEEM LIKE A PRETTY ROTTEN BOSS YOURSELF.
AND IT'S NOT VERY NICE...
....HOW YOU TWO KEEP REJECTING ME.
FOR HEAVEN'S SAKE...
...I'M JUST A MISCHIEVOUS MIDDLE-AGED MAN!
WHAM
EH?
ANSWER MY QUESTION.

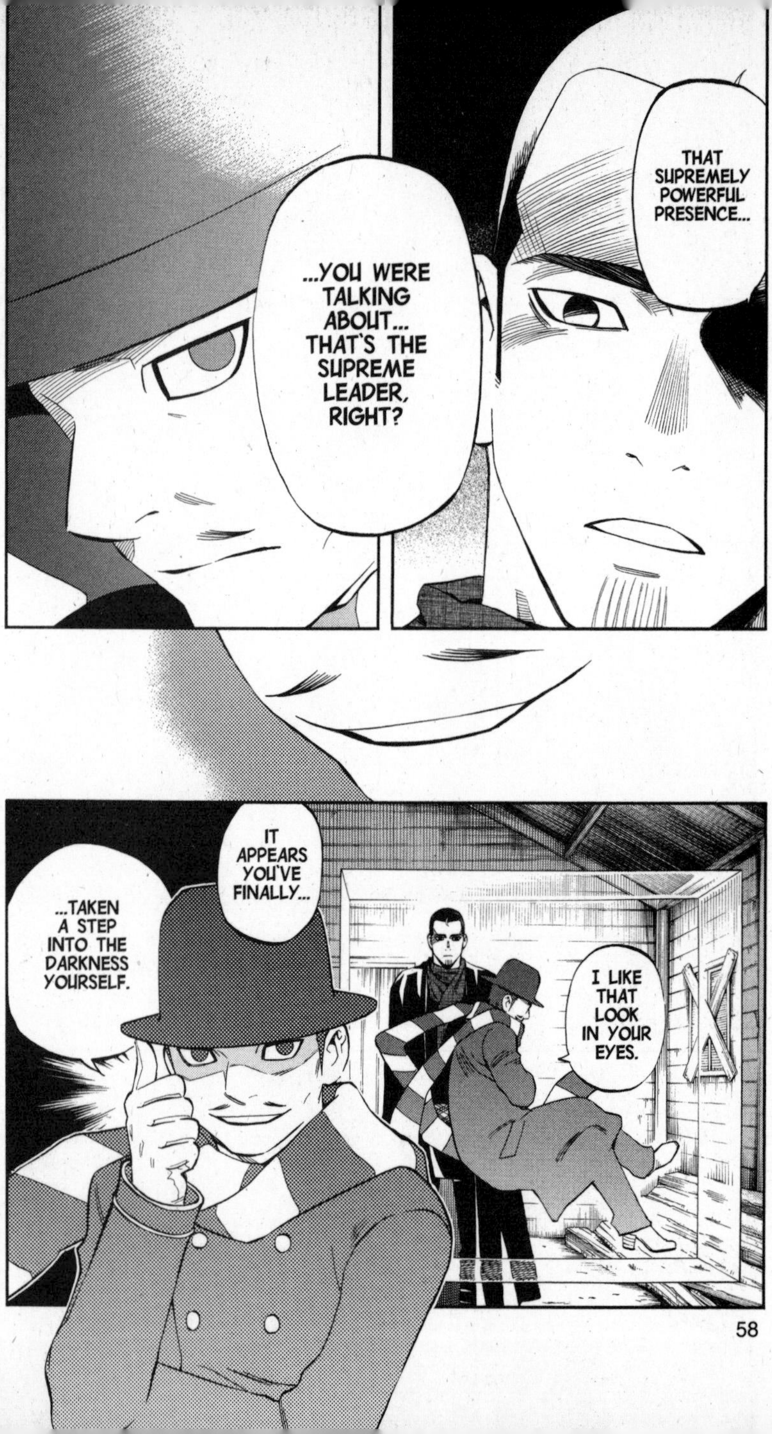
THAT SUPREMELY POWERFUL PRESENCE...
...YOU WERE TALKING ABOUT... THAT'S THE SUPREME LEADER, RIGHT?
IT APPEARS YOU'VE FINALLY...
...TAKEN A STEP INTO THE DARKNESS YOURSELF.
I LIKE THAT LOOK IN YOUR EYES.

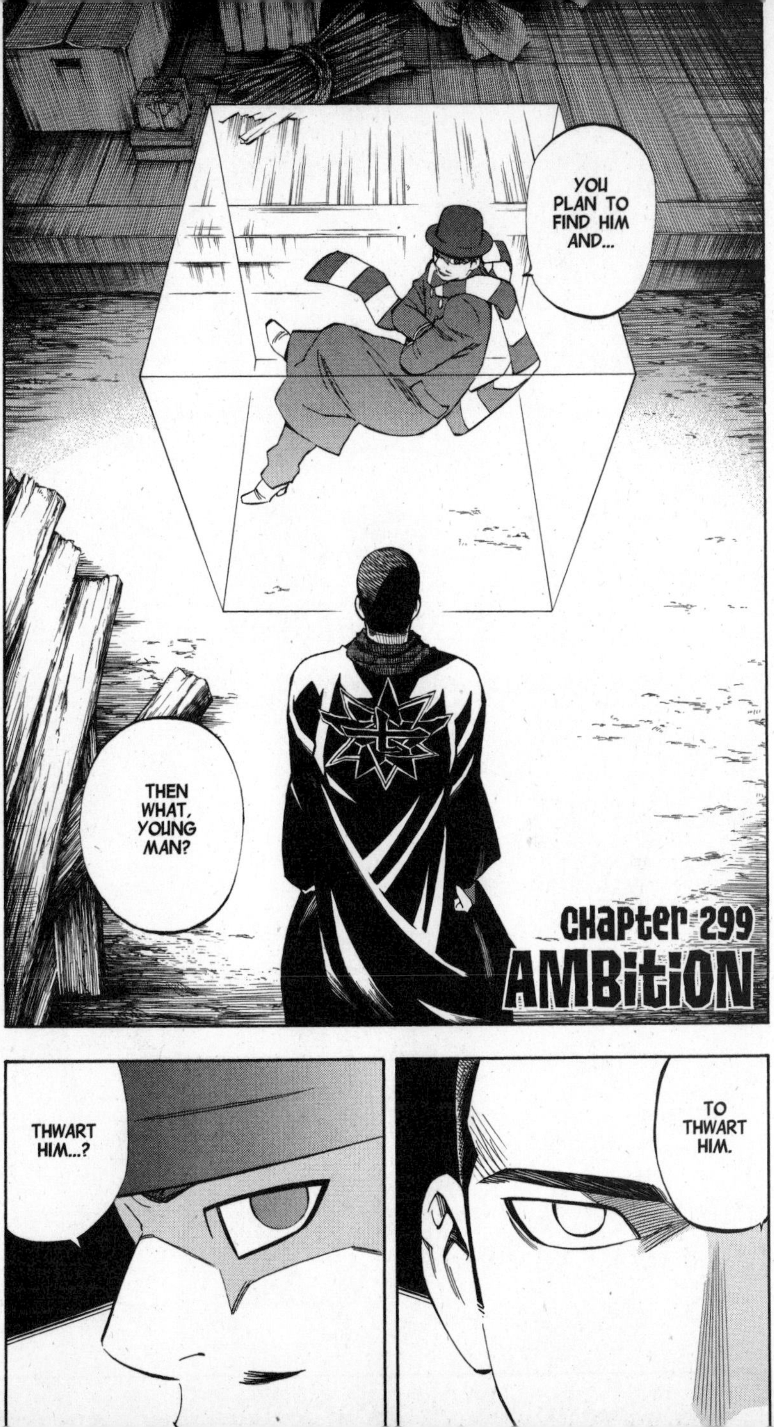
YOU PLAN TO FIND HIM AND...
THEN WHAT, YOUNG MAN?
CHAPTER 299
AMBITION
TO THWART HIM.
THWART HIM...?

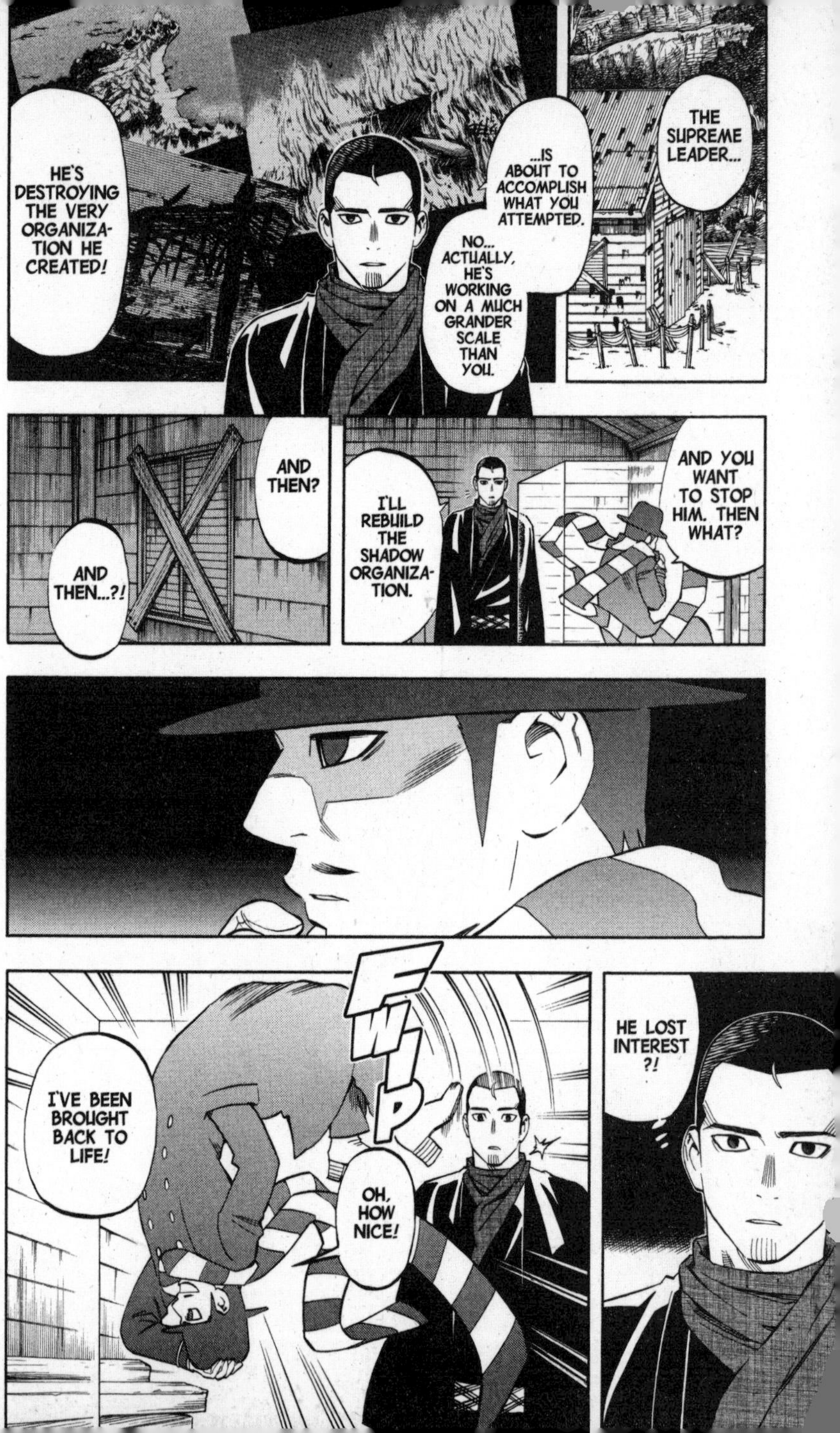
THE SUPREME LEADER...
...IS ABOUT TO ACCOMPLISH WHAT YOU ATTEMPTED.
NO... ACTUALLY, HE'S WORKING ON A MUCH GRANDER SCALE THAN YOU.
HE'S DESTROYING THE VERY ORGANIZATION HE CREATED!
AND YOU WANT TO STOP HIM. THEN WHAT?
I'LL REBUILD THE SHADOW ORGANIZATION.
AND THEN?
AND THEN...?!
HE LOST INTEREST ?!
FWIP
OH, HOW NICE!
I'VE BEEN BROUGHT BACK TO LIFE!

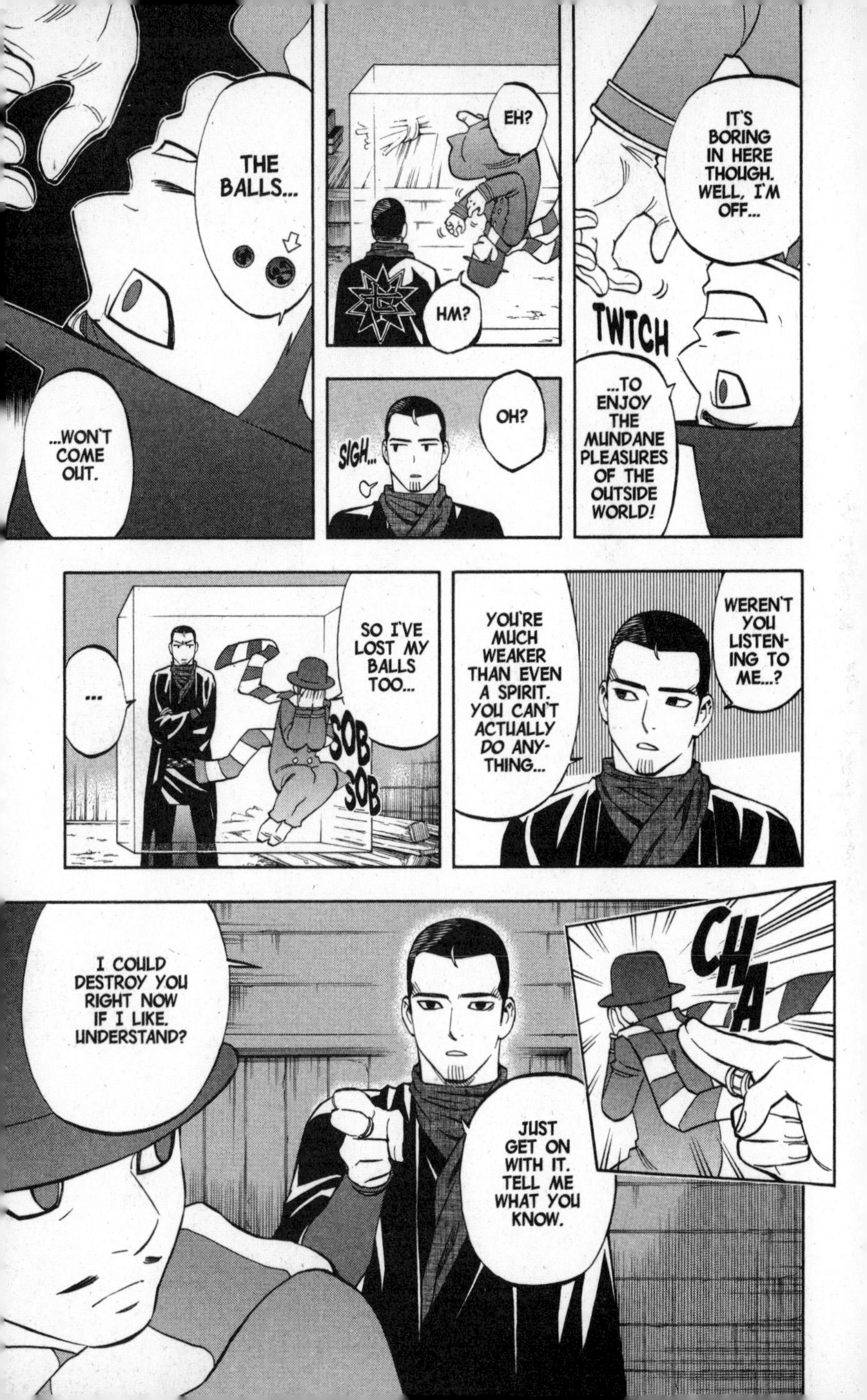
IT'S BORING IN HERE THOUGH. WELL, I'M OFF...
TWTCH
...TO ENJOY THE MUNDANE PLEASURES OF THE OUTSIDE WORLD!
EH?
HM?
OH?
SIGH...
THE BALLS...
...WON'T COME OUT.
WEREN'T YOU LISTENING TO ME...?
YOU'RE MUCH WEAKER THAN EVEN A SPIRIT. YOU CAN'T ACTUALLY DO ANYTHING...
SO I'VE LOST MY BALLS TOO...
SOB SOB
...
CHA
I COULD DESTROY YOU RIGHT NOW IF I LIKE. UNDERSTAND?
JUST GET ON WITH IT. TELL ME WHAT YOU KNOW.

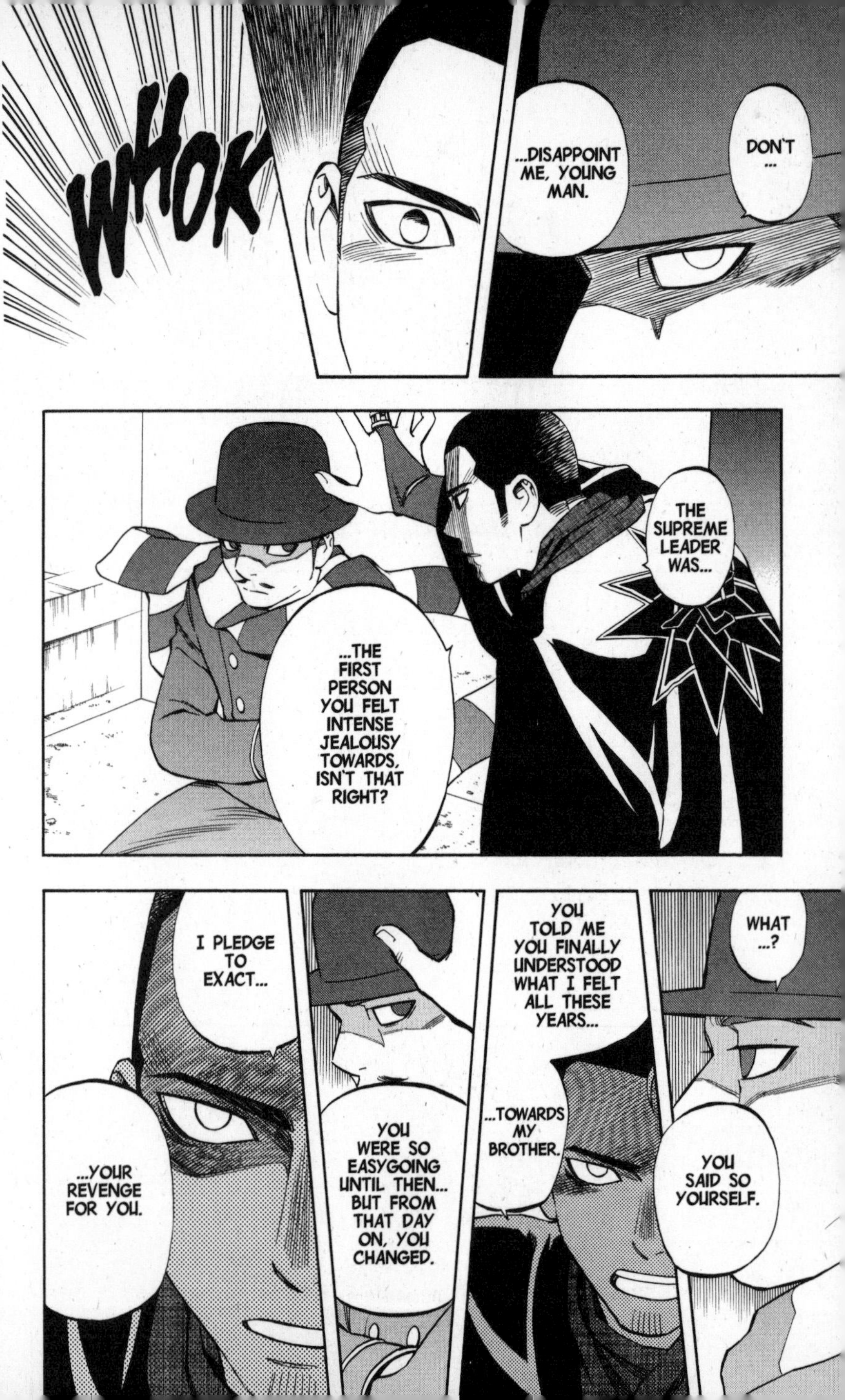
DON'T ...
...DISAPPOINT ME, YOUNG MAN.
WHOK
THE SUPREME LEADER WAS...
...THE FIRST PERSON YOU FELT INTENSE JEALOUSY TOWARDS, ISN'T THAT RIGHT?
WHAT ...?
YOU SAID SO YOURSELF.
YOU TOLD ME YOU FINALLY UNDERSTOOD WHAT I FELT ALL THESE YEARS...
...TOWARDS MY BROTHER.
YOU WERE SO EASYGOING UNTIL THEN... BUT FROM THAT DAY ON, YOU CHANGED.
I PLEDGE TO EXACT...
...YOUR REVENGE FOR YOU.

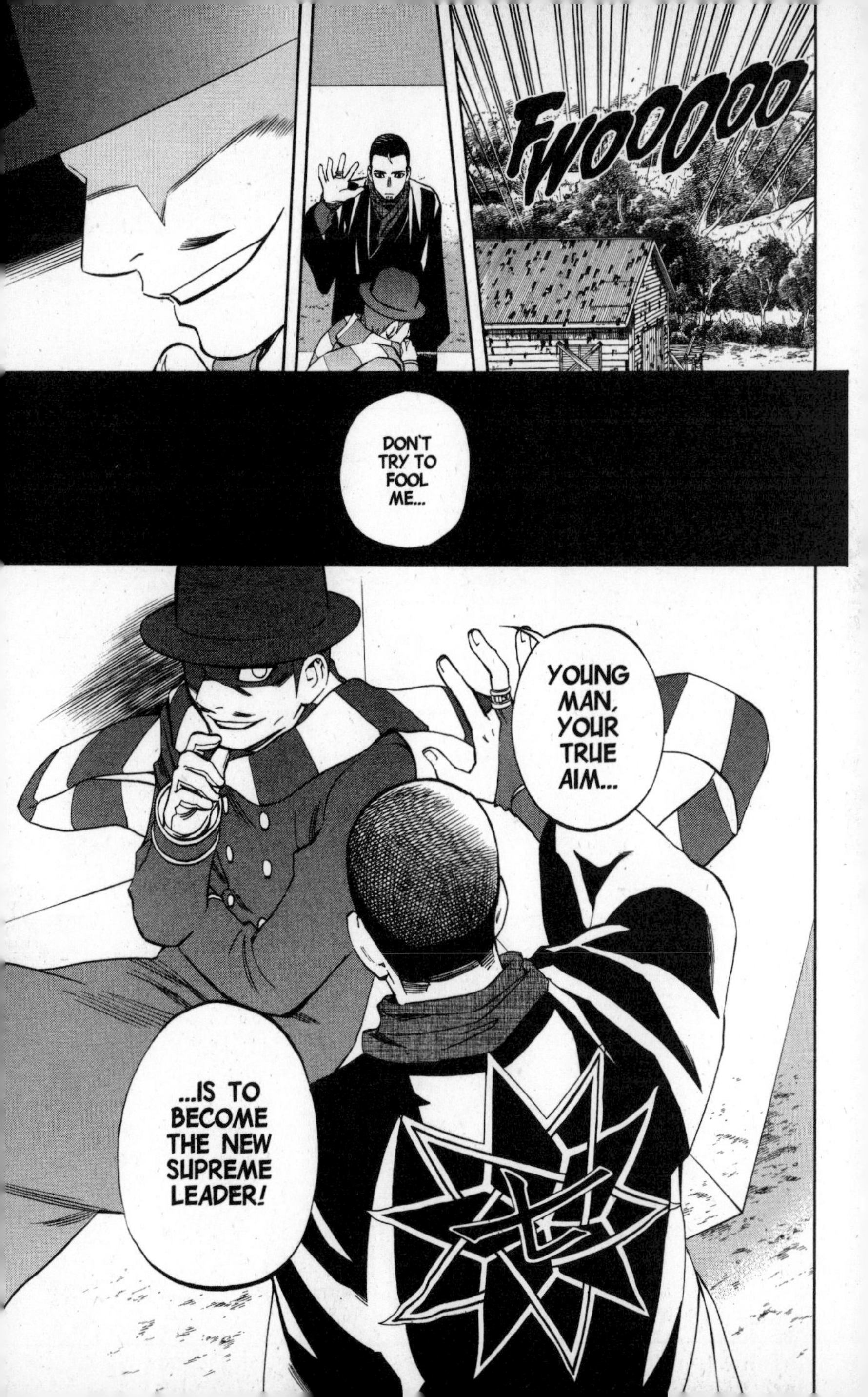
FWOOOOO
DON'T TRY TO FOOL ME...
YOUNG MAN, YOUR TRUE AIM...
...IS TO BECOME THE NEW SUPREME LEADER!

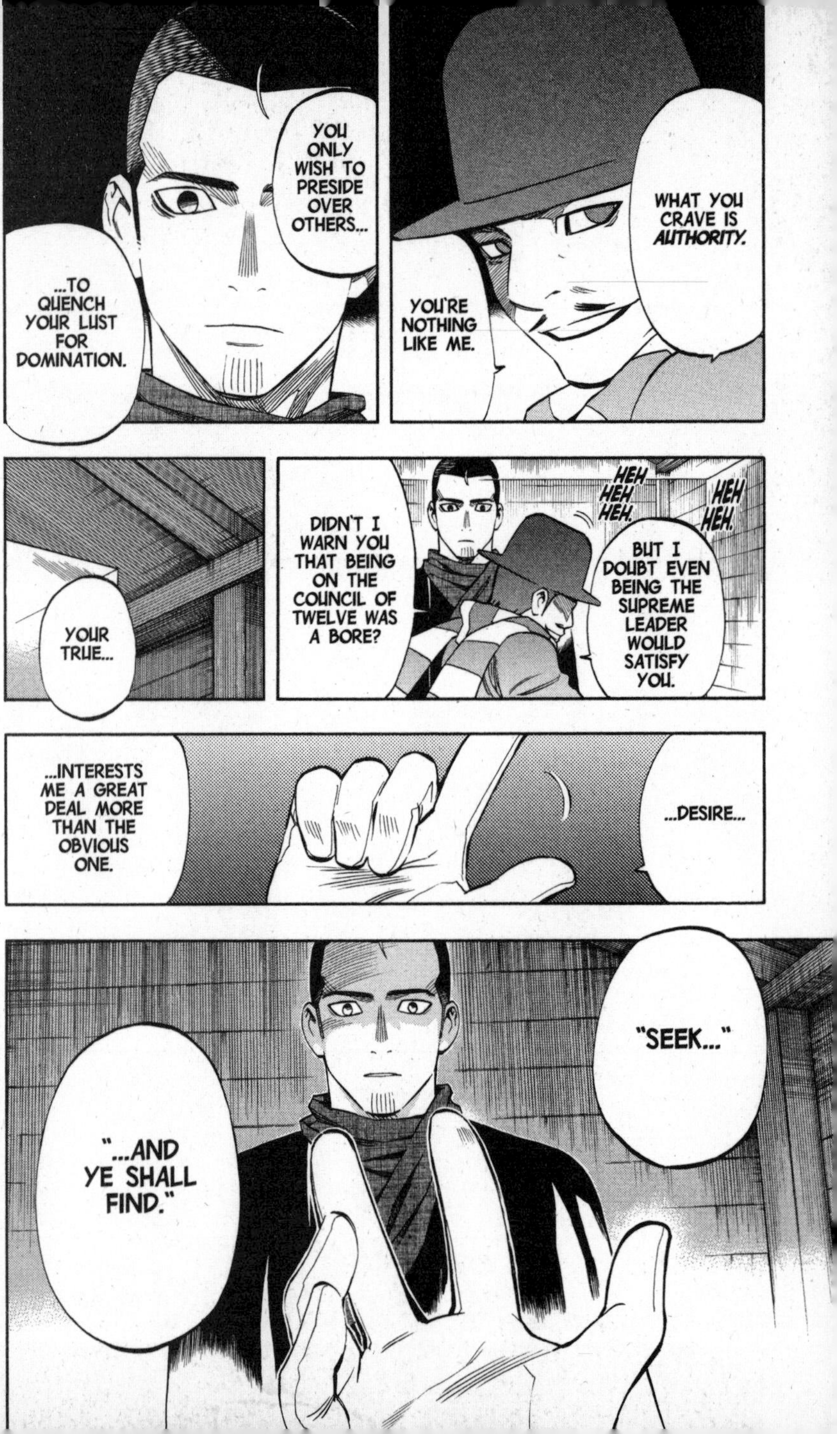
WHAT YOU CRAVE IS *AUTHORITY.*
YOU'RE NOTHING LIKE ME.
YOU ONLY WISH TO PRESIDE OVER OTHERS...
...TO QUENCH YOUR LUST FOR DOMINATION.
HEH HEH HEH.
HEH HEH.
BUT I DOUBT EVEN BEING THE SUPREME LEADER WOULD SATISFY YOU.
DIDN'T I WARN YOU THAT BEING ON THE COUNCIL OF TWELVE WAS A BORE?
YOUR TRUE...
...DESIRE...
...INTERESTS ME A GREAT DEAL MORE THAN THE OBVIOUS ONE.
"SEEK..."
"...AND YE SHALL FIND."

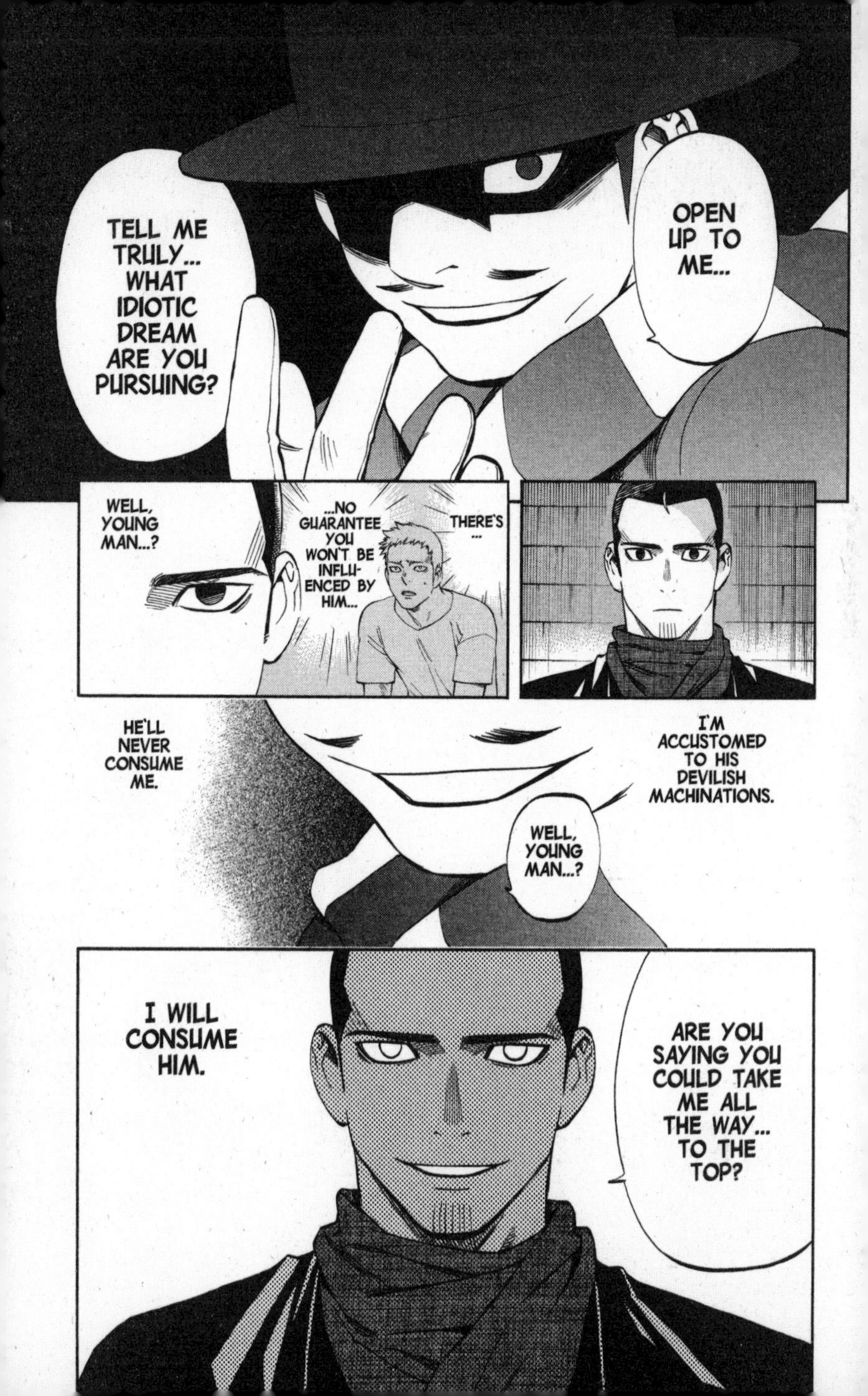
OPEN UP TO ME...
TELL ME TRULY... WHAT IDIOTIC DREAM ARE YOU PURSUING?
THERE'S ...
...NO GUARANTEE YOU WON'T BE INFLU-ENCED BY HIM...
WELL, YOUNG MAN...?
I'M ACCUSTOMED TO HIS DEVILISH MACHINATIONS.
WELL, YOUNG MAN...?
HE'LL NEVER CONSUME ME.
ARE YOU SAYING YOU COULD TAKE ME ALL THE WAY... TO THE TOP?
I WILL CONSUME HIM.

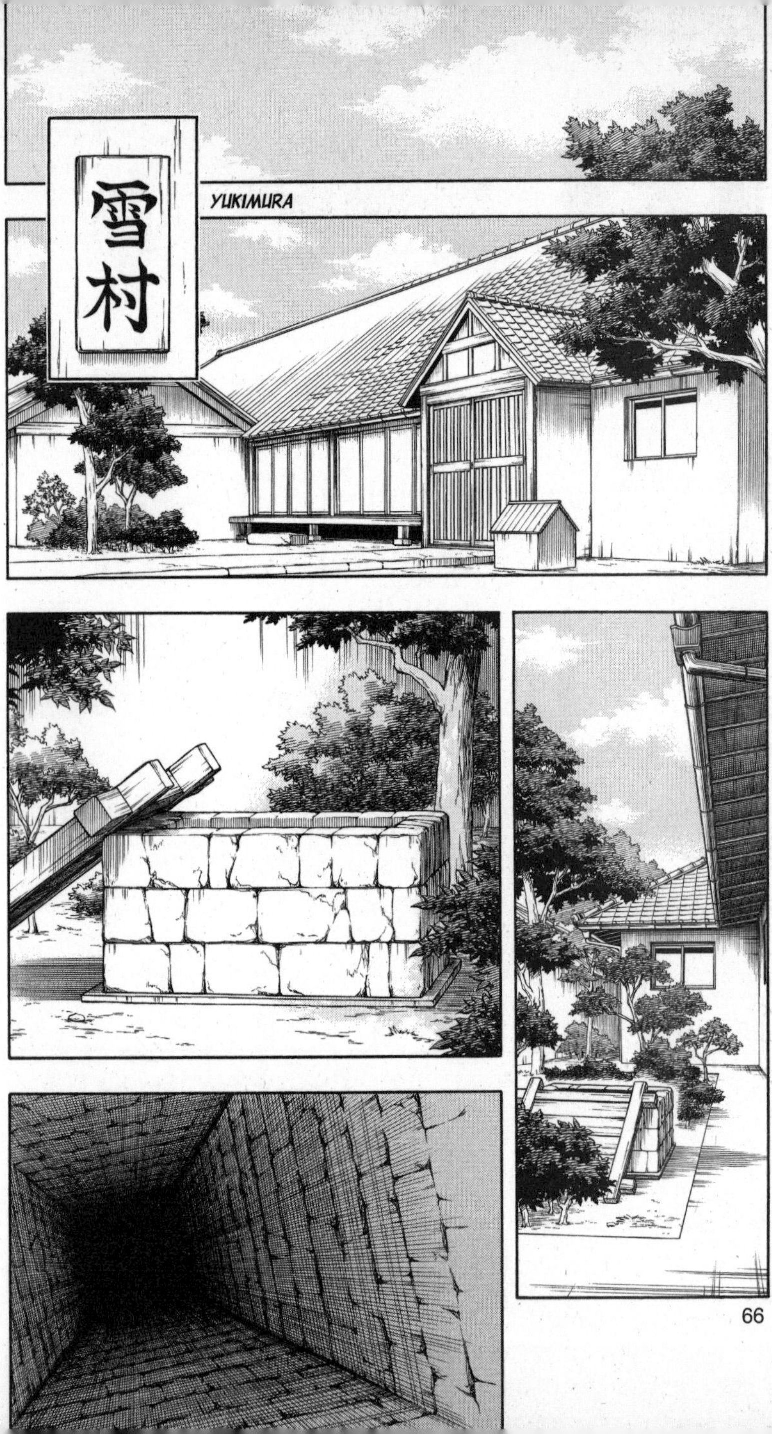
雪村
YUKIMURA

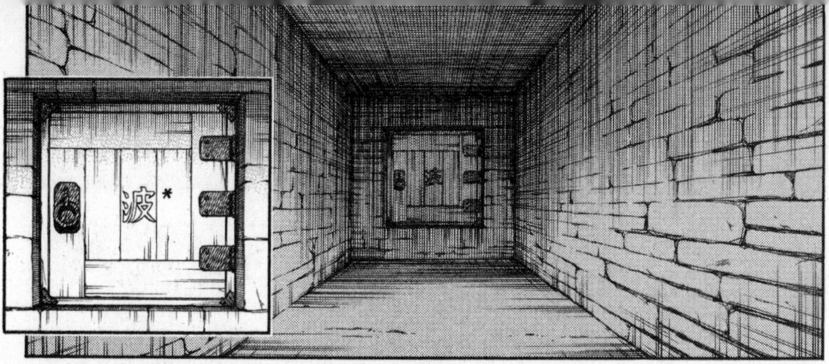
波*

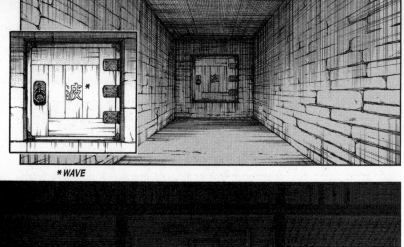

*WAVE

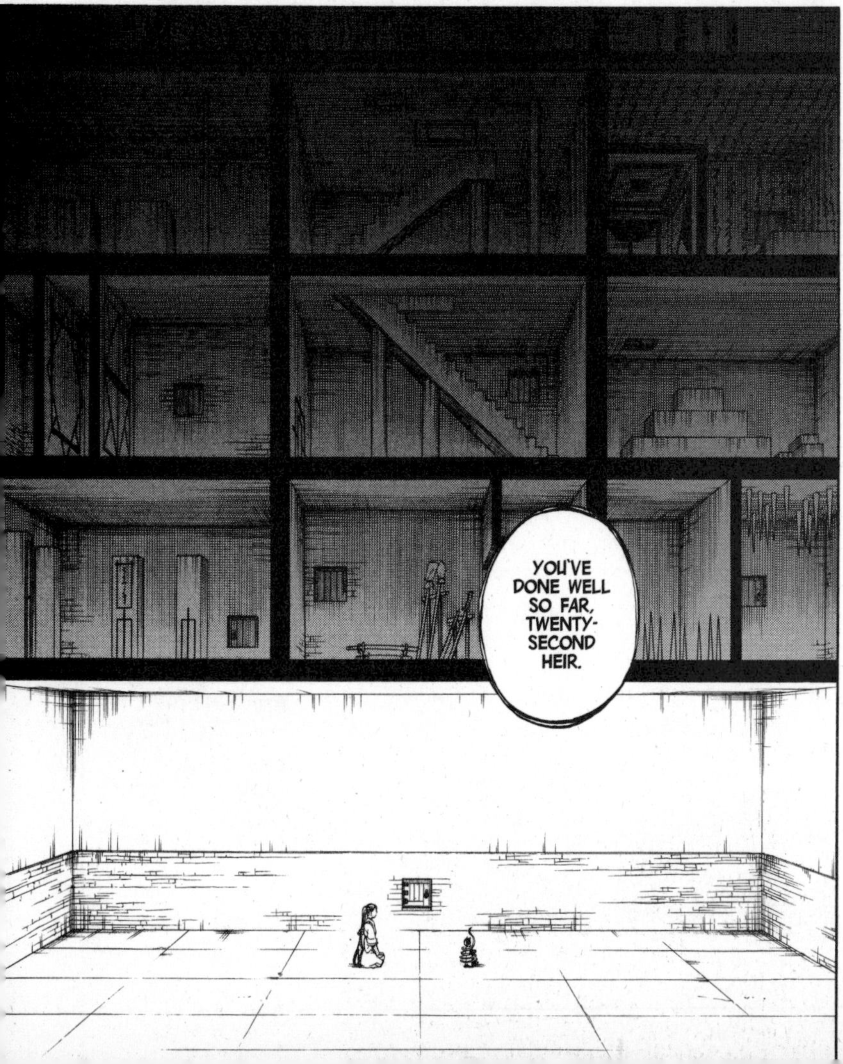
YOU'VE DONE WELL SO FAR, TWENTY-SECOND HEIR.

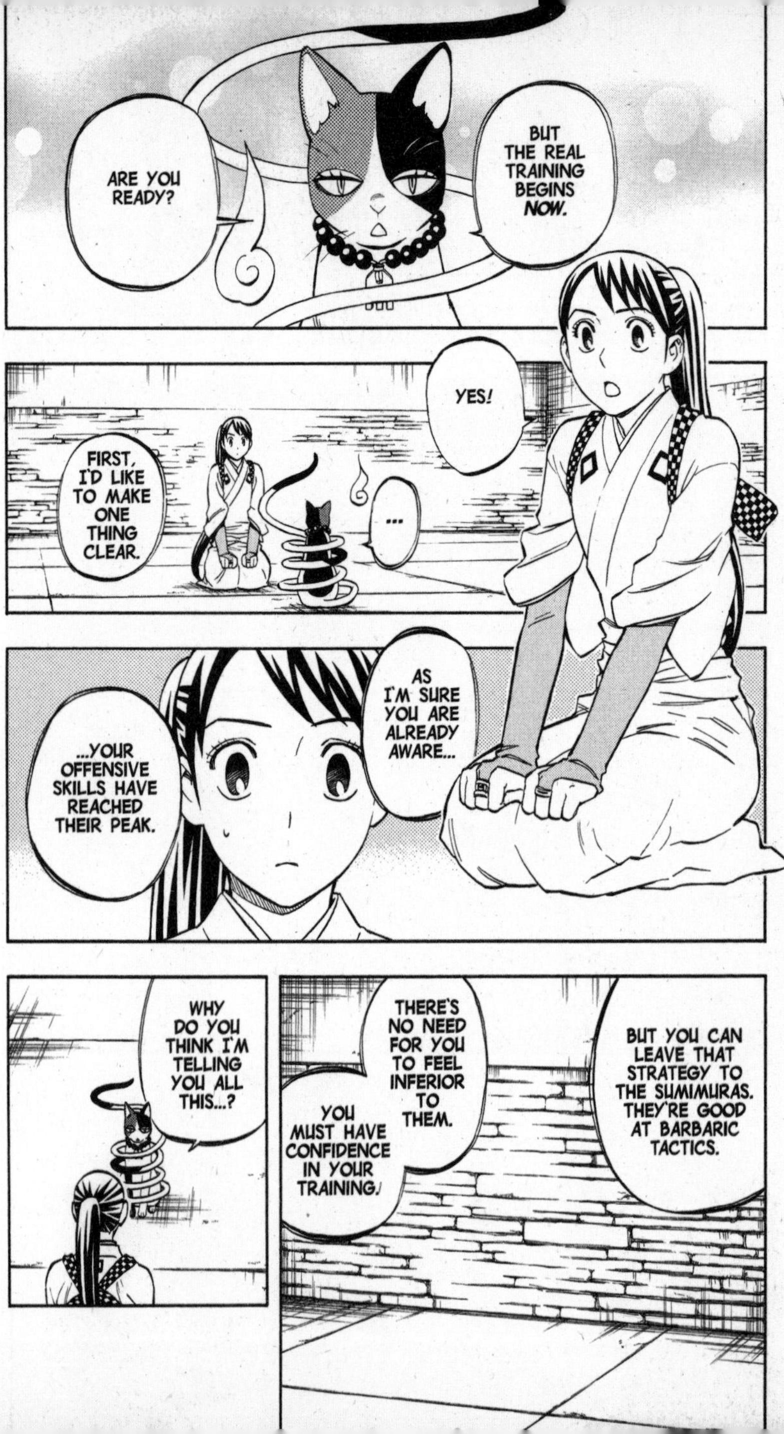
BUT THE REAL TRAINING BEGINS NOW.
ARE YOU READY?
YES!
...
FIRST, I'D LIKE TO MAKE ONE THING CLEAR.
AS I'M SURE YOU ARE ALREADY AWARE...
...YOUR OFFENSIVE SKILLS HAVE REACHED THEIR PEAK.
BUT YOU CAN LEAVE THAT STRATEGY TO THE SUMIMURAS. THEY'RE GOOD AT BARBARIC TACTICS.
THERE'S NO NEED FOR YOU TO FEEL INFERIOR TO THEM.
YOU MUST HAVE CONFIDENCE IN YOUR TRAINING!
WHY DO YOU THINK I'M TELLING YOU ALL THIS...?

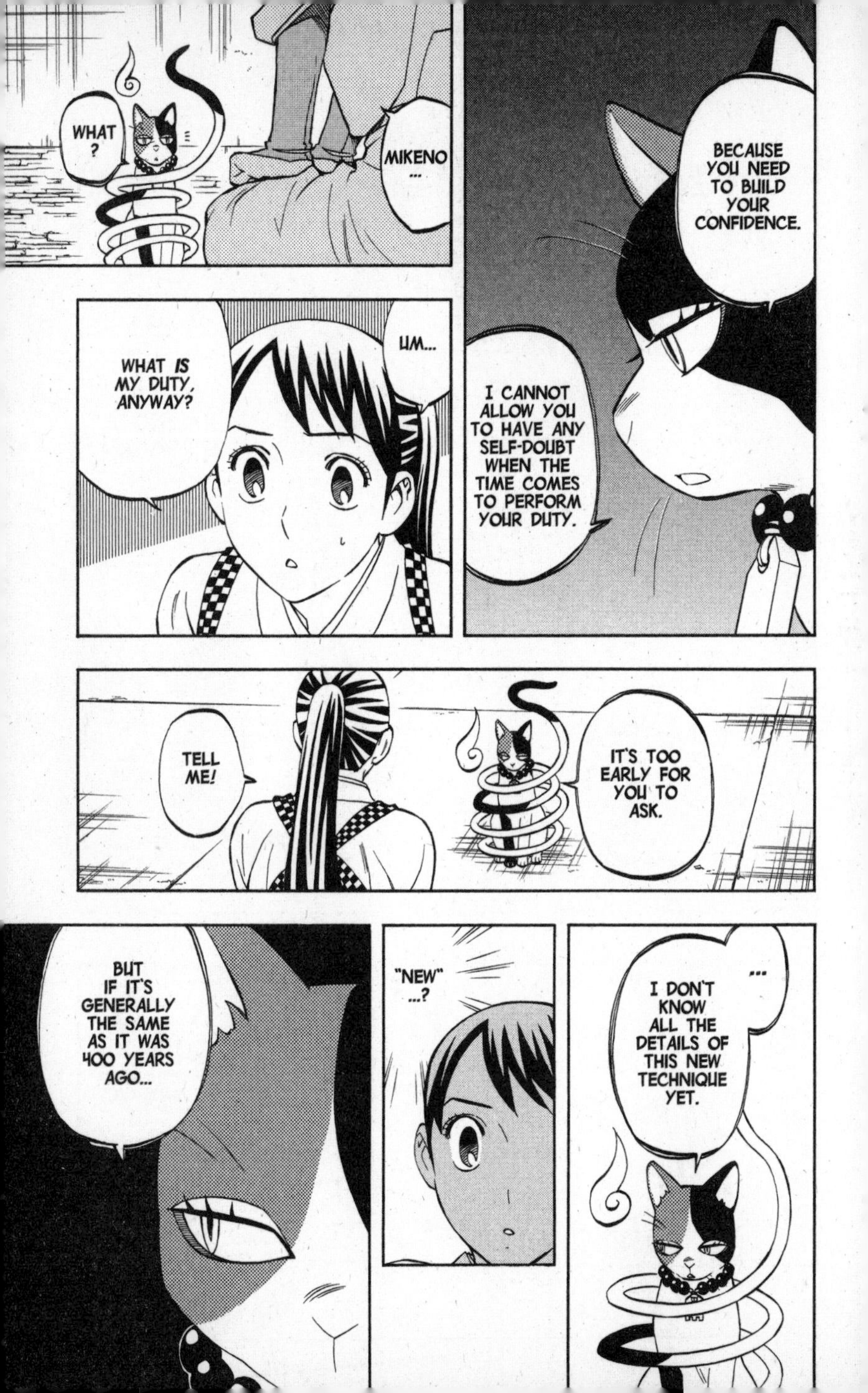
BECAUSE YOU NEED TO BUILD YOUR CONFIDENCE.
I CANNOT ALLOW YOU TO HAVE ANY SELF-DOUBT WHEN THE TIME COMES TO PERFORM YOUR DUTY.
MIKENO ...
WHAT ?
UM...
WHAT *IS* MY DUTY, ANYWAY?
IT'S TOO EARLY FOR YOU TO ASK.
TELL ME!
...
I DON'T KNOW ALL THE DETAILS OF THIS NEW TECHNIQUE YET.
"NEW" ...?
BUT IF IT'S GENERALLY THE SAME AS IT WAS 400 YEARS AGO...

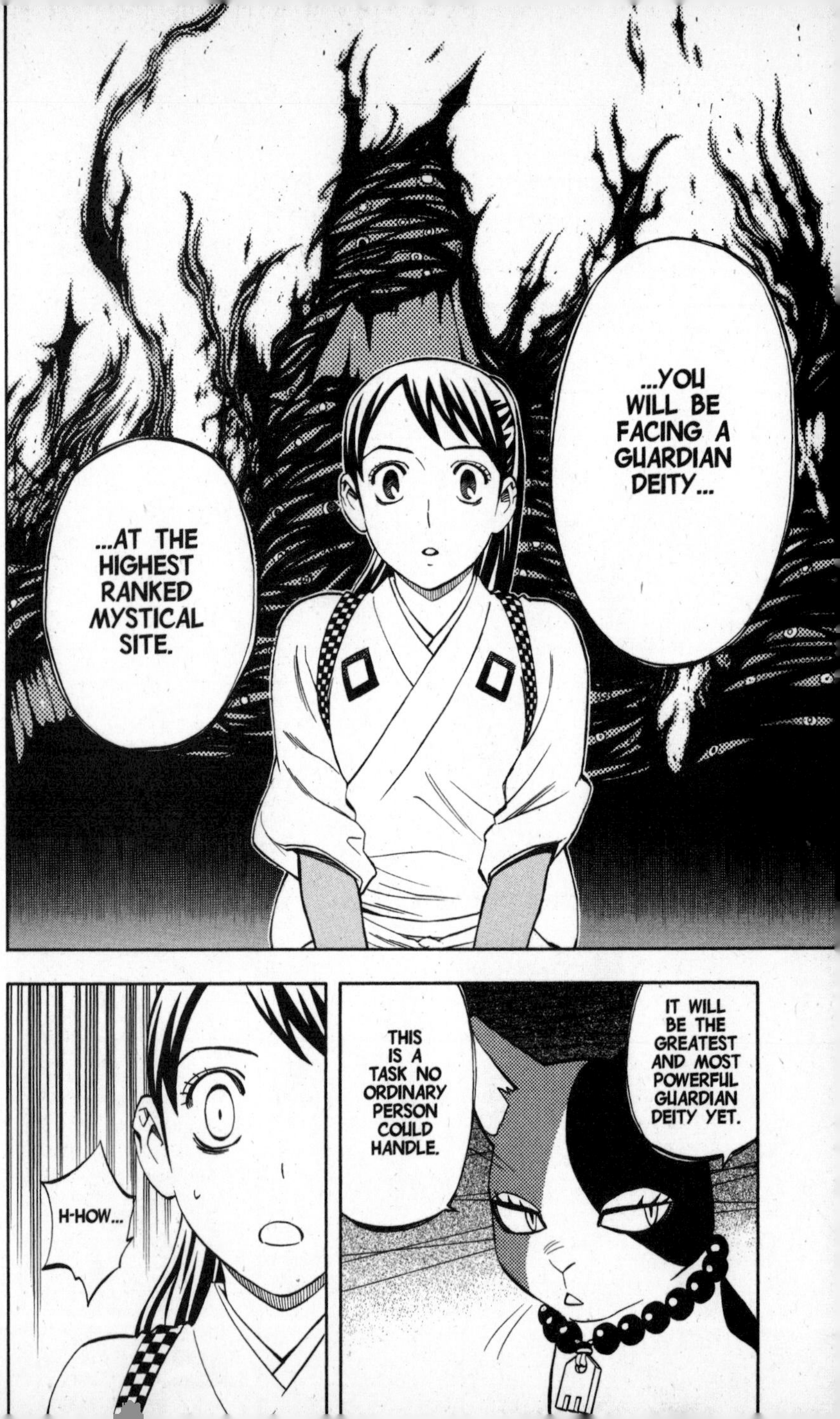
...YOU WILL BE FACING A GUARDIAN DEITY...
...AT THE HIGHEST RANKED MYSTICAL SITE.
IT WILL BE THE GREATEST AND MOST POWERFUL GUARDIAN DEITY YET.
THIS IS A TASK NO ORDINARY PERSON COULD HANDLE.
H-HOW...

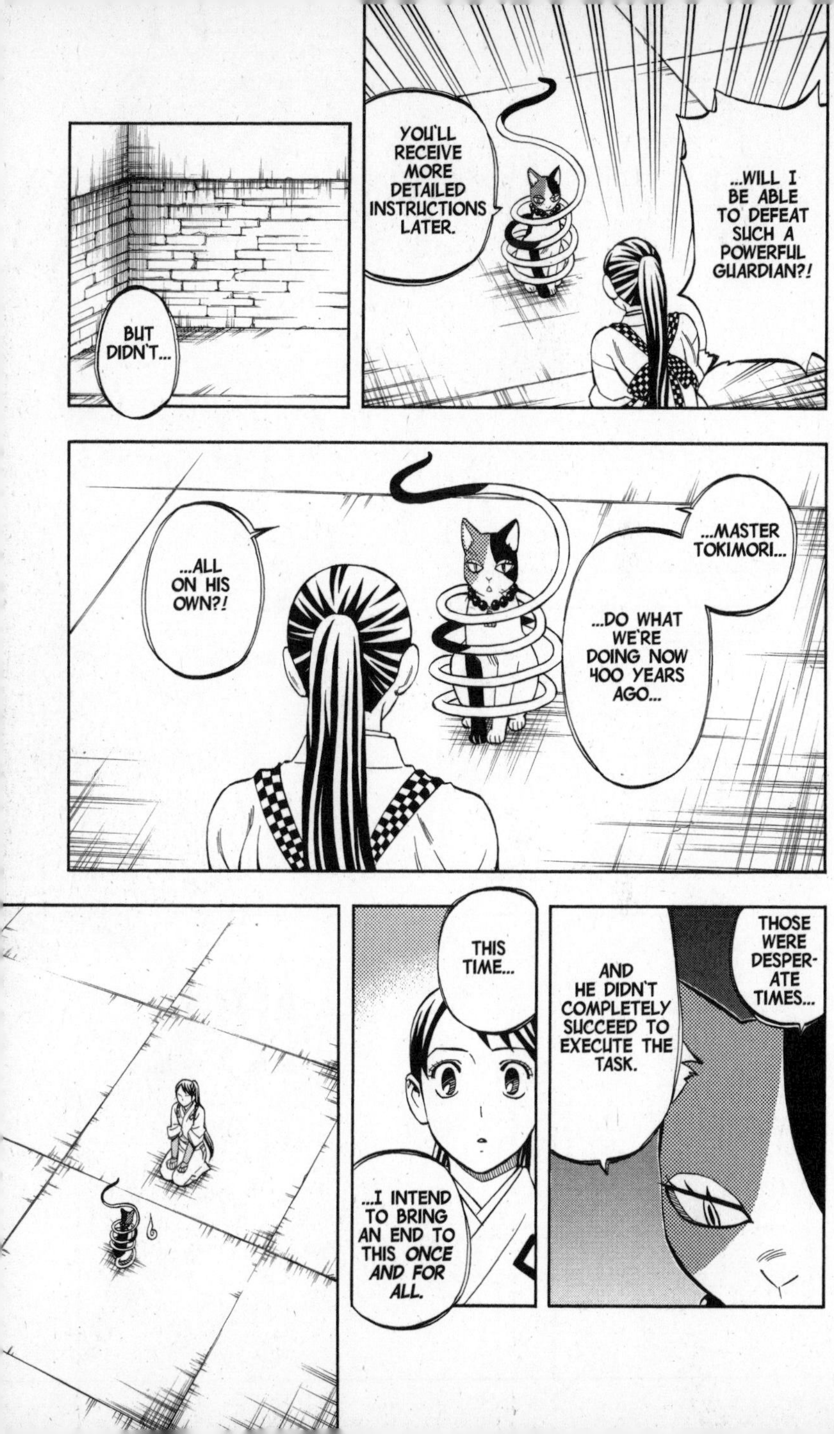
YOU'LL RECEIVE MORE DETAILED INSTRUCTIONS LATER.
...WILL I BE ABLE TO DEFEAT SUCH A POWERFUL GUARDIAN?!
BUT DIDN'T...
...MASTER TOKIMORI...
...DO WHAT WE'RE DOING NOW 400 YEARS AGO...
...ALL ON HIS OWN?!
THOSE WERE DESPER-ATE TIMES...
AND HE DIDN'T COMPLETELY SUCCEED TO EXECUTE THE TASK.
THIS TIME...
...I INTEND TO BRING AN END TO THIS *ONCE* AND FOR ALL.

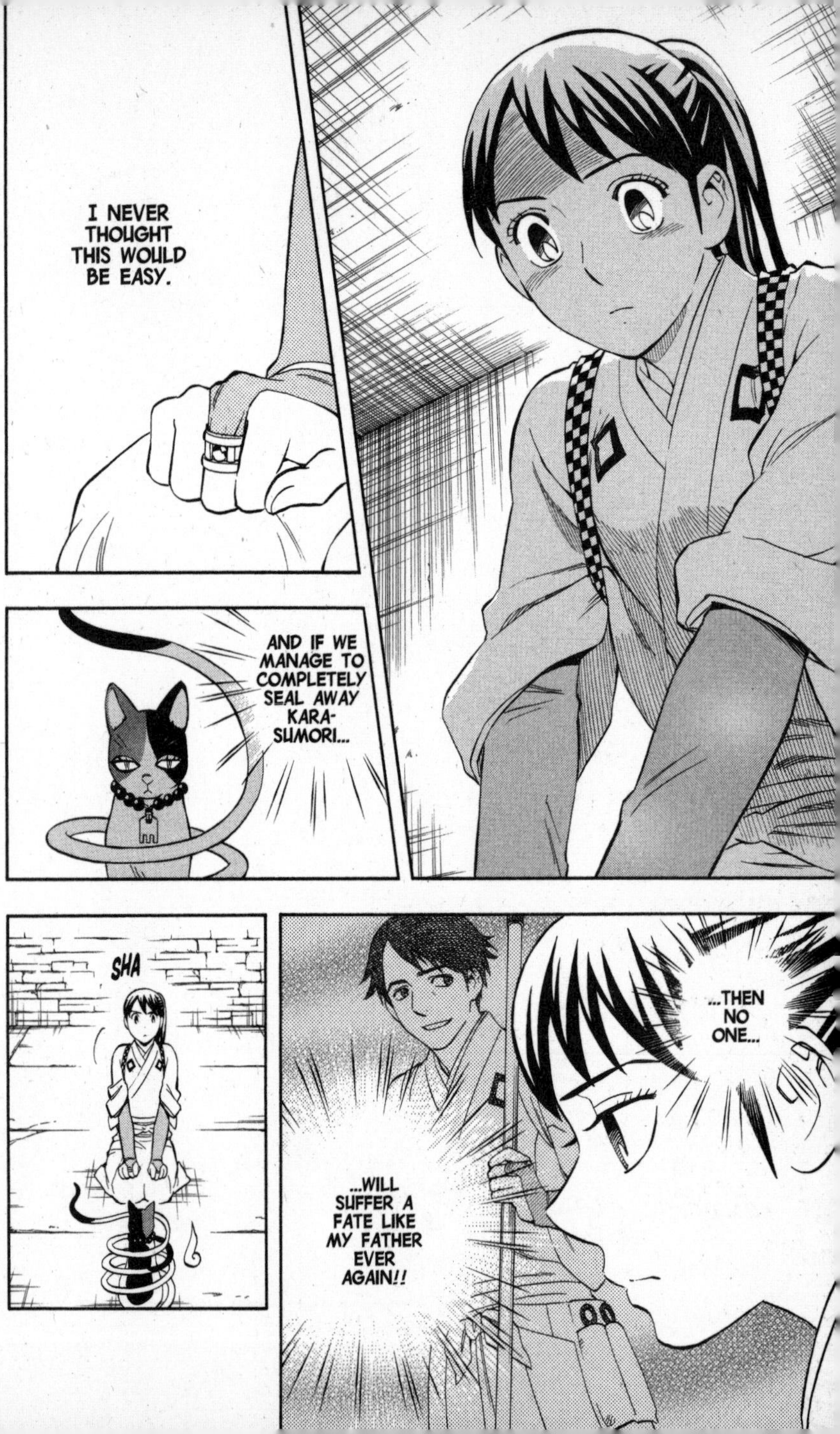
I NEVER THOUGHT THIS WOULD BE EASY.
AND IF WE MANAGE TO COMPLETELY SEAL AWAY KARA-SUMORI...
...THEN NO ONE...
...WILL SUFFER A FATE LIKE MY FATHER EVER AGAIN!!
SHA

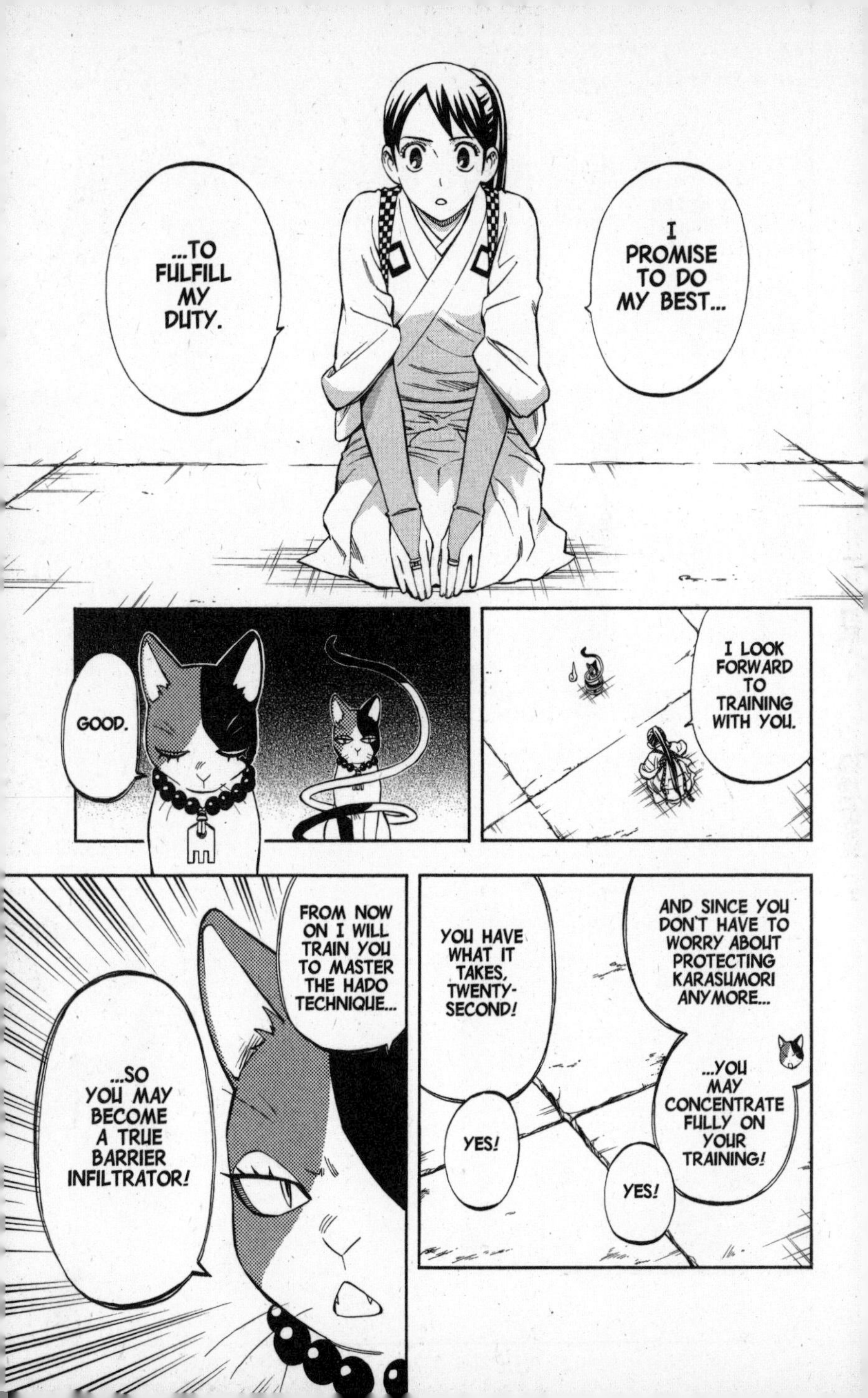
I PROMISE TO DO MY BEST...
...TO FULFILL MY DUTY.
I LOOK FORWARD TO TRAINING WITH YOU.
GOOD.
AND SINCE YOU DON'T HAVE TO WORRY ABOUT PROTECTING KARASUMORI ANYMORE...
...YOU MAY CONCENTRATE FULLY ON YOUR TRAINING!
YES!
YOU HAVE WHAT IT TAKES, TWENTY-SECOND!
YES!
FROM NOW ON I WILL TRAIN YOU TO MASTER THE HADO TECHNIQUE...
...SO YOU MAY BECOME A TRUE BARRIER INFILTRATOR!

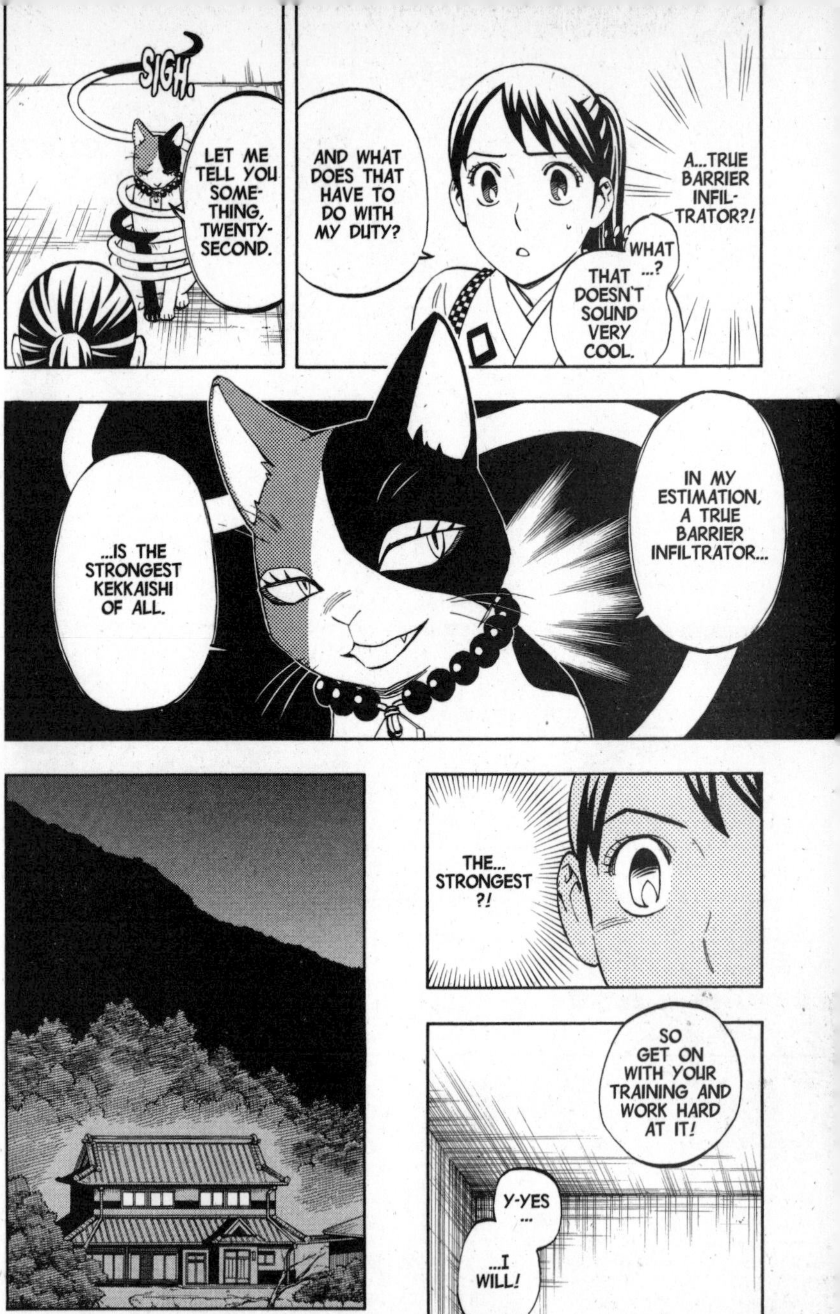
A...TRUE BARRIER INFILTRATOR?!
WHAT ...?
THAT DOESN'T SOUND VERY COOL.
AND WHAT DOES THAT HAVE TO DO WITH MY DUTY?
SIGH.
LET ME TELL YOU SOMETHING, TWENTY-SECOND.
IN MY ESTIMATION, A TRUE BARRIER INFILTRATOR...
...IS THE STRONGEST KEKKAISHI OF ALL.
THE... STRONGEST?!
SO GET ON WITH YOUR TRAINING AND WORK HARD AT IT!
Y-YES...
...I WILL!

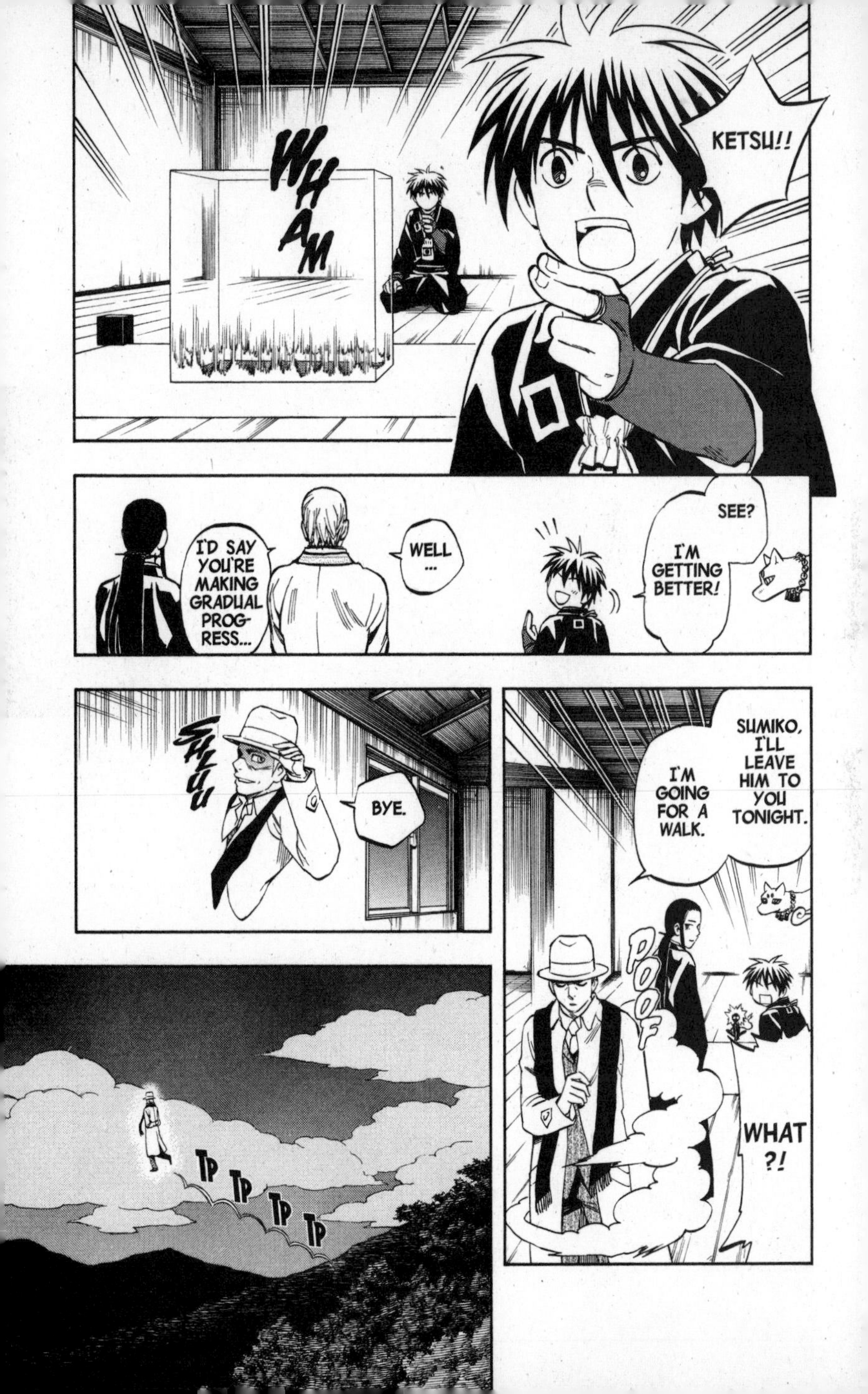
KETSU!!
WHAM
SEE?
I'M GETTING BETTER!
WELL ...
I'D SAY YOU'RE MAKING GRADUAL PROG-RESS...
SUMIKO, I'LL LEAVE HIM TO YOU TONIGHT.
I'M GOING FOR A WALK.
POOF
WHAT ?!
SHUU
BYE.
TP TP TP TP

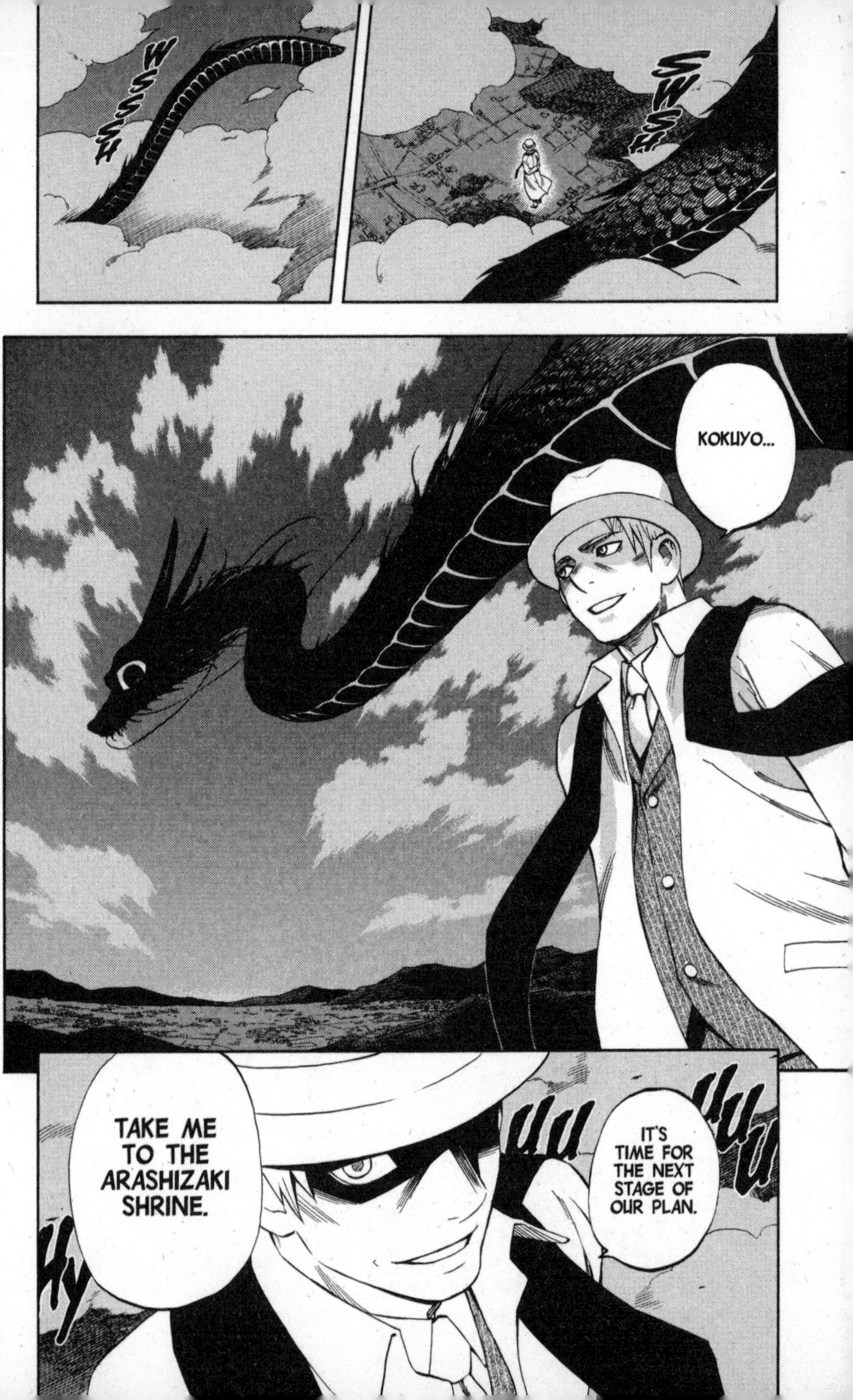
SWSSH
WSSSH
KOKUYO...
IT'S TIME FOR THE NEXT STAGE OF OUR PLAN.
TAKE ME TO THE ARASHIZAKI SHRINE.

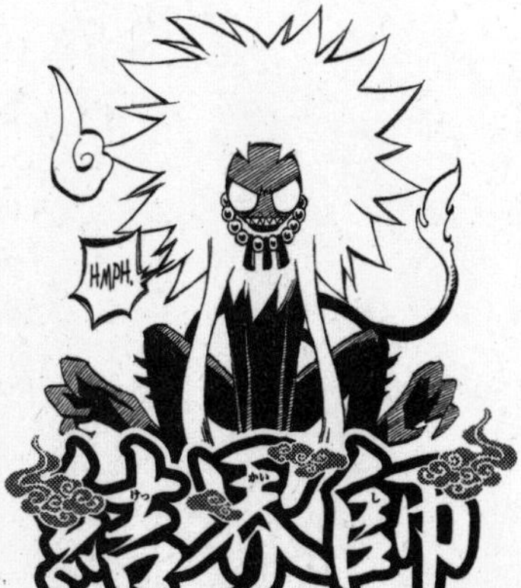
HMPH.
結界師

Chapter 300 Arashizaki Shrine

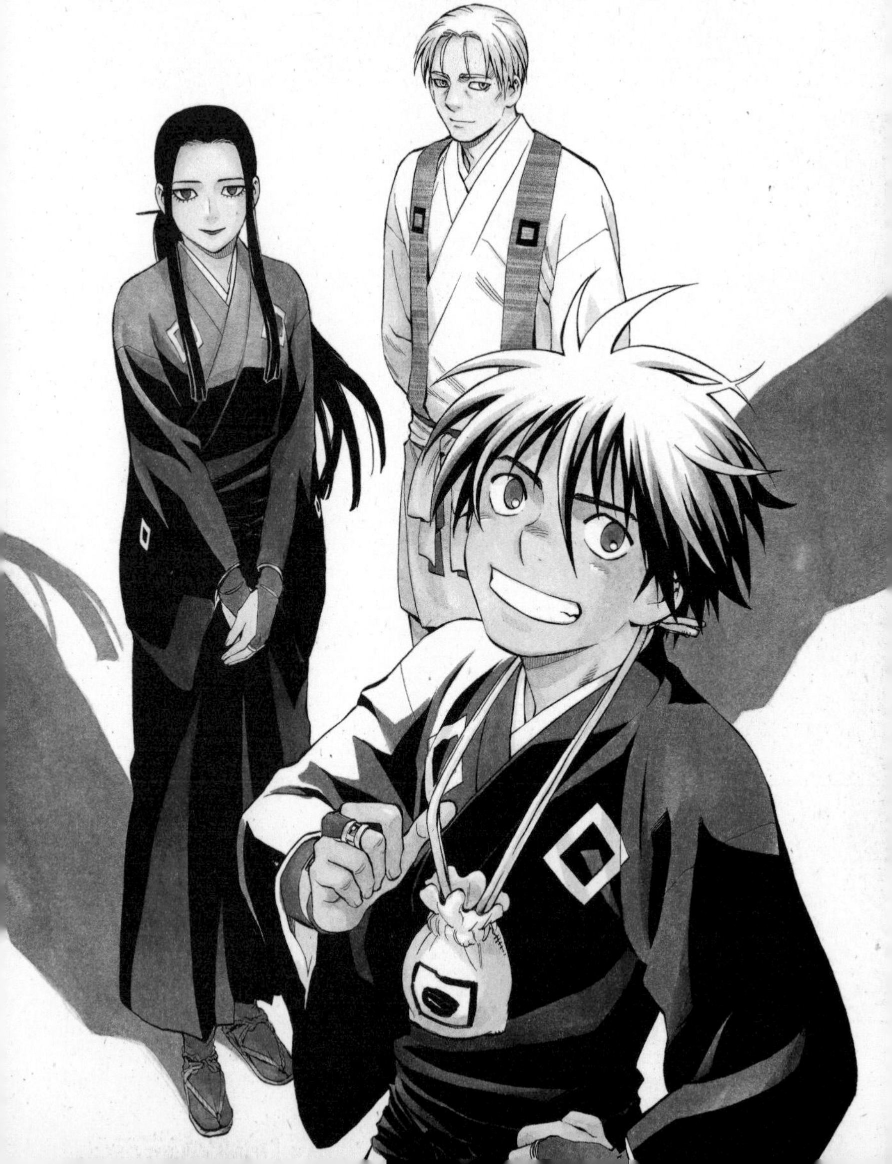

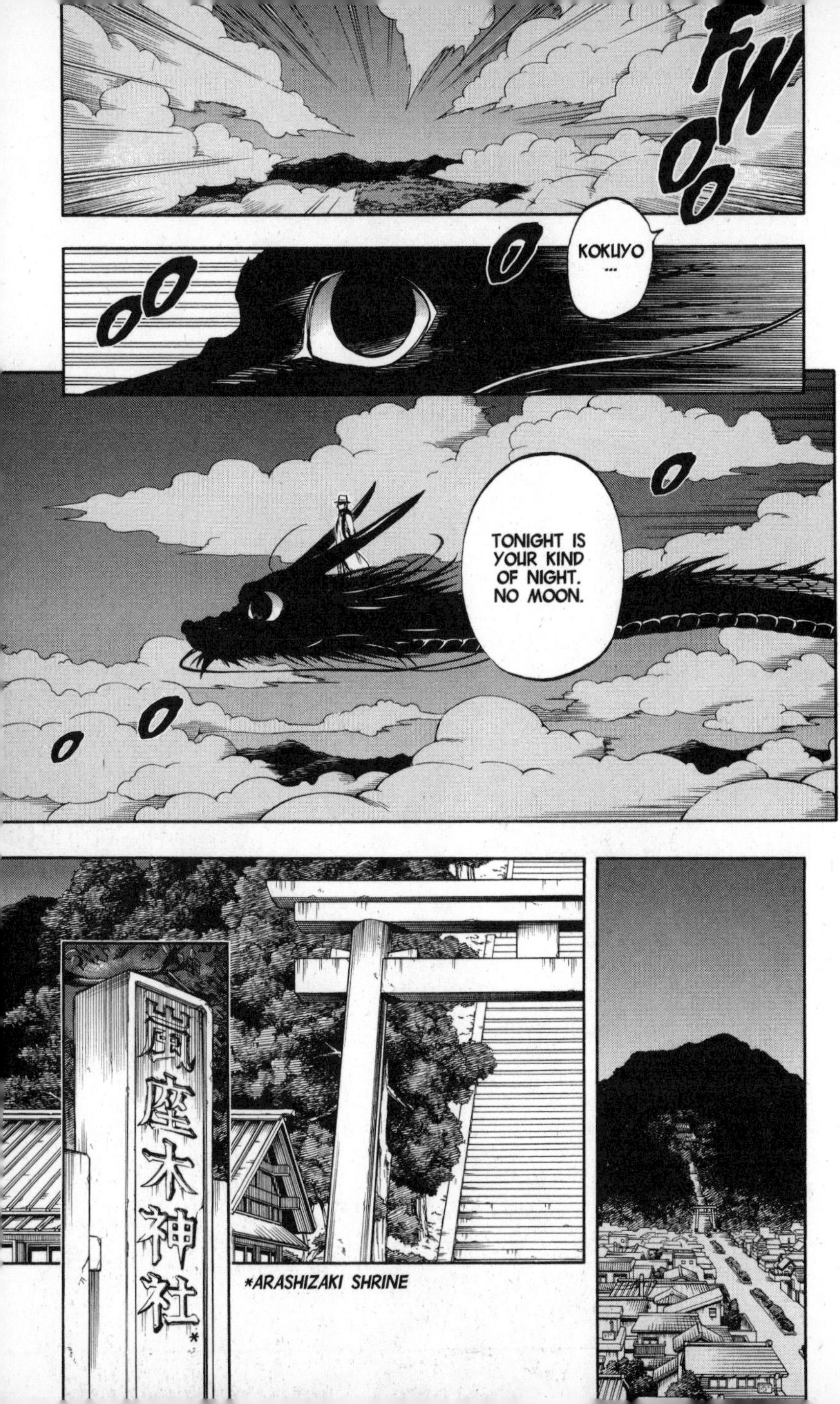
FWOOO
KOKUYO...
TONIGHT IS YOUR KIND OF NIGHT. NO MOON.
嵐座木神社*
*ARASHIZAKI SHRINE

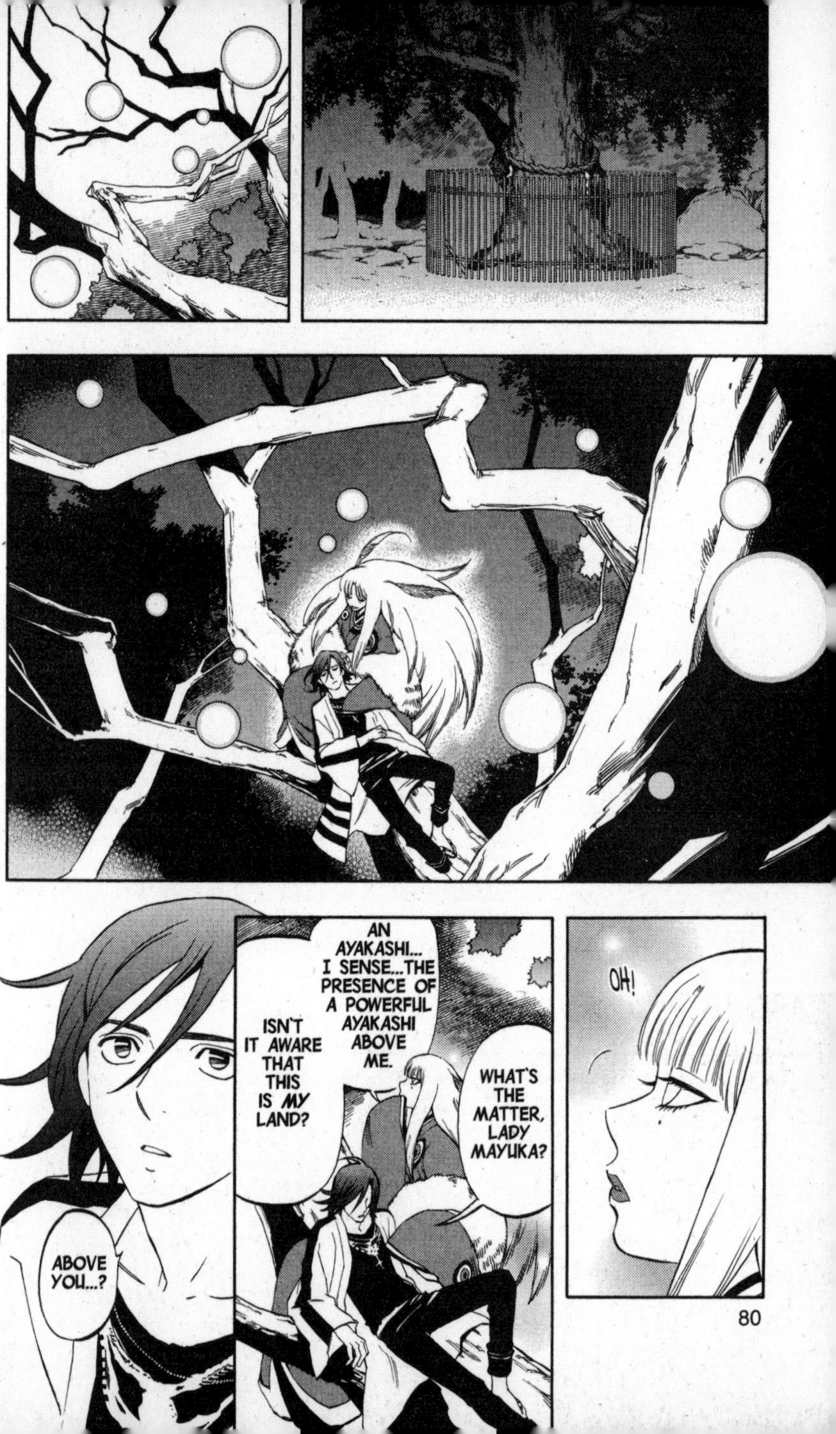
OH!
WHAT'S THE MATTER, LADY MAYUKA?
AN AYAKASHI... I SENSE...THE PRESENCE OF A POWERFUL AYAKASHI ABOVE ME.
ISN'T IT AWARE THAT THIS IS *MY* LAND?
ABOVE YOU...?

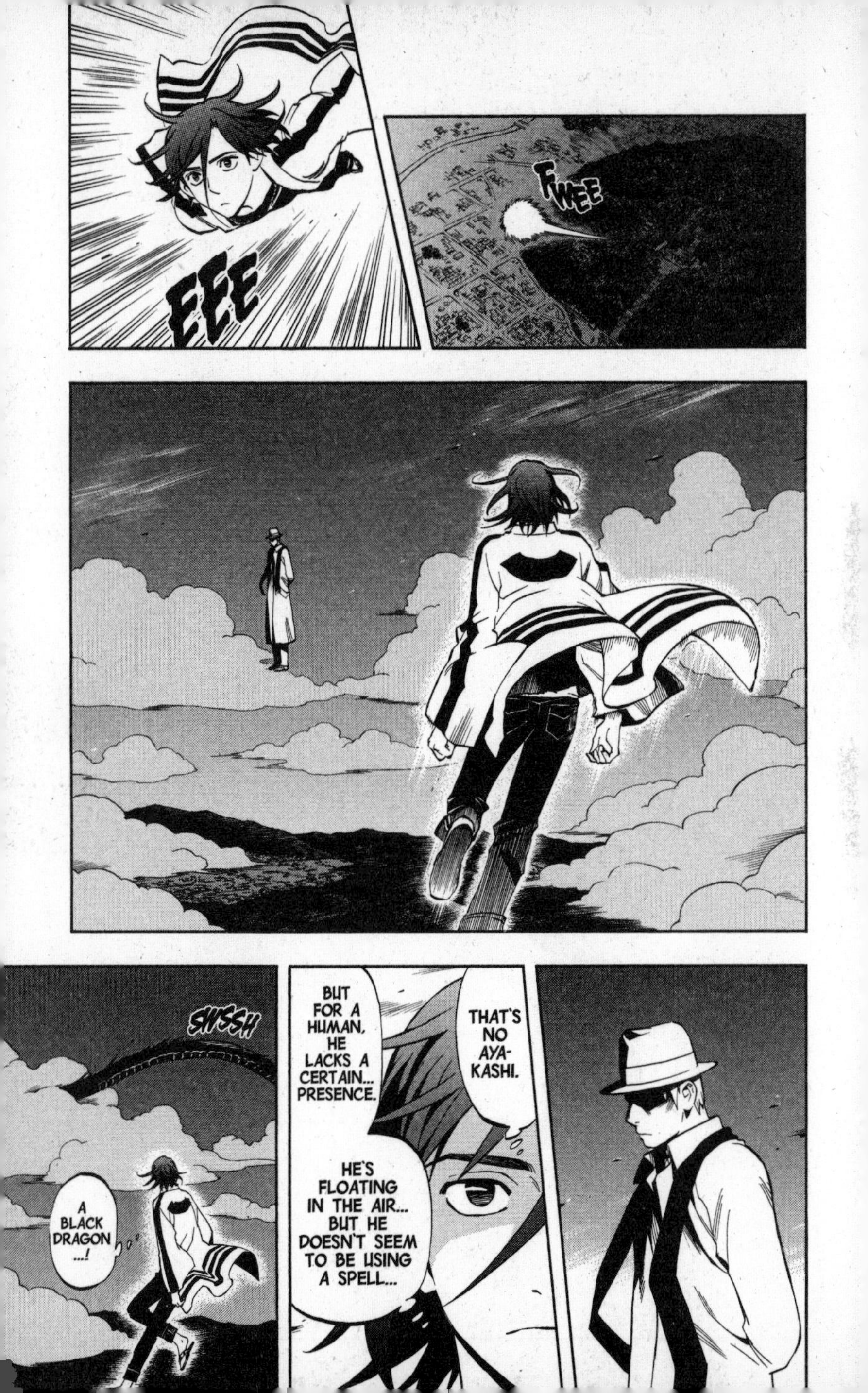
FWEE
EEE
THAT'S NO AYA-KASHI.
BUT FOR A HUMAN, HE LACKS A CERTAIN... PRESENCE.
HE'S FLOATING IN THE AIR... BUT HE DOESN'T SEEM TO BE USING A SPELL...
SWSSH
A BLACK DRAGON ...!

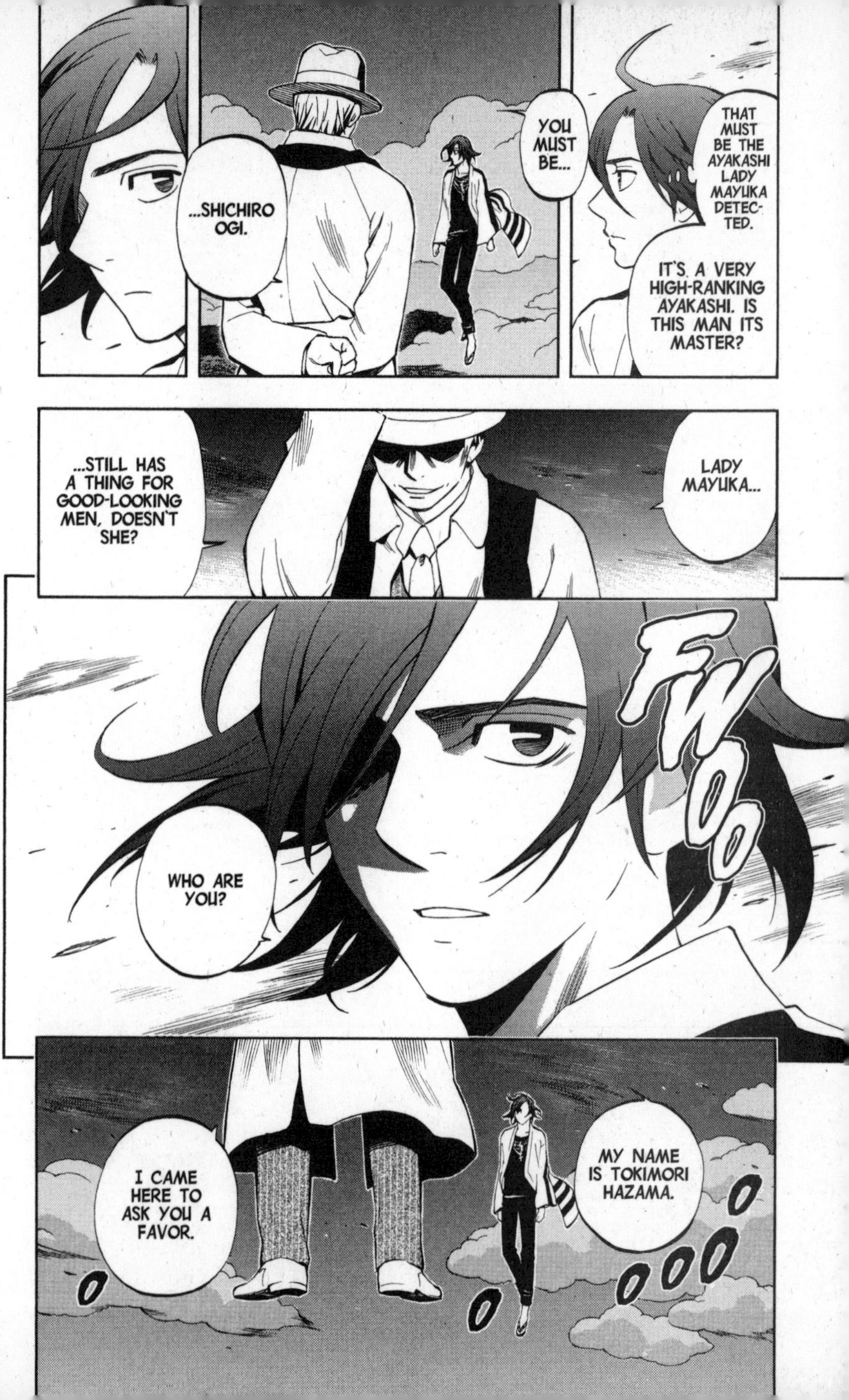
THAT MUST BE THE AYAKASHI LADY MAYUKA DETECTED.
IT'S A VERY HIGH-RANKING AYAKASHI. IS THIS MAN ITS MASTER?
YOU MUST BE...
...SHICHIRO OGI.
LADY MAYUKA...
...STILL HAS A THING FOR GOOD-LOOKING MEN, DOESN'T SHE?
FWOO
WHO ARE YOU?
MY NAME IS TOKIMORI HAZAMA.
I CAME HERE TO ASK YOU A FAVOR.

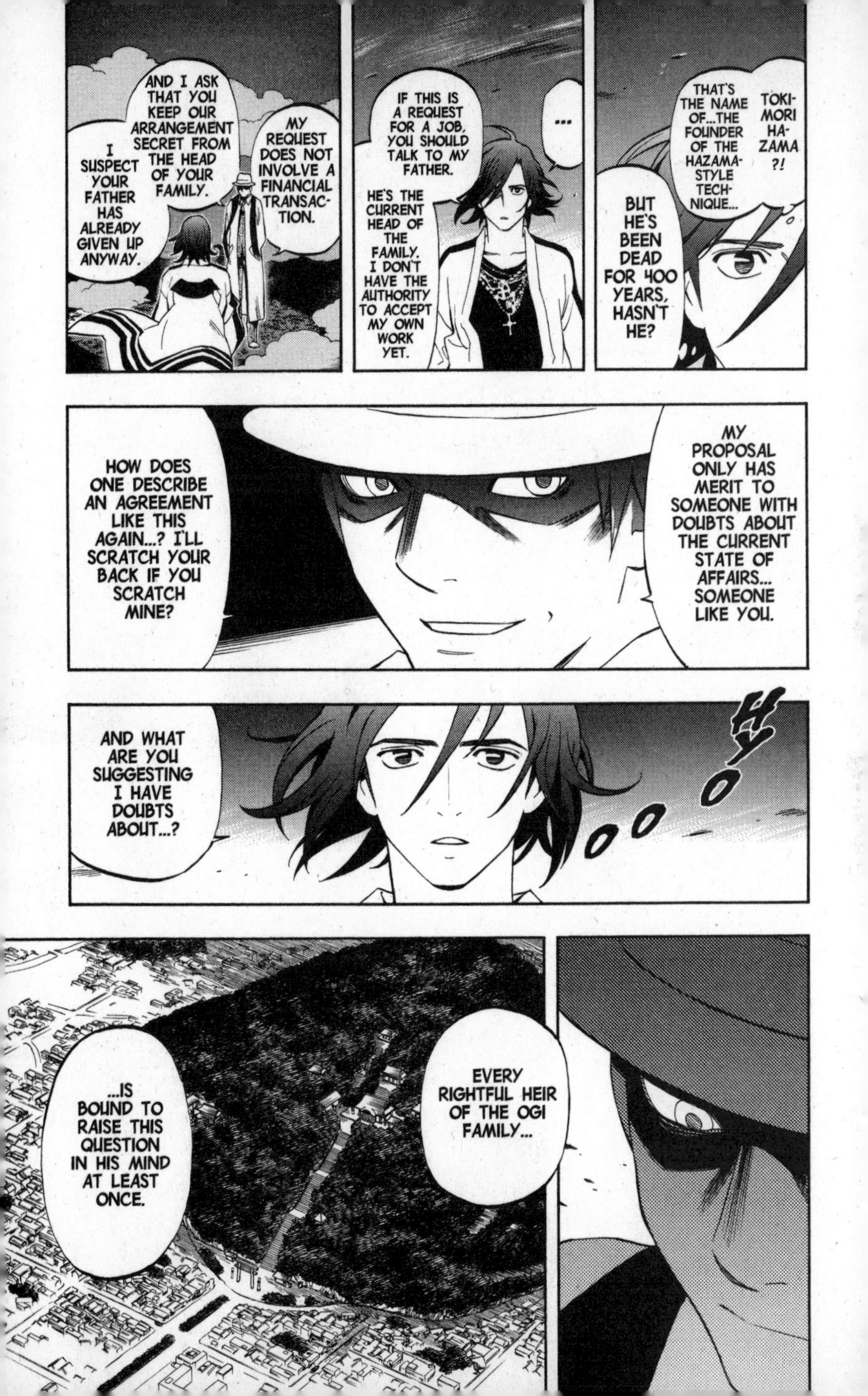
TOKIMORI HAZAMA ?!
THAT'S THE NAME OF...THE FOUNDER OF THE HAZAMA-STYLE TECHNIQUE...
BUT HE'S BEEN DEAD FOR 400 YEARS, HASN'T HE?
...
IF THIS IS A REQUEST FOR A JOB, YOU SHOULD TALK TO MY FATHER.
HE'S THE CURRENT HEAD OF THE FAMILY. I DON'T HAVE THE AUTHORITY TO ACCEPT MY OWN WORK YET.
MY REQUEST DOES NOT INVOLVE A FINANCIAL TRANSACTION.
AND I ASK THAT YOU KEEP OUR ARRANGEMENT SECRET FROM THE HEAD OF YOUR FAMILY.
I SUSPECT YOUR FATHER HAS ALREADY GIVEN UP ANYWAY.
MY PROPOSAL ONLY HAS MERIT TO SOMEONE WITH DOUBTS ABOUT THE CURRENT STATE OF AFFAIRS... SOMEONE LIKE YOU.
HOW DOES ONE DESCRIBE AN AGREEMENT LIKE THIS AGAIN...? I'LL SCRATCH YOUR BACK IF YOU SCRATCH MINE?
AND WHAT ARE YOU SUGGESTING I HAVE DOUBTS ABOUT...?
EVERY RIGHTFUL HEIR OF THE OGI FAMILY...
...IS BOUND TO RAISE THIS QUESTION IN HIS MIND AT LEAST ONCE.

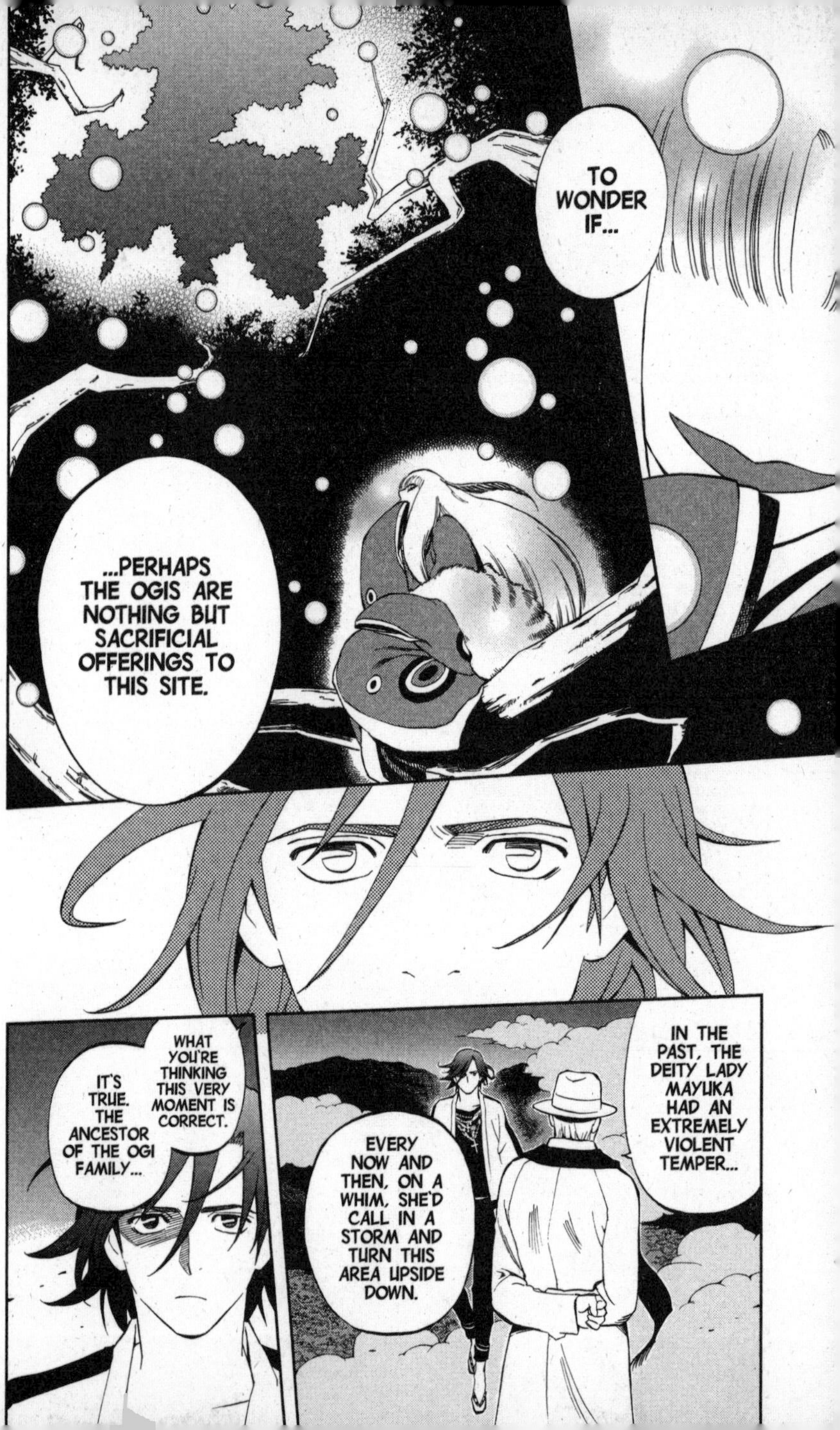
TO WONDER IF...
...PERHAPS THE OGIS ARE NOTHING BUT SACRIFICIAL OFFERINGS TO THIS SITE.
IN THE PAST, THE DEITY LADY MAYUKA HAD AN EXTREMELY VIOLENT TEMPER...
EVERY NOW AND THEN, ON A WHIM, SHE'D CALL IN A STORM AND TURN THIS AREA UPSIDE DOWN.
WHAT YOU'RE THINKING THIS VERY MOMENT IS CORRECT.
IT'S TRUE. THE ANCESTOR OF THE OGI FAMILY...

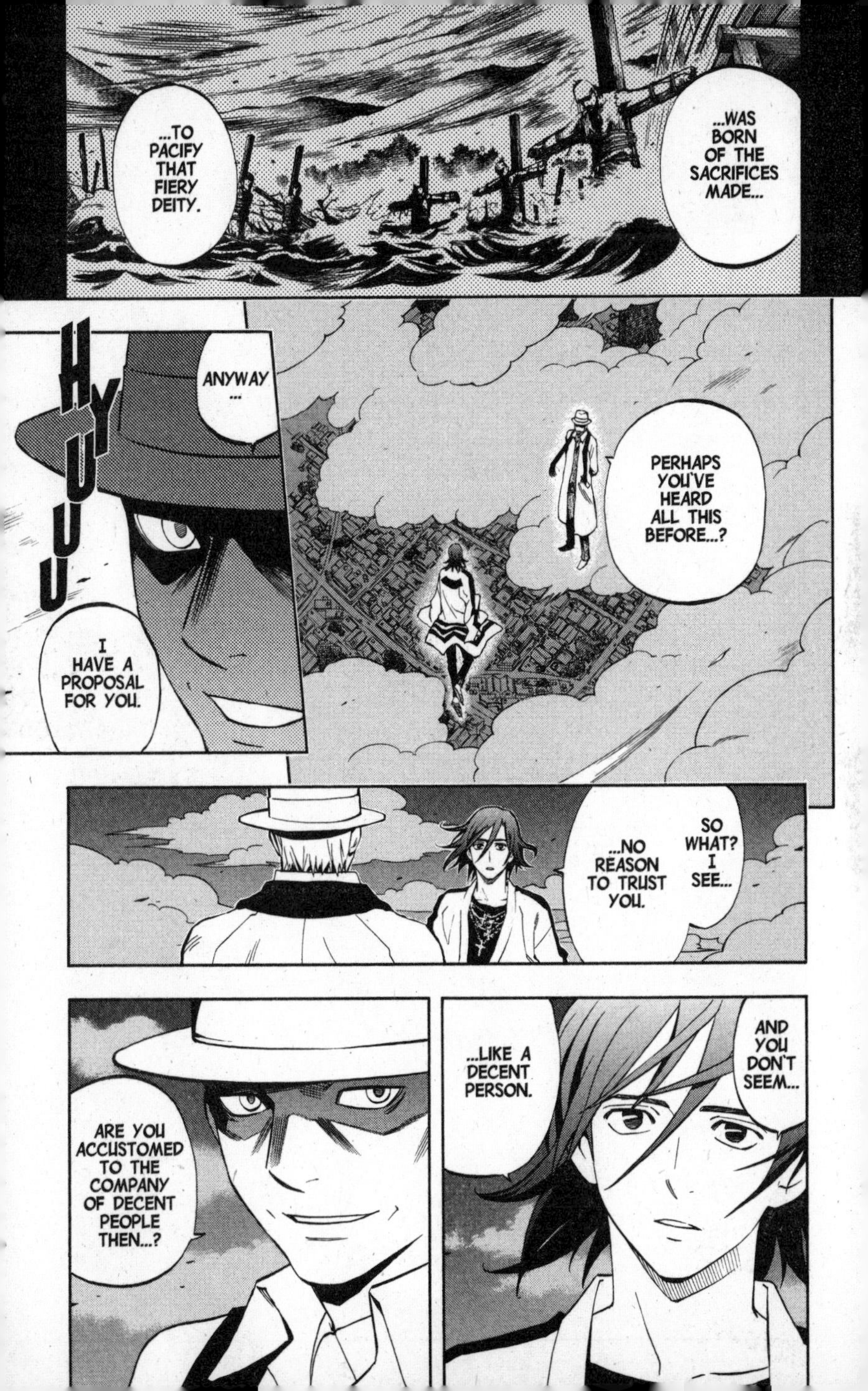
...WAS BORN OF THE SACRIFICES MADE...
...TO PACIFY THAT FIERY DEITY.
PERHAPS YOU'VE HEARD ALL THIS BEFORE...?
ANYWAY...
HYUUUU
I HAVE A PROPOSAL FOR YOU.
SO WHAT? I SEE...
...NO REASON TO TRUST YOU.
AND YOU DON'T SEEM...
...LIKE A DECENT PERSON.
ARE YOU ACCUSTOMED TO THE COMPANY OF DECENT PEOPLE THEN...?

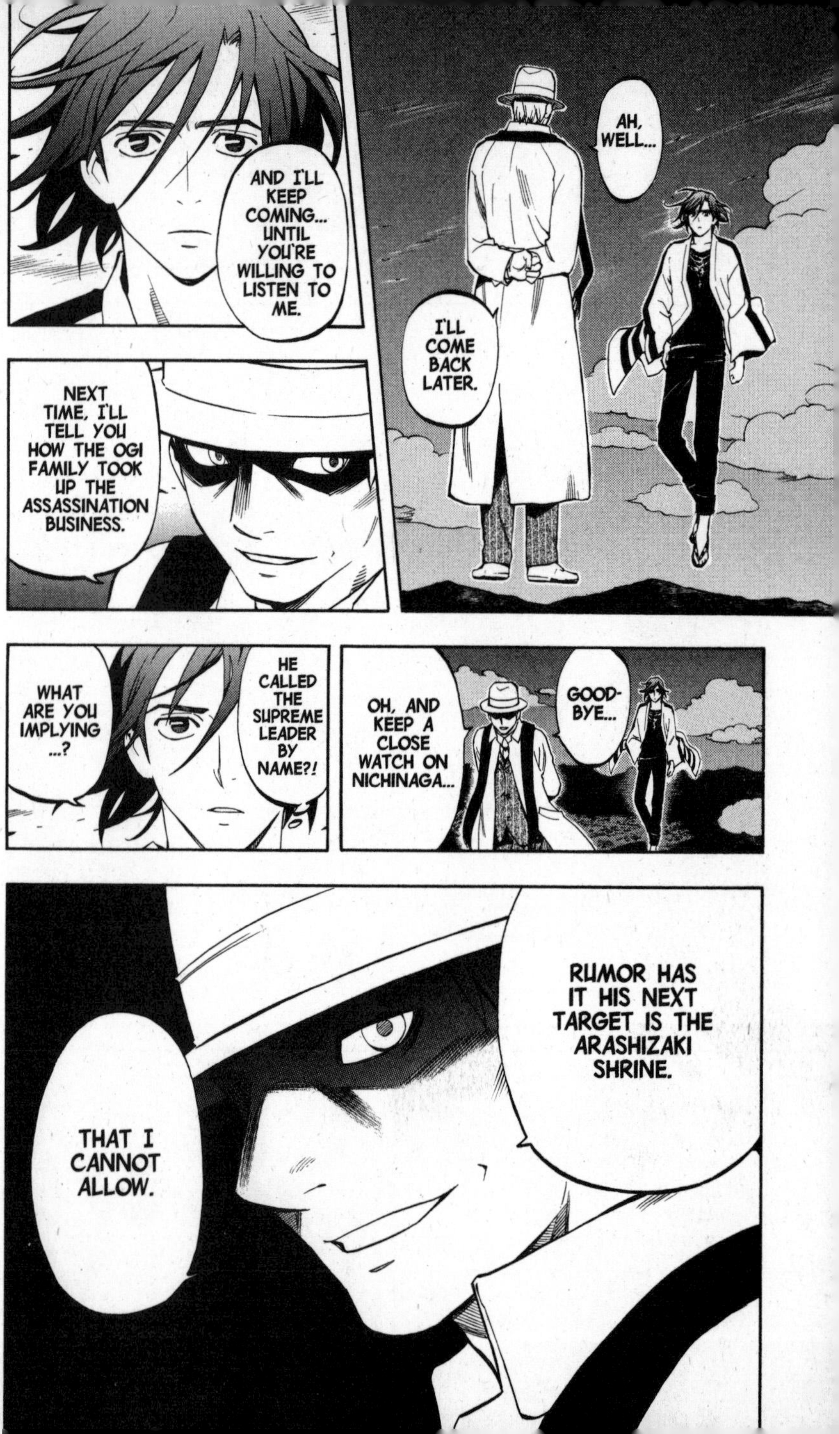
AH, WELL...
I'LL COME BACK LATER.
AND I'LL KEEP COMING... UNTIL YOU'RE WILLING TO LISTEN TO ME.
NEXT TIME, I'LL TELL YOU HOW THE OGI FAMILY TOOK UP THE ASSASSINATION BUSINESS.
GOOD-BYE...
OH, AND KEEP A CLOSE WATCH ON NICHINAGA...
HE CALLED THE SUPREME LEADER BY NAME?!
WHAT ARE YOU IMPLYING ...?
RUMOR HAS IT HIS NEXT TARGET IS THE ARASHIZAKI SHRINE.
THAT I CANNOT ALLOW.

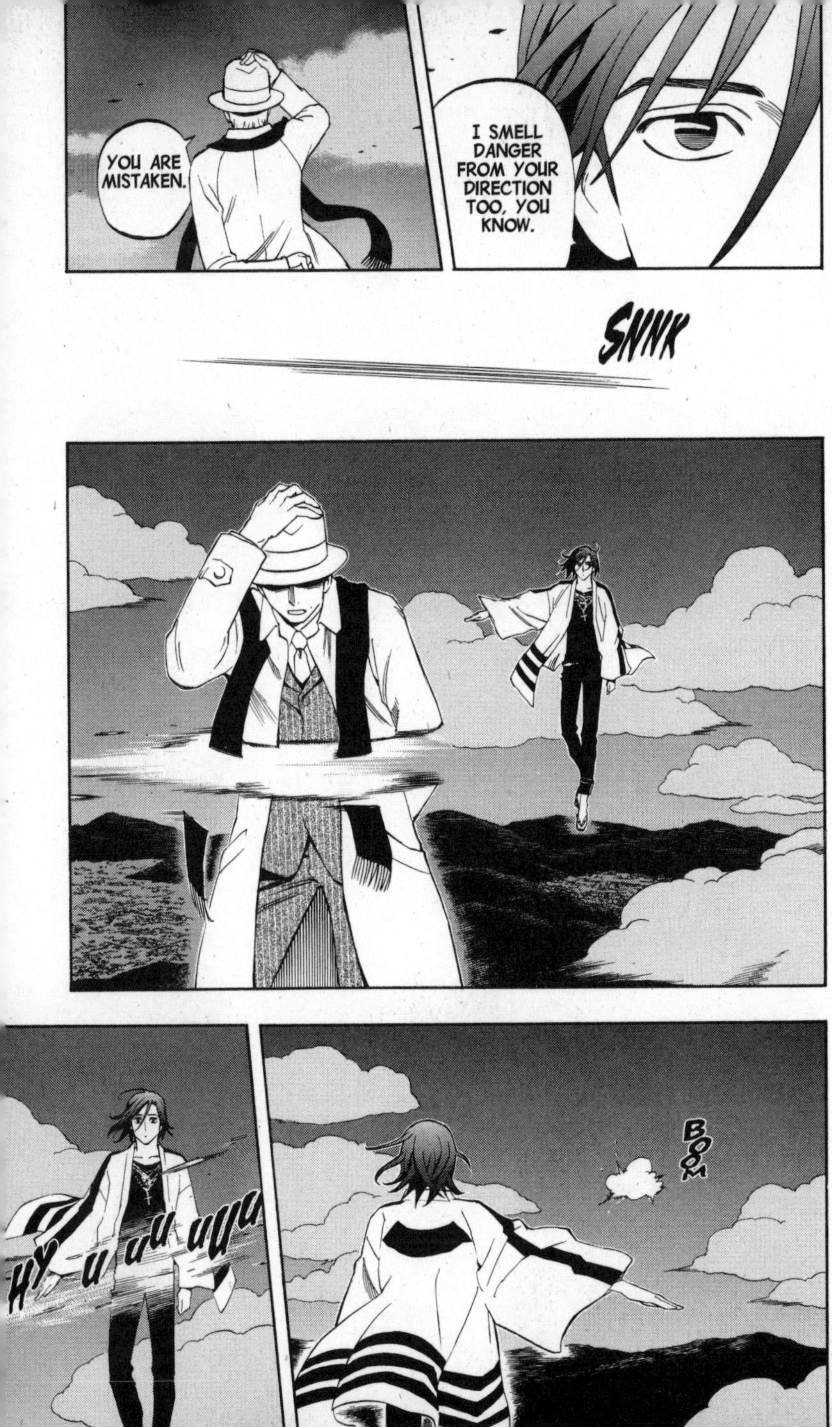
I SMELL DANGER FROM YOUR DIRECTION TOO, YOU KNOW.
YOU ARE MISTAKEN.
SNNK
BOOM
HYUUUUUUU

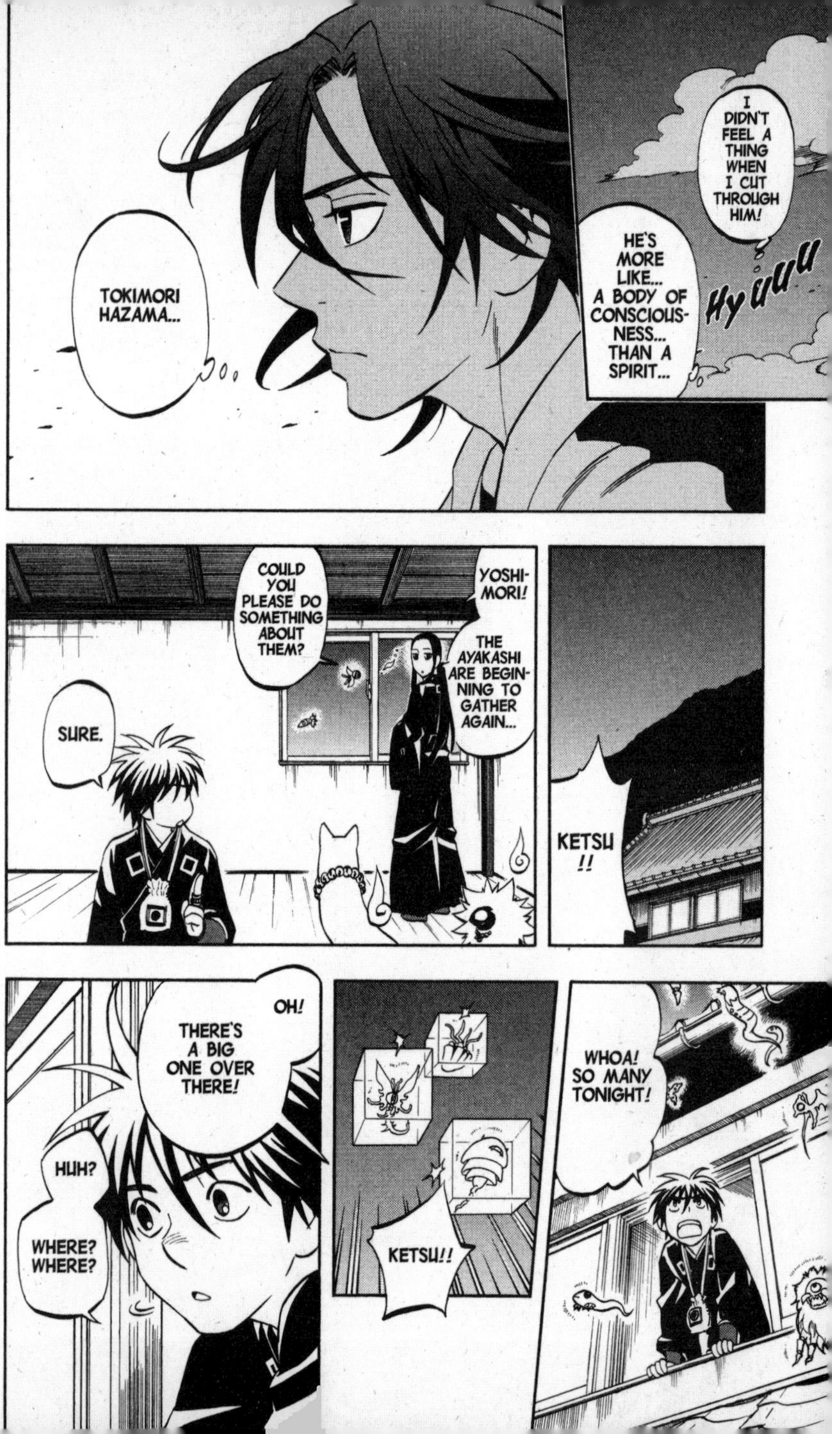

I DIDN'T FEEL A THING WHEN I CUT THROUGH HIM!
HE'S MORE LIKE... A BODY OF CONSCIOUSNESS... THAN A SPIRIT...
Hy uuu
TOKIMORI HAZAMA...
KETSU!!
YOSHI-MORI!
THE AYAKASHI ARE BEGINNING TO GATHER AGAIN...
COULD YOU PLEASE DO SOMETHING ABOUT THEM?
SURE.
WHOA! SO MANY TONIGHT!
KETSU!!
OH!
THERE'S A BIG ONE OVER THERE!
HUH?
WHERE? WHERE?

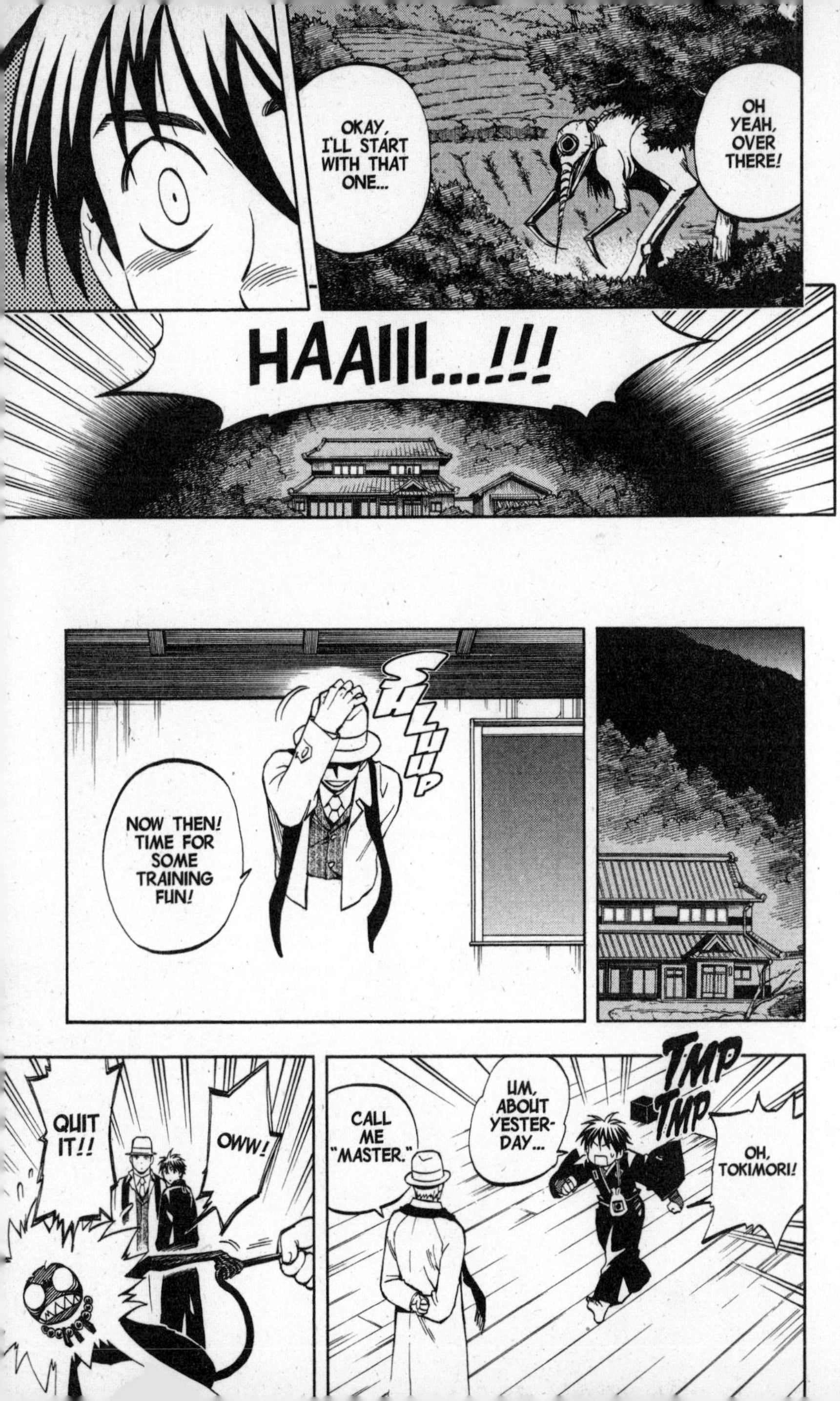
OH YEAH, OVER THERE!
OKAY, I'LL START WITH THAT ONE...
HAAIII...!!!
SHLUUP
NOW THEN! TIME FOR SOME TRAINING FUN!
TMP TMP
OH, TOKIMORI!
UM, ABOUT YESTER-DAY...
CALL ME "MASTER."
OWW!
QUIT IT!!

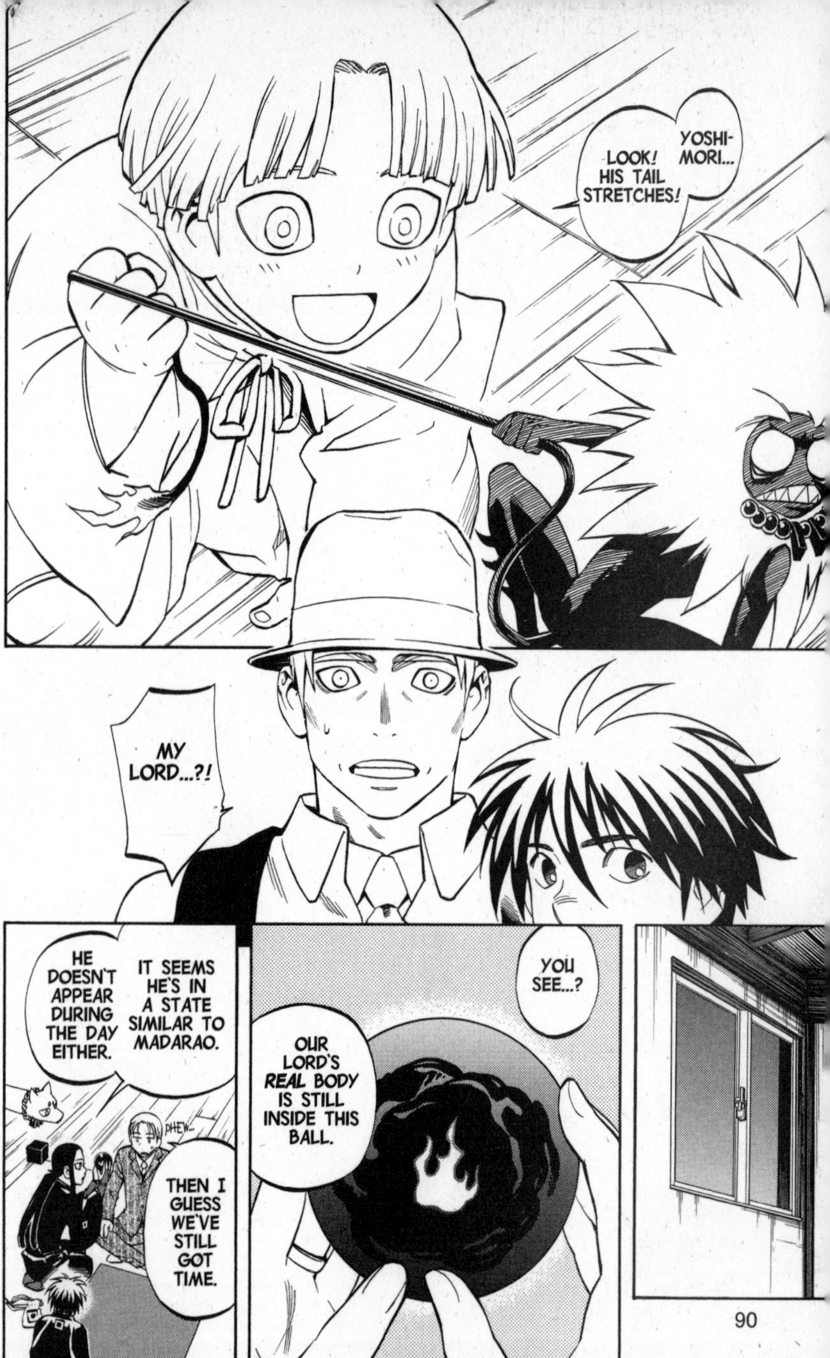
YOSHI-MORI... LOOK! HIS TAIL STRETCHES!
MY LORD...?!
YOU SEE...?
OUR LORD'S *REAL* BODY IS STILL INSIDE THIS BALL.
IT SEEMS HE'S IN A STATE SIMILAR TO MADARAO.
HE DOESN'T APPEAR DURING THE DAY EITHER.
PHEW...
THEN I GUESS WE'VE STILL GOT TIME.

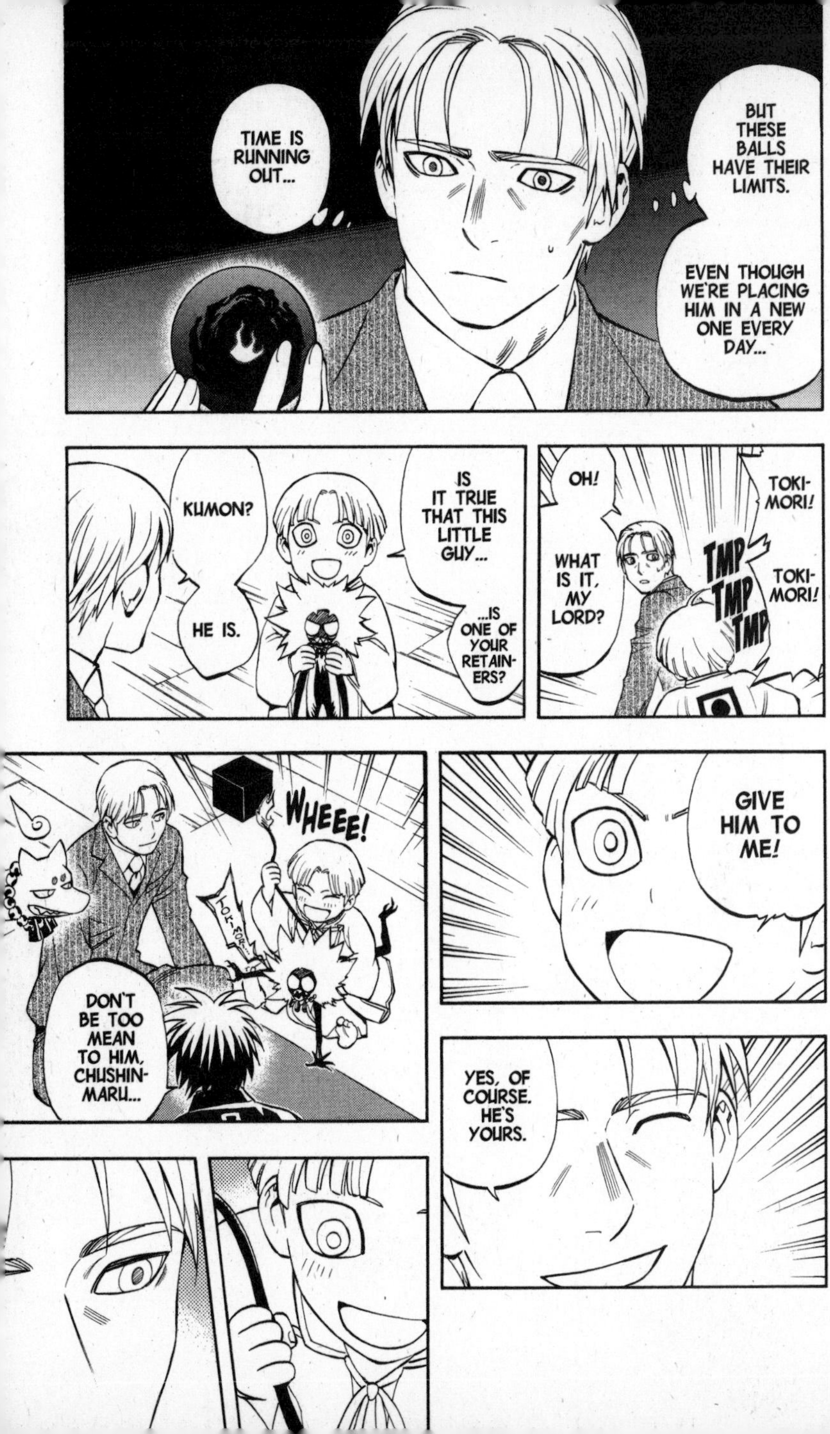
BUT THESE BALLS HAVE THEIR LIMITS.
EVEN THOUGH WE'RE PLACING HIM IN A NEW ONE EVERY DAY...
TIME IS RUNNING OUT...
TOKI-MORI!
TOKI-MORI!
TMP TMP TMP
OH!
WHAT IS IT, MY LORD?
IS IT TRUE THAT THIS LITTLE GUY...
...IS ONE OF YOUR RETAINERS?
KUMON?
HE IS.
GIVE HIM TO ME!
YES, OF COURSE. HE'S YOURS.
WHEEE!
TOKIMORI!!
DON'T BE TOO MEAN TO HIM, CHUSHIN-MARU...

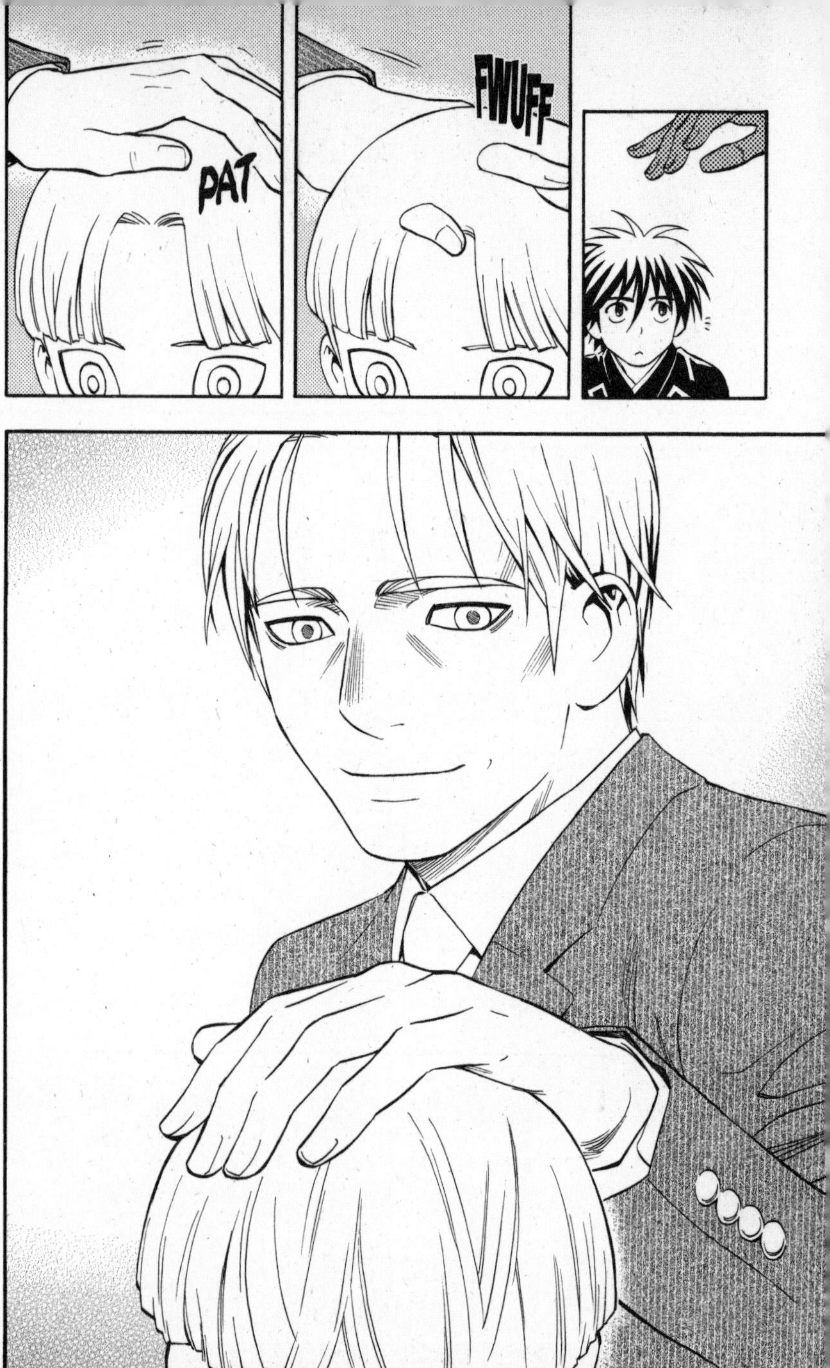
FWUFF
PAT

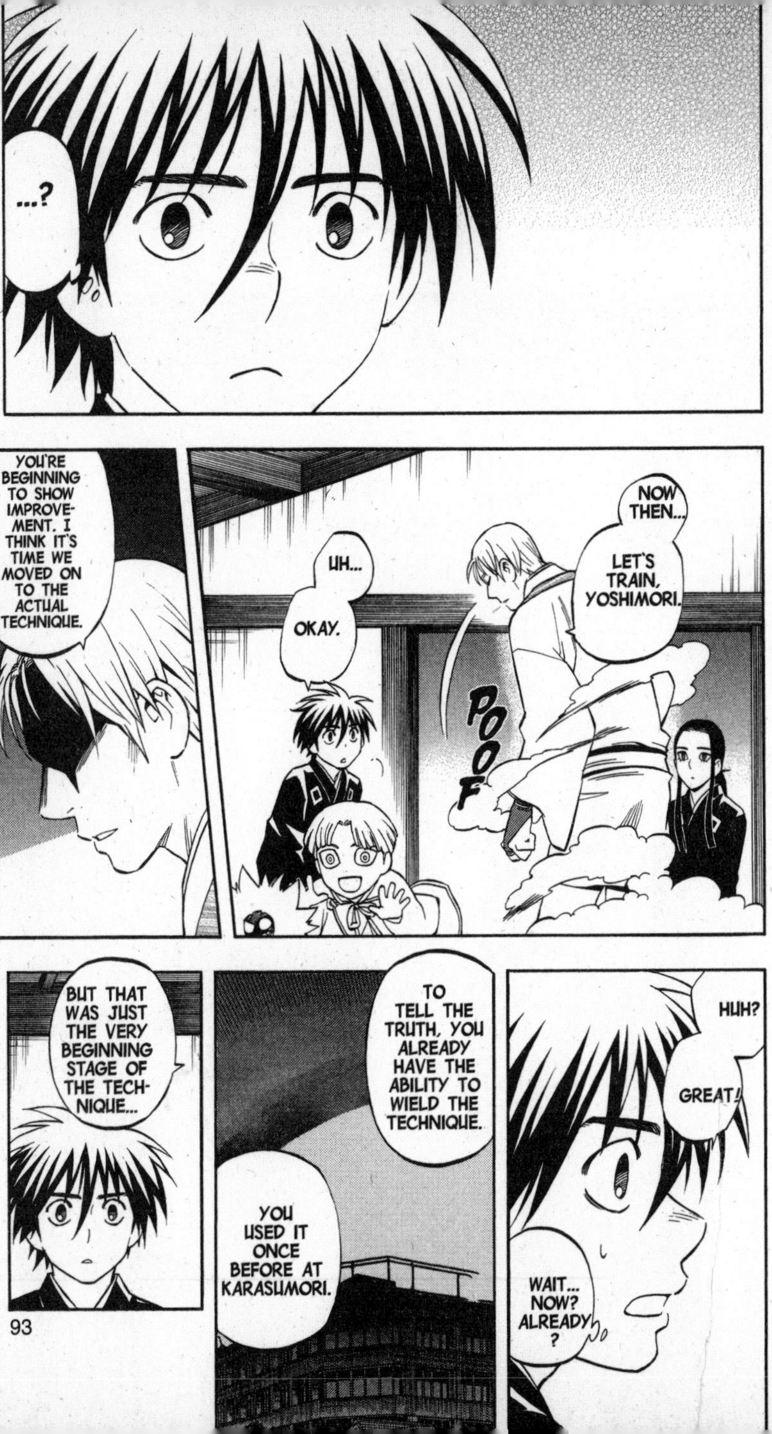
...?
NOW THEN...
LET'S TRAIN, YOSHIMORI.
UH...
OKAY.
POOF
YOU'RE BEGINNING TO SHOW IMPROVEMENT. I THINK IT'S TIME WE MOVED ON TO THE ACTUAL TECHNIQUE.
HUH?
GREAT!
WAIT... NOW? ALREADY?
TO TELL THE TRUTH, YOU ALREADY HAVE THE ABILITY TO WIELD THE TECHNIQUE.
YOU USED IT ONCE BEFORE AT KARASUMORI.
BUT THAT WAS JUST THE VERY BEGINNING STAGE OF THE TECHNIQUE...

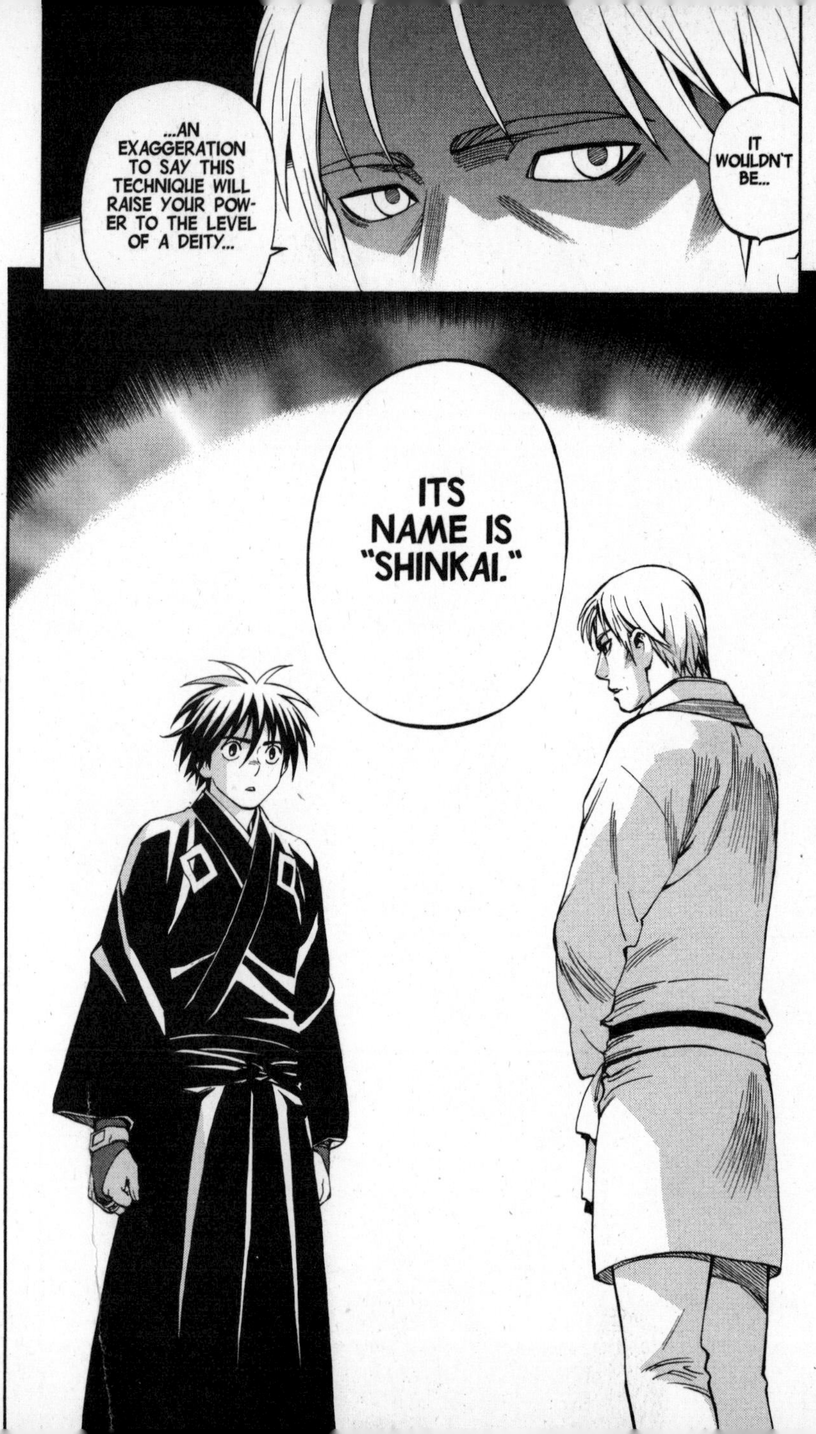
IT WOULDN'T BE...
...AN EXAGGERATION TO SAY THIS TECHNIQUE WILL RAISE YOUR POW-ER TO THE LEVEL OF A DEITY...
ITS NAME IS "SHINKAI."

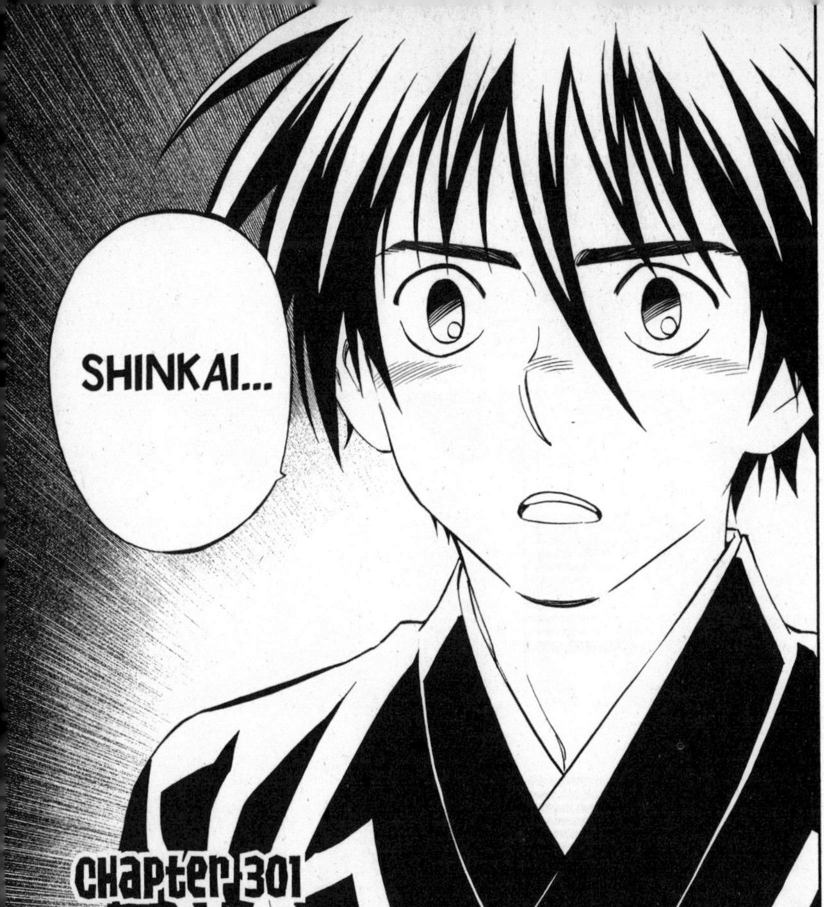
SHINKAI...
Chapter 301
SHINKAI
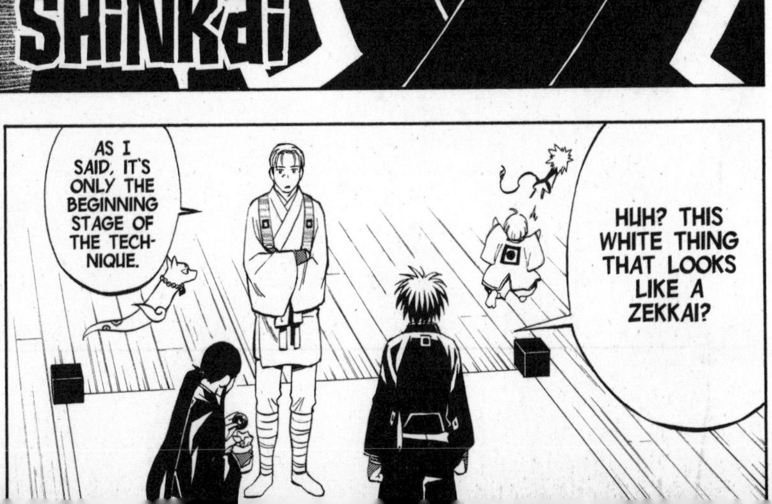
HUH? THIS WHITE THING THAT LOOKS LIKE A ZEKKAI?
AS I SAID, IT'S ONLY THE BEGINNING STAGE OF THE TECH-NIQUE.

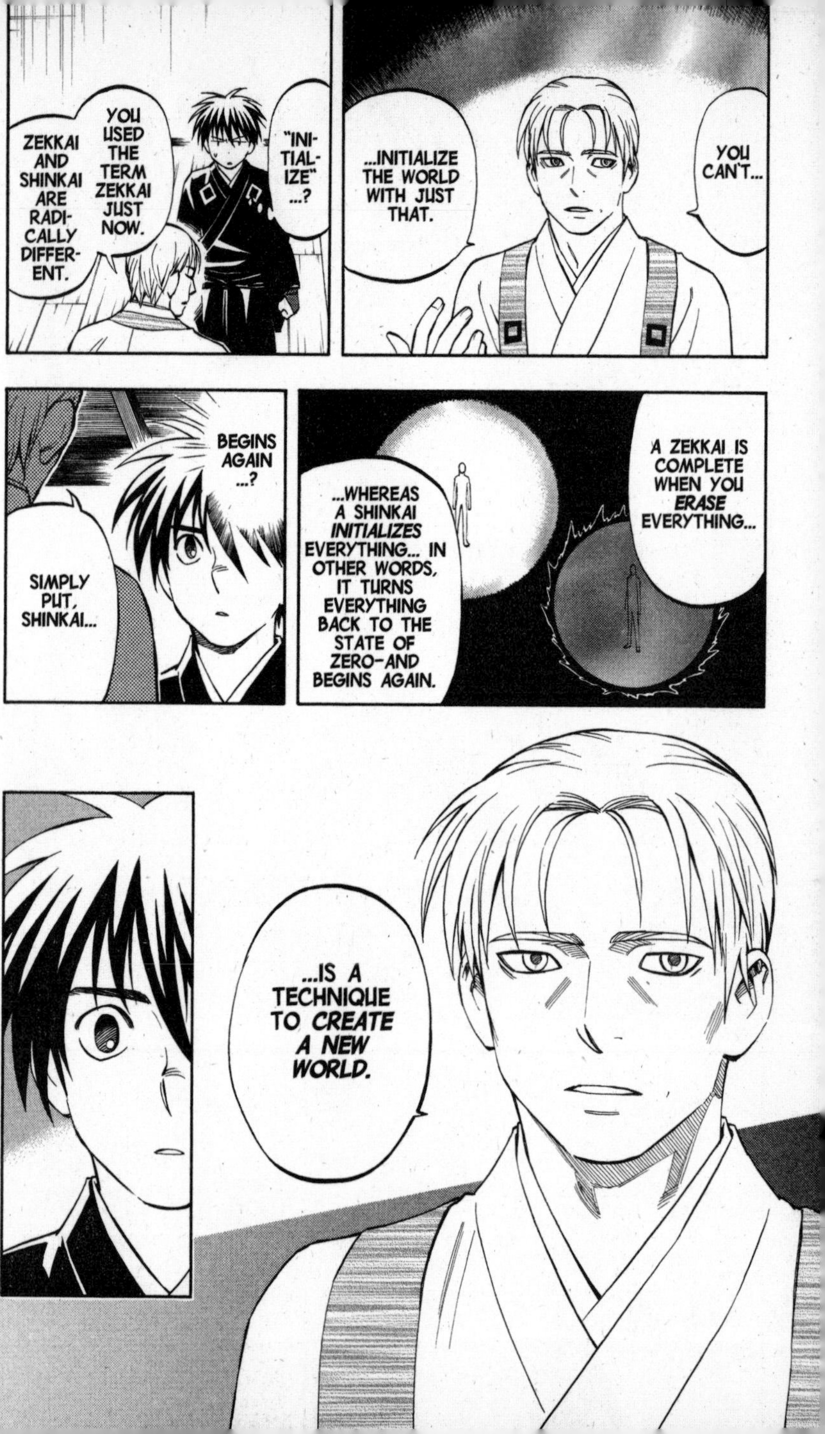
YOU CAN'T...
...INITIALIZE THE WORLD WITH JUST THAT.
"INITIALIZE"...?
YOU USED THE TERM ZEKKAI JUST NOW.
ZEKKAI AND SHINKAI ARE RADICALLY DIFFERENT.
A ZEKKAI IS COMPLETE WHEN YOU *ERASE* EVERYTHING...
...WHEREAS A SHINKAI *INITIALIZES* EVERYTHING... IN OTHER WORDS, IT TURNS EVERYTHING BACK TO THE STATE OF ZERO—AND BEGINS AGAIN.
BEGINS AGAIN...?
SIMPLY PUT, SHINKAI...
...IS A TECHNIQUE TO *CREATE A NEW WORLD.*

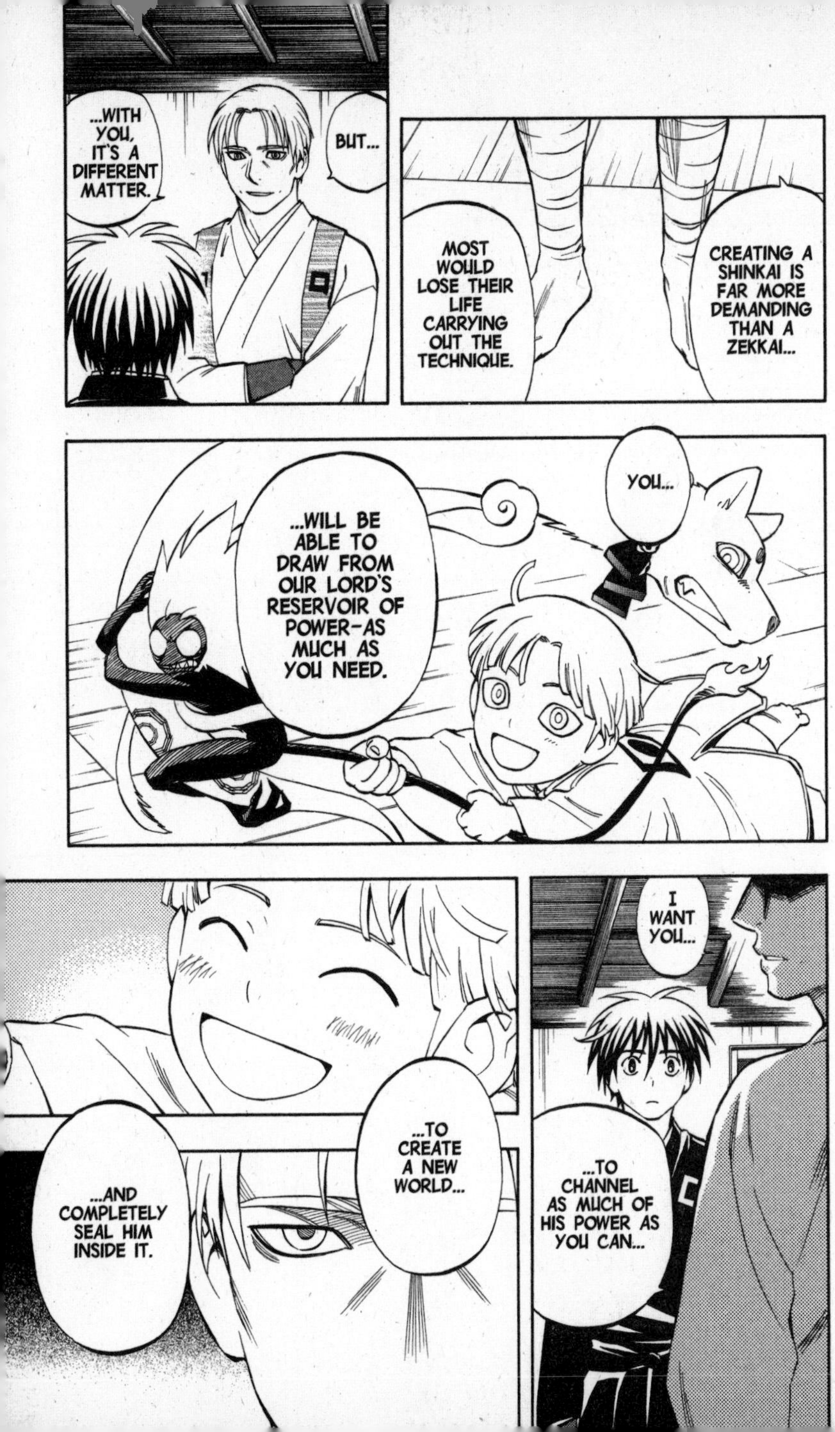
CREATING A SHINKAI IS FAR MORE DEMANDING THAN A ZEKKAI...
MOST WOULD LOSE THEIR LIFE CARRYING OUT THE TECHNIQUE.
BUT...
...WITH YOU, IT'S A DIFFERENT MATTER.
YOU...
...WILL BE ABLE TO DRAW FROM OUR LORD'S RESERVOIR OF POWER–AS MUCH AS YOU NEED.
I WANT YOU...
...TO CHANNEL AS MUCH OF HIS POWER AS YOU CAN...
...TO CREATE A NEW WORLD...
...AND COMPLETELY SEAL HIM INSIDE IT.

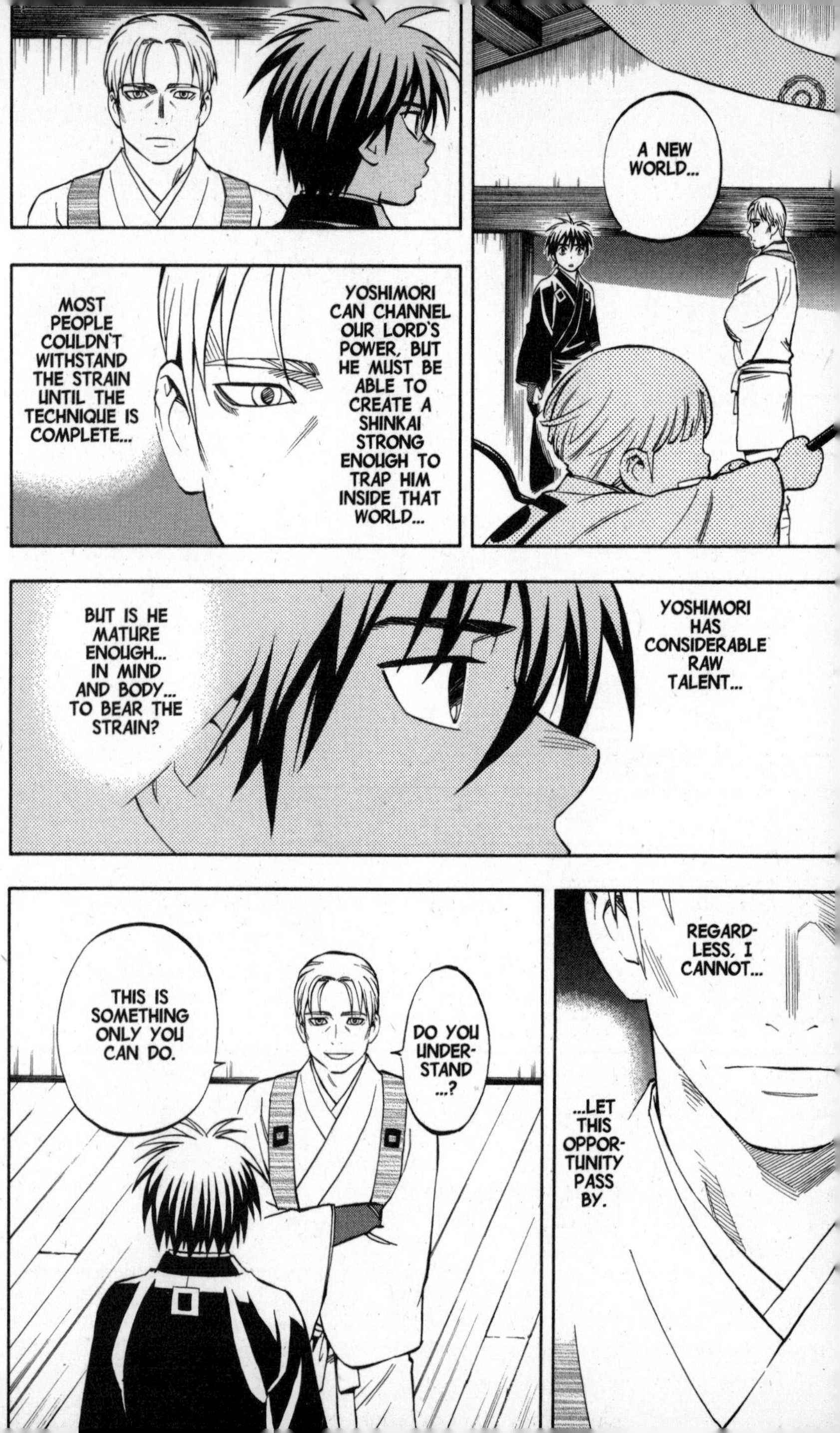
A NEW WORLD...
YOSHIMORI CAN CHANNEL OUR LORD'S POWER, BUT HE MUST BE ABLE TO CREATE A SHINKAI STRONG ENOUGH TO TRAP HIM INSIDE THAT WORLD...
MOST PEOPLE COULDN'T WITHSTAND THE STRAIN UNTIL THE TECHNIQUE IS COMPLETE...
YOSHIMORI HAS CONSIDERABLE RAW TALENT...
BUT IS HE MATURE ENOUGH... IN MIND AND BODY... TO BEAR THE STRAIN?
REGARDLESS, I CANNOT...
...LET THIS OPPORTUNITY PASS BY.
DO YOU UNDERSTAND...?
THIS IS SOMETHING ONLY YOU CAN DO.

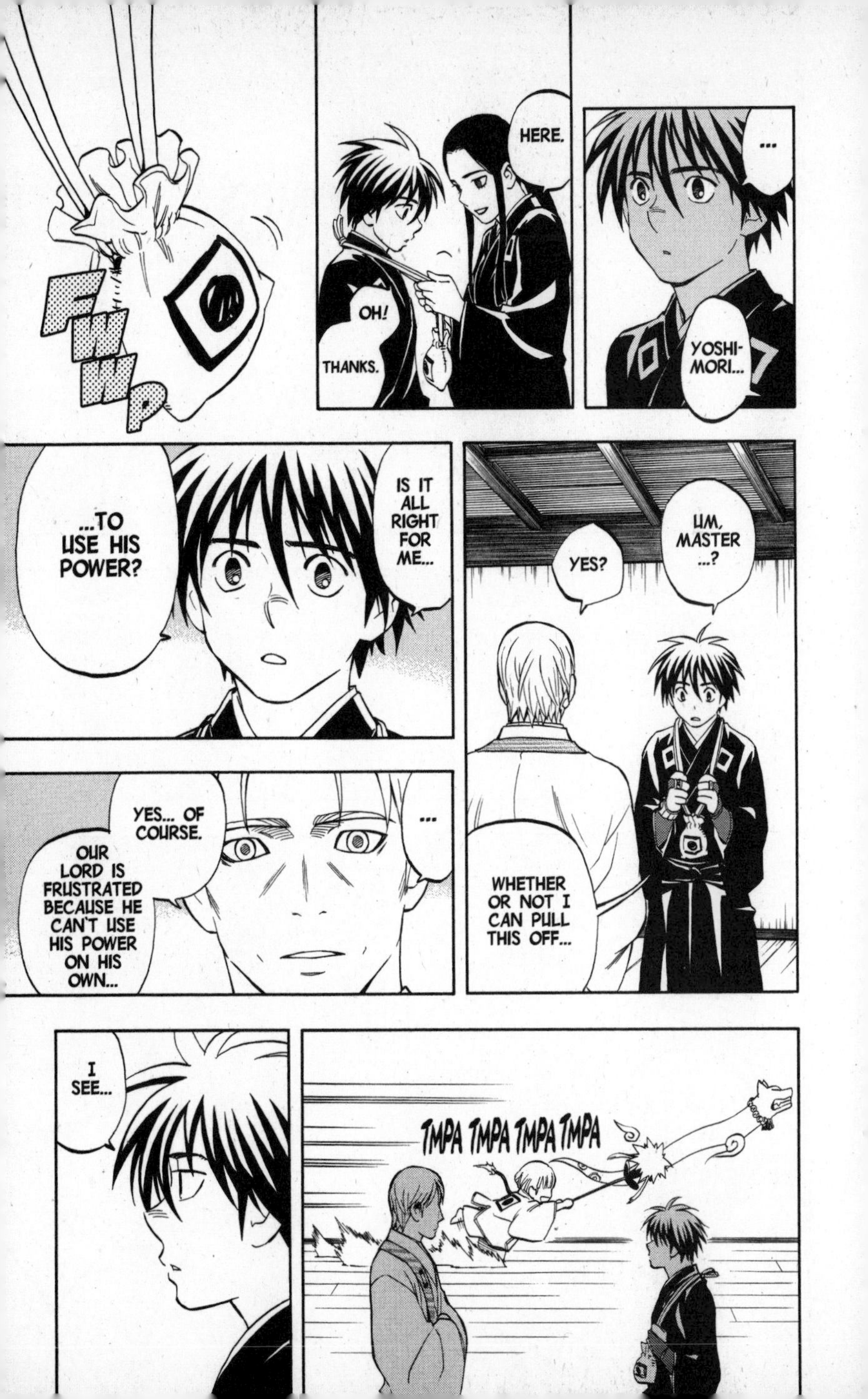
...
YOSHI-MORI...
HERE.
OH!
THANKS.
FWHP
UM, MASTER ...?
YES?
WHETHER OR NOT I CAN PULL THIS OFF...
IS IT ALL RIGHT FOR ME...
...TO USE HIS POWER?
...
YES... OF COURSE.
OUR LORD IS FRUSTRATED BECAUSE HE CAN'T USE HIS POWER ON HIS OWN...
TMPA TMPA TMPA TMPA
I SEE...

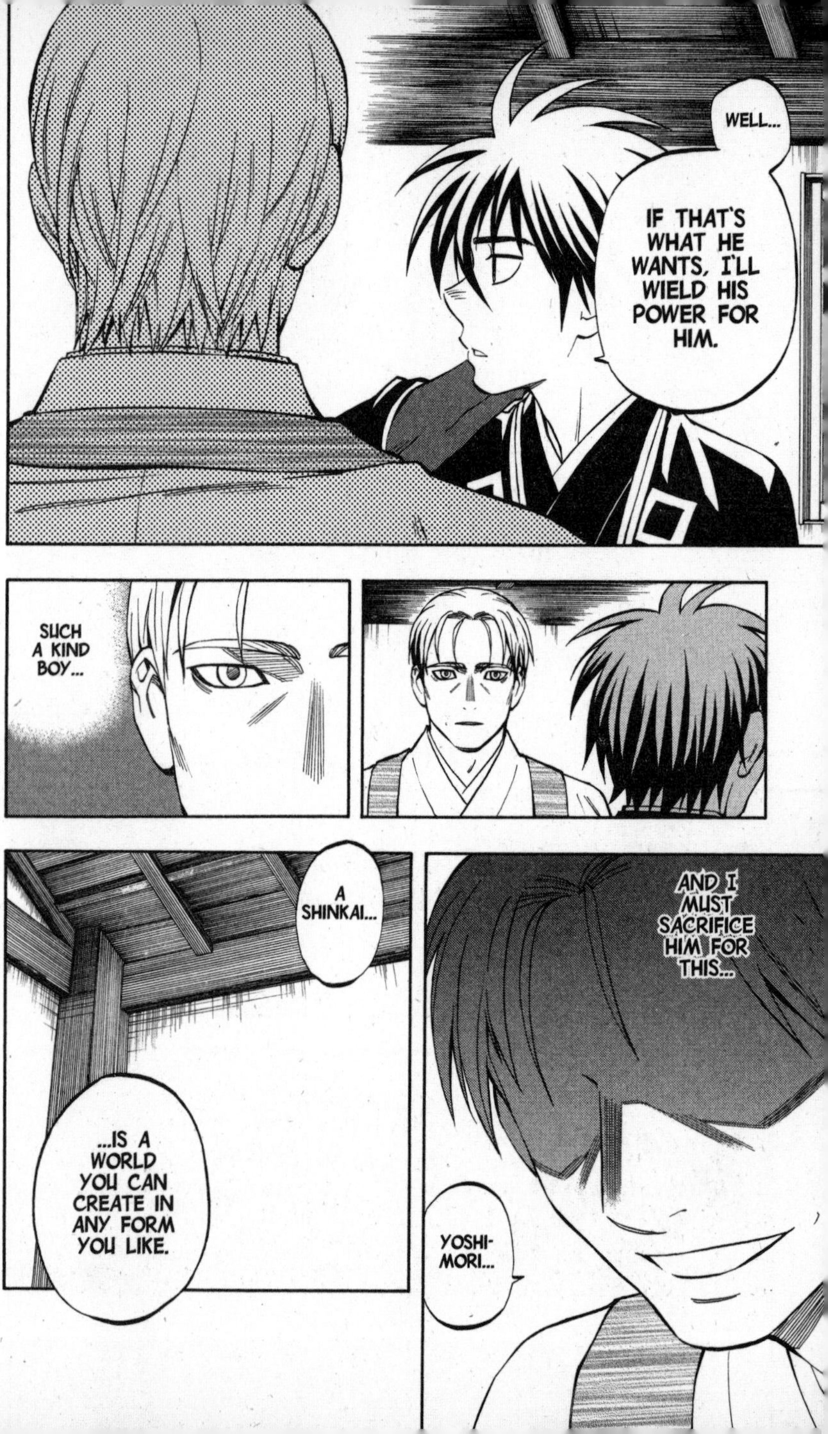
WELL...
IF THAT'S WHAT HE WANTS, I'LL WIELD HIS POWER FOR HIM.
SUCH A KIND BOY...
AND I MUST SACRIFICE HIM FOR THIS...
YOSHI-MORI...
A SHINKAI...
...IS A WORLD YOU CAN CREATE IN ANY FORM YOU LIKE.

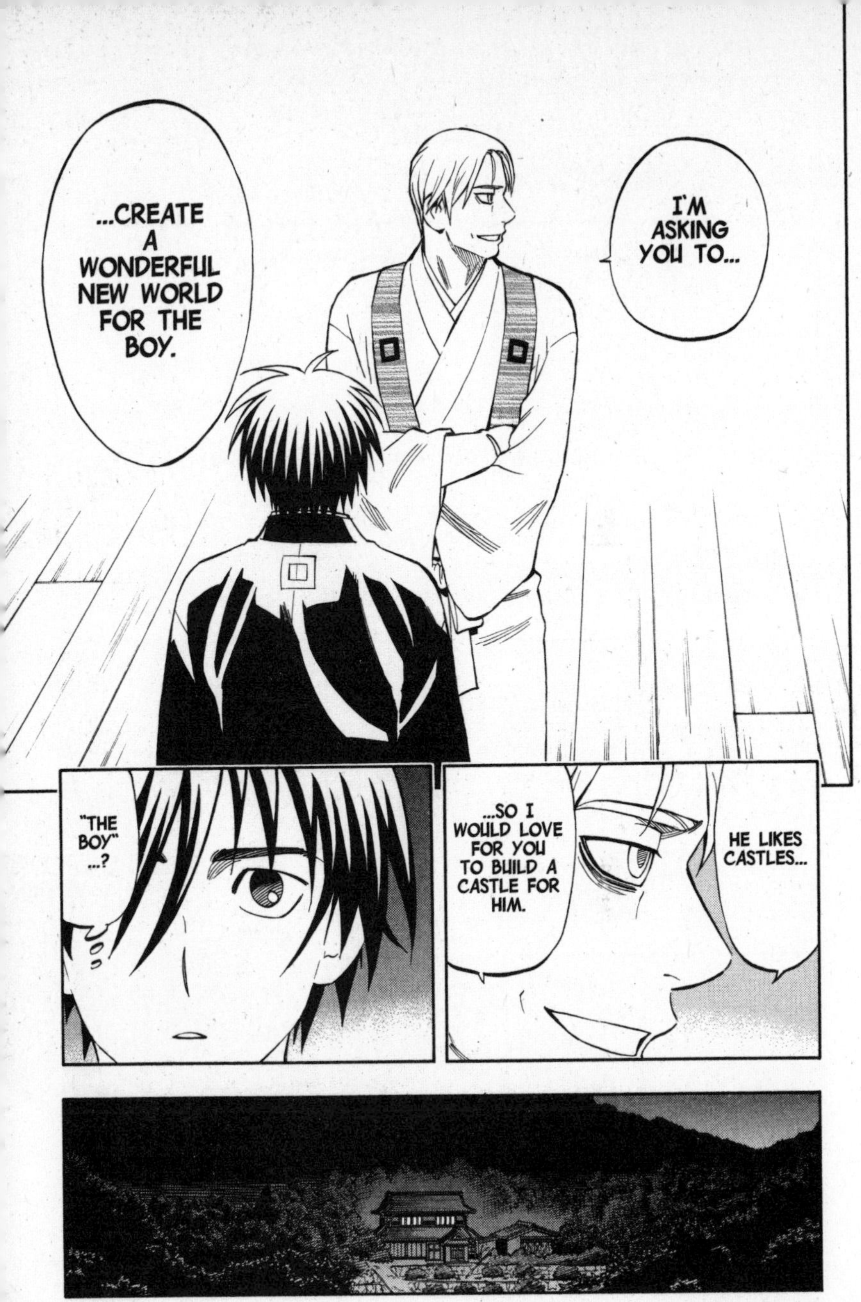
I'M ASKING YOU TO...
...CREATE A WONDERFUL NEW WORLD FOR THE BOY.
HE LIKES CASTLES...
...SO I WOULD LOVE FOR YOU TO BUILD A CASTLE FOR HIM.
"THE BOY" ...?

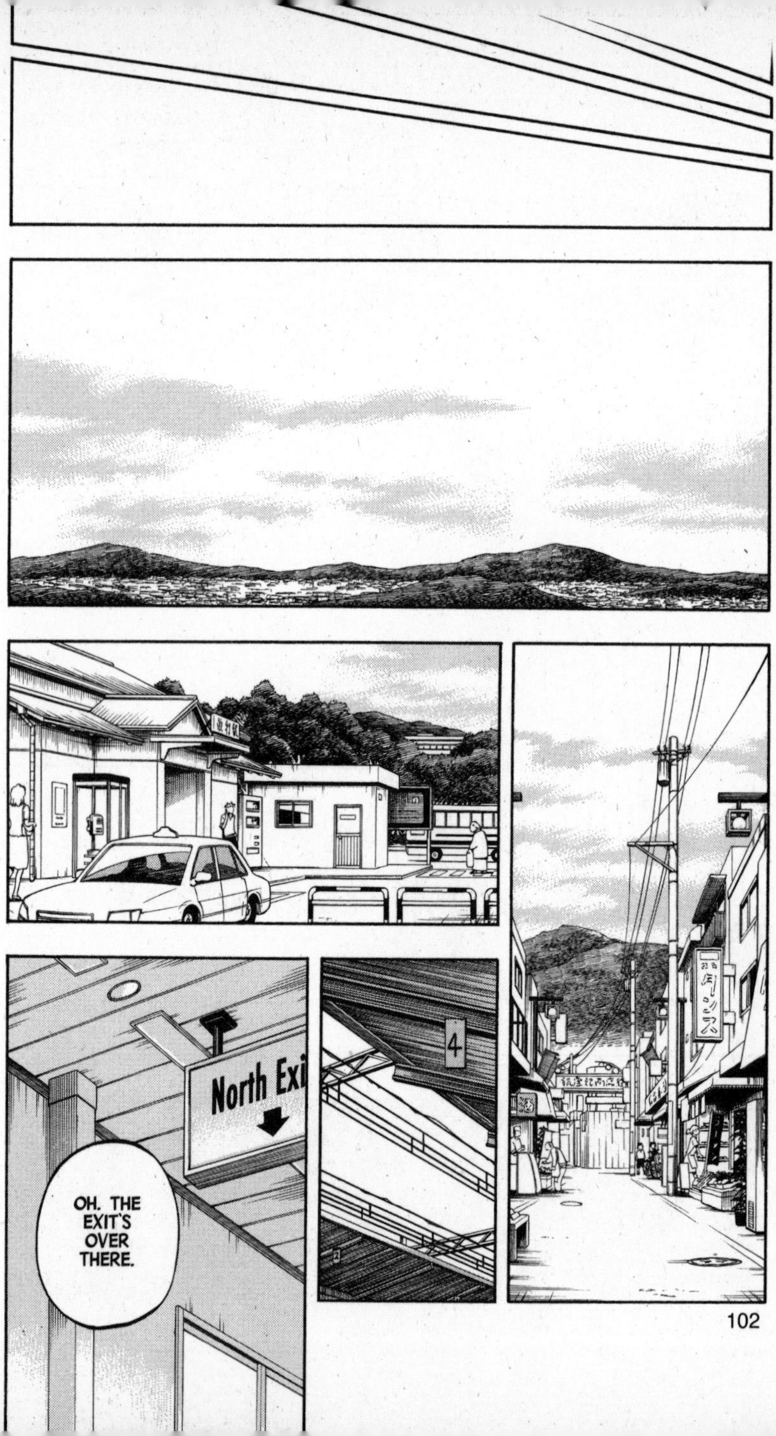
North Exi
4
OH. THE EXIT'S OVER THERE.

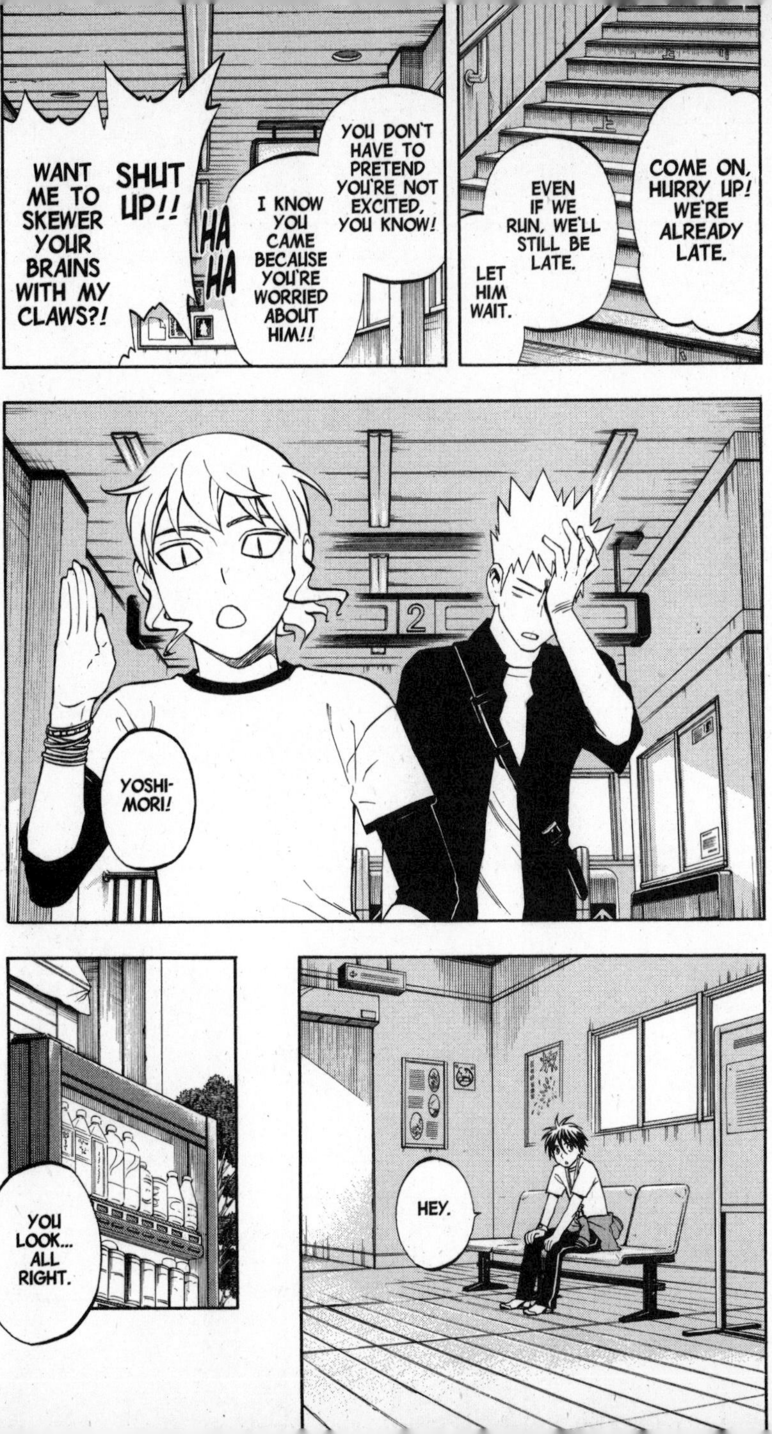
COME ON, HURRY UP! WE'RE ALREADY LATE.
EVEN IF WE RUN, WE'LL STILL BE LATE.
LET HIM WAIT.
YOU DON'T HAVE TO PRETEND YOU'RE NOT EXCITED, YOU KNOW!
I KNOW YOU CAME BECAUSE YOU'RE WORRIED ABOUT HIM!!
HA HA
SHUT UP!!
WANT ME TO SKEWER YOUR BRAINS WITH MY CLAWS?!
YOSHI-MORI!
HEY.
YOU LOOK... ALL RIGHT.

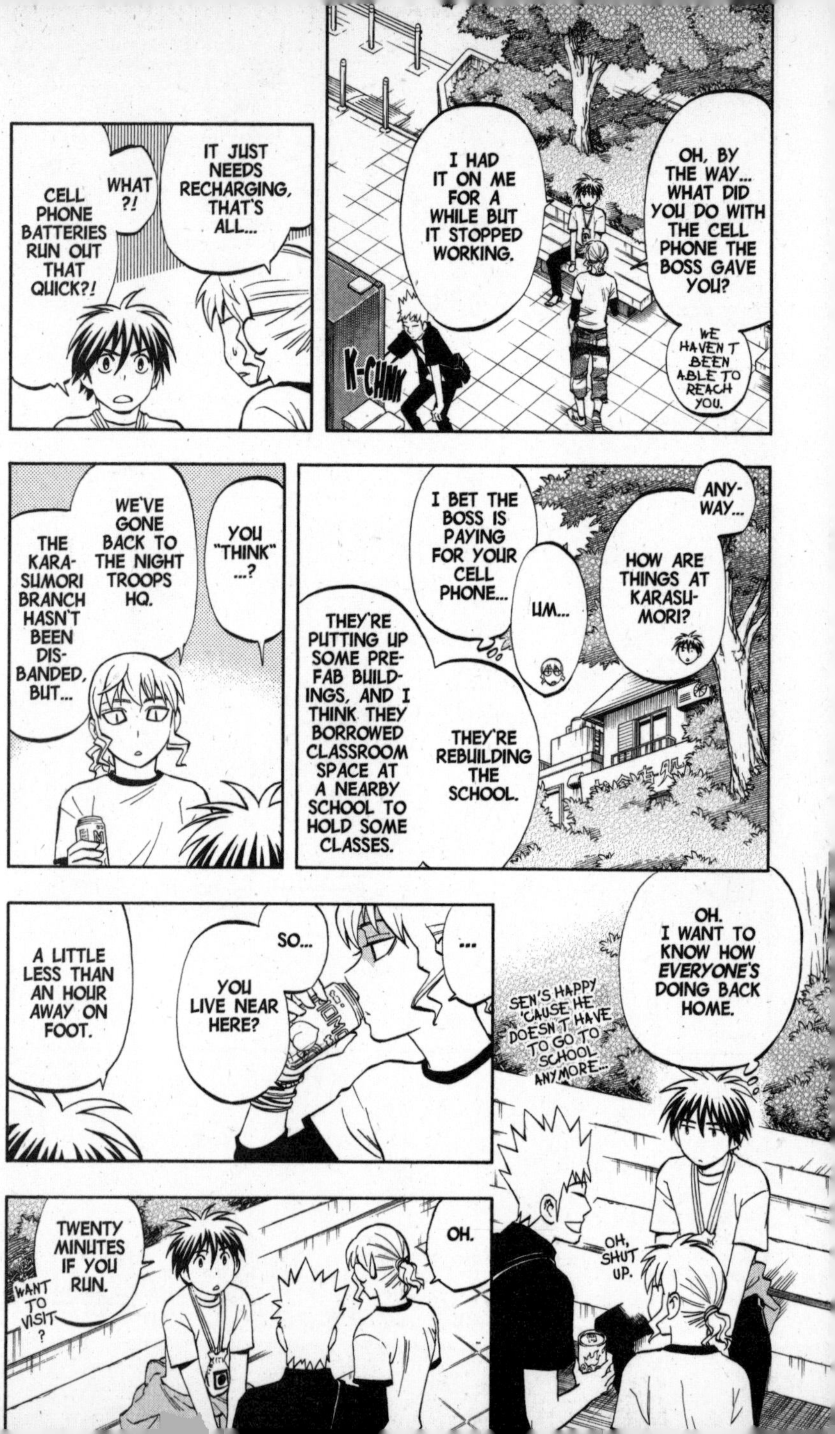
OH, BY THE WAY... WHAT DID YOU DO WITH THE CELL PHONE THE BOSS GAVE YOU?
WE HAVEN'T BEEN ABLE TO REACH YOU.
I HAD IT ON ME FOR A WHILE BUT IT STOPPED WORKING.
K-CHNK
IT JUST NEEDS RECHARGING, THAT'S ALL...
WHAT?!
CELL PHONE BATTERIES RUN OUT THAT QUICK?!
ANYWAY...
HOW ARE THINGS AT KARASUMORI?
I BET THE BOSS IS PAYING FOR YOUR CELL PHONE...
UM...
THEY'RE REBUILDING THE SCHOOL.
THEY'RE PUTTING UP SOME PREFAB BUILDINGS, AND I THINK THEY BORROWED CLASSROOM SPACE AT A NEARBY SCHOOL TO HOLD SOME CLASSES.
YOU "THINK" ...?
WE'VE GONE BACK TO THE NIGHT TROOPS HQ.
THE KARASUMORI BRANCH HASN'T BEEN DISBANDED, BUT...
OH. I WANT TO KNOW HOW EVERYONE'S DOING BACK HOME.
SEN'S HAPPY 'CAUSE HE DOESN'T HAVE TO GO TO SCHOOL ANYMORE...
OH, SHUT UP.
...
SO...
YOU LIVE NEAR HERE?
A LITTLE LESS THAN AN HOUR AWAY ON FOOT.
OH.
TWENTY MINUTES IF YOU RUN.
WANT TO VISIT?

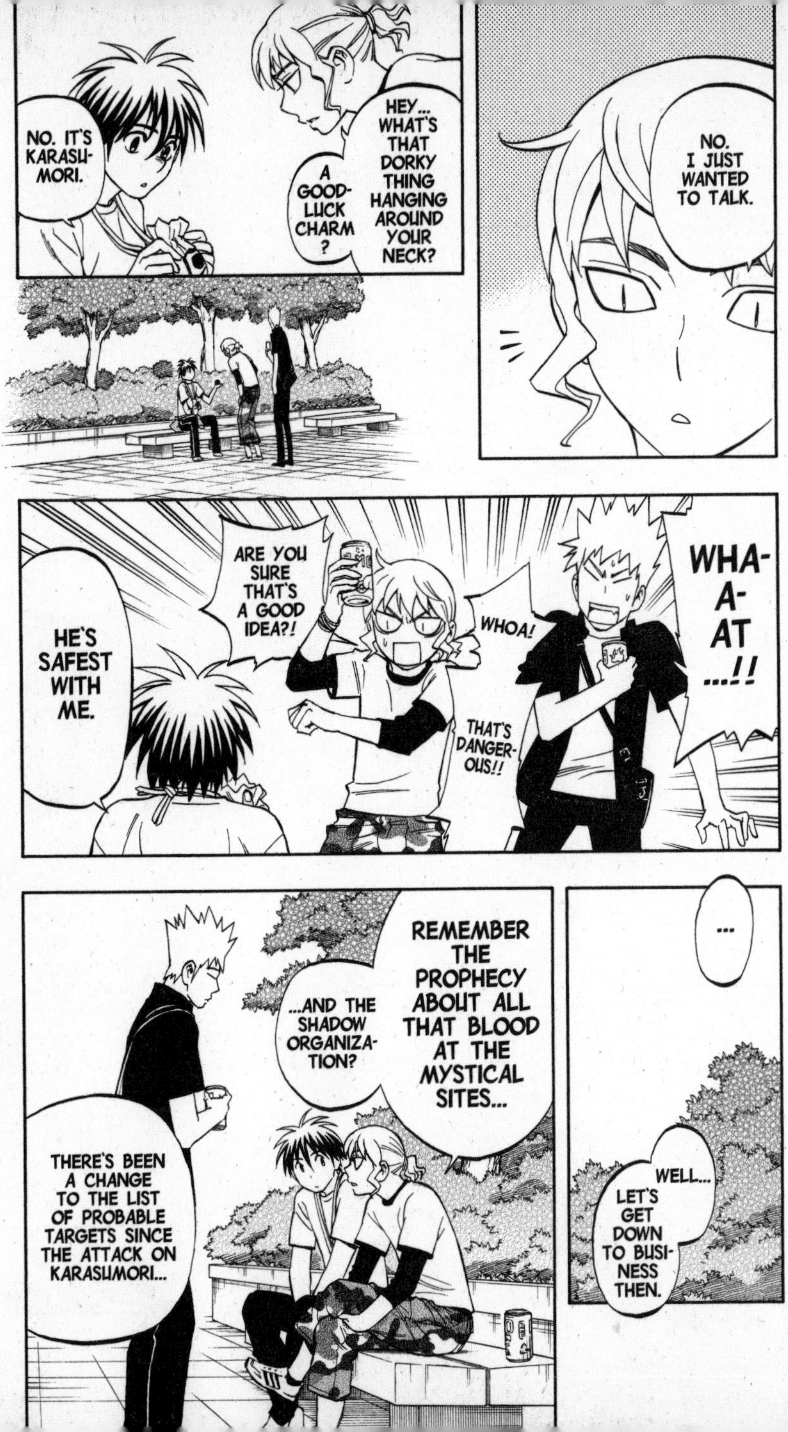
NO. I JUST WANTED TO TALK.
HEY... WHAT'S THAT DORKY THING HANGING AROUND YOUR NECK?
A GOOD-LUCK CHARM?
NO. IT'S KARASUMORI.
WHA-A-AT...!!
WHOA!
THAT'S DANGEROUS!!
ARE YOU SURE THAT'S A GOOD IDEA?!
HE'S SAFEST WITH ME.
...
WELL... LET'S GET DOWN TO BUSINESS THEN.
REMEMBER THE PROPHECY ABOUT ALL THAT BLOOD AT THE MYSTICAL SITES...
...AND THE SHADOW ORGANIZATION?
THERE'S BEEN A CHANGE TO THE LIST OF PROBABLE TARGETS SINCE THE ATTACK ON KARASUMORI...

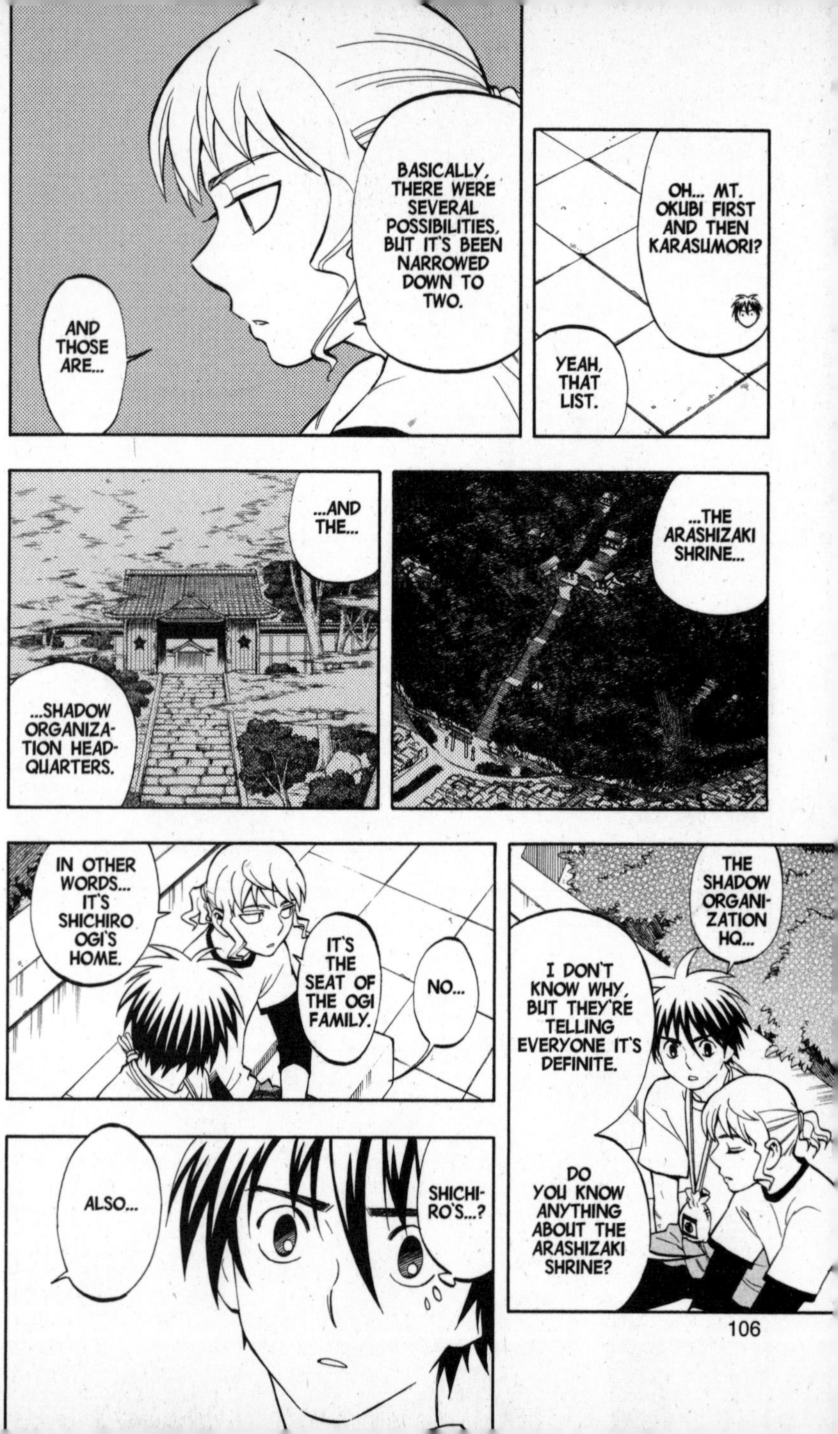
OH... MT. OKUBI FIRST AND THEN KARASUMORI?
YEAH, THAT LIST.
BASICALLY, THERE WERE SEVERAL POSSIBILITIES, BUT IT'S BEEN NARROWED DOWN TO TWO.
AND THOSE ARE...
...THE ARASHIZAKI SHRINE...
...AND THE...
...SHADOW ORGANIZATION HEADQUARTERS.
THE SHADOW ORGANIZATION HQ...
I DON'T KNOW WHY, BUT THEY'RE TELLING EVERYONE IT'S DEFINITE.
DO YOU KNOW ANYTHING ABOUT THE ARASHIZAKI SHRINE?
NO...
IT'S THE SEAT OF THE OGI FAMILY.
IN OTHER WORDS... IT'S SHICHIRO OGI'S HOME.
SHICHIRO'S...?
ALSO...

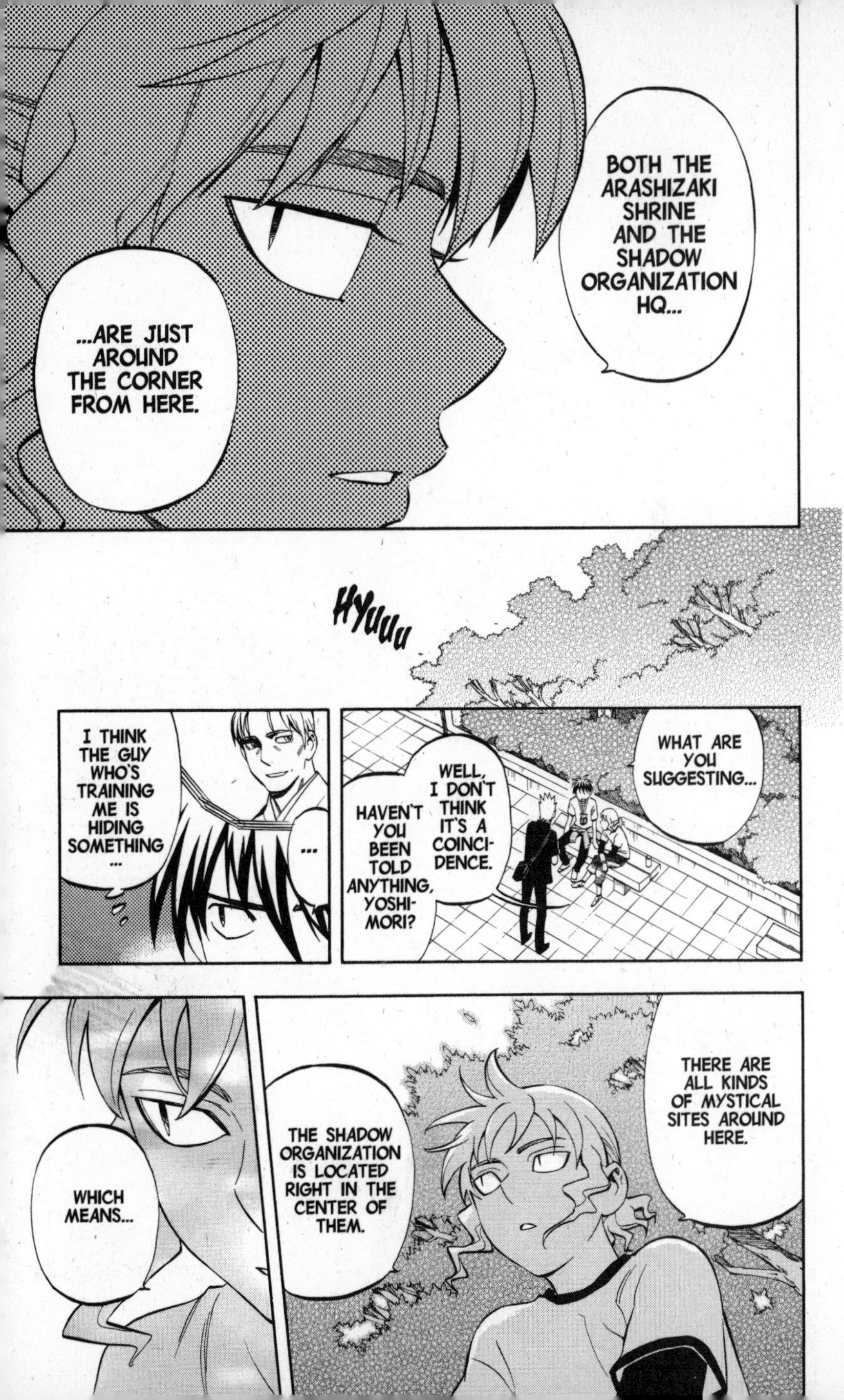
BOTH THE ARASHIZAKI SHRINE AND THE SHADOW ORGANIZATION HQ...
...ARE JUST AROUND THE CORNER FROM HERE.
HYUUU
WHAT ARE YOU SUGGESTING...
WELL, I DON'T THINK IT'S A COINCI-DENCE.
HAVEN'T YOU BEEN TOLD ANYTHING, YOSHI-MORI?
...
I THINK THE GUY WHO'S TRAINING ME IS HIDING SOMETHING...
THERE ARE ALL KINDS OF MYSTICAL SITES AROUND HERE.
THE SHADOW ORGANIZATION IS LOCATED RIGHT IN THE CENTER OF THEM.
WHICH MEANS...

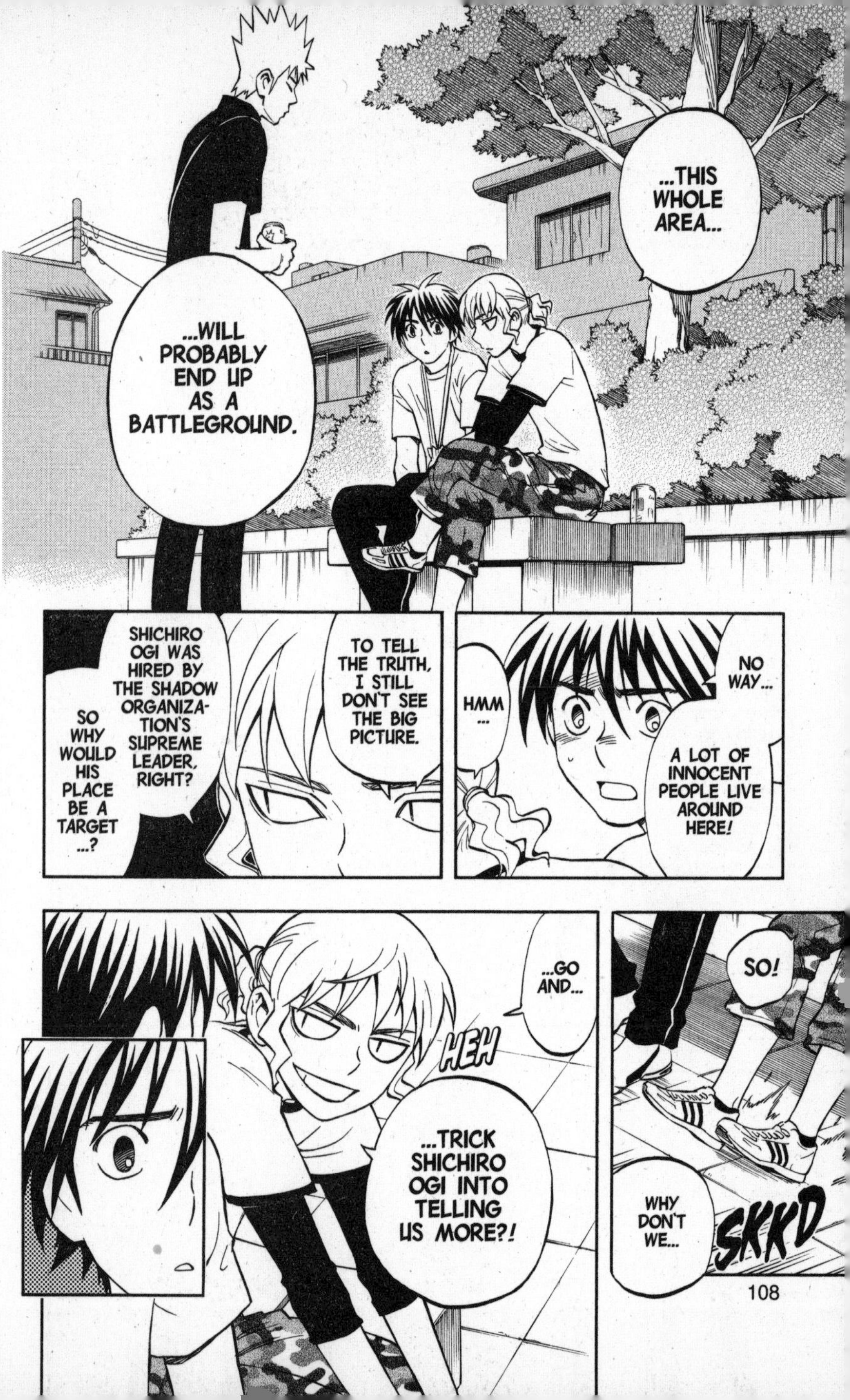
...THIS WHOLE AREA...
...WILL PROBABLY END UP AS A BATTLEGROUND.
NO WAY...
A LOT OF INNOCENT PEOPLE LIVE AROUND HERE!
HMM...
TO TELL THE TRUTH, I STILL DON'T SEE THE BIG PICTURE.
SHICHIRO OGI WAS HIRED BY THE SHADOW ORGANIZATION'S SUPREME LEADER, RIGHT?
SO WHY WOULD HIS PLACE BE A TARGET...?
SO!
SKKD
WHY DON'T WE...
HEH
...GO AND...
...TRICK SHICHIRO OGI INTO TELLING US MORE?!

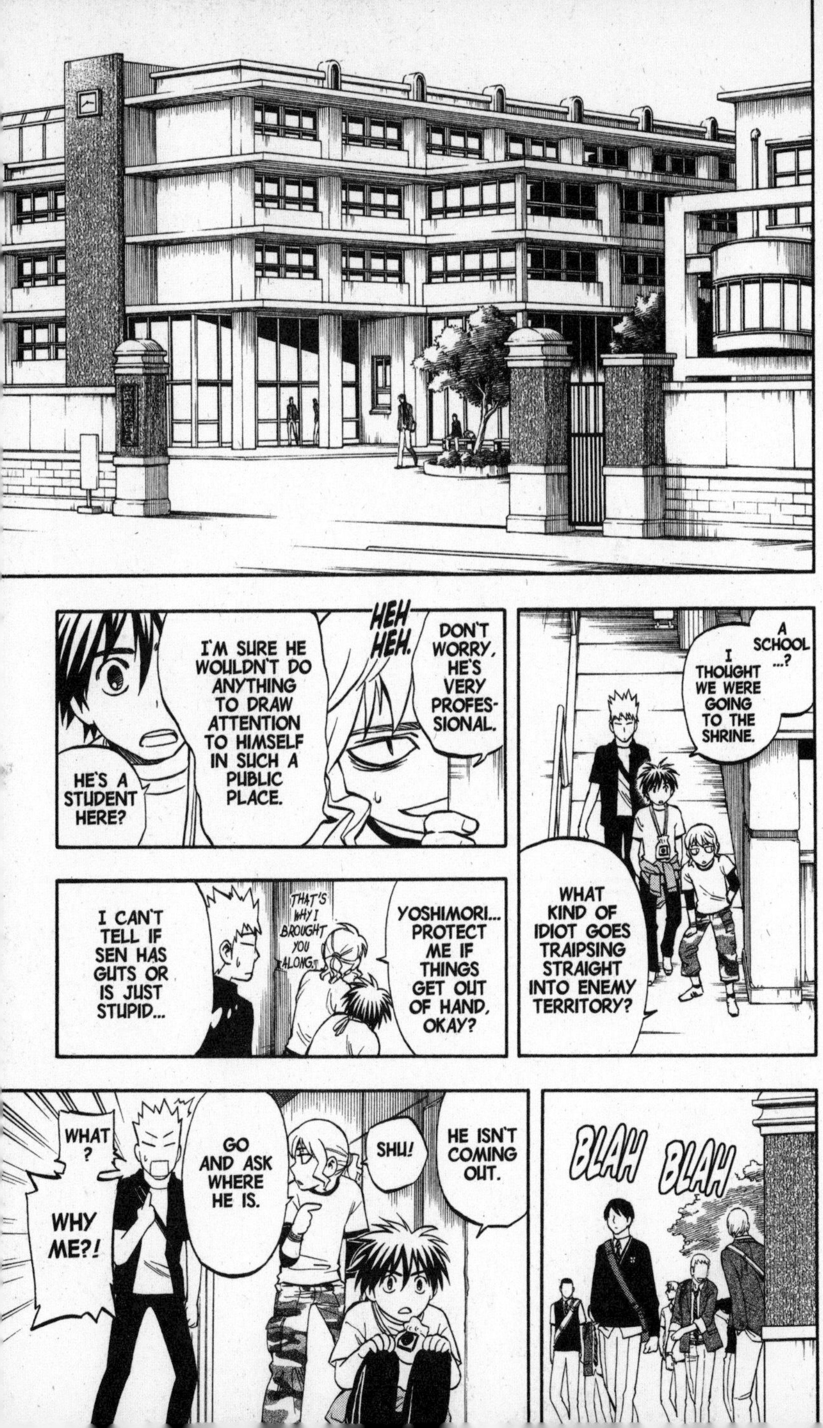
A SCHOOL ...?
I THOUGHT WE WERE GOING TO THE SHRINE.
WHAT KIND OF IDIOT GOES TRAIPSING STRAIGHT INTO ENEMY TERRITORY?
HEH HEH.
DON'T WORRY, HE'S VERY PROFES-SIONAL.
I'M SURE HE WOULDN'T DO ANYTHING TO DRAW ATTENTION TO HIMSELF IN SUCH A PUBLIC PLACE.
HE'S A STUDENT HERE?
YOSHIMORI... PROTECT ME IF THINGS GET OUT OF HAND, OKAY?
THAT'S WHY I BROUGHT YOU ALONG.
I CAN'T TELL IF SEN HAS GUTS OR IS JUST STUPID...
BLAH BLAH
HE ISN'T COMING OUT.
SHU!
GO AND ASK WHERE HE IS.
WHAT?
WHY ME?!

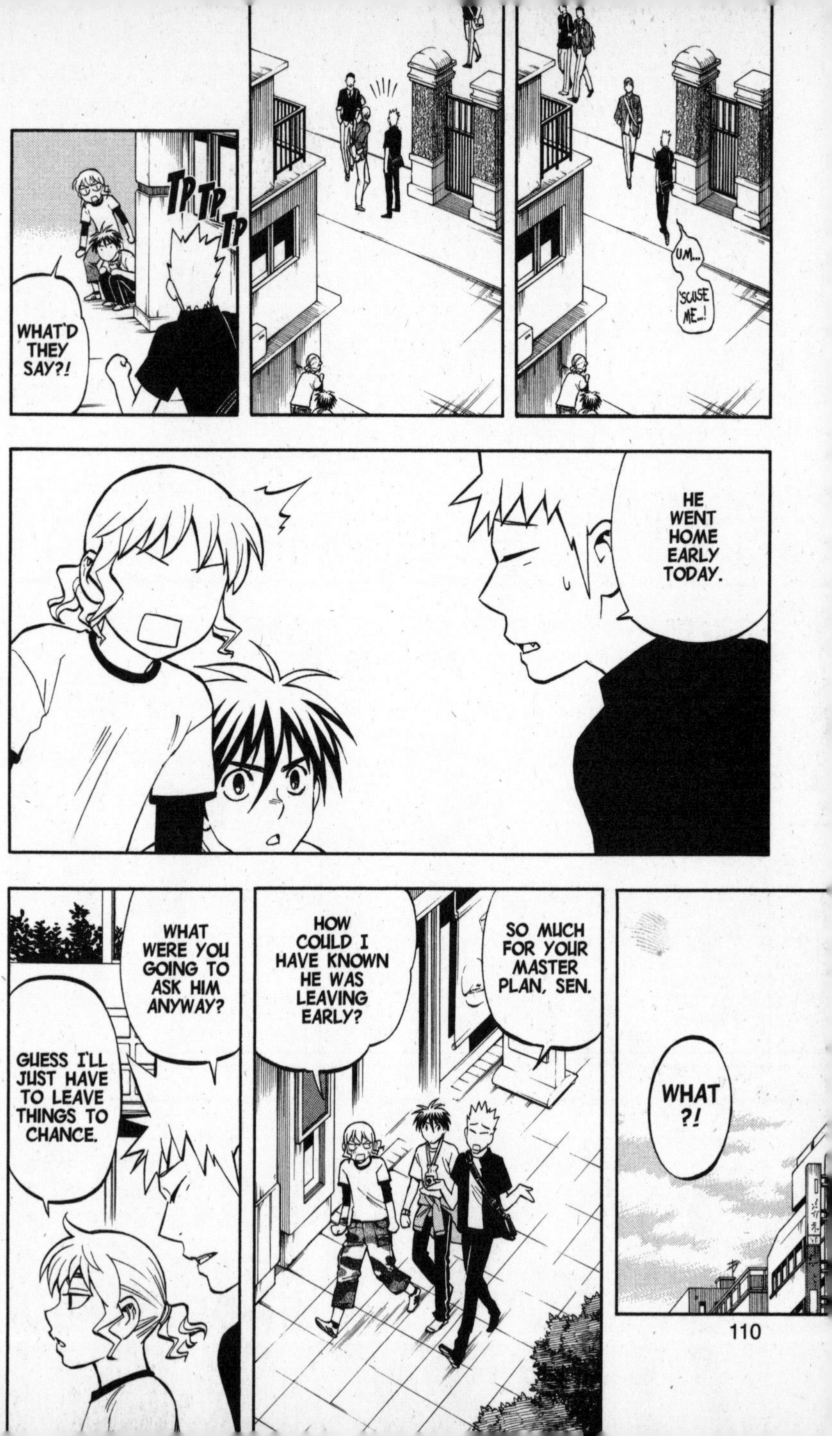
UM... 'SCUSE ME...!
TP TP TP
WHAT'D THEY SAY?!
HE WENT HOME EARLY TODAY.
WHAT?!
SO MUCH FOR YOUR MASTER PLAN, SEN.
HOW COULD I HAVE KNOWN HE WAS LEAVING EARLY?
WHAT WERE YOU GOING TO ASK HIM ANYWAY?
GUESS I'LL JUST HAVE TO LEAVE THINGS TO CHANCE.

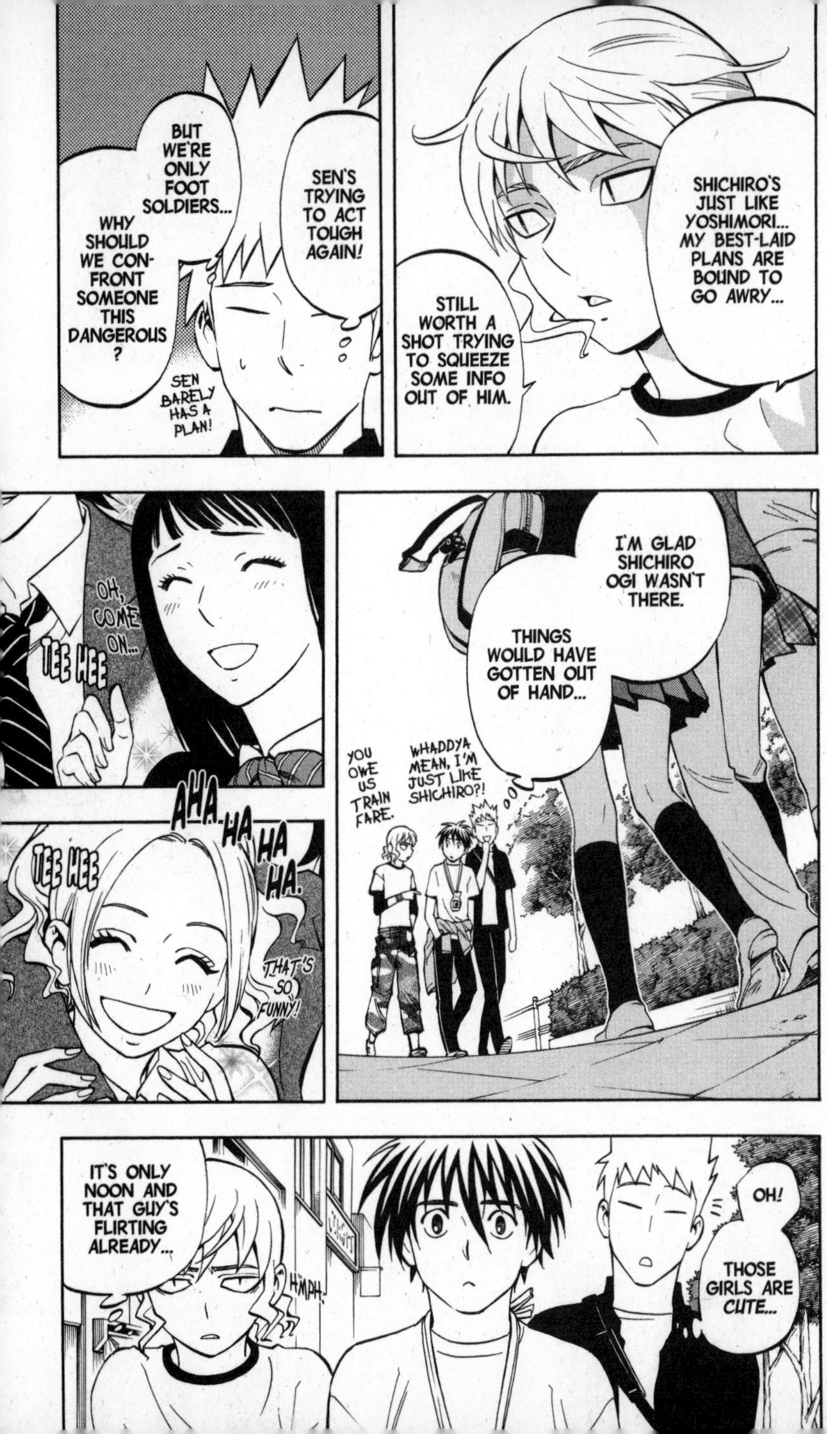
SHICHIRO'S JUST LIKE YOSHIMORI... MY BEST-LAID PLANS ARE BOUND TO GO AWRY...
STILL WORTH A SHOT TRYING TO SQUEEZE SOME INFO OUT OF HIM.
SEN'S TRYING TO ACT TOUGH AGAIN!
BUT WE'RE ONLY FOOT SOLDIERS...
WHY SHOULD WE CON-FRONT SOMEONE THIS DANGEROUS?
SEN BARELY HAS A PLAN!
I'M GLAD SHICHIRO OGI WASN'T THERE.
THINGS WOULD HAVE GOTTEN OUT OF HAND...
WHADDYA MEAN, I'M JUST LIKE SHICHIRO?!
YOU OWE US TRAIN FARE.
OH, COME ON...
TEE HEE
AHAHAHA.
TEE HEE
THAT'S SO FUNNY!
OH!
THOSE GIRLS ARE CUTE...
IT'S ONLY NOON AND THAT GUY'S FLIRTING ALREADY...
HMPH!

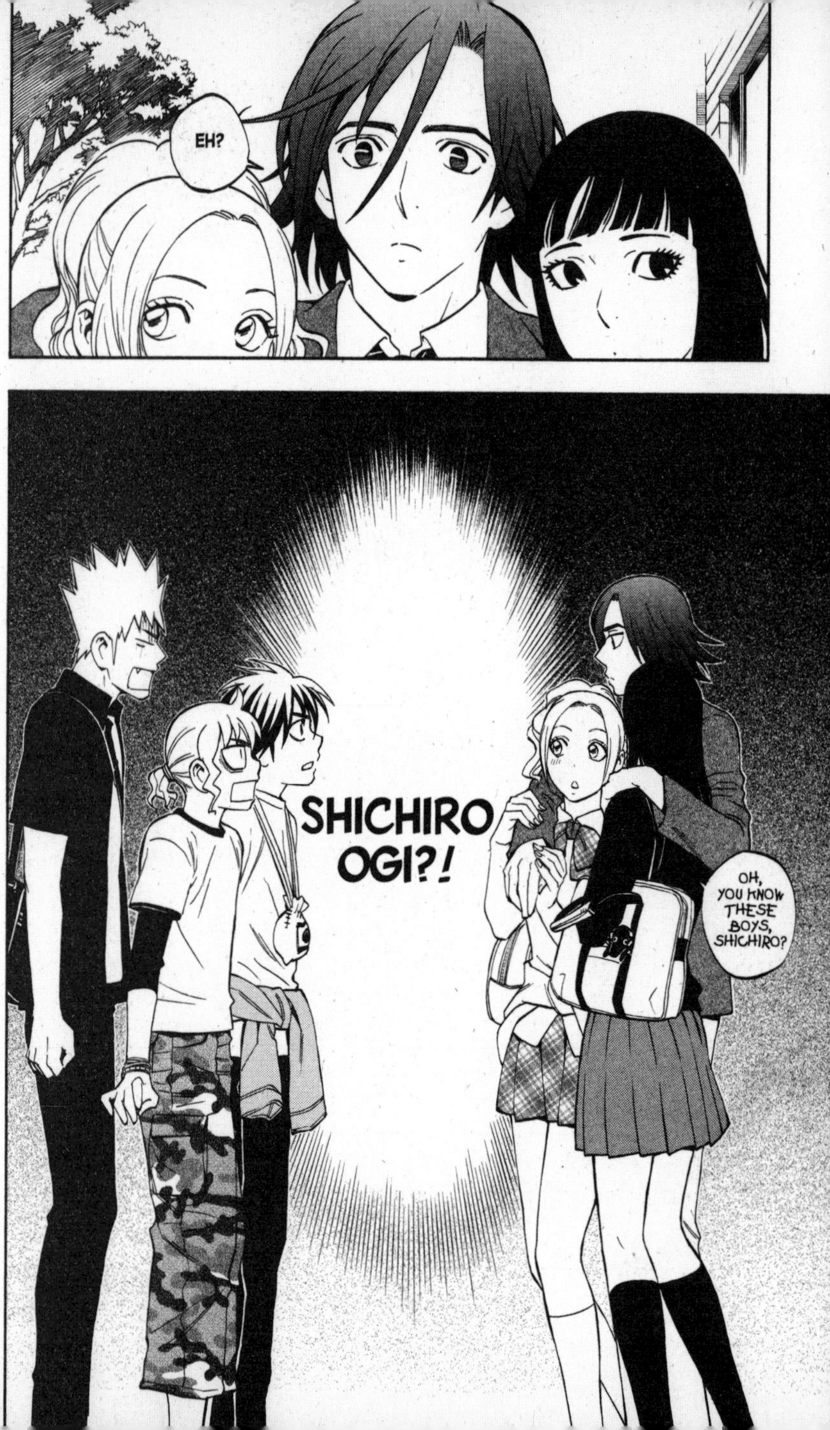
EH?
OH, YOU KNOW THESE BOYS, SHICHIRO?
SHICHIRO OGI?!

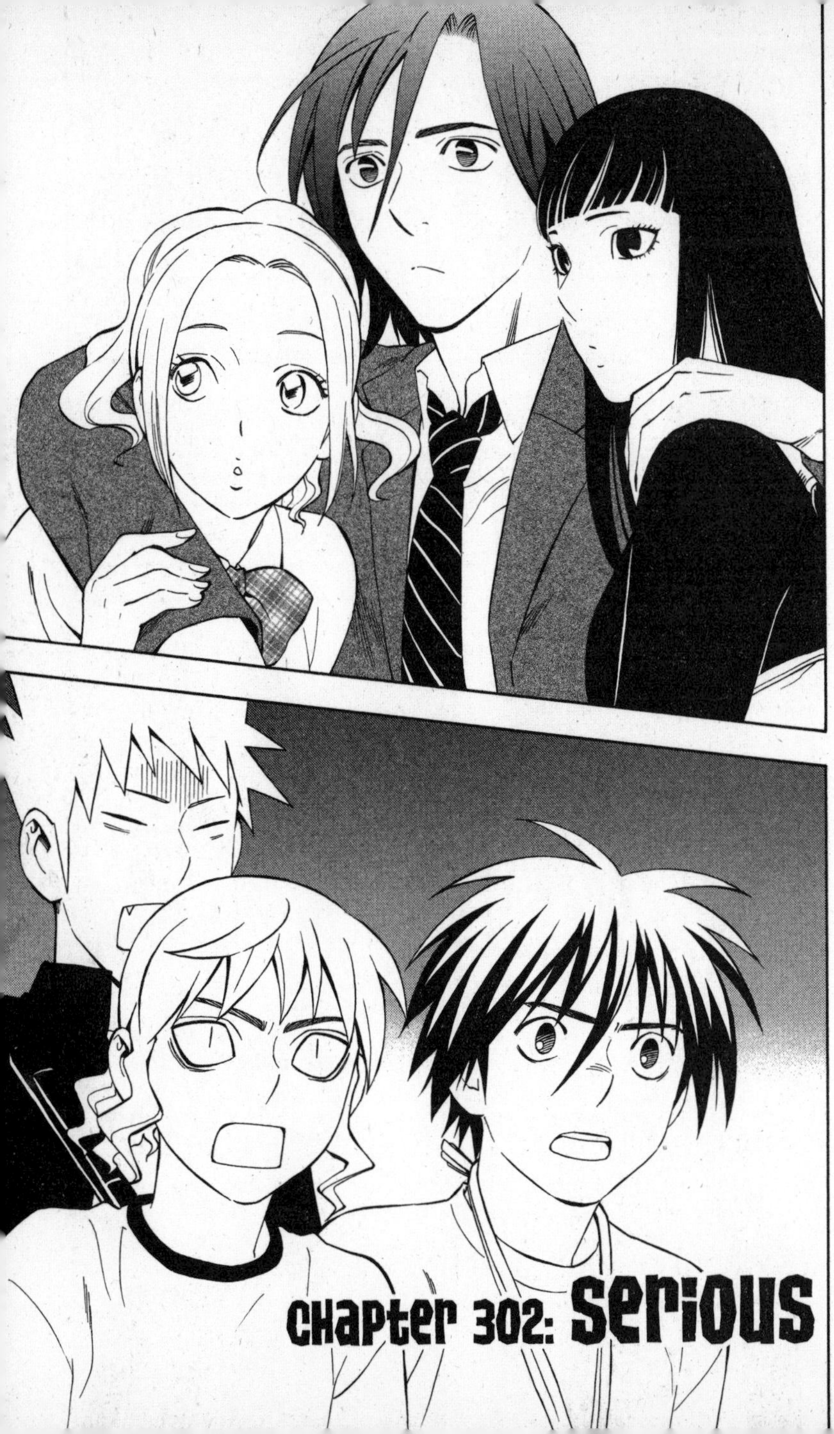
Chapter 302: Serious

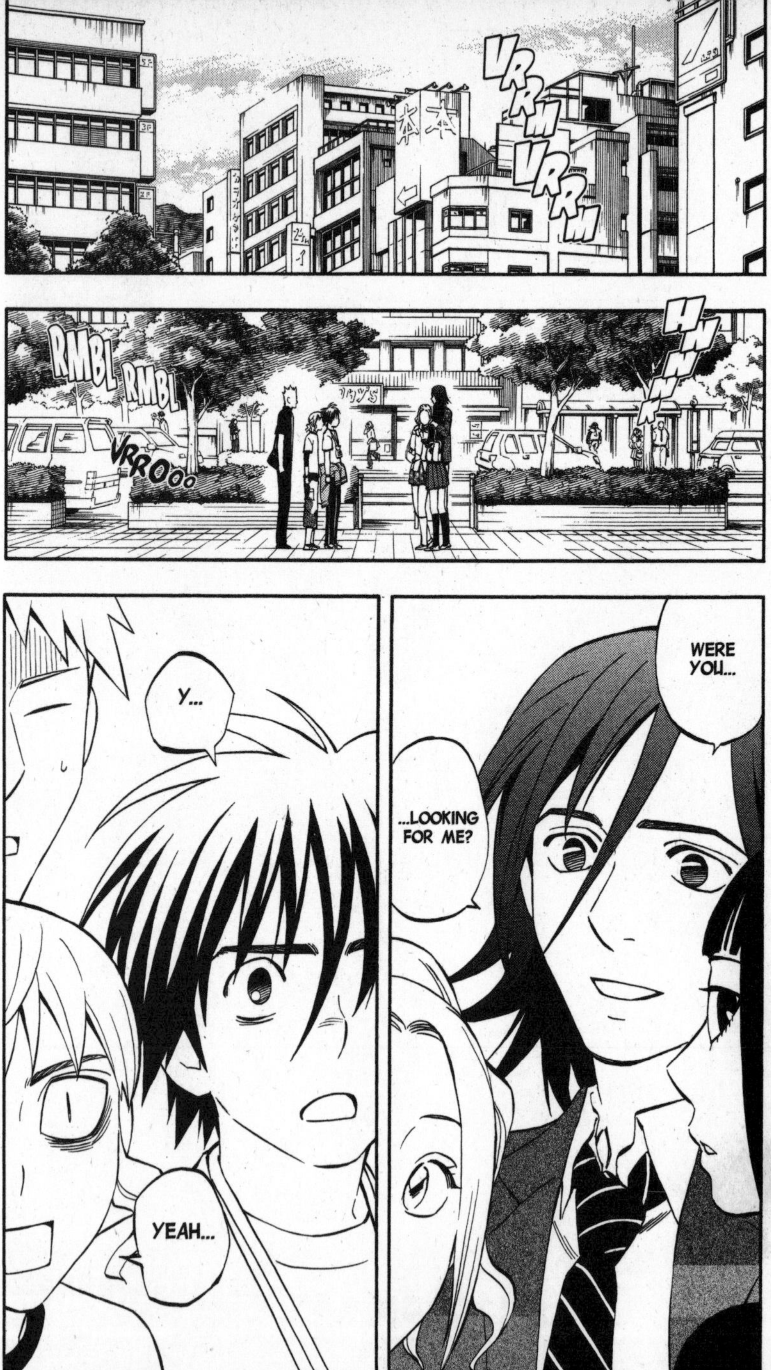
VRRM
VRRRM
HNNNK
RMBL RMBL
VRROooo
WERE YOU...
...LOOKING FOR ME?
Y...
YEAH...

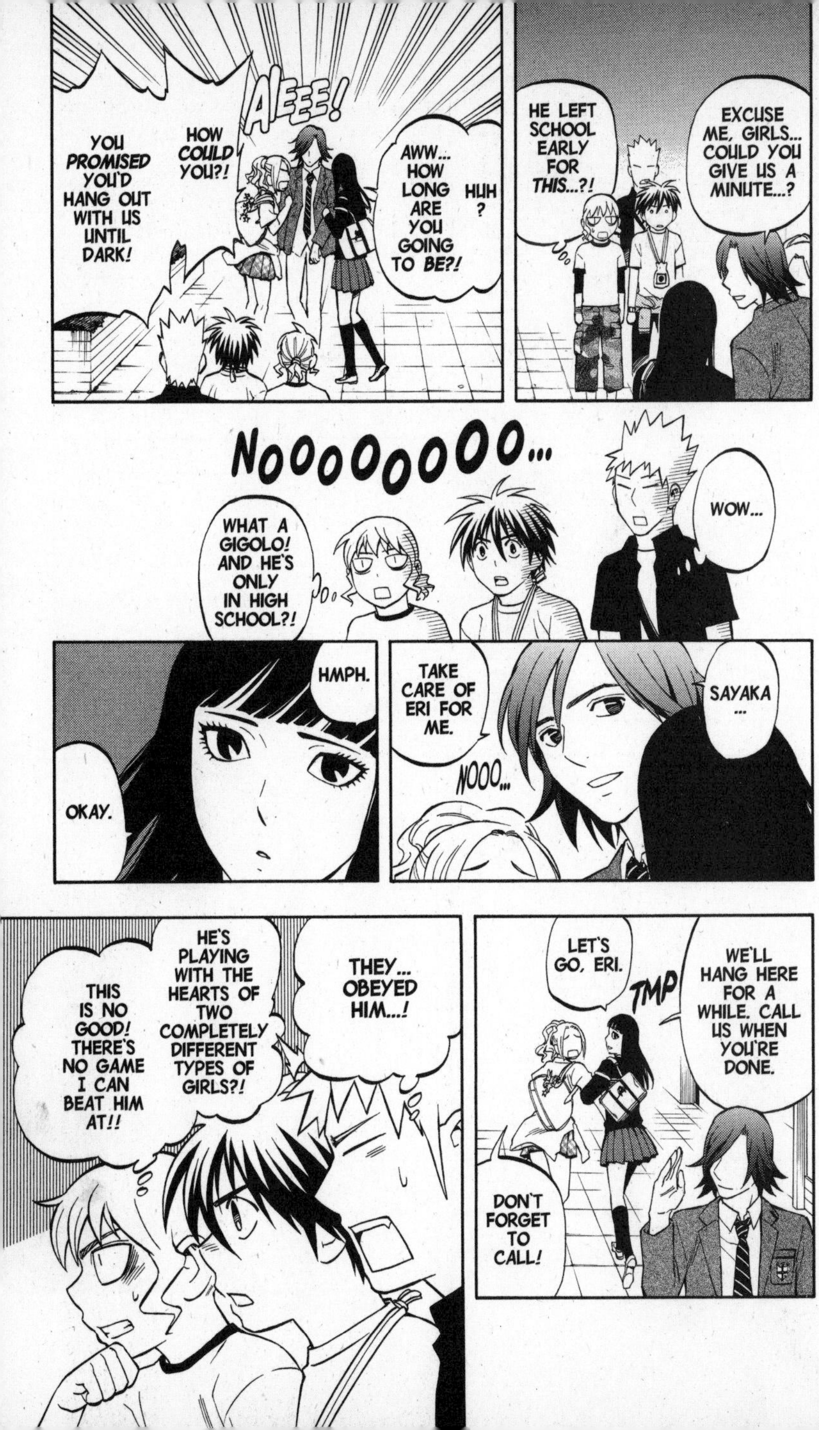
EXCUSE ME, GIRLS... COULD YOU GIVE US A MINUTE...?
HE LEFT SCHOOL EARLY FOR THIS...?!
HUH?
AWW... HOW LONG ARE YOU GOING TO BE?!
AIEEE!
HOW COULD YOU?!
YOU PROMISED YOU'D HANG OUT WITH US UNTIL DARK!
NOOOOOOOOO...
WOW...
WHAT A GIGOLO! AND HE'S ONLY IN HIGH SCHOOL?!
SAYAKA...
TAKE CARE OF ERI FOR ME.
NOOO...
HMPH.
OKAY.
WE'LL HANG HERE FOR A WHILE. CALL US WHEN YOU'RE DONE.
LET'S GO, ERI.
TMP
DON'T FORGET TO CALL!
THEY... OBEYED HIM...!
HE'S PLAYING WITH THE HEARTS OF TWO COMPLETELY DIFFERENT TYPES OF GIRLS?!
THIS IS NO GOOD! THERE'S NO GAME I CAN BEAT HIM AT!!

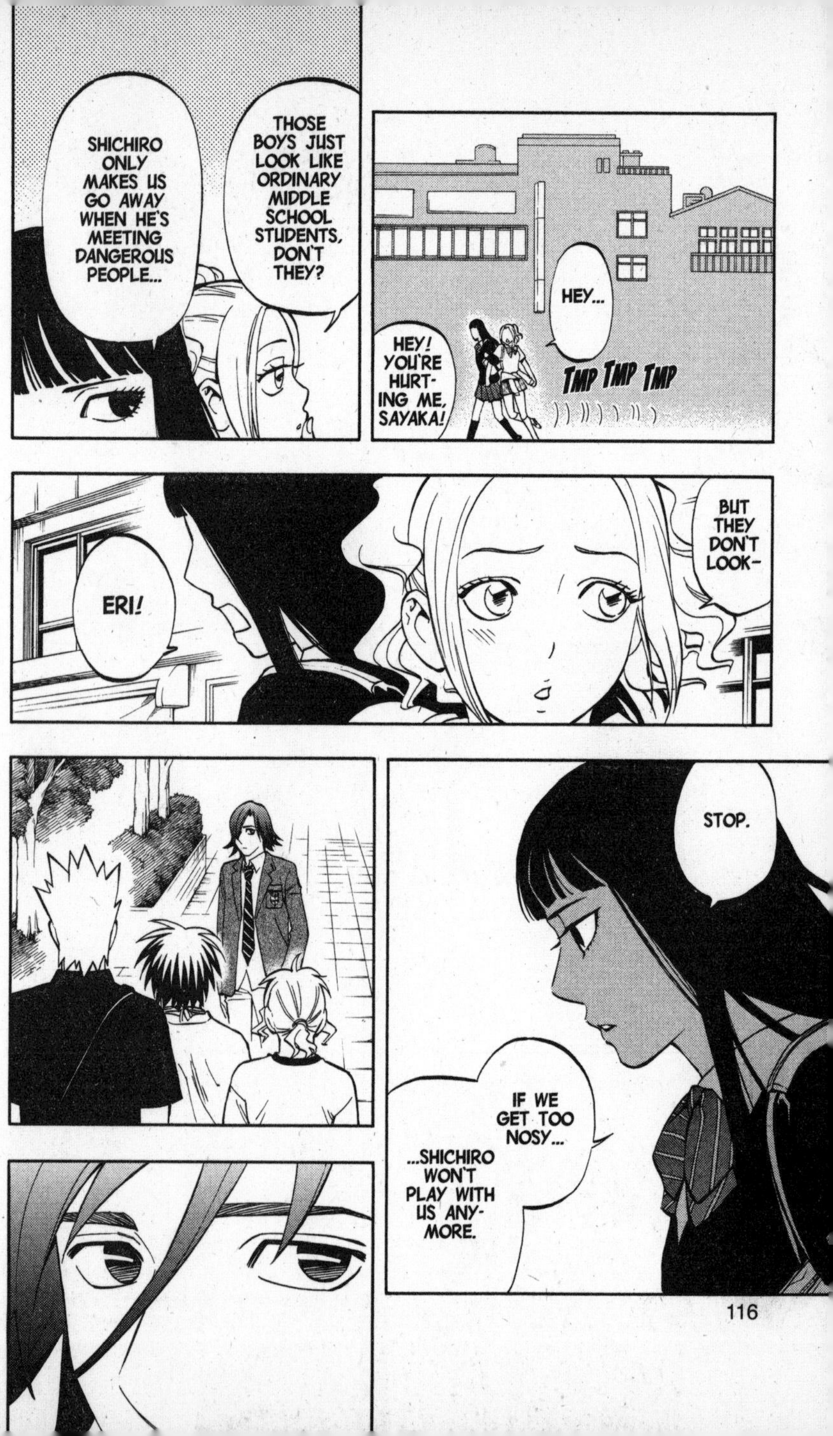
HEY...
HEY! YOU'RE HURT-ING ME, SAYAKA!
TMP TMP TMP
THOSE BOYS JUST LOOK LIKE ORDINARY MIDDLE SCHOOL STUDENTS, DON'T THEY?
SHICHIRO ONLY MAKES US GO AWAY WHEN HE'S MEETING DANGEROUS PEOPLE...
BUT THEY DON'T LOOK-
ERI!
STOP.
IF WE GET TOO NOSY...
...SHICHIRO WON'T PLAY WITH US ANY-MORE.

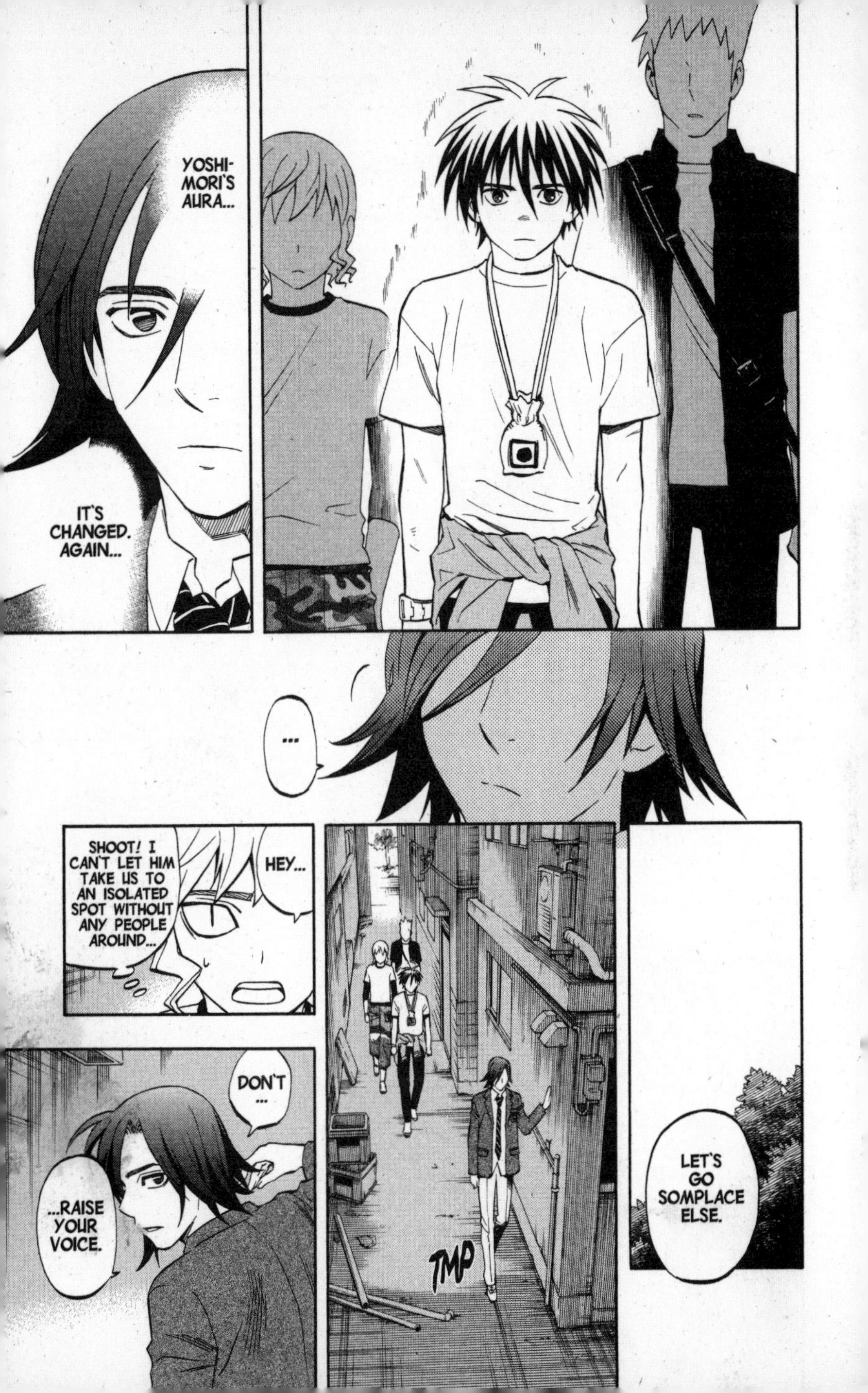
YOSHI-MORI'S AURA...
IT'S CHANGED. AGAIN...
...
LET'S GO SOMPLACE ELSE.
TMP
HEY...
SHOOT! I CAN'T LET HIM TAKE US TO AN ISOLATED SPOT WITHOUT ANY PEOPLE AROUND...
DON'T ...
...RAISE YOUR VOICE.

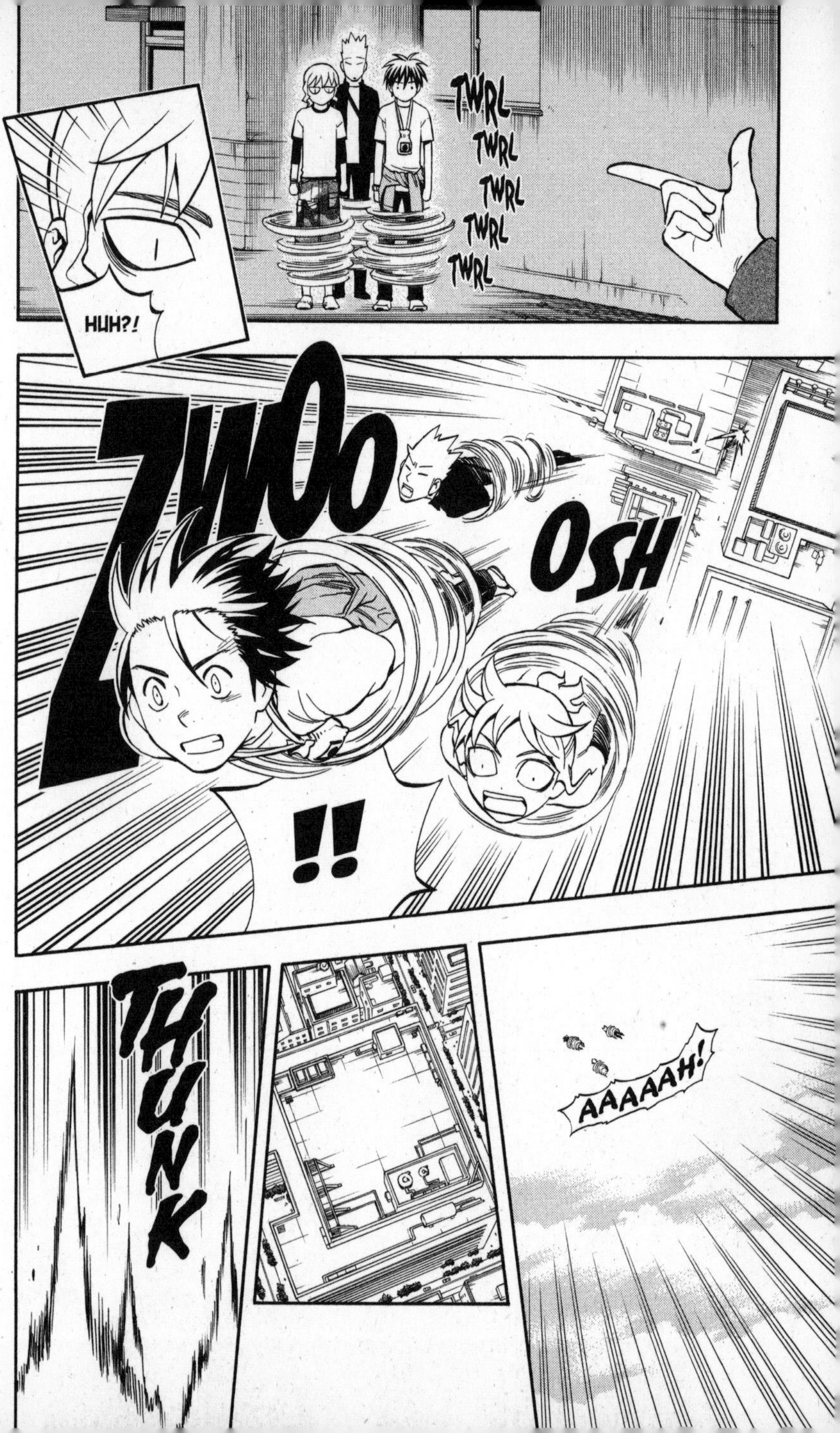
TWRL
TWRL
TWRL
TWRL
TWRL
HUH?!
ZWOOOSH
!!
AAAAAH!
THUNK

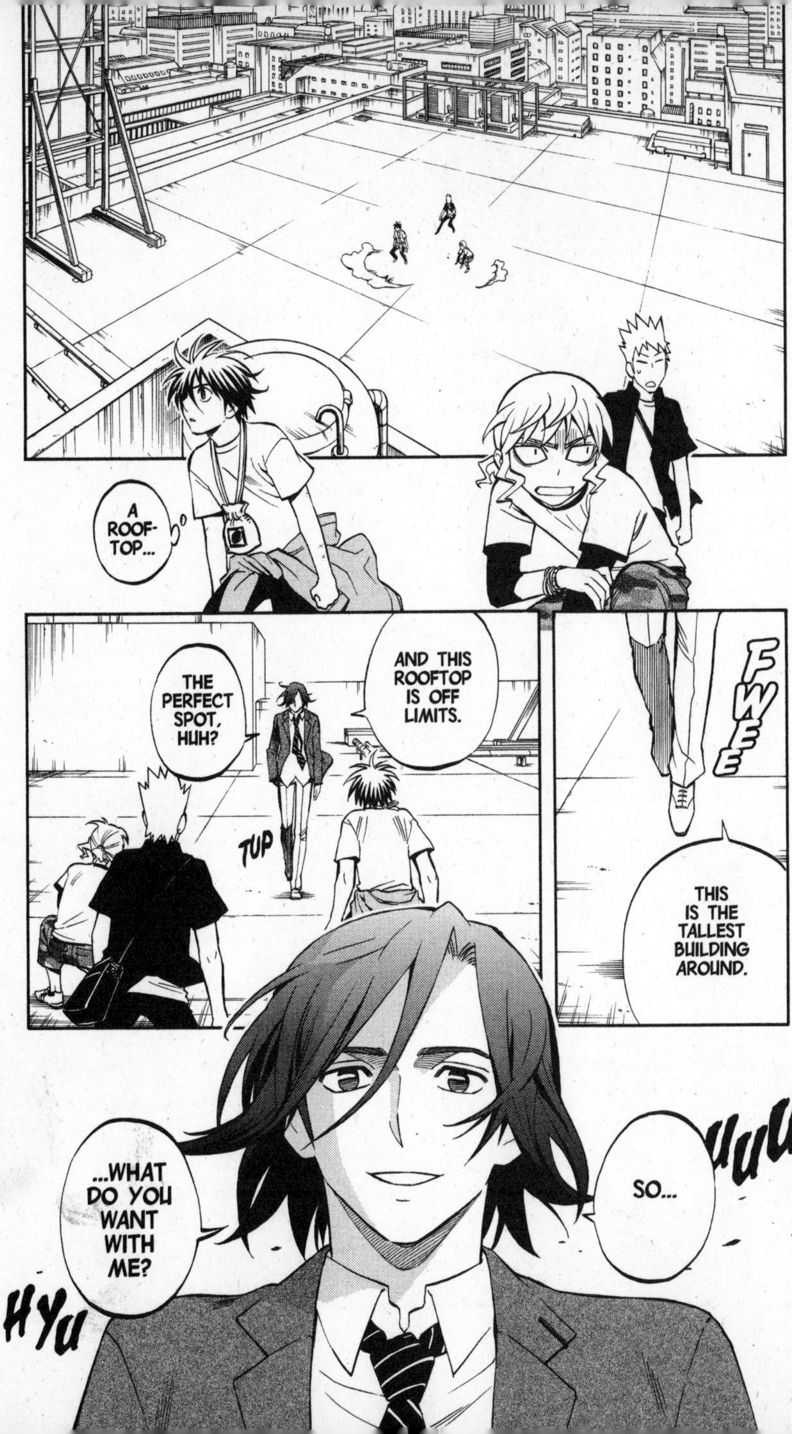
A ROOFTOP...
FWEE
THIS IS THE TALLEST BUILDING AROUND.
AND THIS ROOFTOP IS OFF LIMITS.
THE PERFECT SPOT, HUH?
TUP
UUUU
SO...
...WHAT DO YOU WANT WITH ME?
HYU

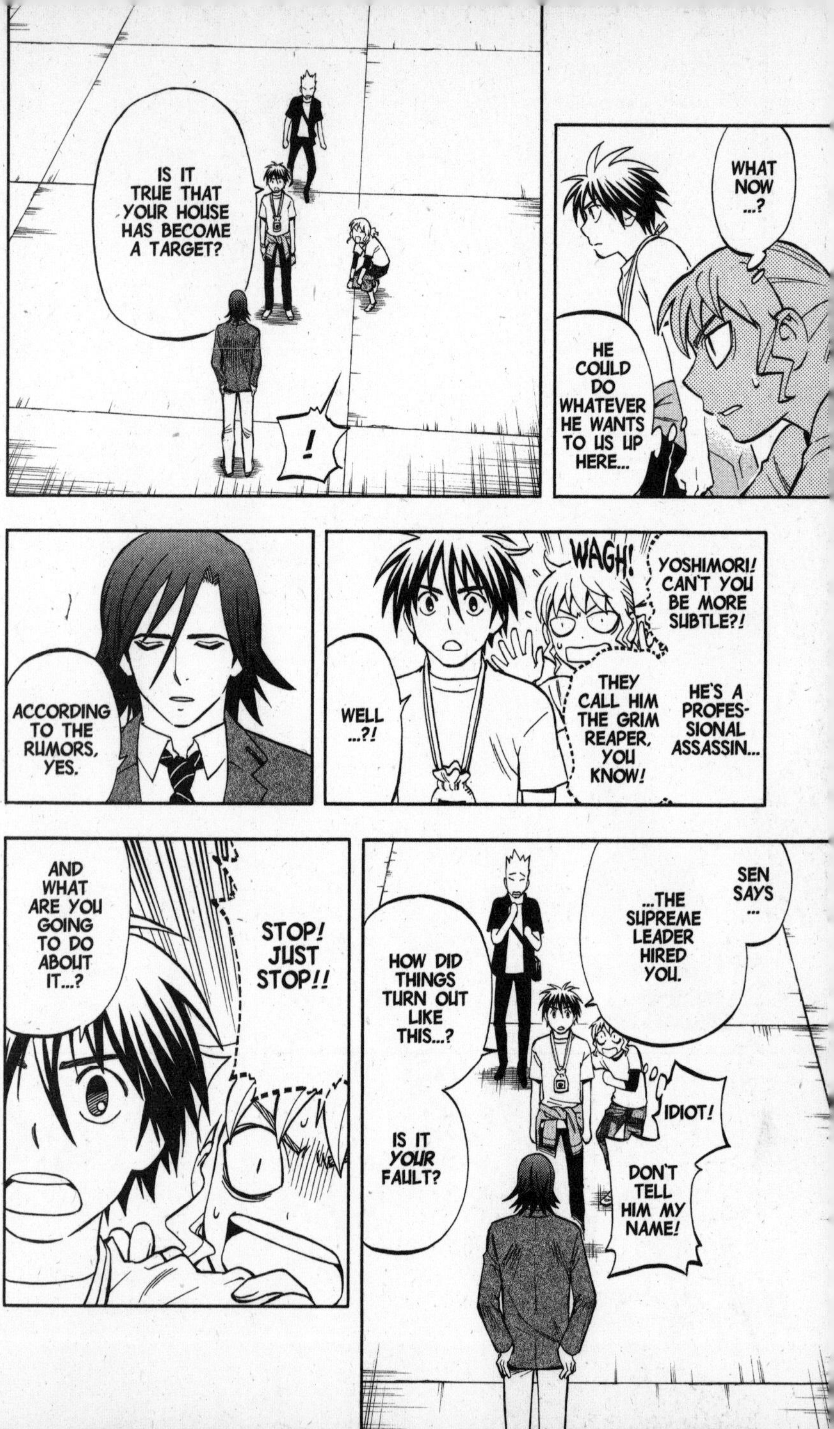
WHAT NOW ...?
HE COULD DO WHATEVER HE WANTS TO US UP HERE...
IS IT TRUE THAT YOUR HOUSE HAS BECOME A TARGET?
!
WAGH!
YOSHIMORI! CAN'T YOU BE MORE SUBTLE?!
HE'S A PROFESSIONAL ASSASSIN...
THEY CALL HIM THE GRIM REAPER, YOU KNOW!
WELL ...?!
ACCORDING TO THE RUMORS, YES.
SEN SAYS ...
...THE SUPREME LEADER HIRED YOU.
IDIOT!
DON'T TELL HIM MY NAME!
HOW DID THINGS TURN OUT LIKE THIS...?
IS IT *YOUR* FAULT?
STOP! JUST STOP!!
AND WHAT ARE YOU GOING TO DO ABOUT IT...?

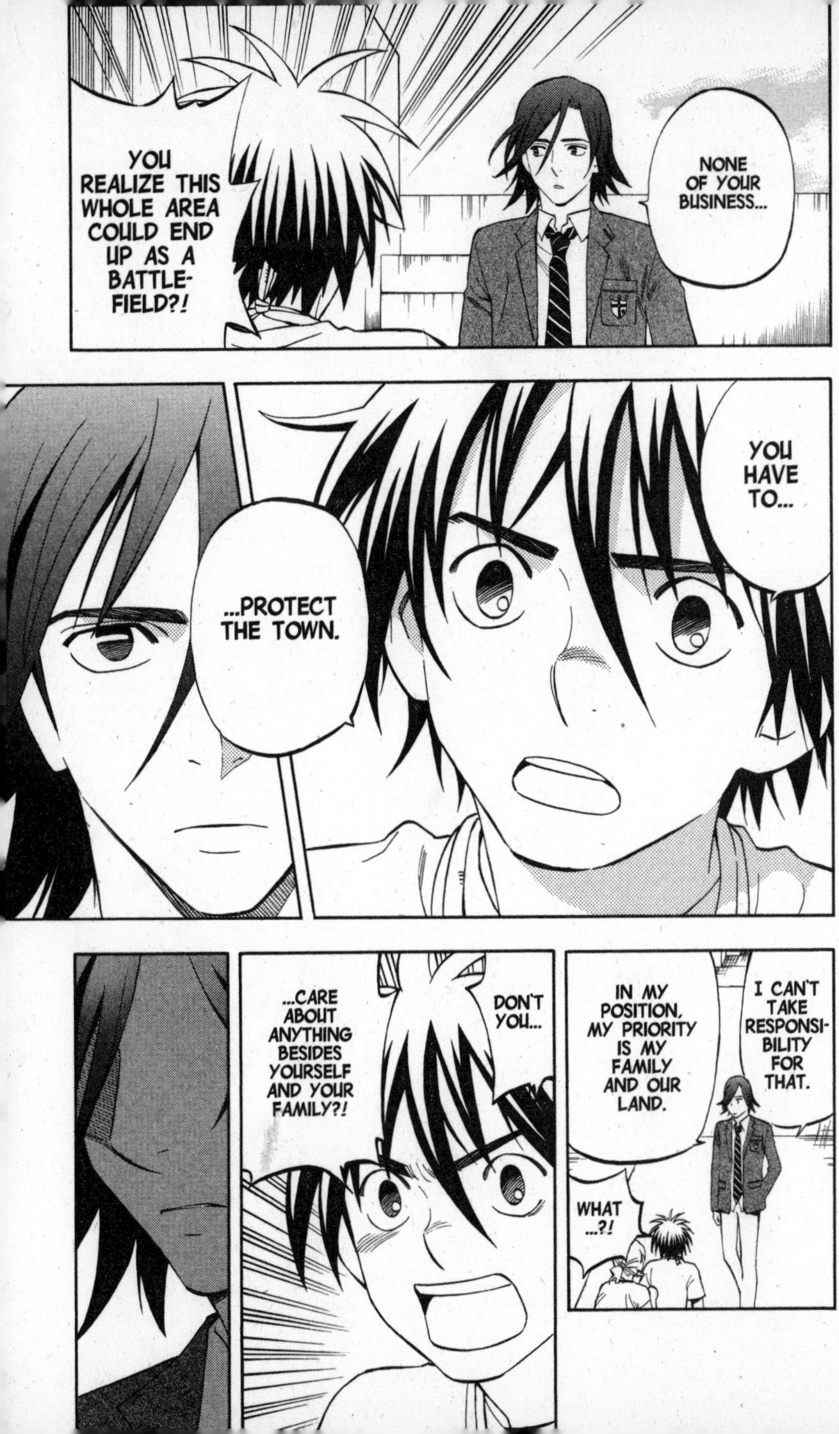
NONE OF YOUR BUSINESS...
YOU REALIZE THIS WHOLE AREA COULD END UP AS A BATTLE-FIELD?!
YOU HAVE TO...
...PROTECT THE TOWN.
I CAN'T TAKE RESPONSI-BILITY FOR THAT.
IN MY POSITION, MY PRIORITY IS MY FAMILY AND OUR LAND.
WHAT ...?!
DON'T YOU...
...CARE ABOUT ANYTHING BESIDES YOURSELF AND YOUR FAMILY?!

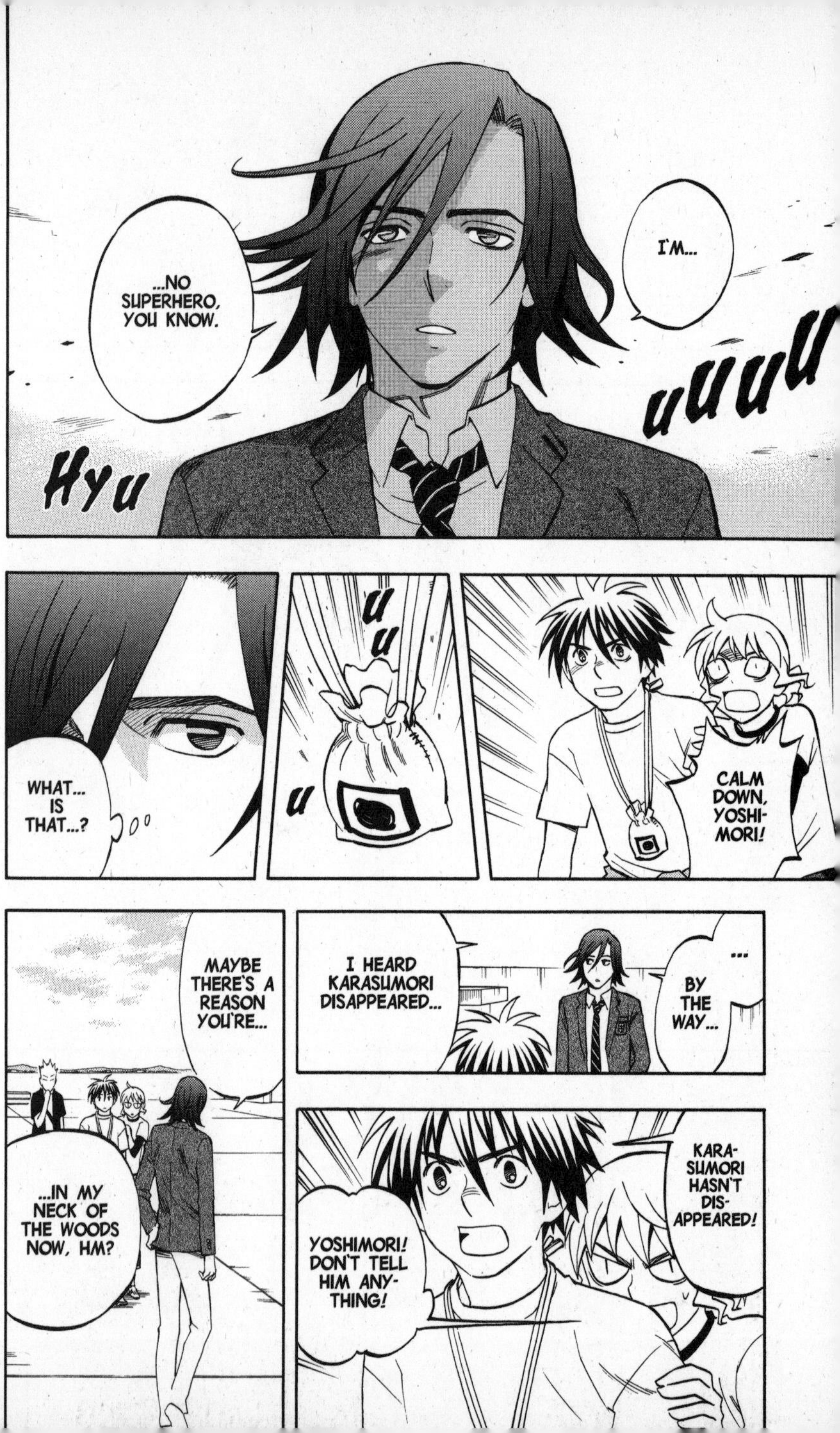
I'M...
UUUUU
...NO SUPERHERO, YOU KNOW.
Hyu
CALM DOWN, YOSHIMORI!
U
U
U
WHAT... IS THAT...?
... BY THE WAY...
I HEARD KARASUMORI DISAPPEARED...
KARA-SUMORI HASN'T DIS-APPEARED!
YOSHIMORI! DON'T TELL HIM ANY-THING!
MAYBE THERE'S A REASON YOU'RE...
...IN MY NECK OF THE WOODS NOW, HM?

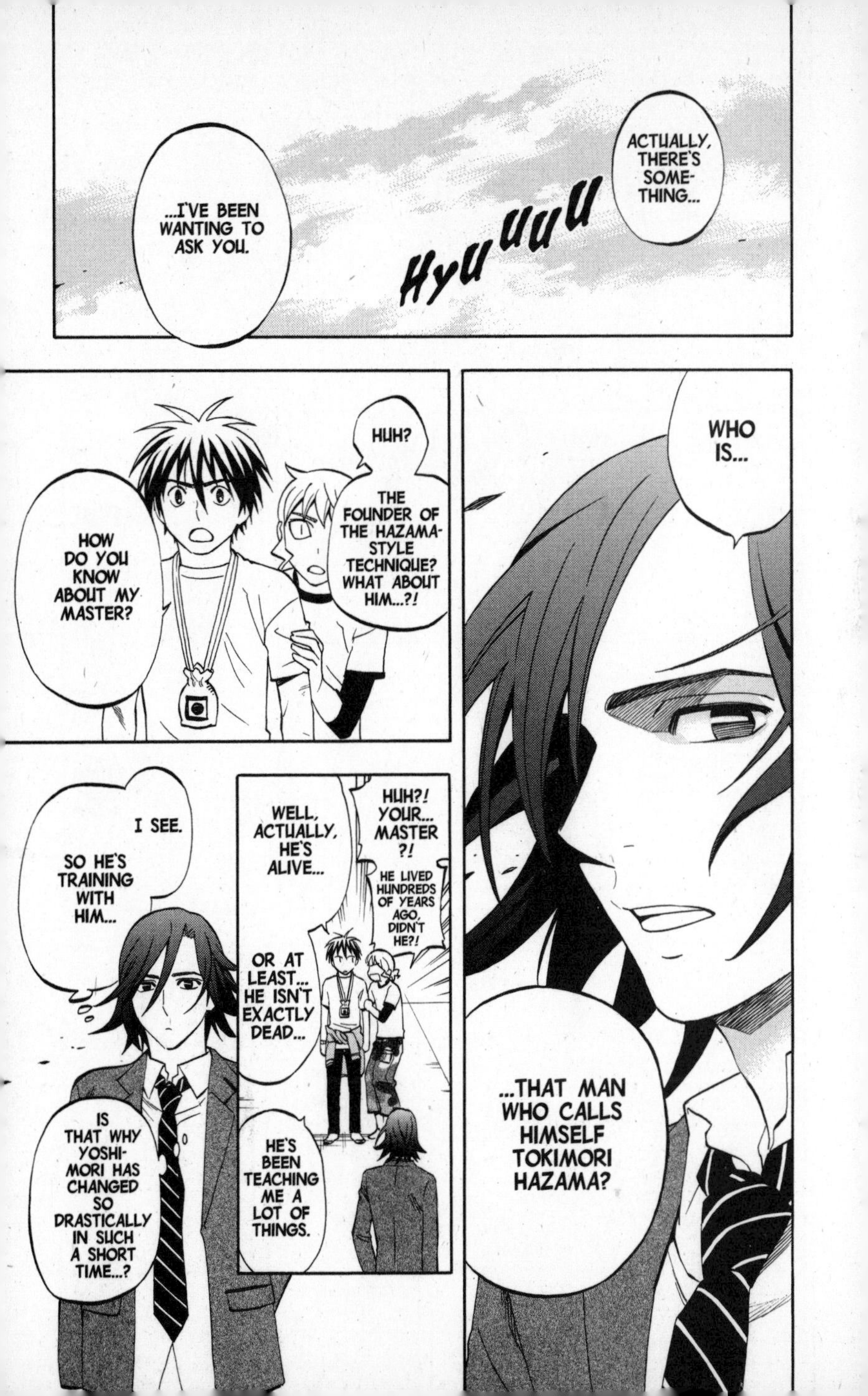
ACTUALLY, THERE'S SOMETHING...
HYUUUU
...I'VE BEEN WANTING TO ASK YOU.
WHO IS...
...THAT MAN WHO CALLS HIMSELF TOKIMORI HAZAMA?
HUH?
THE FOUNDER OF THE HAZAMA-STYLE TECHNIQUE? WHAT ABOUT HIM...?!
HOW DO YOU KNOW ABOUT MY MASTER?
HUH?! YOUR... MASTER?!
HE LIVED HUNDREDS OF YEARS AGO, DIDN'T HE?!
WELL, ACTUALLY, HE'S ALIVE...
OR AT LEAST... HE ISN'T EXACTLY DEAD...
HE'S BEEN TEACHING ME A LOT OF THINGS.
I SEE.
SO HE'S TRAINING WITH HIM...
IS THAT WHY YOSHIMORI HAS CHANGED SO DRASTICALLY IN SUCH A SHORT TIME...?

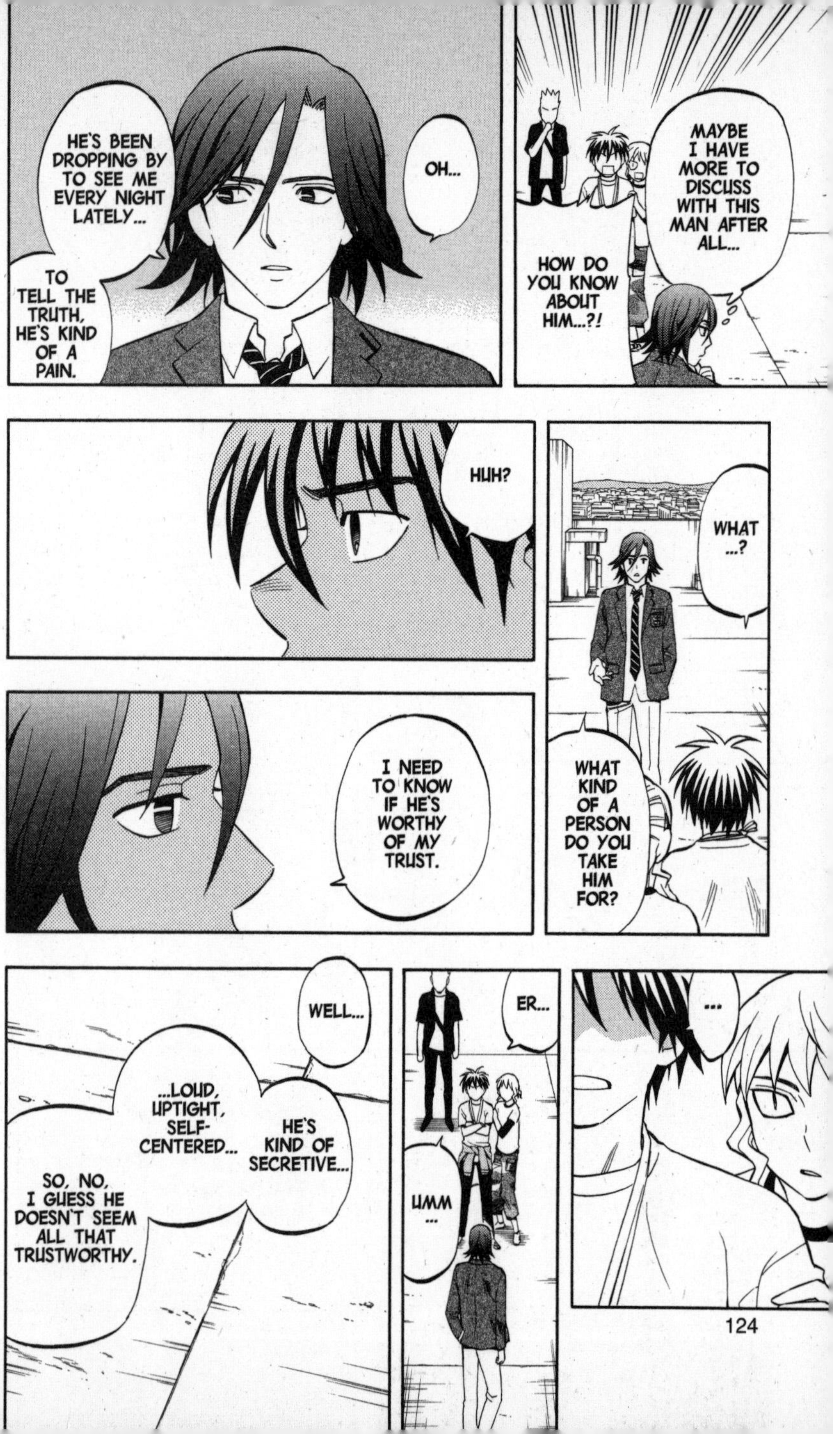
MAYBE I HAVE MORE TO DISCUSS WITH THIS MAN AFTER ALL...
HOW DO YOU KNOW ABOUT HIM...?!
OH...
HE'S BEEN DROPPING BY TO SEE ME EVERY NIGHT LATELY...
TO TELL THE TRUTH, HE'S KIND OF A PAIN.
WHAT ...?
WHAT KIND OF A PERSON DO YOU TAKE HIM FOR?
HUH?
I NEED TO KNOW IF HE'S WORTHY OF MY TRUST.
...
ER...
UMM ...
WELL...
HE'S KIND OF SECRETIVE...
...LOUD, UPTIGHT, SELF-CENTERED...
SO, NO, I GUESS HE DOESN'T SEEM ALL THAT TRUSTWORTHY.

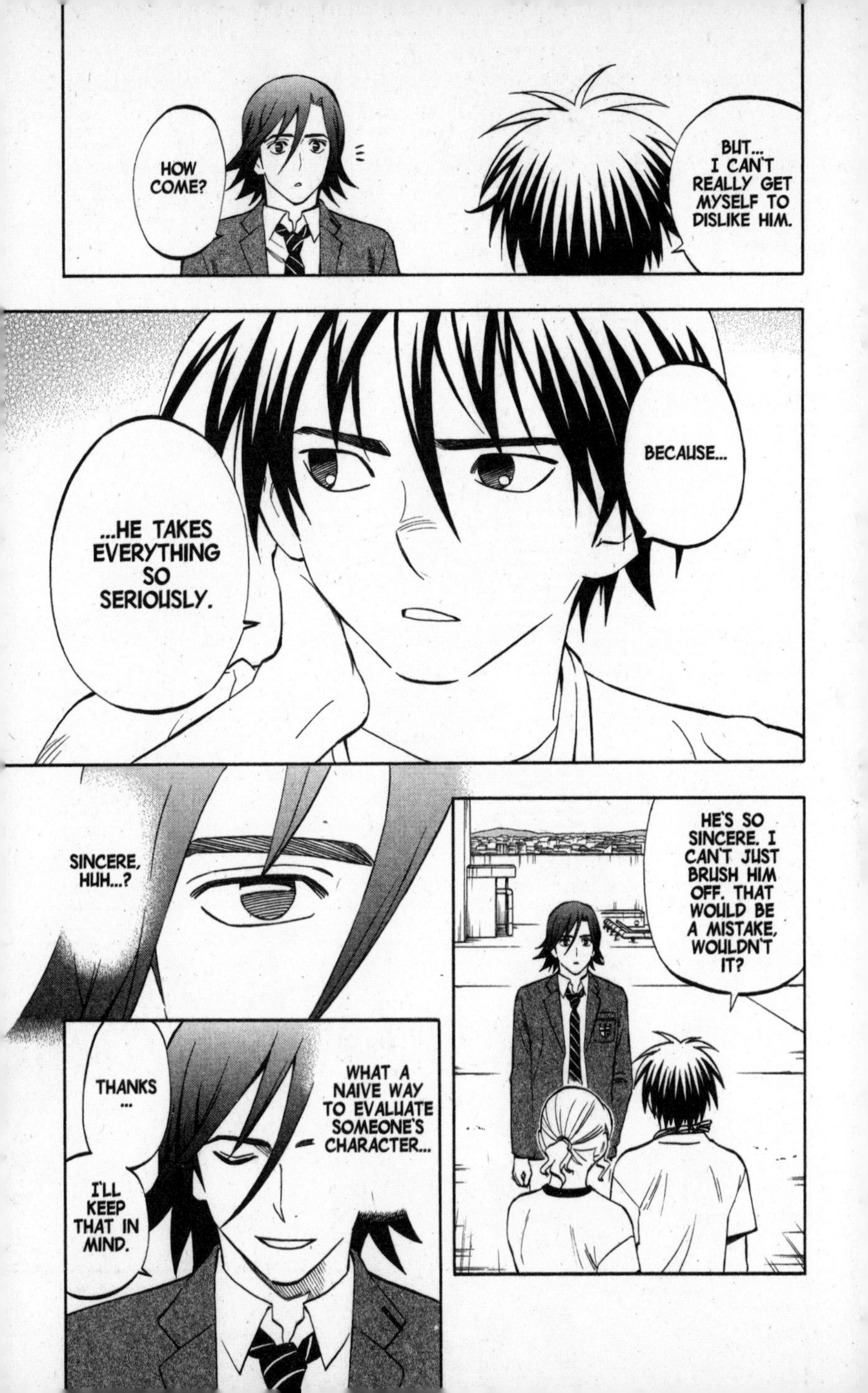
BUT... I CAN'T REALLY GET MYSELF TO DISLIKE HIM.
HOW COME?
BECAUSE...
...HE TAKES EVERYTHING SO SERIOUSLY.
HE'S SO SINCERE. I CAN'T JUST BRUSH HIM OFF. THAT WOULD BE A MISTAKE, WOULDN'T IT?
SINCERE, HUH...?
WHAT A NAIVE WAY TO EVALUATE SOMEONE'S CHARACTER...
THANKS...
I'LL KEEP THAT IN MIND.

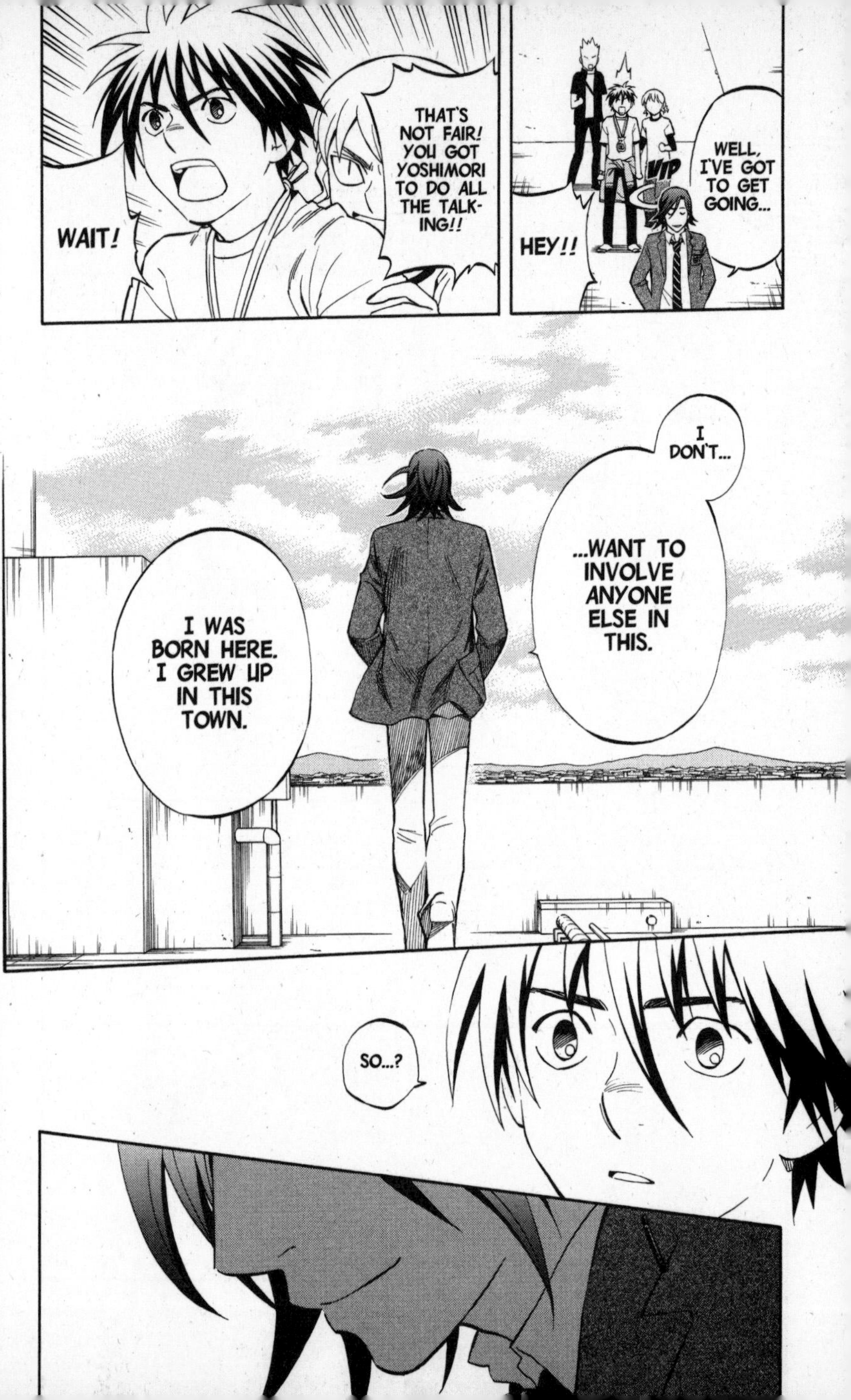
WELL, I'VE GOT TO GET GOING...
VIP
HEY!!
THAT'S NOT FAIR! YOU GOT YOSHIMORI TO DO ALL THE TALKING!!
WAIT!
I DON'T...
...WANT TO INVOLVE ANYONE ELSE IN THIS.
I WAS BORN HERE. I GREW UP IN THIS TOWN.
SO...?

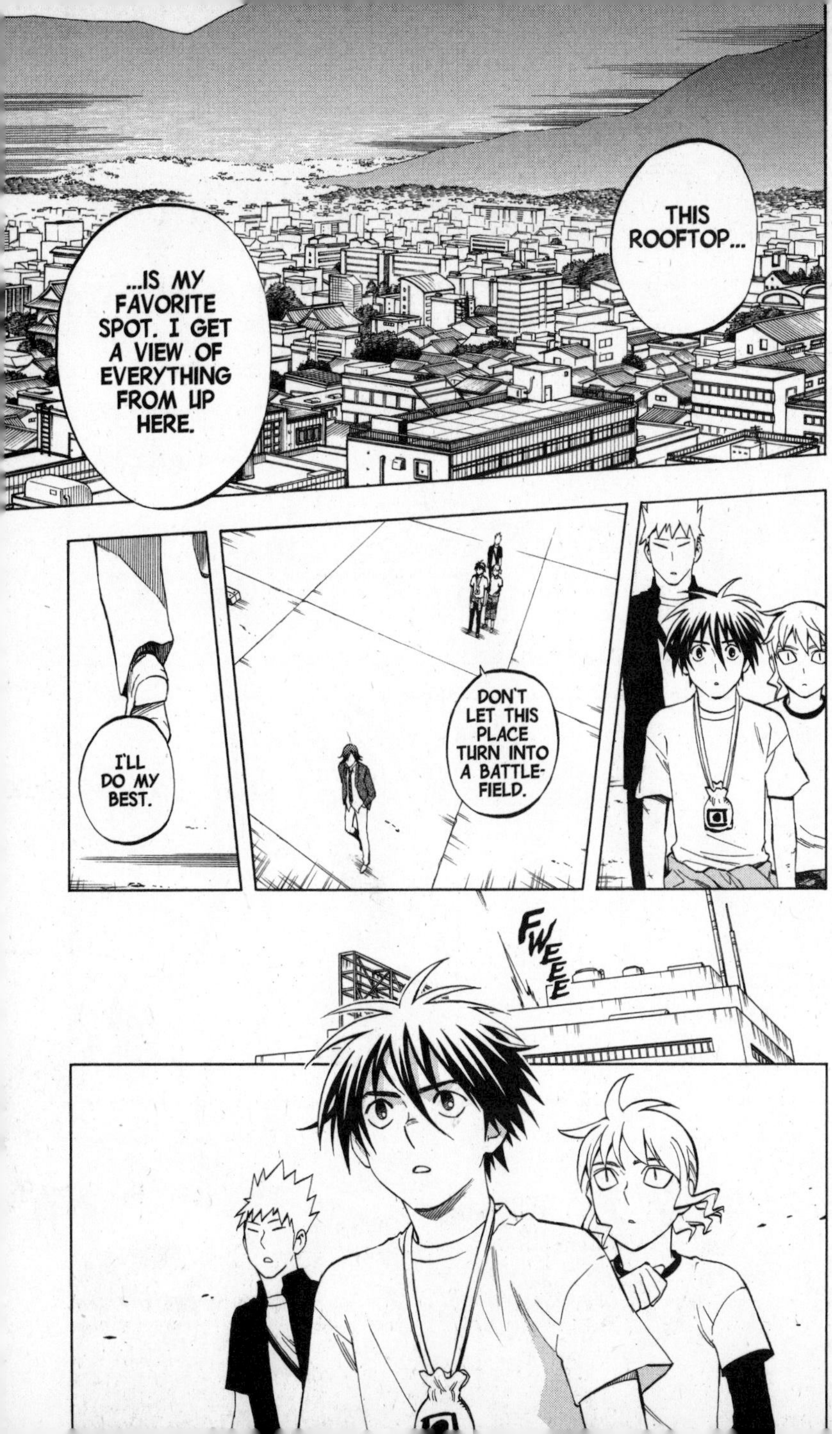
THIS ROOFTOP...
...IS MY FAVORITE SPOT. I GET A VIEW OF EVERYTHING FROM UP HERE.
DON'T LET THIS PLACE TURN INTO A BATTLE-FIELD.
I'LL DO MY BEST.
FWEEE

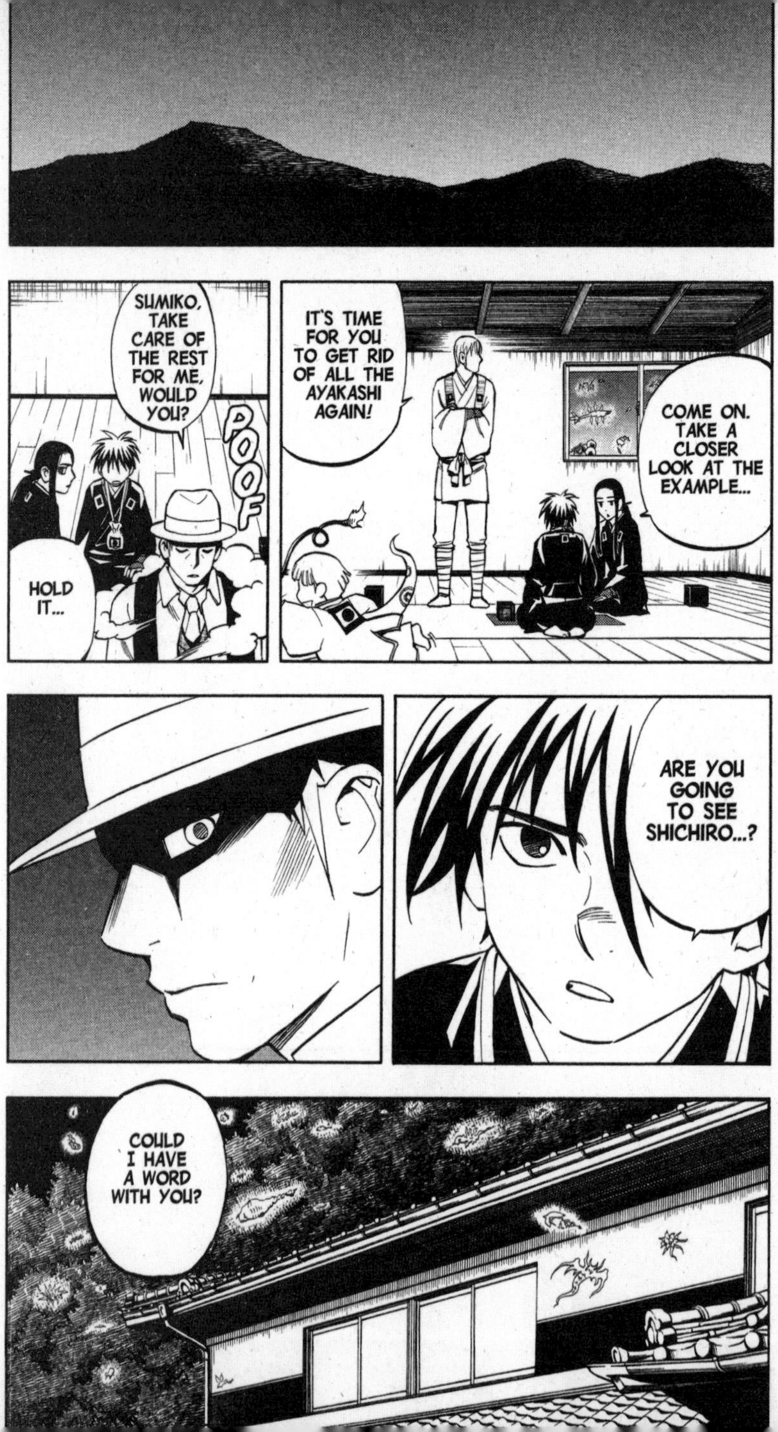
COME ON. TAKE A CLOSER LOOK AT THE EXAMPLE...
IT'S TIME FOR YOU TO GET RID OF ALL THE AYAKASHI AGAIN!
SUMIKO, TAKE CARE OF THE REST FOR ME, WOULD YOU?
POOF
HOLD IT...
ARE YOU GOING TO SEE SHICHIRO...?
COULD I HAVE A WORD WITH YOU?

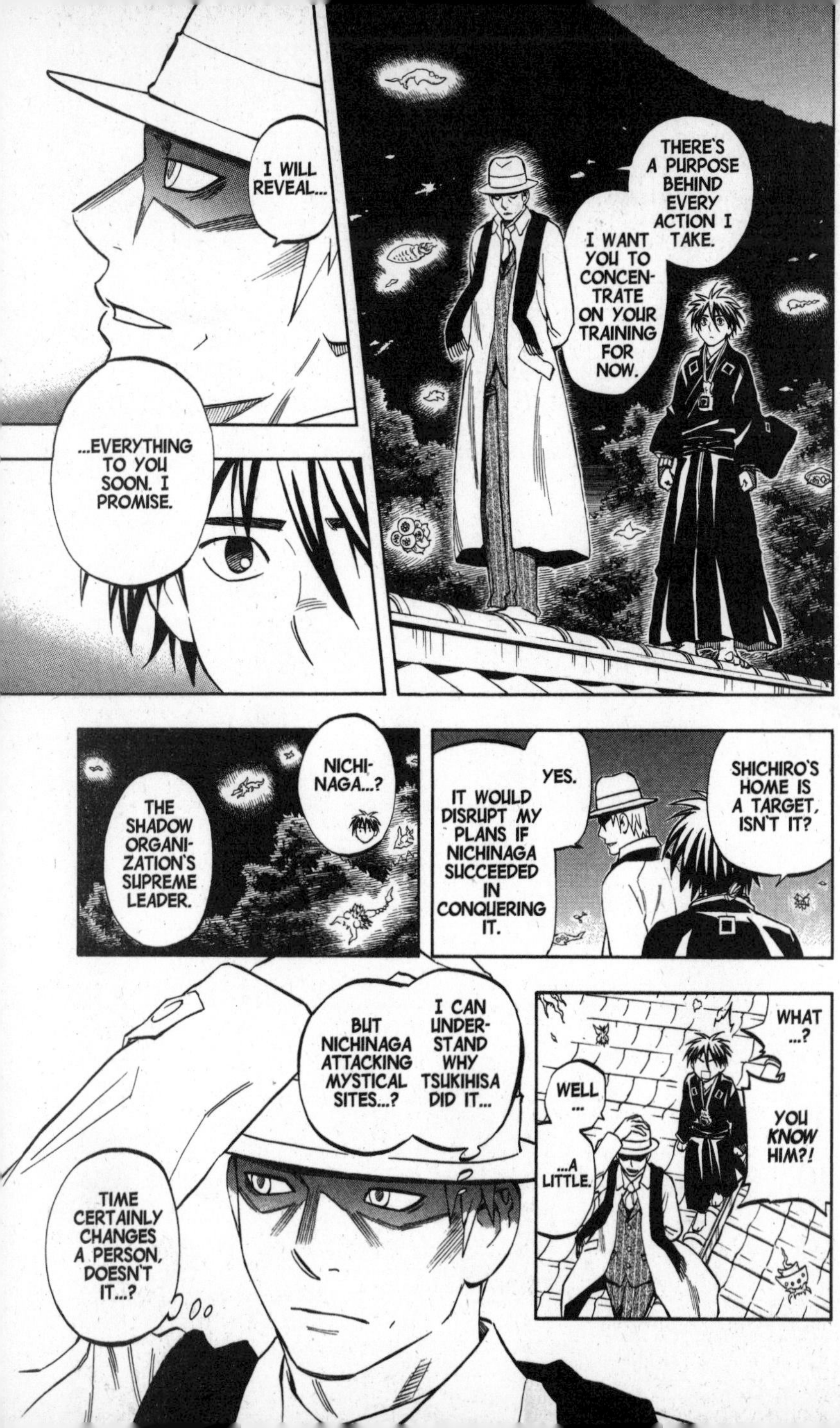
THERE'S A PURPOSE BEHIND EVERY ACTION I TAKE.
I WANT YOU TO CONCENTRATE ON YOUR TRAINING FOR NOW.
I WILL REVEAL...
...EVERYTHING TO YOU SOON. I PROMISE.
SHICHIRO'S HOME IS A TARGET, ISN'T IT?
YES.
IT WOULD DISRUPT MY PLANS IF NICHINAGA SUCCEEDED IN CONQUERING IT.
NICHINAGA...?
THE SHADOW ORGANIZATION'S SUPREME LEADER.
WHAT ...?
YOU KNOW HIM?!
WELL ...
...A LITTLE.
I CAN UNDERSTAND WHY TSUKIHISA DID IT...
BUT NICHINAGA ATTACKING MYSTICAL SITES...?
TIME CERTAINLY CHANGES A PERSON, DOESN'T IT...?

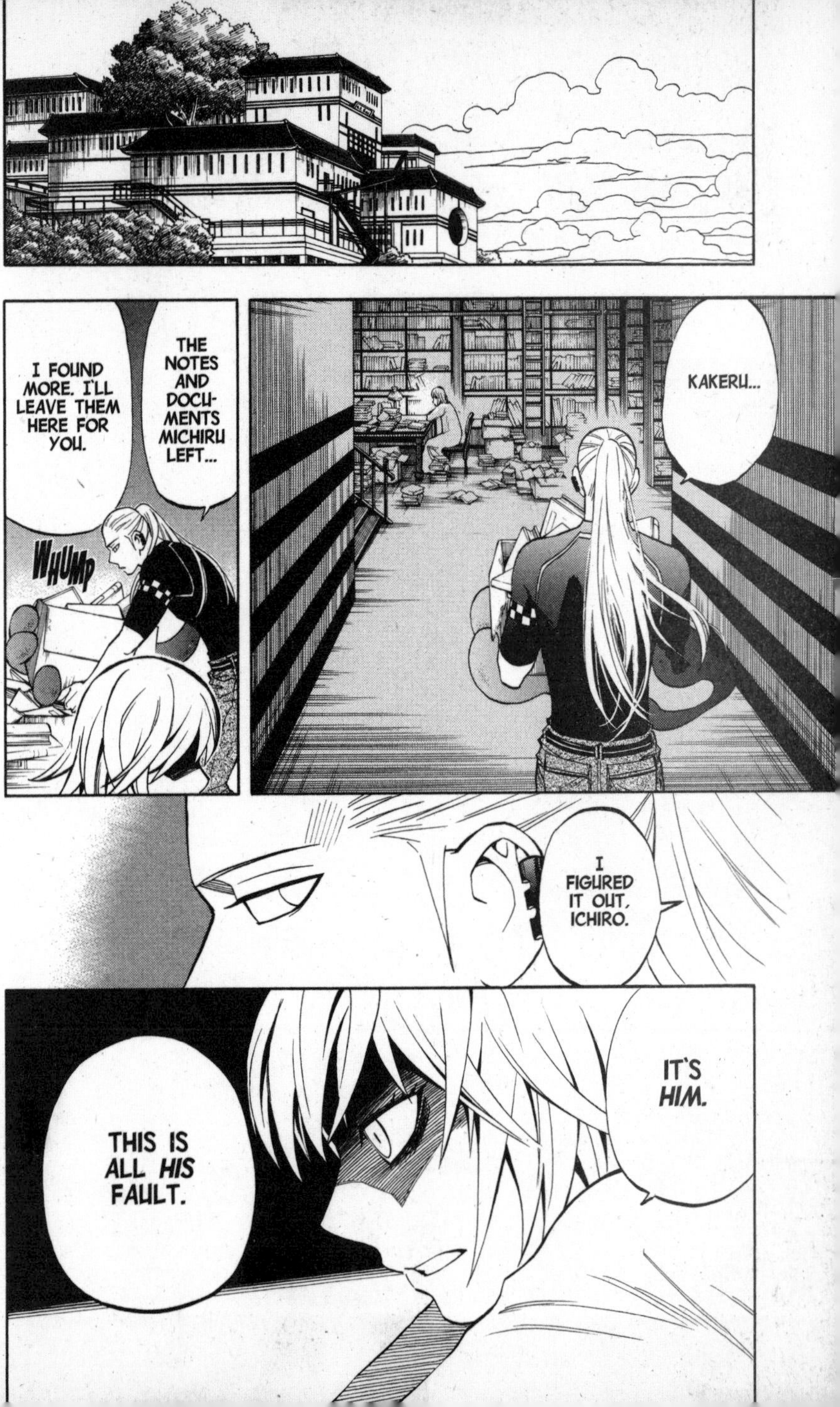
KAKERU...
THE NOTES AND DOCUMENTS MICHIRU LEFT...
I FOUND MORE. I'LL LEAVE THEM HERE FOR YOU.
WHUMP
I FIGURED IT OUT, ICHIRO.
IT'S *HIM*.
THIS IS ALL *HIS* FAULT.

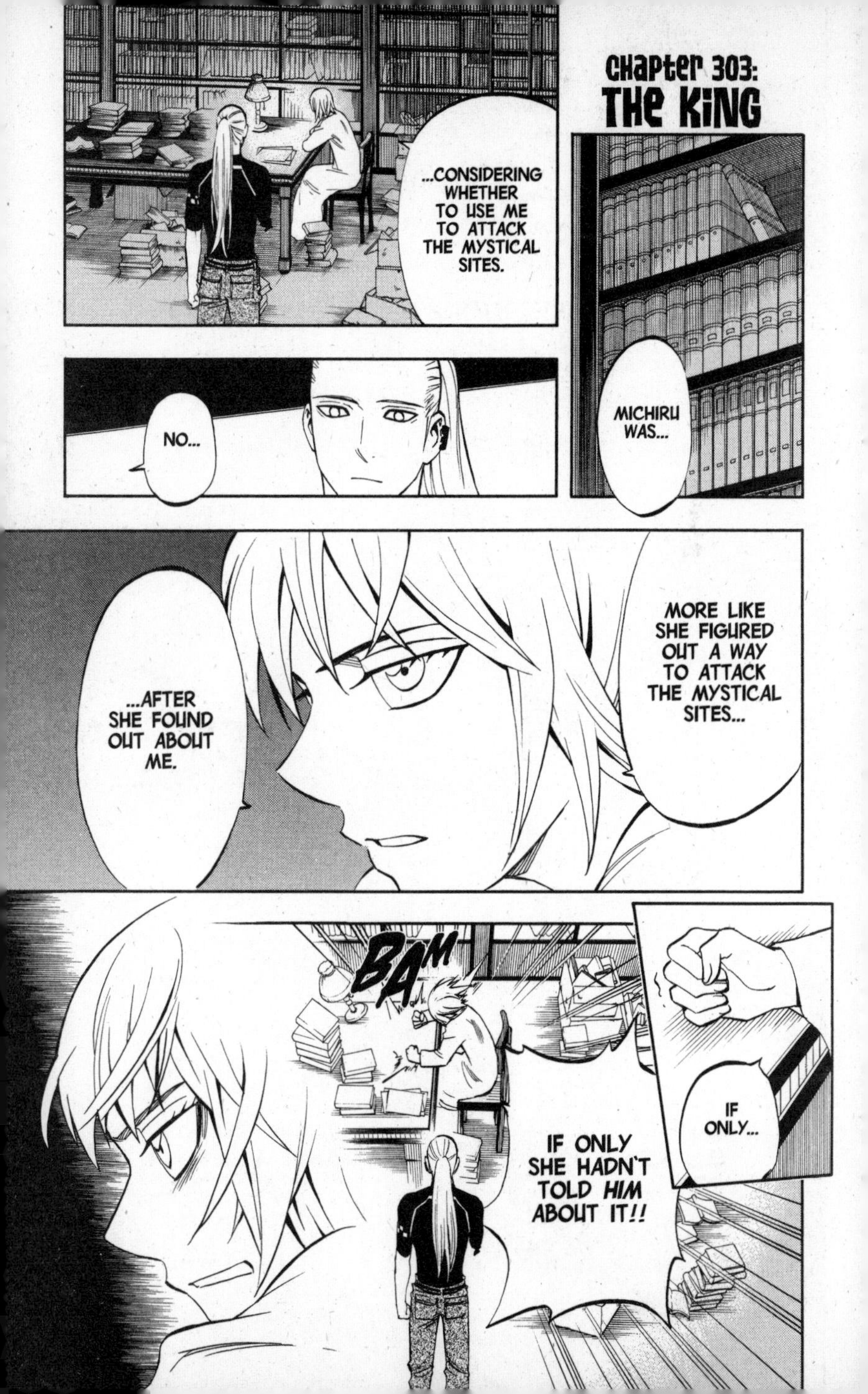
Chapter 303:
The King
MICHIRU WAS...
...CONSIDERING WHETHER TO USE ME TO ATTACK THE MYSTICAL SITES.
NO...
MORE LIKE SHE FIGURED OUT A WAY TO ATTACK THE MYSTICAL SITES...
...AFTER SHE FOUND OUT ABOUT ME.
IF ONLY...
BAM
IF ONLY SHE HADN'T TOLD *HIM* ABOUT IT!!

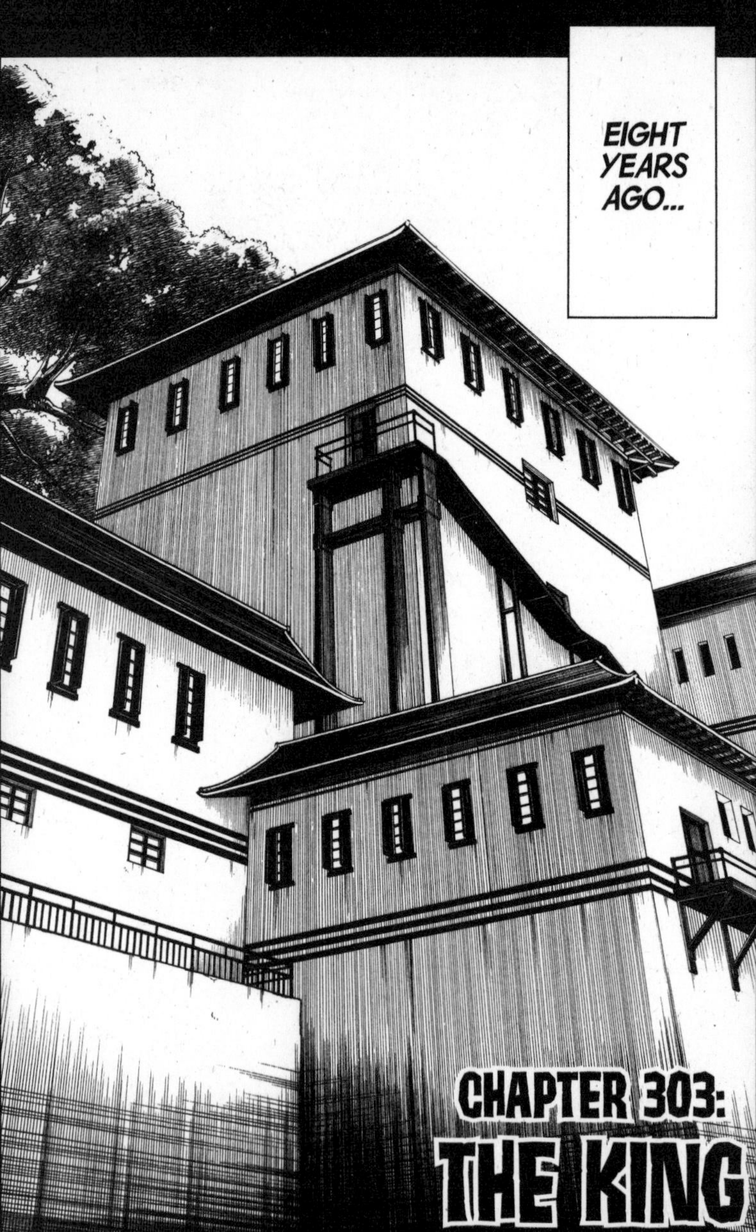
EIGHT YEARS AGO...
CHAPTER 303:
THE KING

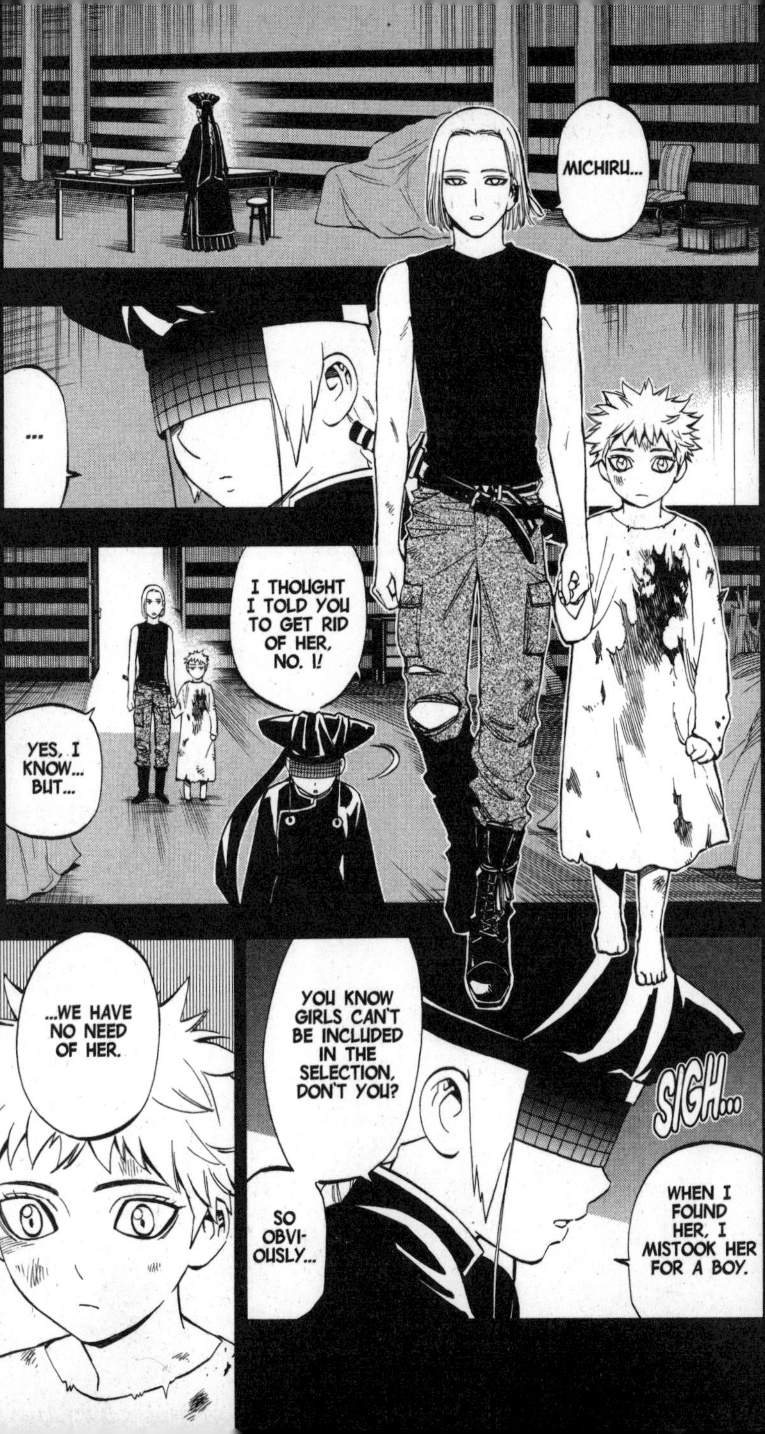
MICHIRU...
...
I THOUGHT I TOLD YOU TO GET RID OF HER, NO. 1!
YES, I KNOW... BUT...
WHEN I FOUND HER, I MISTOOK HER FOR A BOY.
SIGH...
YOU KNOW GIRLS CAN'T BE INCLUDED IN THE SELECTION, DON'T YOU?
SO OBVI-OUSLY...
...WE HAVE NO NEED OF HER.

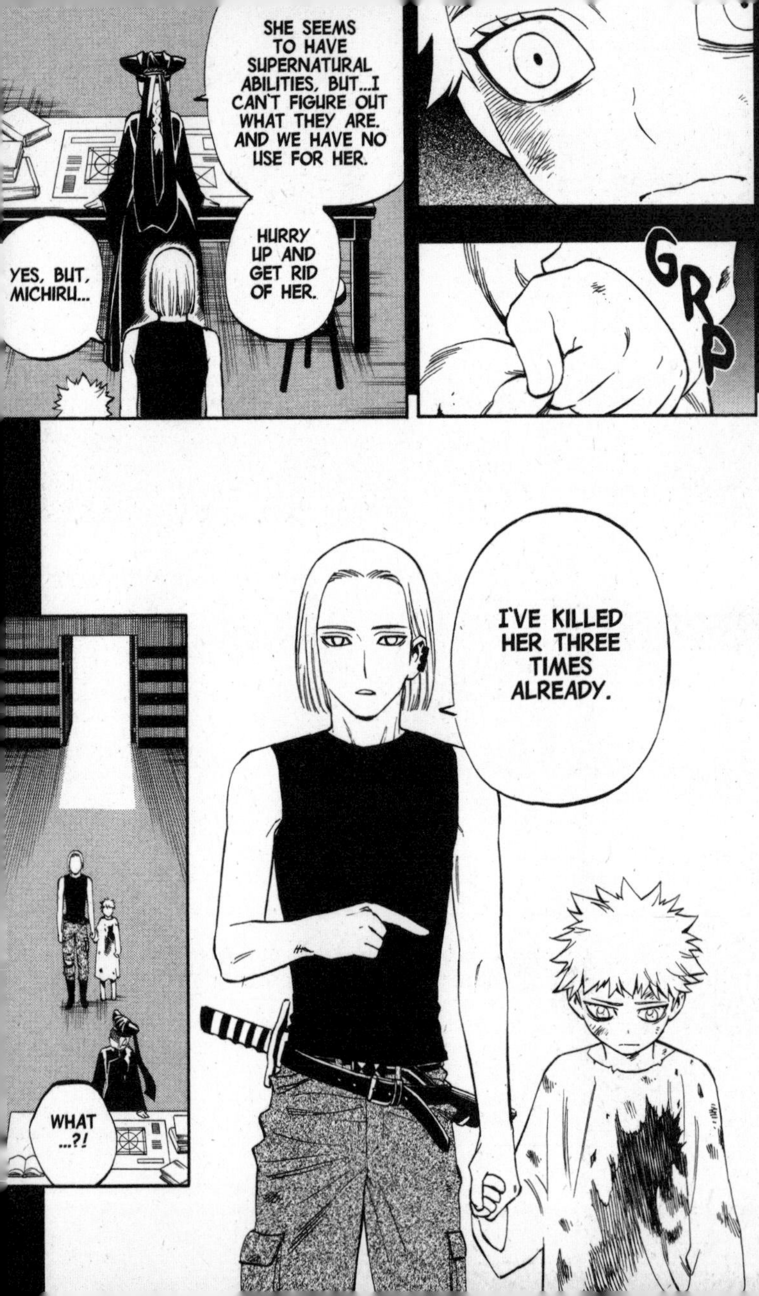
GRP
SHE SEEMS TO HAVE SUPERNATURAL ABILITIES, BUT...I CAN'T FIGURE OUT WHAT THEY ARE. AND WE HAVE NO USE FOR HER.
HURRY UP AND GET RID OF HER.
YES, BUT, MICHIRU...
I'VE KILLED HER THREE TIMES ALREADY.
WHAT ...?!

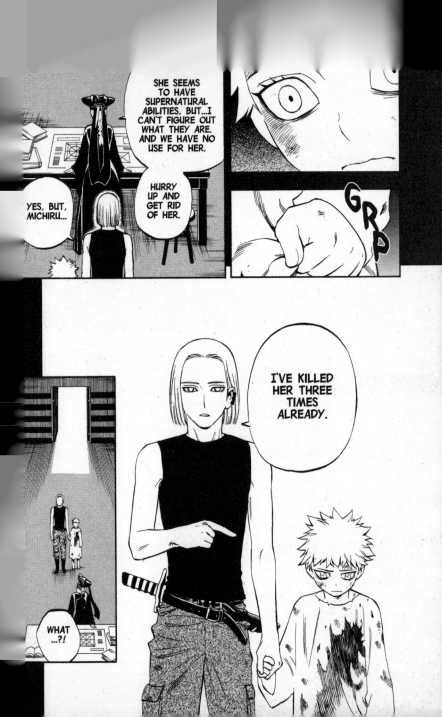

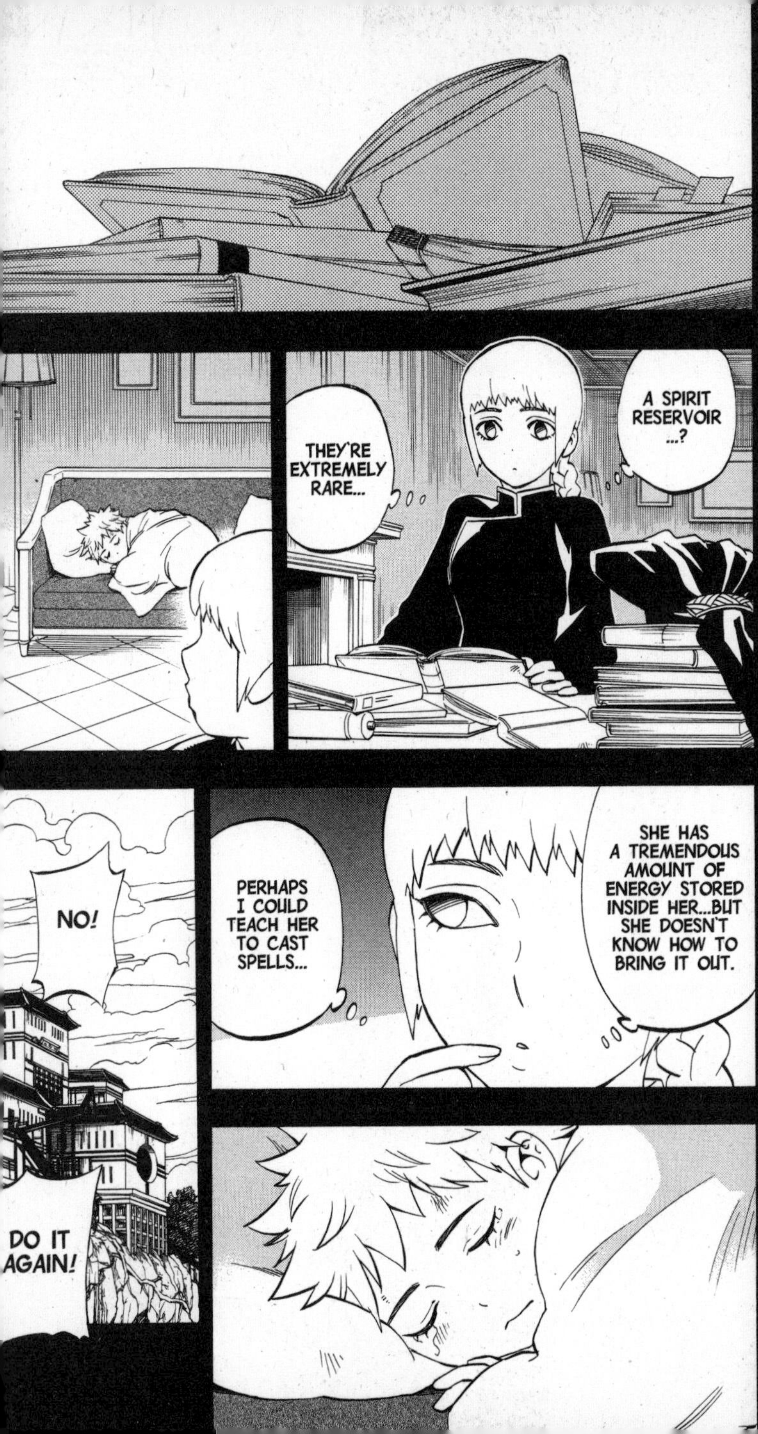
A SPIRIT RESERVOIR ...?
THEY'RE EXTREMELY RARE...
SHE HAS A TREMENDOUS AMOUNT OF ENERGY STORED INSIDE HER...BUT SHE DOESN'T KNOW HOW TO BRING IT OUT.
PERHAPS I COULD TEACH HER TO CAST SPELLS...
NO!
DO IT AGAIN!

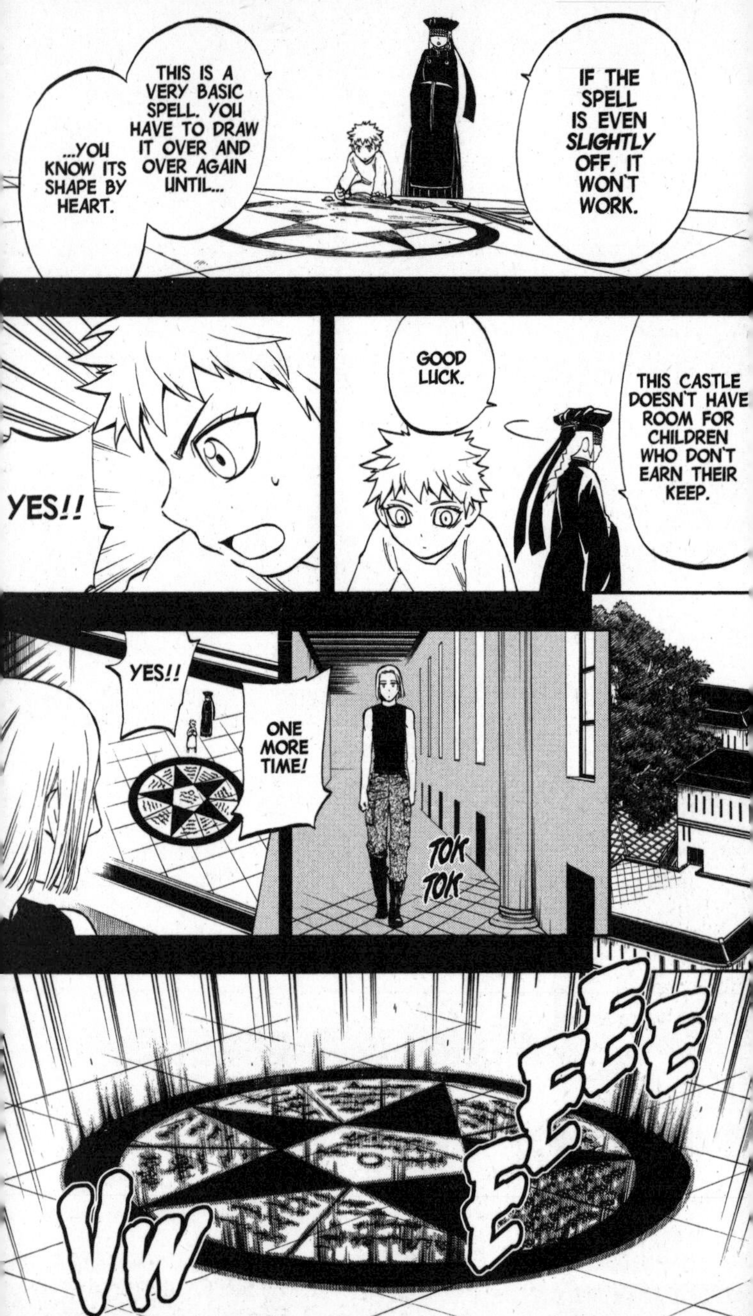
IF THE SPELL IS EVEN *SLIGHTLY* OFF, IT WON'T WORK.
THIS IS A VERY BASIC SPELL. YOU HAVE TO DRAW IT OVER AND OVER AGAIN UNTIL...
...YOU KNOW ITS SHAPE BY HEART.
THIS CASTLE DOESN'T HAVE ROOM FOR CHILDREN WHO DON'T EARN THEIR KEEP.
GOOD LUCK.
YES!!
TOK TOK
YES!!
ONE MORE TIME!
VWEEEEE

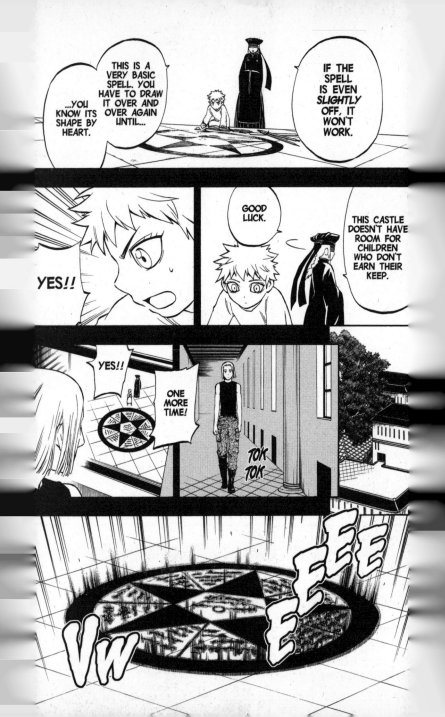

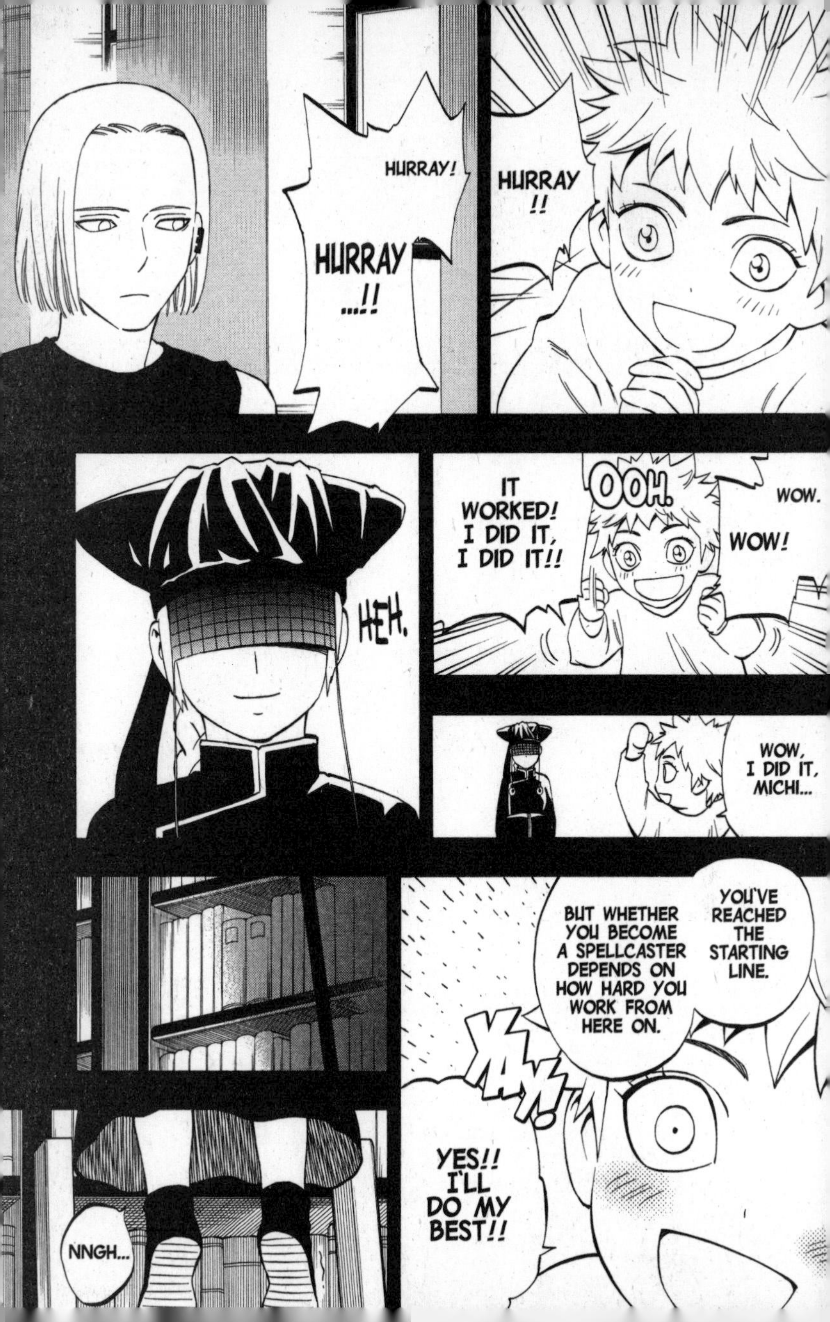
HURRAY !!
HURRAY!
HURRAY ...!!
WOW.
WOW!
OOH.
IT WORKED! I DID IT, I DID IT!!
WOW, I DID IT, MICHI...
HEH.
YOU'VE REACHED THE STARTING LINE.
BUT WHETHER YOU BECOME A SPELLCASTER DEPENDS ON HOW HARD YOU WORK FROM HERE ON.
YAY!
YES!! I'LL DO MY BEST!!
NNGH...

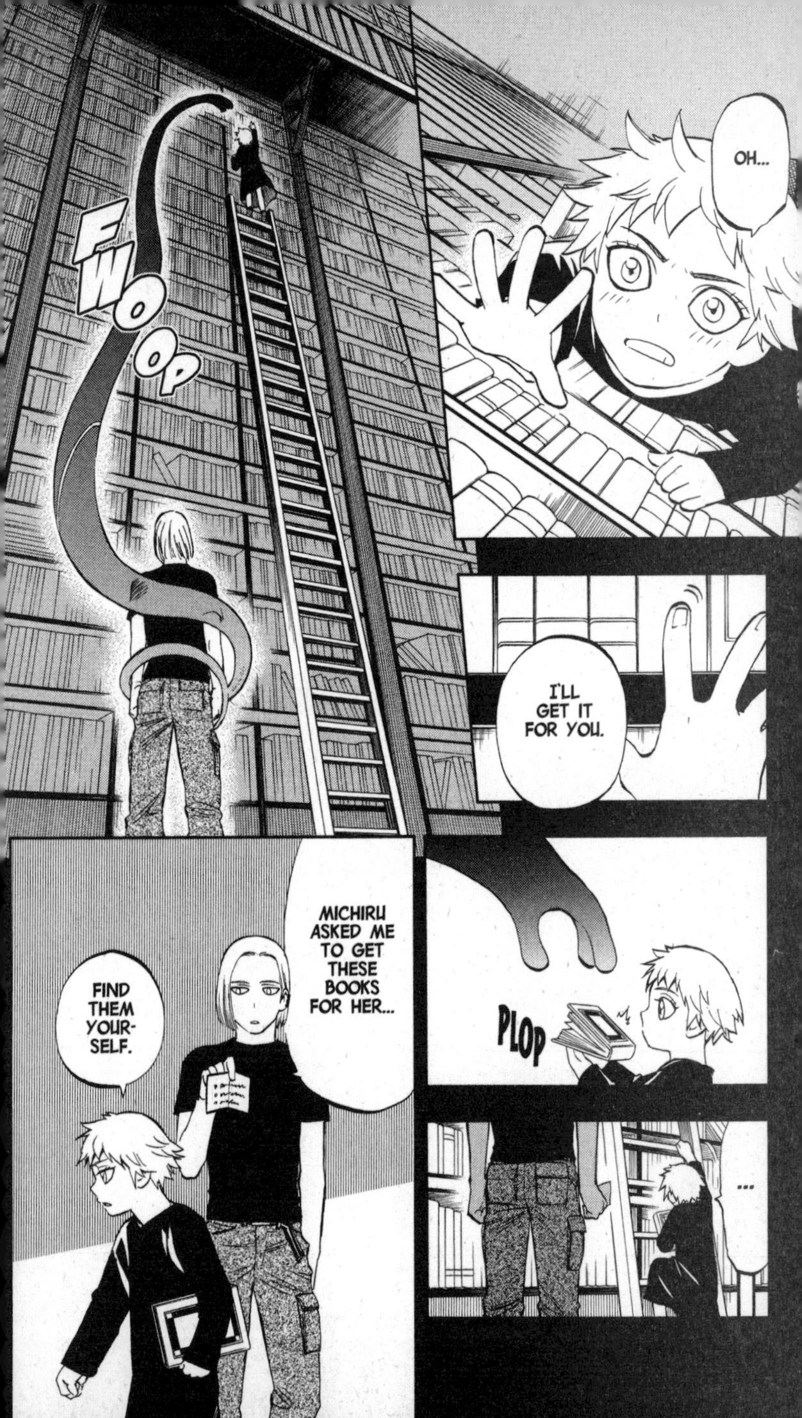
OH...
I'LL GET IT FOR YOU.
FWOOOP
PLOP
...
MICHIRU ASKED ME TO GET THESE BOOKS FOR HER...
FIND THEM YOUR-SELF.

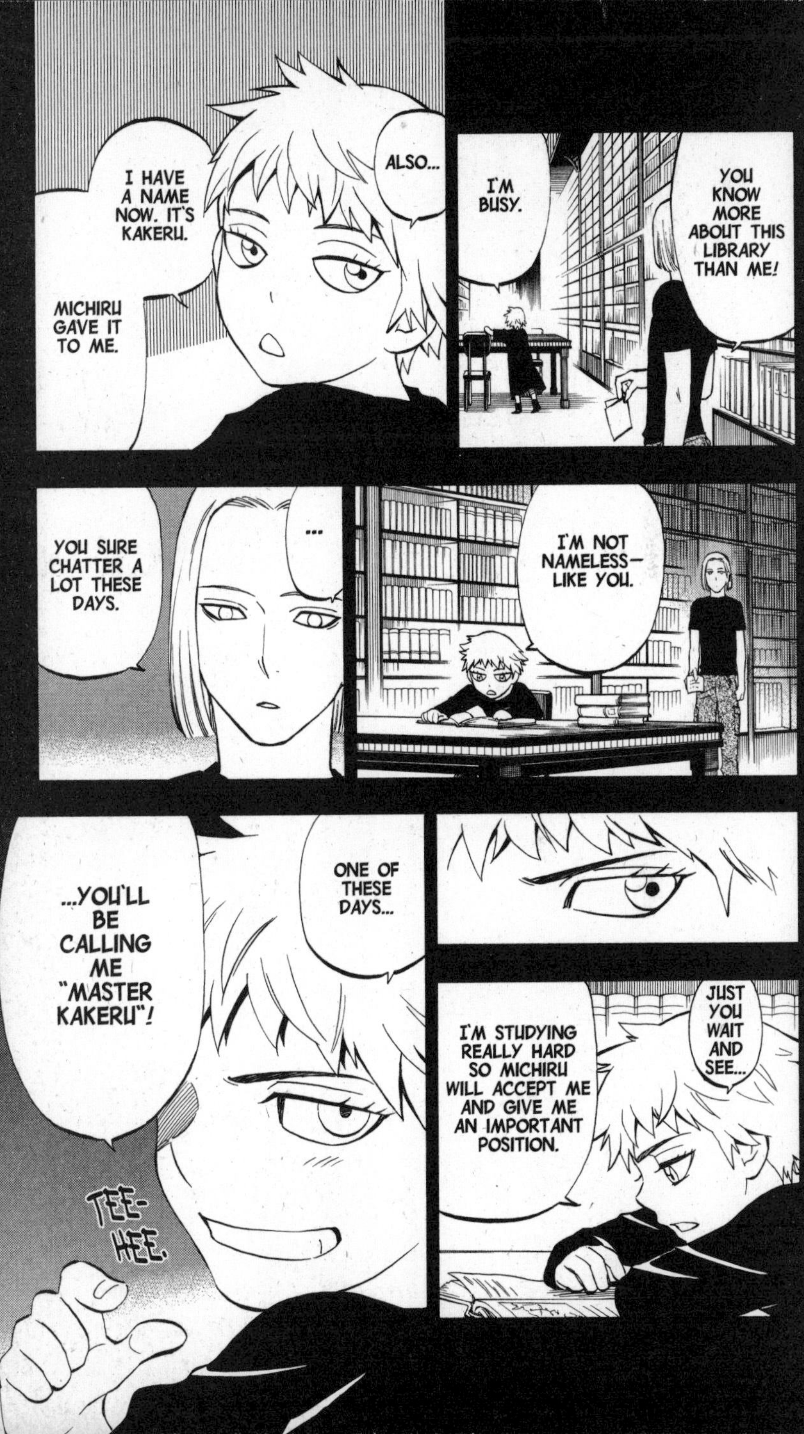
YOU KNOW MORE ABOUT THIS LIBRARY THAN ME!
I'M BUSY.
ALSO...
I HAVE A NAME NOW. IT'S KAKERU.
MICHIRU GAVE IT TO ME.
I'M NOT NAMELESS— LIKE YOU.
...
YOU SURE CHATTER A LOT THESE DAYS.
JUST YOU WAIT AND SEE...
I'M STUDYING REALLY HARD SO MICHIRU WILL ACCEPT ME AND GIVE ME AN IMPORTANT POSITION.
ONE OF THESE DAYS...
...YOU'LL BE CALLING ME "MASTER KAKERU"!
TEE-HEE.

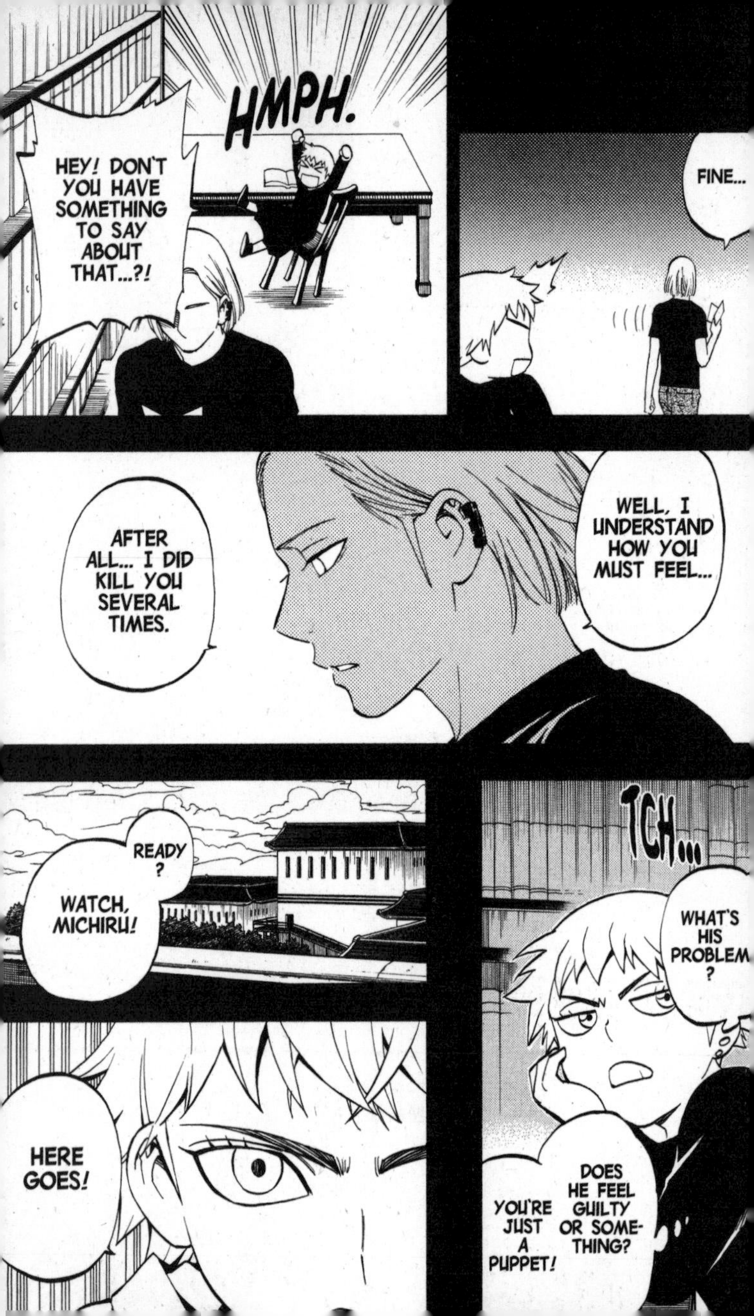
FINE...
HMPH.
HEY! DON'T YOU HAVE SOMETHING TO SAY ABOUT THAT...?!
WELL, I UNDERSTAND HOW YOU MUST FEEL...
AFTER ALL... I DID KILL YOU SEVERAL TIMES.
TCH...
WHAT'S HIS PROBLEM?
DOES HE FEEL GUILTY OR SOME-THING?
YOU'RE JUST A PUPPET!
READY?
WATCH, MICHIRU!
HERE GOES!

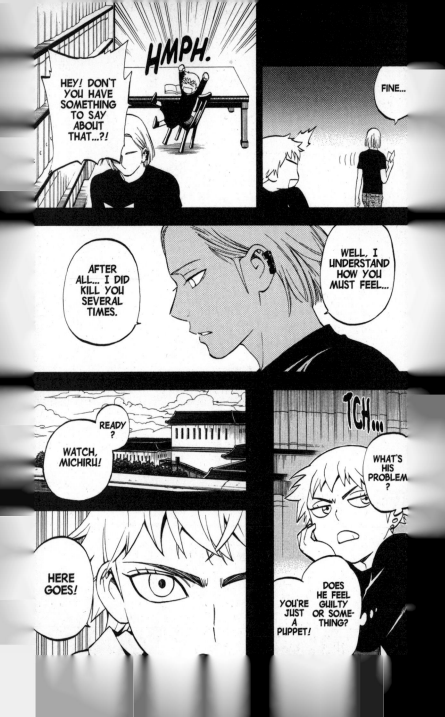

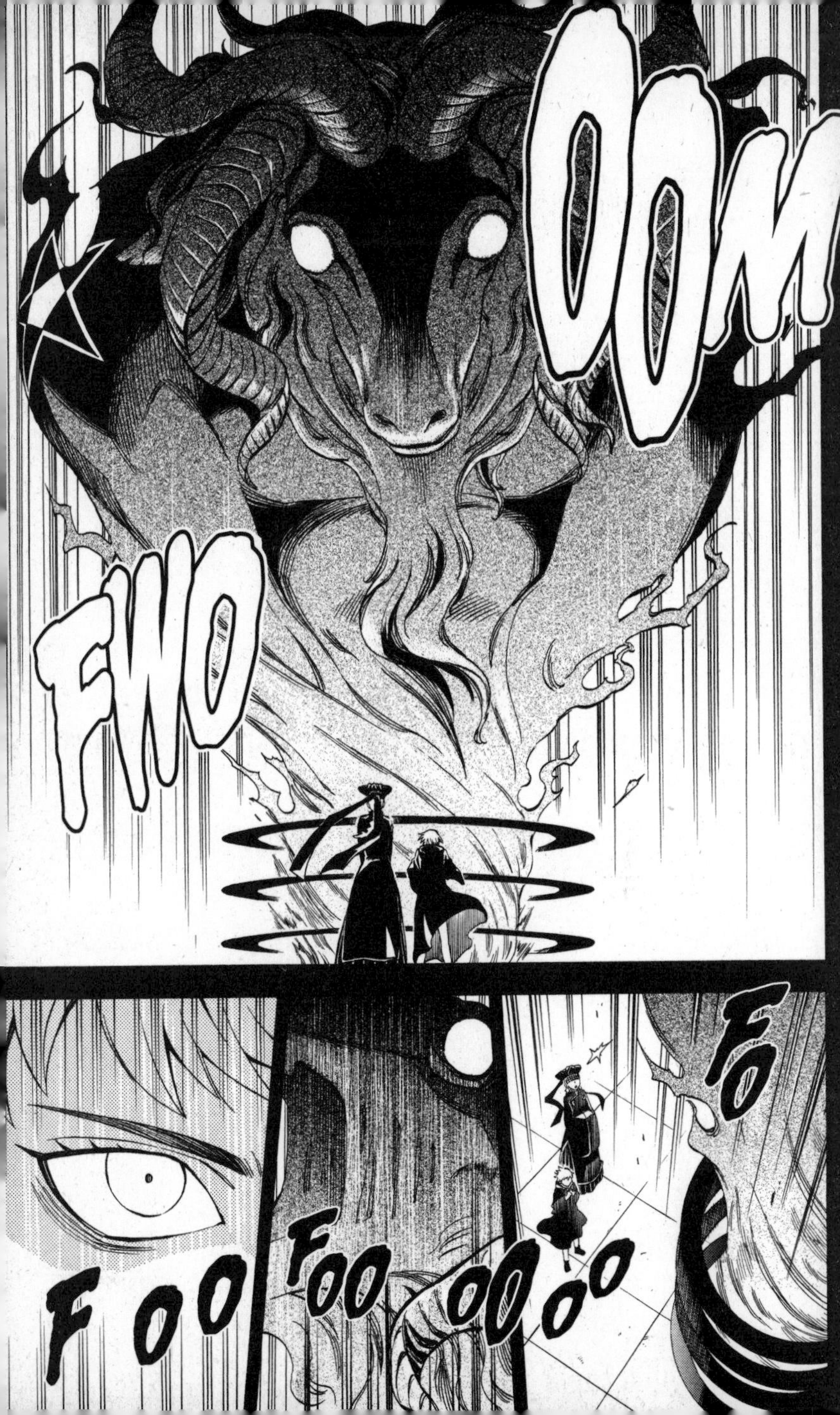
FWO
OOM
FO
OOOO
FOO
FOO

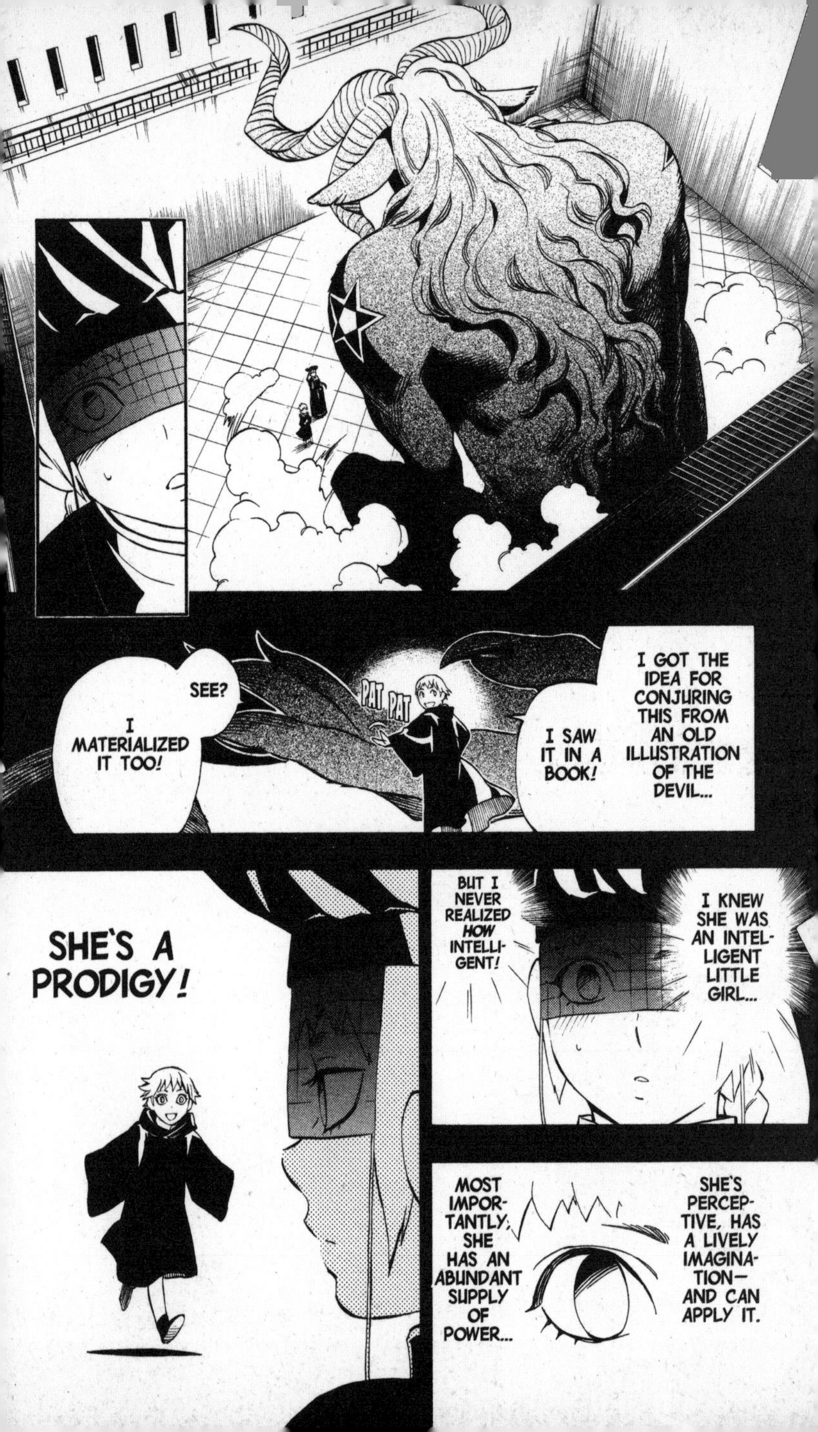
I GOT THE IDEA FOR CONJURING THIS FROM AN OLD ILLUSTRATION OF THE DEVIL...
I SAW IT IN A BOOK!
PAT PAT
SEE?
I MATERIALIZED IT TOO!
I KNEW SHE WAS AN INTELLIGENT LITTLE GIRL...
BUT I NEVER REALIZED *HOW* INTELLIGENT!
SHE'S PERCEPTIVE, HAS A LIVELY IMAGINATION— AND CAN APPLY IT.
MOST IMPORTANTLY, SHE HAS AN ABUNDANT SUPPLY OF POWER...
SHE'S A PRODIGY!

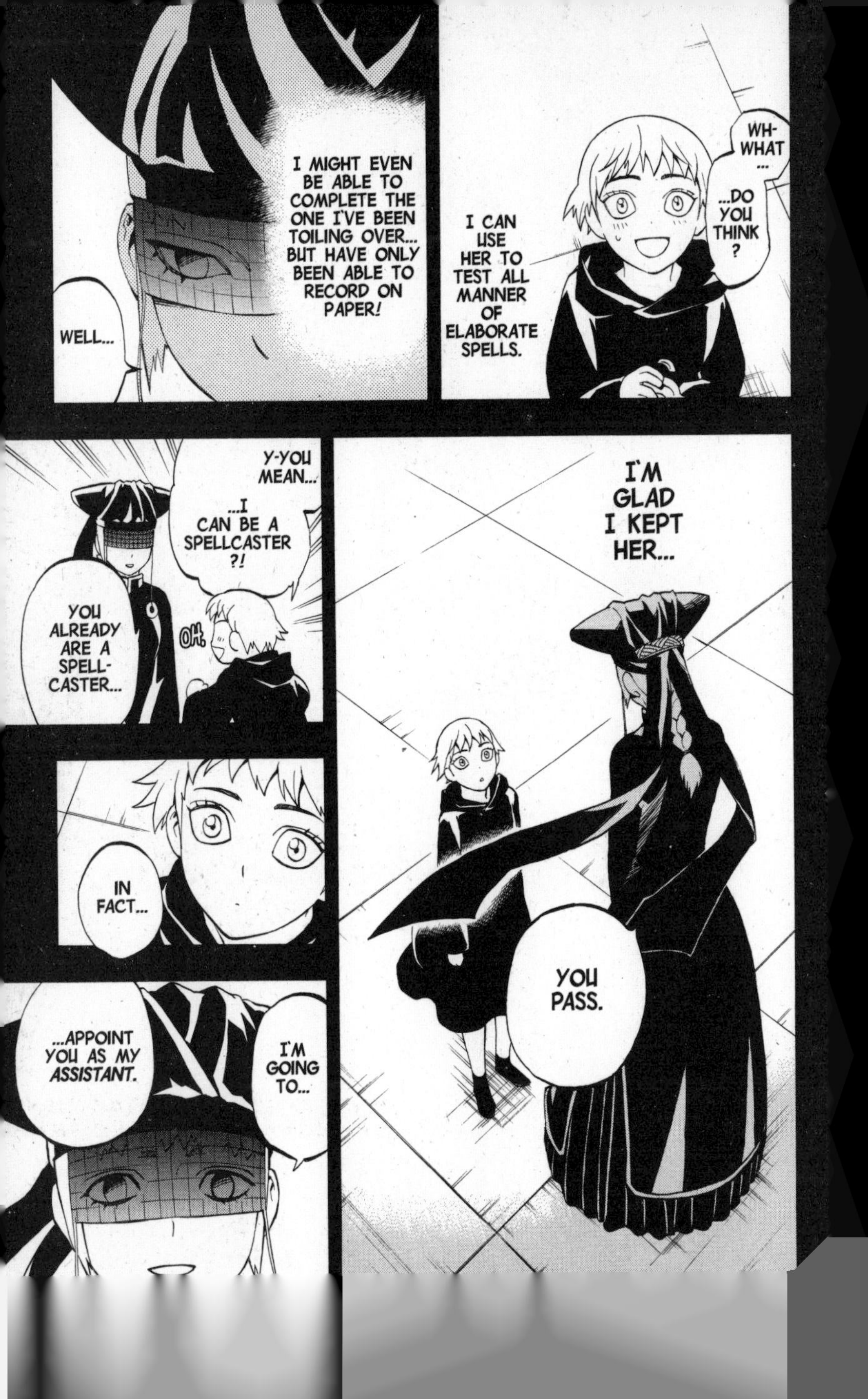
WH-WHAT...
...DO YOU THINK?
I CAN USE HER TO TEST ALL MANNER OF ELABORATE SPELLS.
I MIGHT EVEN BE ABLE TO COMPLETE THE ONE I'VE BEEN TOILING OVER... BUT HAVE ONLY BEEN ABLE TO RECORD ON PAPER!
WELL...
I'M GLAD I KEPT HER...
YOU PASS.
Y-YOU MEAN...
...I CAN BE A SPELLCASTER?!
OH,
YOU ALREADY ARE A SPELL-CASTER...
IN FACT...
I'M GOING TO...
...APPOINT YOU AS MY *ASSISTANT*.

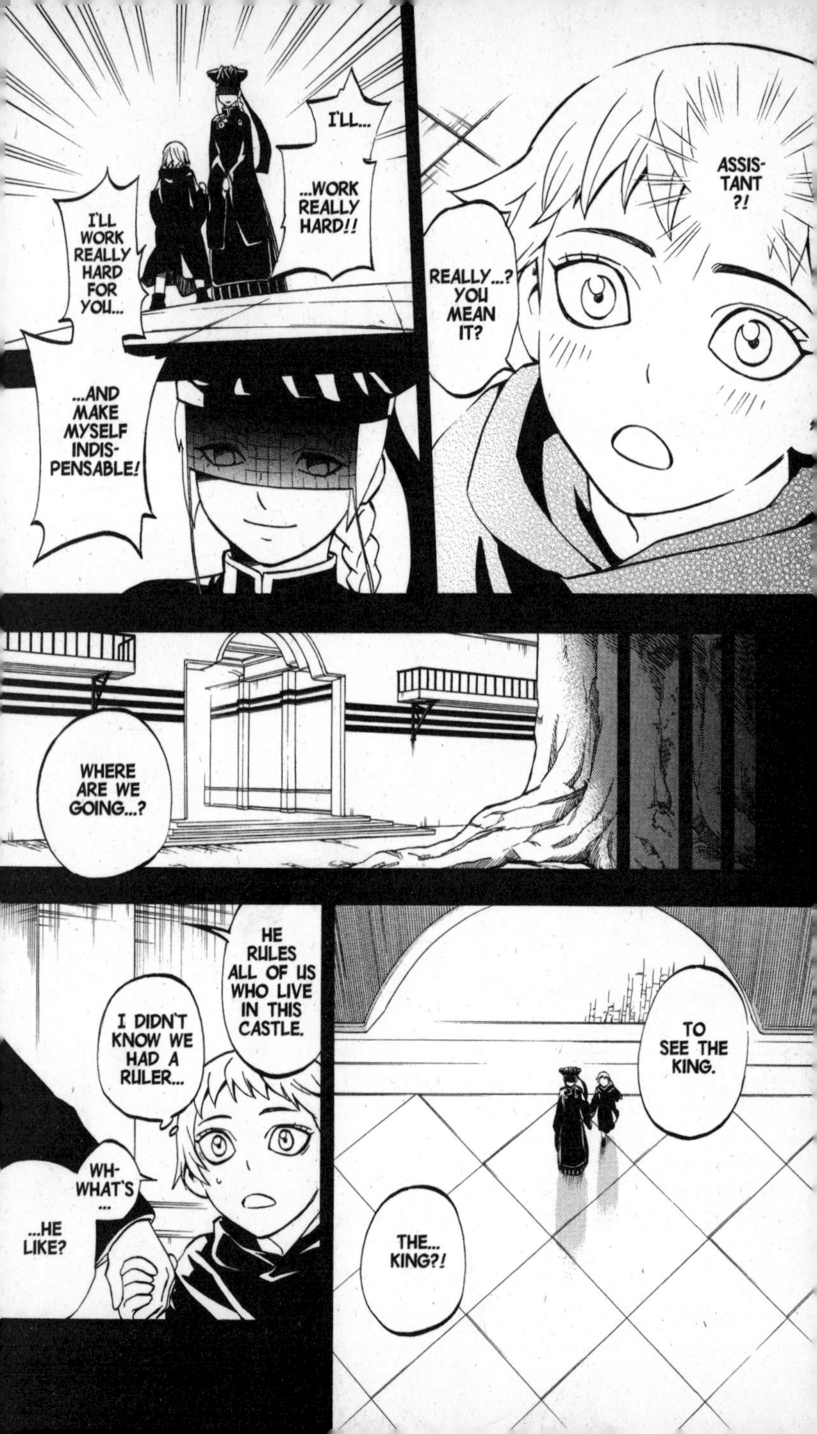
ASSIS-TANT?!
REALLY...? YOU MEAN IT?
I'LL...
...WORK REALLY HARD!!
I'LL WORK REALLY HARD FOR YOU...
...AND MAKE MYSELF INDIS-PENSABLE!
WHERE ARE WE GOING...?
TO SEE THE KING.
THE... KING?!
HE RULES ALL OF US WHO LIVE IN THIS CASTLE.
I DIDN'T KNOW WE HAD A RULER...
WH-WHAT'S...
...HE LIKE?

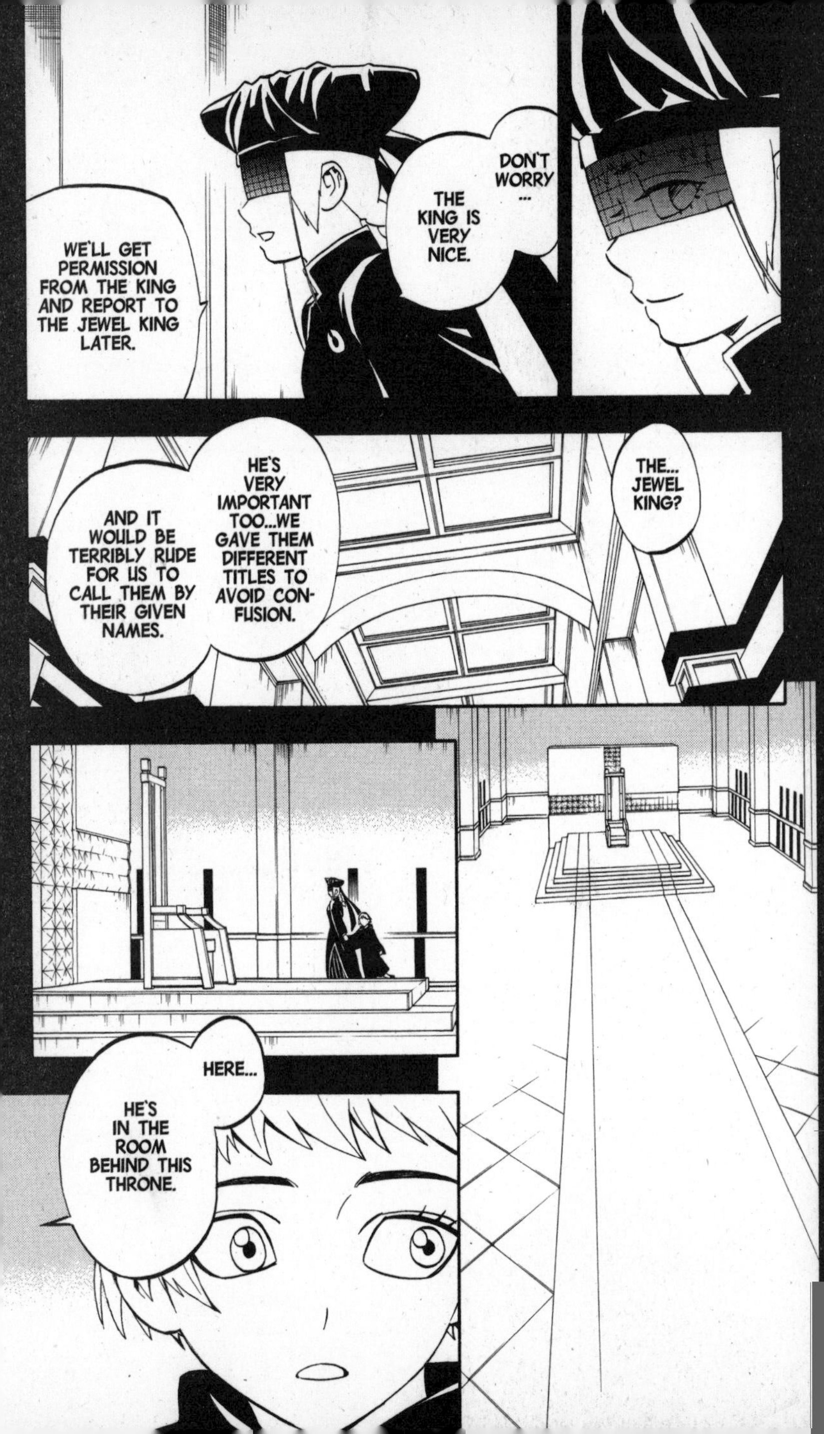
DON'T WORRY...
THE KING IS VERY NICE.
WE'LL GET PERMISSION FROM THE KING AND REPORT TO THE JEWEL KING LATER.
THE... JEWEL KING?
HE'S VERY IMPORTANT TOO...WE GAVE THEM DIFFERENT TITLES TO AVOID CON-FUSION.
AND IT WOULD BE TERRIBLY RUDE FOR US TO CALL THEM BY THEIR GIVEN NAMES.
HERE...
HE'S IN THE ROOM BEHIND THIS THRONE.

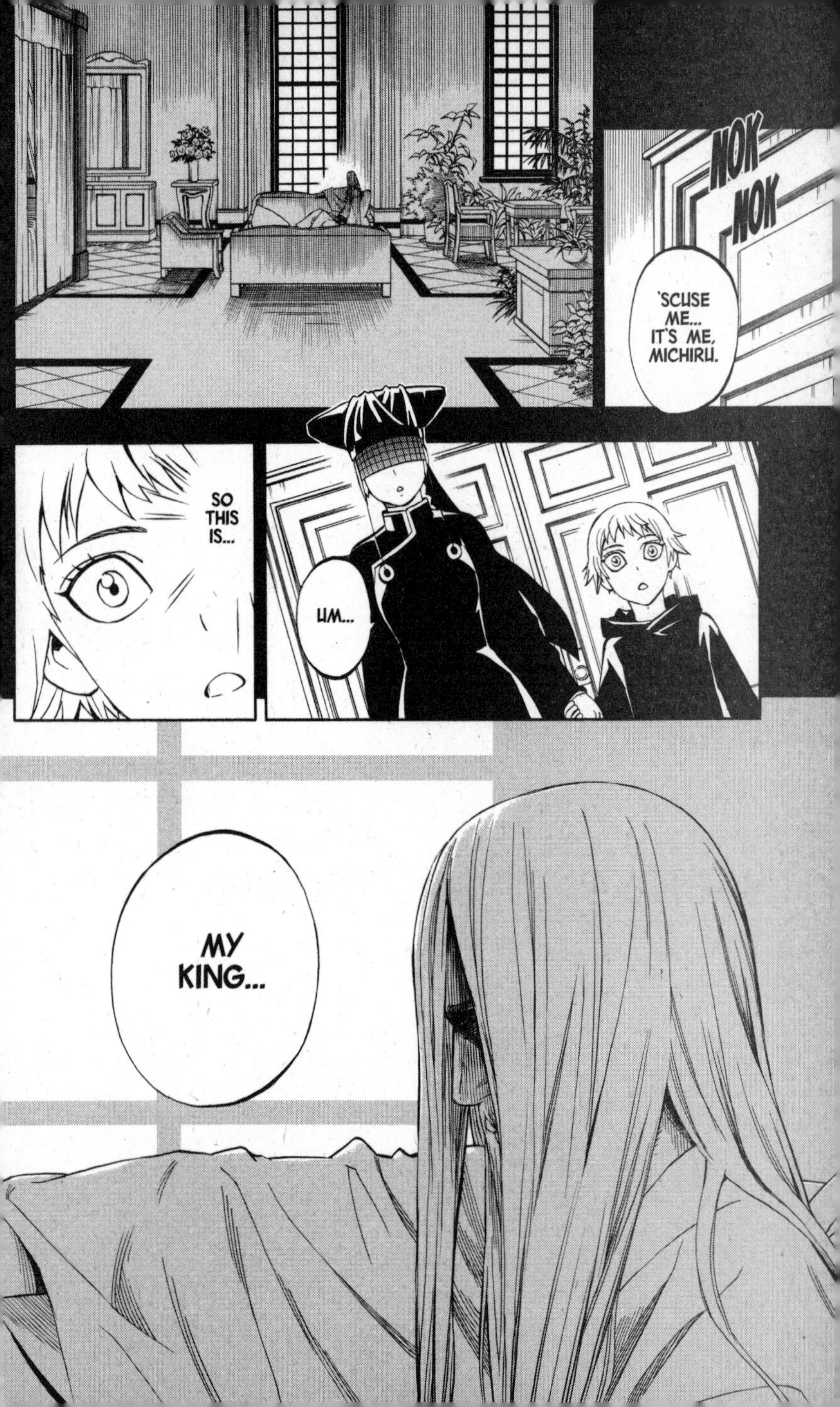
NOK NOK
'SCUSE ME... IT'S ME, MICHIRU.
UM...
SO THIS IS...
MY KING...

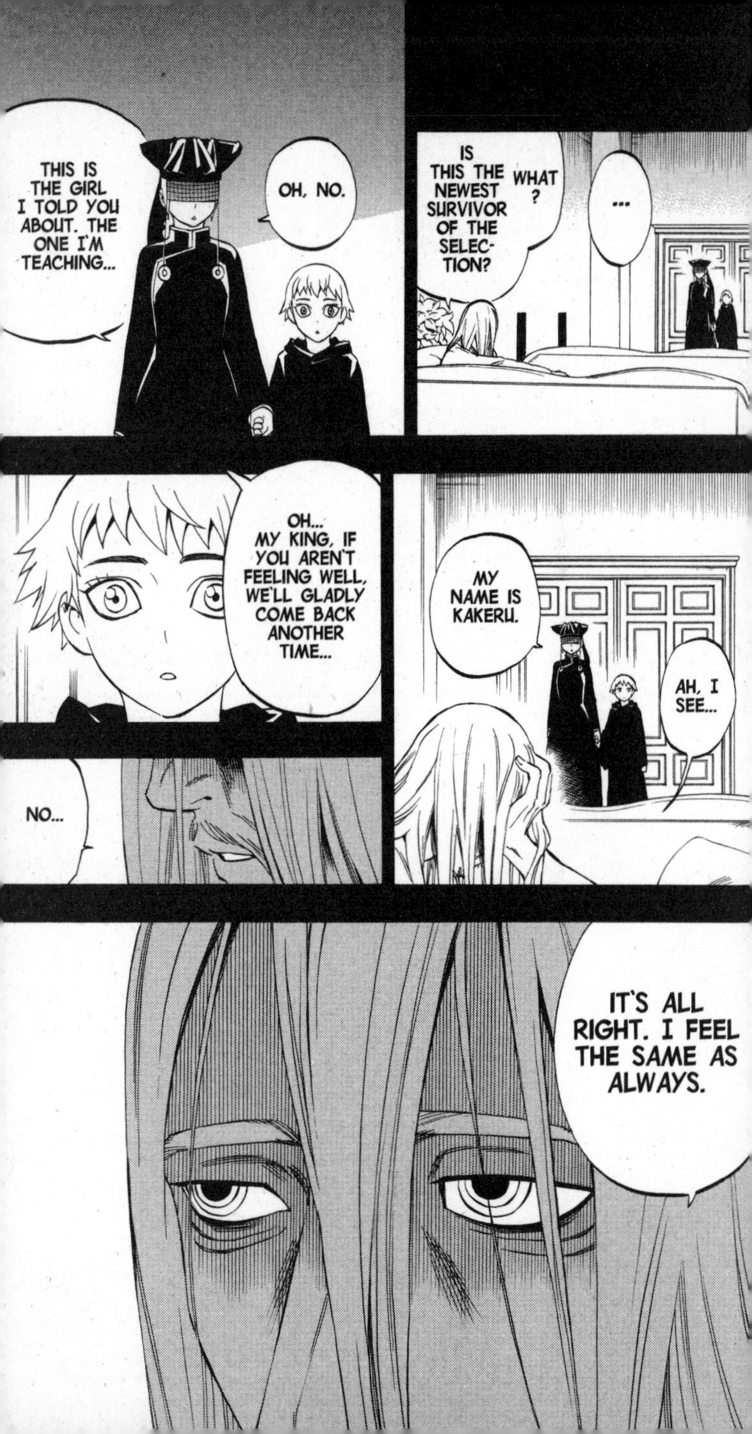
...
WHAT?
IS THIS THE NEWEST SURVIVOR OF THE SELECTION?
OH, NO.
THIS IS THE GIRL I TOLD YOU ABOUT. THE ONE I'M TEACHING...
MY NAME IS KAKERU.
AH, I SEE...
OH... MY KING, IF YOU AREN'T FEELING WELL, WE'LL GLADLY COME BACK ANOTHER TIME...
NO...
IT'S ALL RIGHT. I FEEL THE SAME AS ALWAYS.

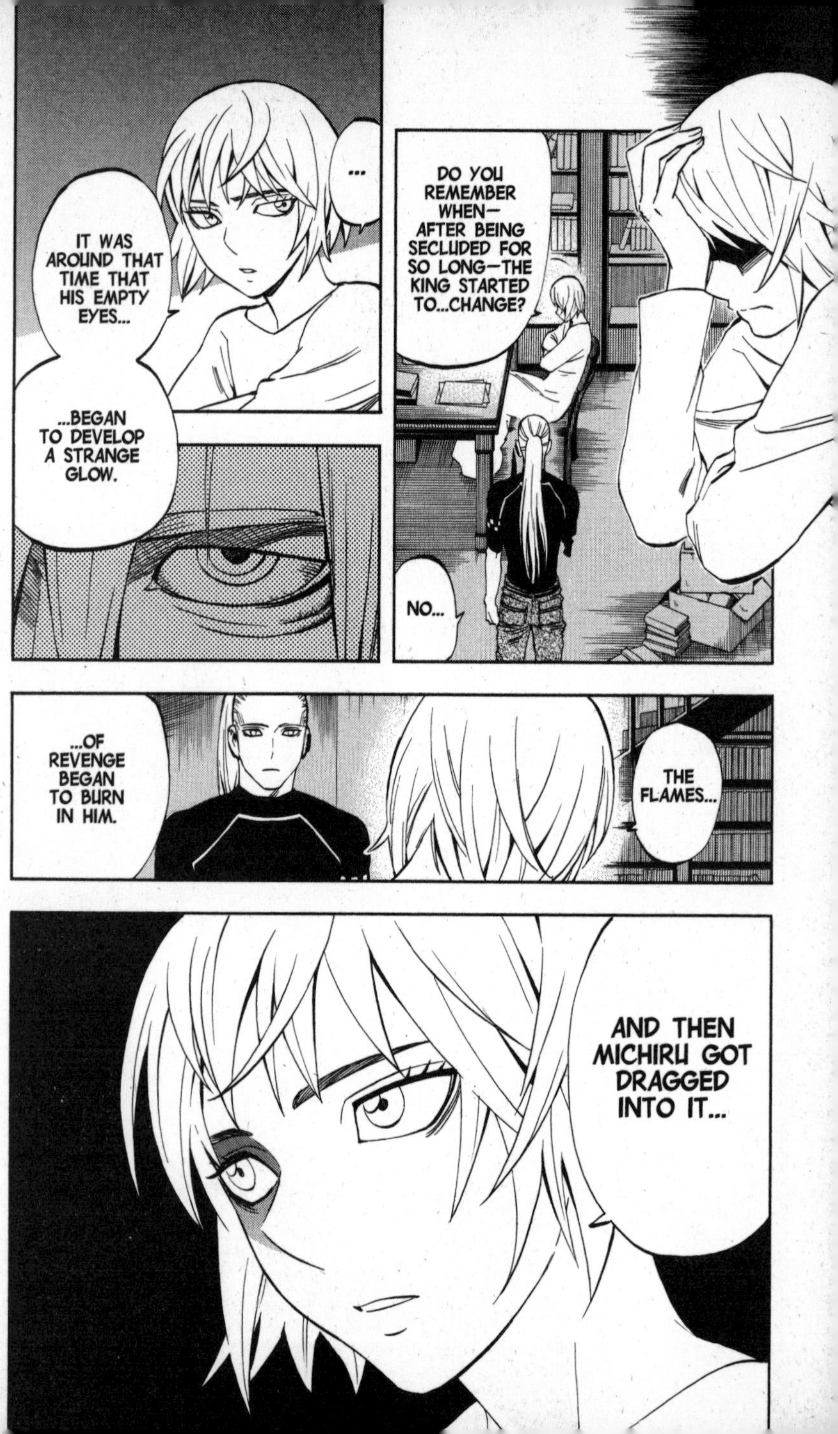
DO YOU REMEMBER WHEN—AFTER BEING SECLUDED FOR SO LONG—THE KING STARTED TO...CHANGE?
NO...
...
IT WAS AROUND THAT TIME THAT HIS EMPTY EYES...
...BEGAN TO DEVELOP A STRANGE GLOW.
THE FLAMES...
...OF REVENGE BEGAN TO BURN IN HIM.
AND THEN MICHIRU GOT DRAGGED INTO IT...

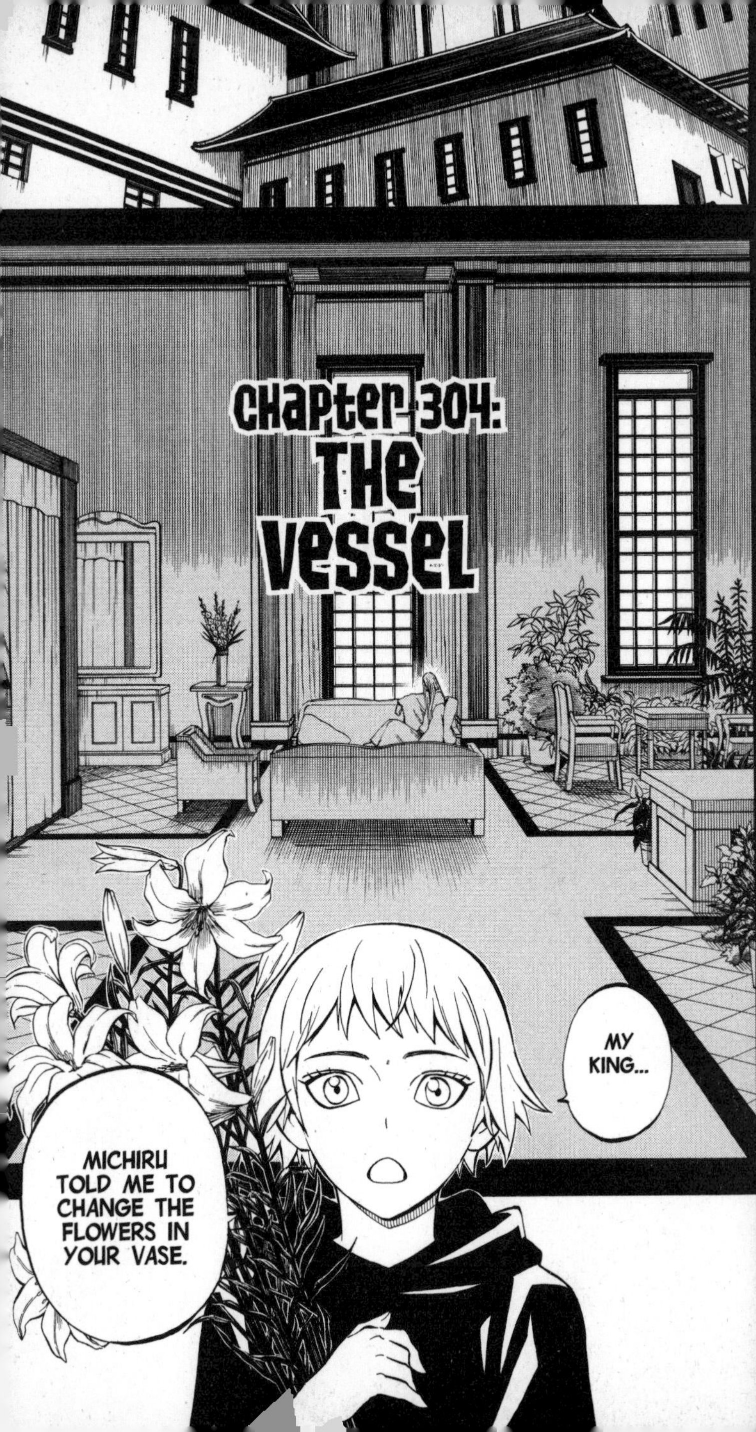
CHAPTER 304:
THE VESSEL
MY KING...
MICHIRU TOLD ME TO CHANGE THE FLOWERS IN YOUR VASE.

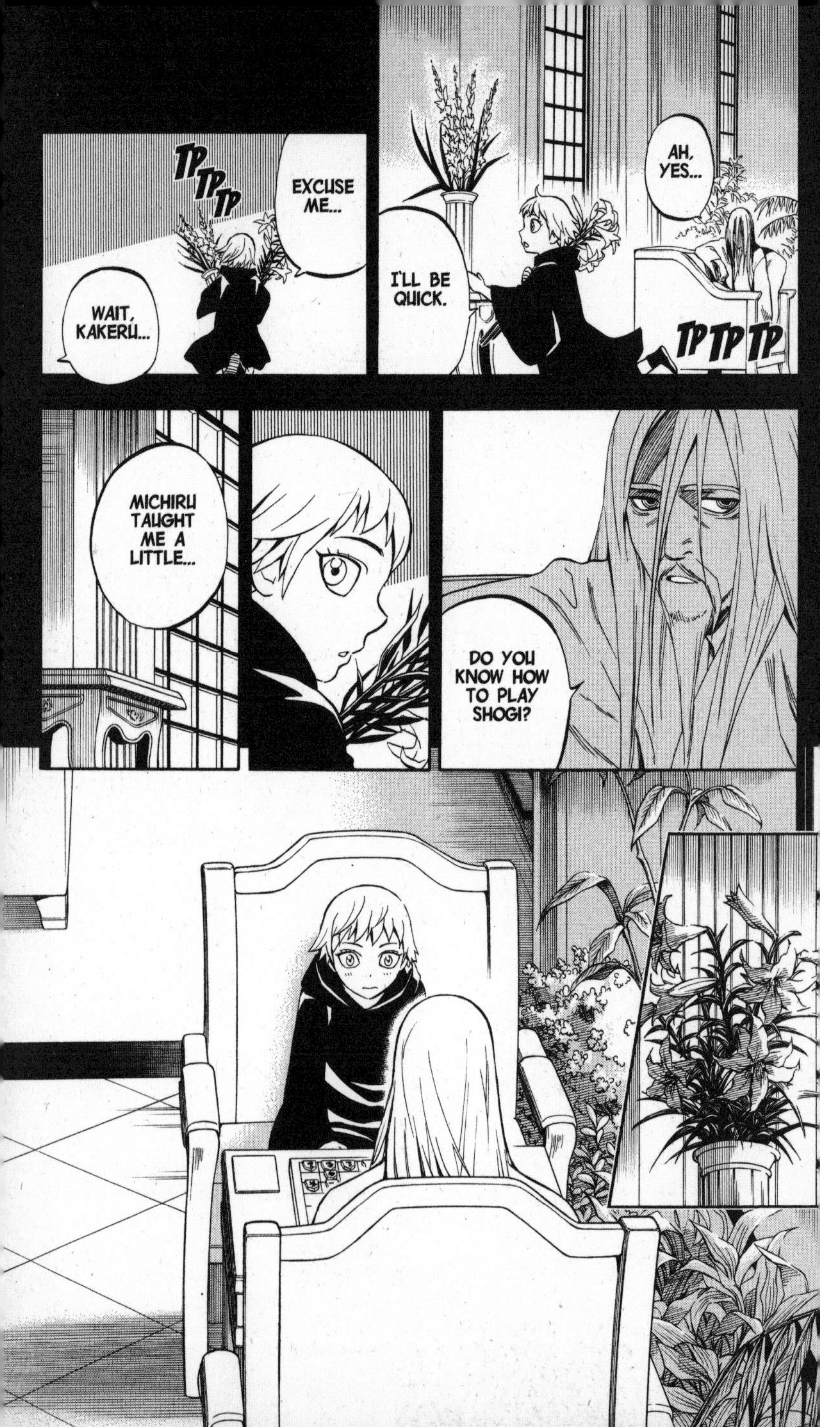
AH, YES...
I'LL BE QUICK.
TP TP TP
EXCUSE ME...
TP TP TP
WAIT, KAKERU...
DO YOU KNOW HOW TO PLAY SHOGI?
MICHIRU TAUGHT ME A LITTLE...

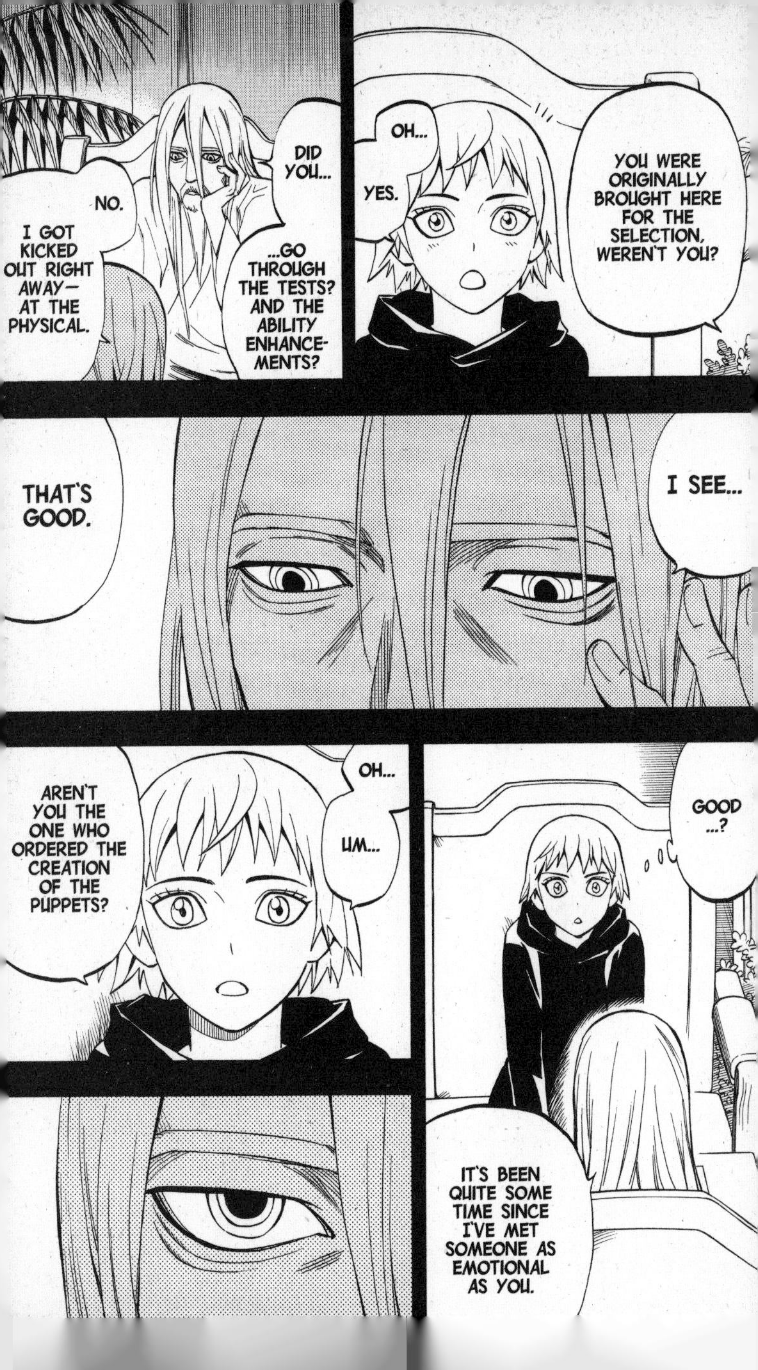
YOU WERE ORIGINALLY BROUGHT HERE FOR THE SELECTION, WEREN'T YOU?
OH...
YES.
DID YOU...
...GO THROUGH THE TESTS? AND THE ABILITY ENHANCEMENTS?
NO.
I GOT KICKED OUT RIGHT AWAY—AT THE PHYSICAL.
I SEE...
THAT'S GOOD.
GOOD ...?
IT'S BEEN QUITE SOME TIME SINCE I'VE MET SOMEONE AS EMOTIONAL AS YOU.
OH...
UM...
AREN'T YOU THE ONE WHO ORDERED THE CREATION OF THE PUPPETS?

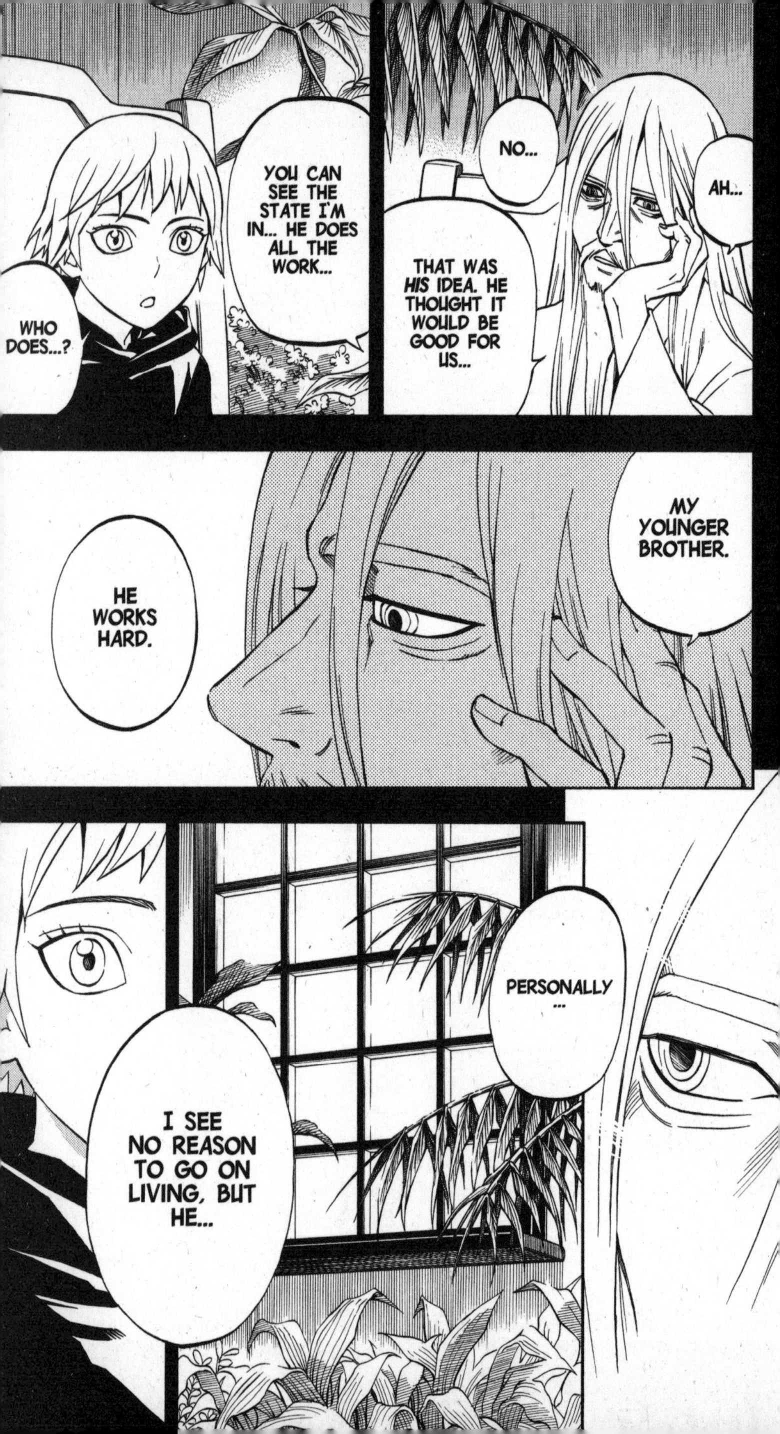
AH...
NO...
THAT WAS *HIS* IDEA. HE THOUGHT IT WOULD BE GOOD FOR US...
YOU CAN SEE THE STATE I'M IN... HE DOES ALL THE WORK...
WHO DOES...?
MY YOUNGER BROTHER.
HE WORKS HARD.
PERSONALLY...
I SEE NO REASON TO GO ON LIVING, BUT HE...

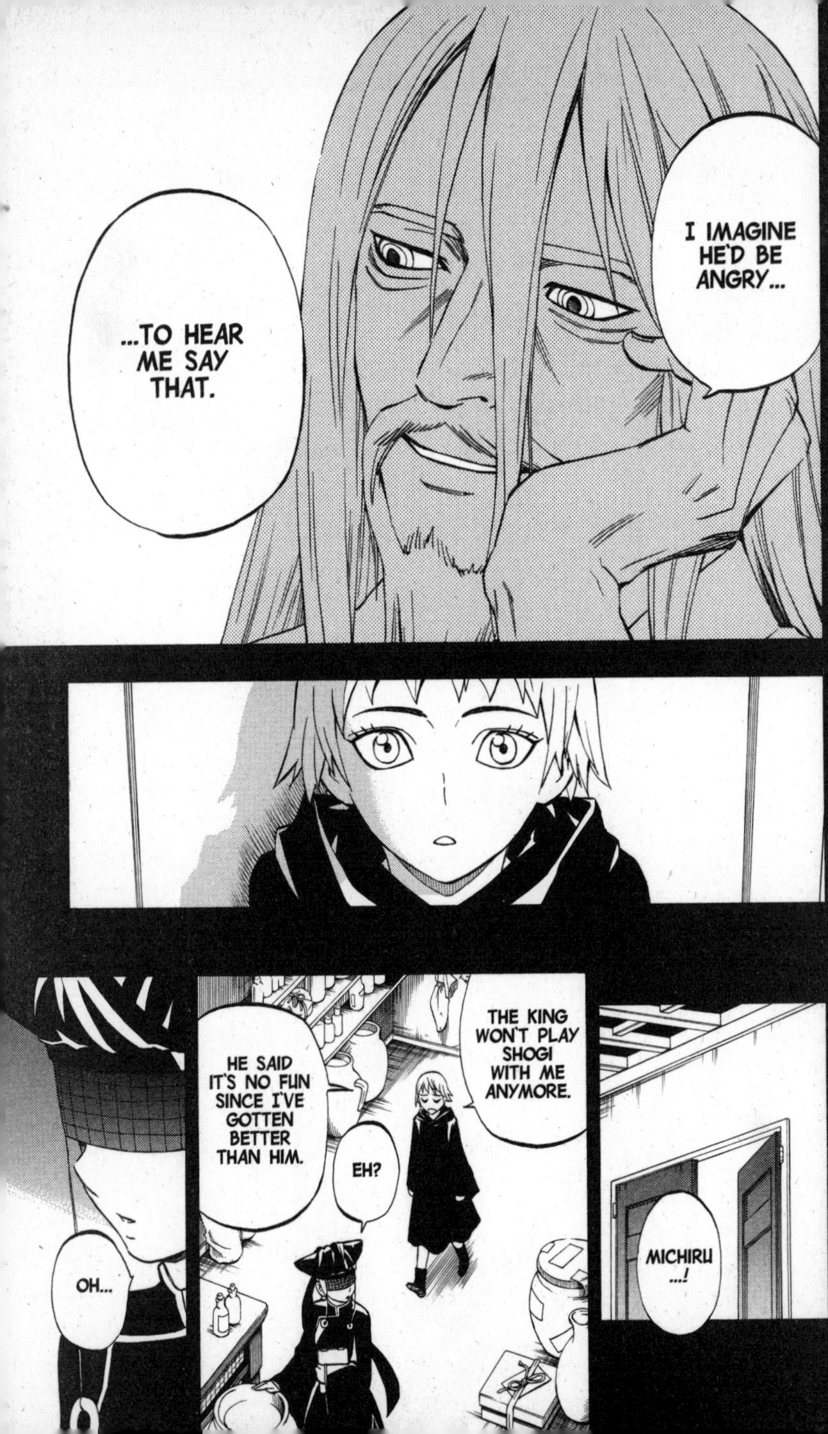
I IMAGINE HE'D BE ANGRY...
...TO HEAR ME SAY THAT.
MICHIRU ...!
THE KING WON'T PLAY SHOGI WITH ME ANYMORE.
HE SAID IT'S NO FUN SINCE I'VE GOTTEN BETTER THAN HIM.
EH?
OH...

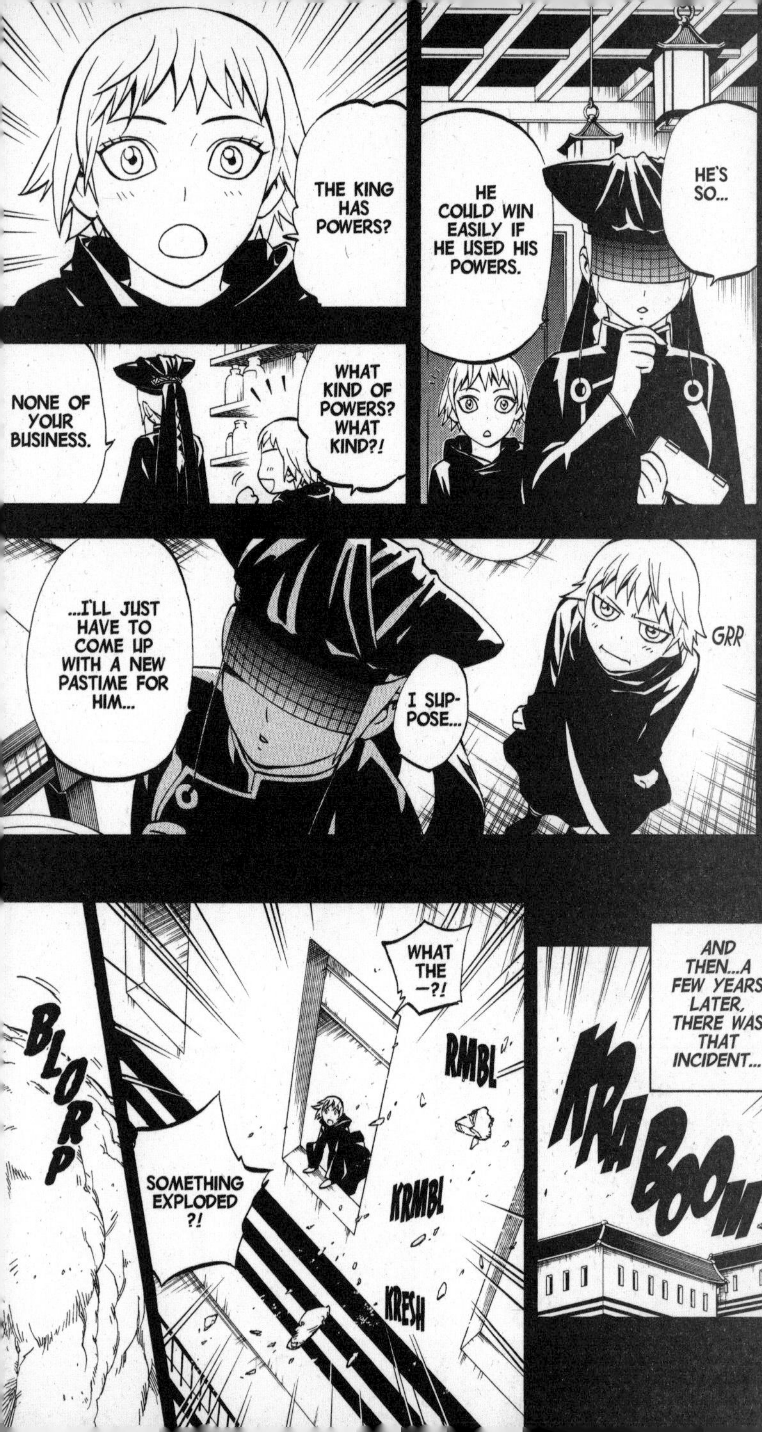
HE'S SO...
HE COULD WIN EASILY IF HE USED HIS POWERS.
THE KING HAS POWERS?
WHAT KIND OF POWERS? WHAT KIND?!
NONE OF YOUR BUSINESS.
GRR
I SUP-POSE...
...I'LL JUST HAVE TO COME UP WITH A NEW PASTIME FOR HIM...
AND THEN...A FEW YEARS LATER, THERE WAS THAT INCIDENT...
KRA BOOM
WHAT THE—?!
RMBL
KRMBL
KRESH
SOMETHING EXPLODED?!
BLORP

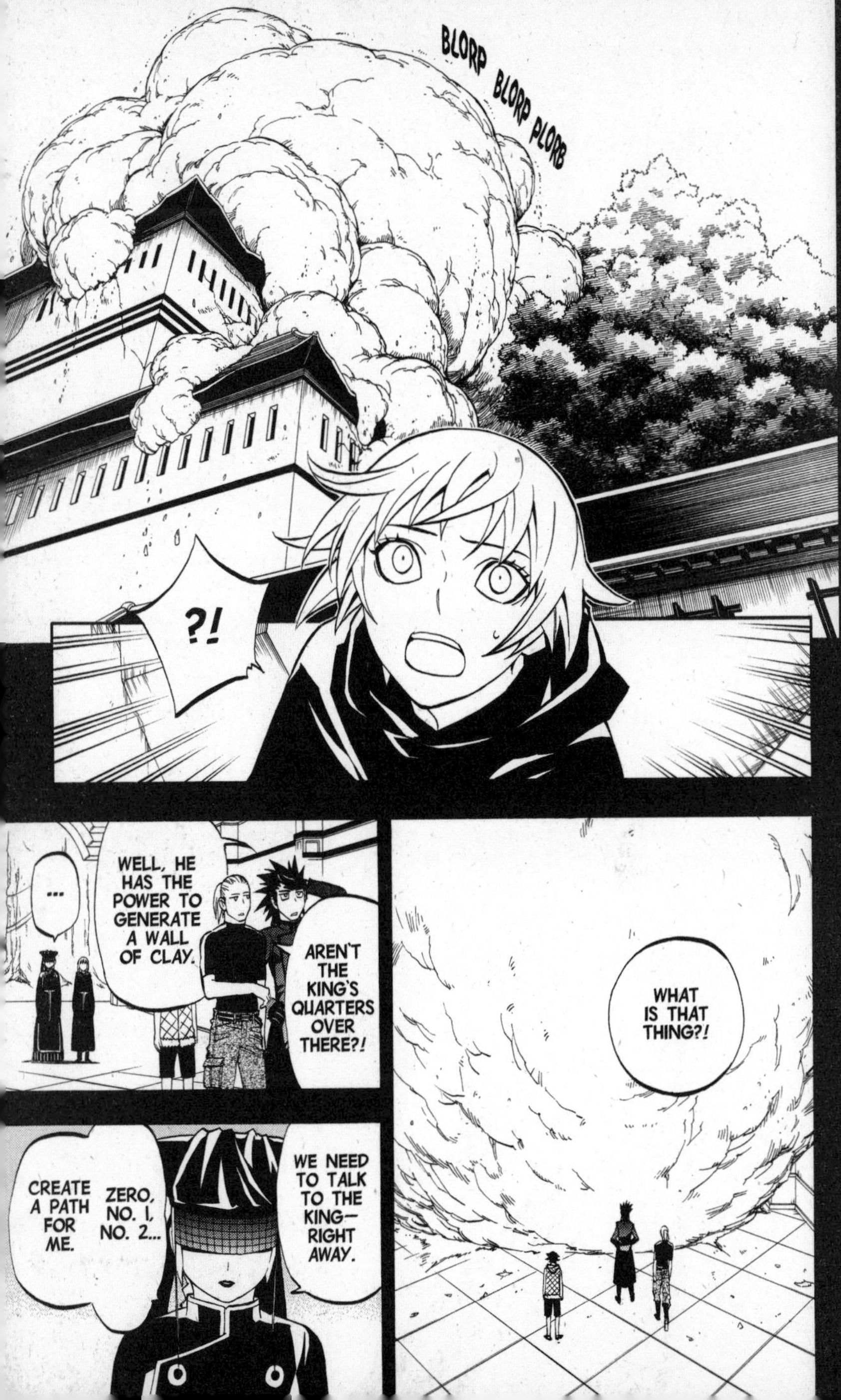
BLORP BLORP PLORB
?!
WHAT IS THAT THING?!
AREN'T THE KING'S QUARTERS OVER THERE?!
WELL, HE HAS THE POWER TO GENERATE A WALL OF CLAY.
...
WE NEED TO TALK TO THE KING— RIGHT AWAY.
ZERO, NO. 1, NO. 2...
CREATE A PATH FOR ME.

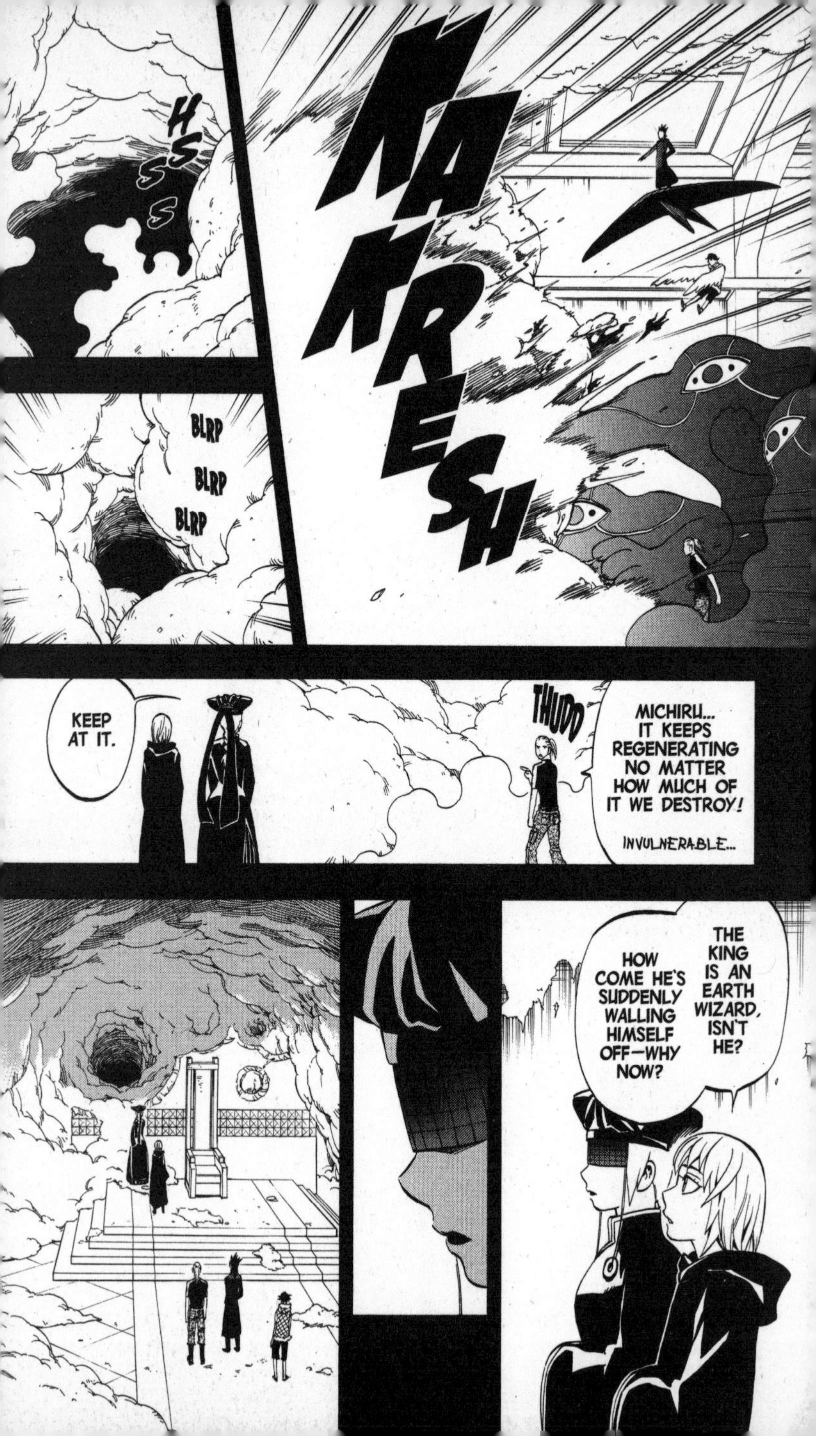
KAKRESH
HSSS
BLRP
BLRP
BLRP
MICHIRU... IT KEEPS REGENERATING NO MATTER HOW MUCH OF IT WE DESTROY!
THUDD
INVULNERABLE...
KEEP AT IT.
THE KING IS AN EARTH WIZARD, ISN'T HE?
HOW COME HE'S SUDDENLY WALLING HIMSELF OFF—WHY NOW?

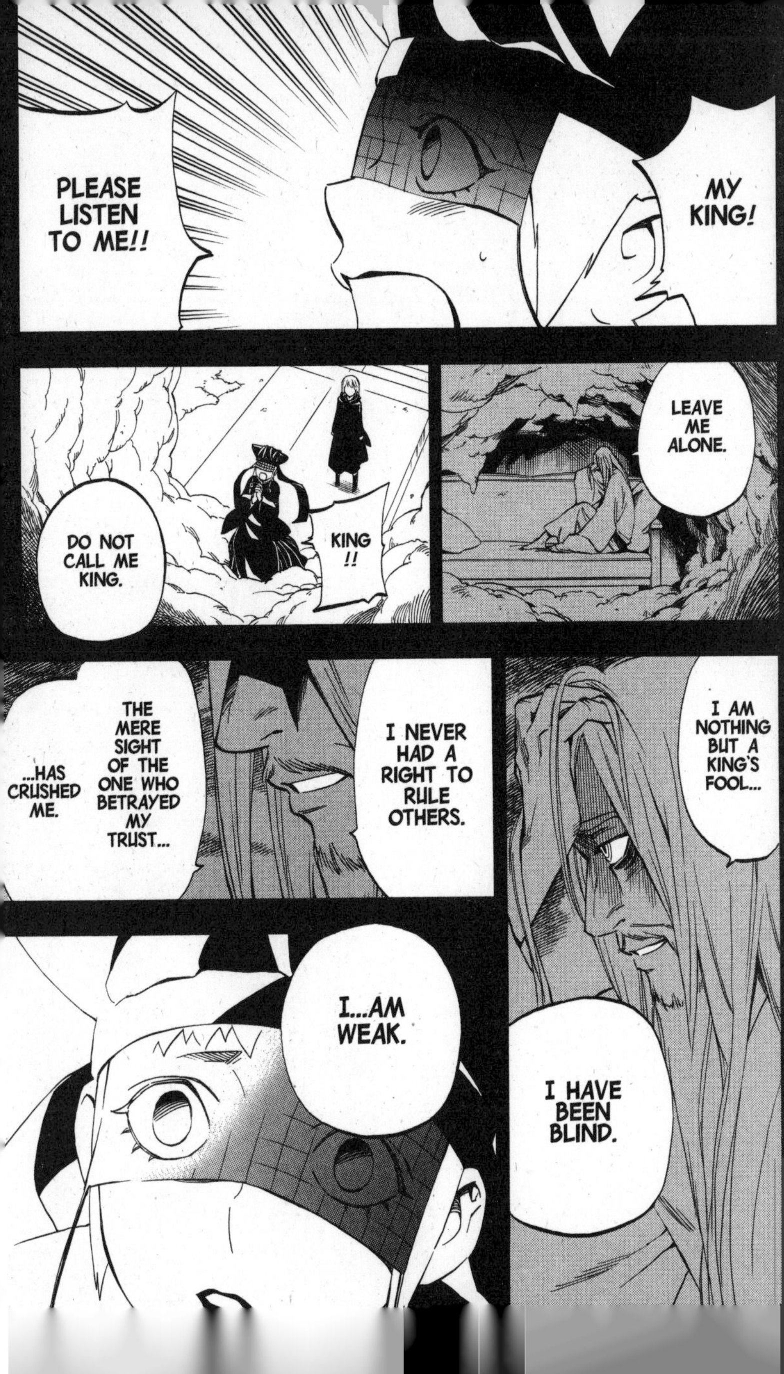
MY KING!
PLEASE LISTEN TO ME!!
LEAVE ME ALONE.
KING!!
DO NOT CALL ME KING.
I AM NOTHING BUT A KING'S FOOL...
I HAVE BEEN BLIND.
I NEVER HAD A RIGHT TO RULE OTHERS.
THE MERE SIGHT OF THE ONE WHO BETRAYED MY TRUST...
...HAS CRUSHED ME.
I...AM WEAK.

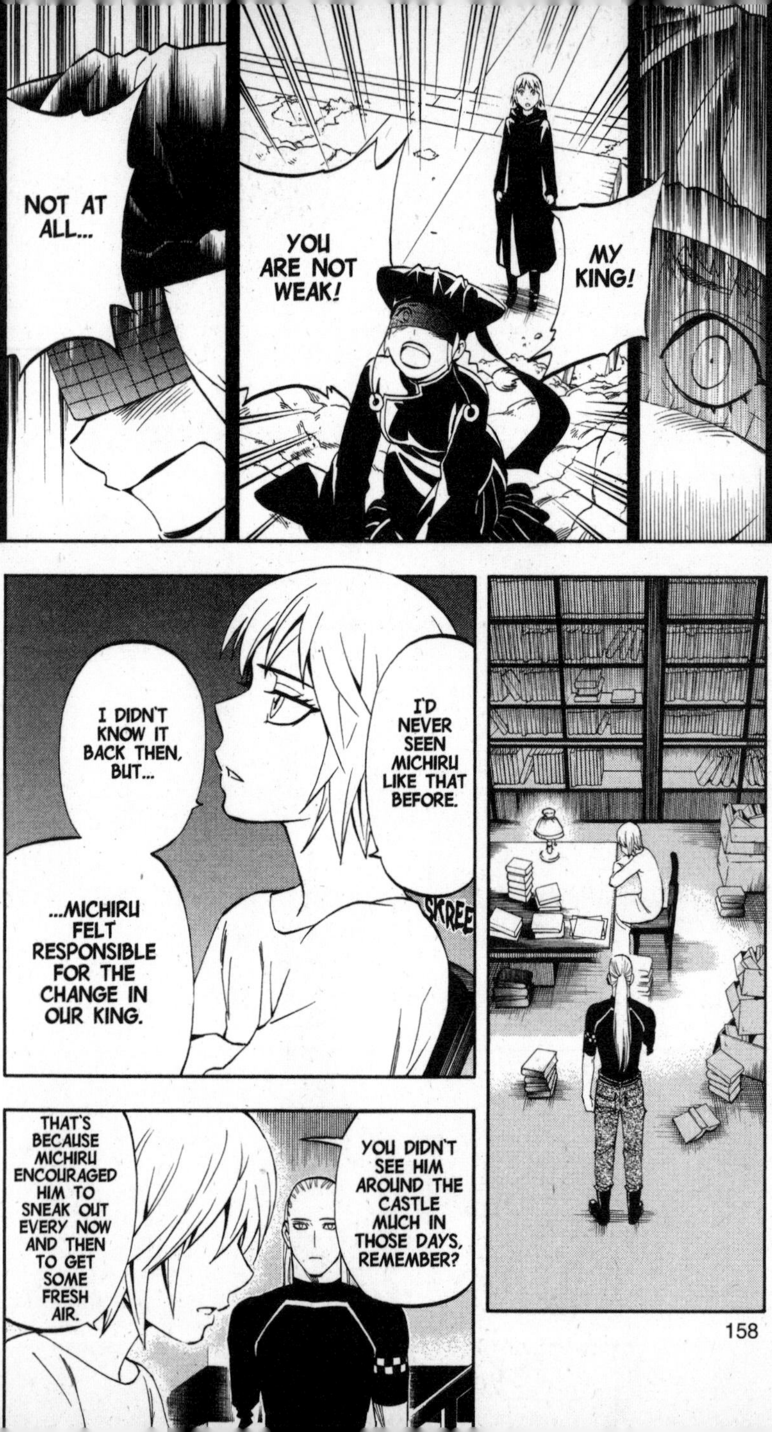
MY KING!
YOU ARE NOT WEAK!
NOT AT ALL...
SKREE
I'D NEVER SEEN MICHIRU LIKE THAT BEFORE.
I DIDN'T KNOW IT BACK THEN, BUT...
...MICHIRU FELT RESPONSIBLE FOR THE CHANGE IN OUR KING.
YOU DIDN'T SEE HIM AROUND THE CASTLE MUCH IN THOSE DAYS, REMEMBER?
THAT'S BECAUSE MICHIRU ENCOURAGED HIM TO SNEAK OUT EVERY NOW AND THEN TO GET SOME FRESH AIR.

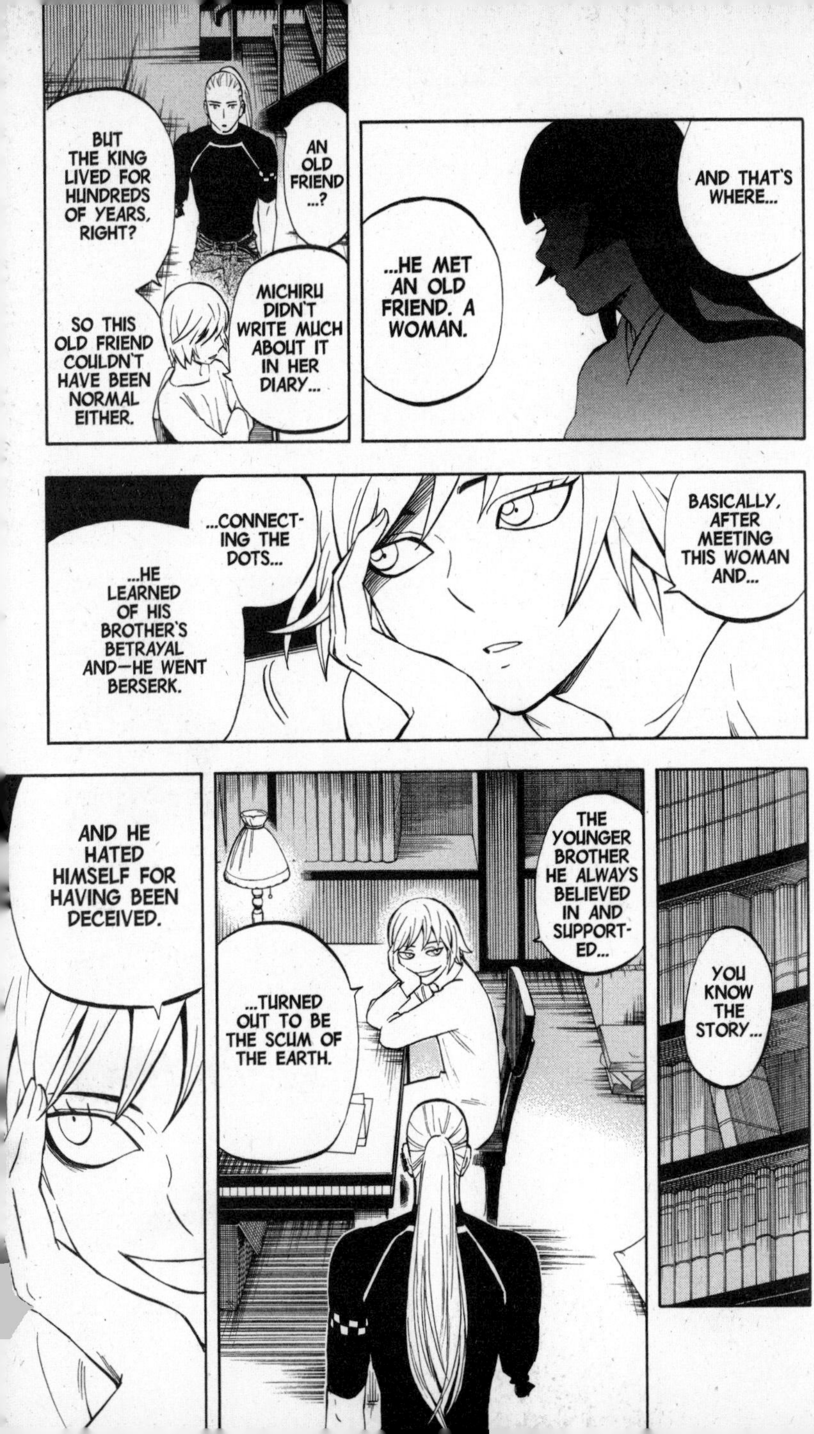
AND THAT'S WHERE...
...HE MET AN OLD FRIEND. A WOMAN.
AN OLD FRIEND...?
BUT THE KING LIVED FOR HUNDREDS OF YEARS, RIGHT?
MICHIRU DIDN'T WRITE MUCH ABOUT IT IN HER DIARY...
SO THIS OLD FRIEND COULDN'T HAVE BEEN NORMAL EITHER.
BASICALLY, AFTER MEETING THIS WOMAN AND...
...CONNECTING THE DOTS...
...HE LEARNED OF HIS BROTHER'S BETRAYAL AND—HE WENT BERSERK.
YOU KNOW THE STORY...
THE YOUNGER BROTHER HE ALWAYS BELIEVED IN AND SUPPORTED...
...TURNED OUT TO BE THE SCUM OF THE EARTH.
AND HE HATED HIMSELF FOR HAVING BEEN DECEIVED.

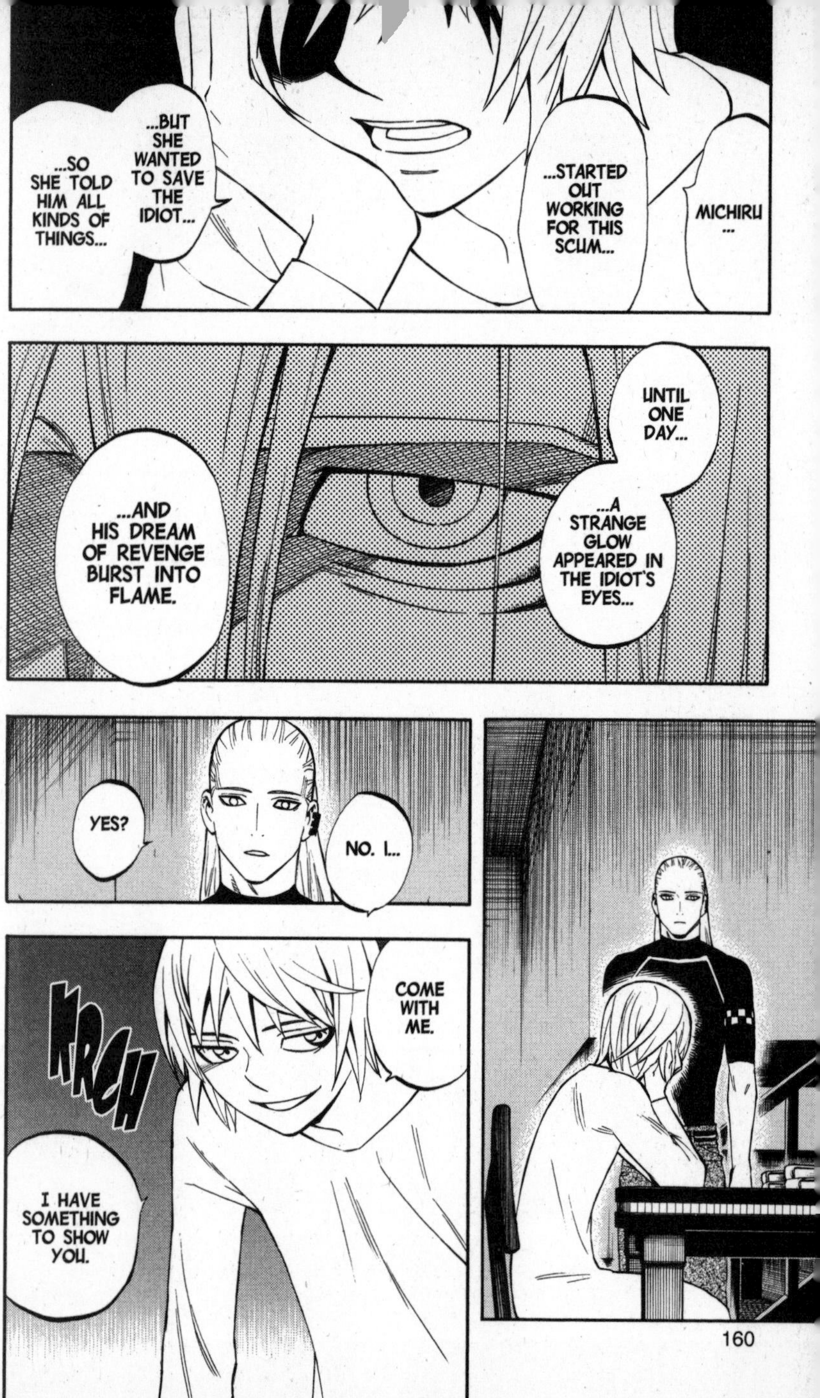
MICHIRU ...
...STARTED OUT WORKING FOR THIS SCUM...
...BUT SHE WANTED TO SAVE THE IDIOT...
...SO SHE TOLD HIM ALL KINDS OF THINGS...
UNTIL ONE DAY...
...A STRANGE GLOW APPEARED IN THE IDIOT'S EYES...
...AND HIS DREAM OF REVENGE BURST INTO FLAME.
NO. I...
YES?
COME WITH ME.
KRCH
I HAVE SOMETHING TO SHOW YOU.

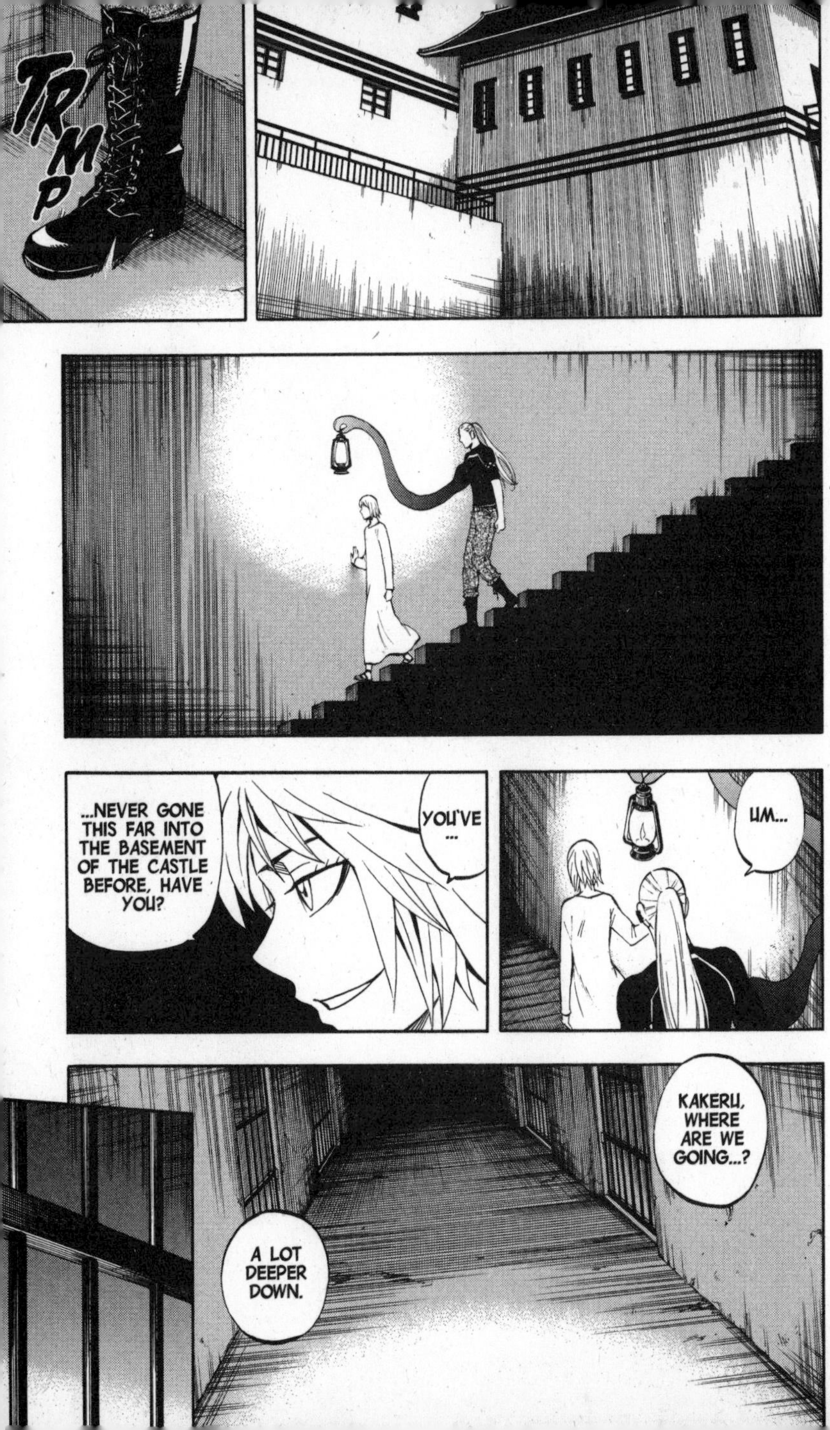
TRMP
UM...
YOU'VE ...
...NEVER GONE THIS FAR INTO THE BASEMENT OF THE CASTLE BEFORE, HAVE YOU?
KAKERU, WHERE ARE WE GOING...?
A LOT DEEPER DOWN.

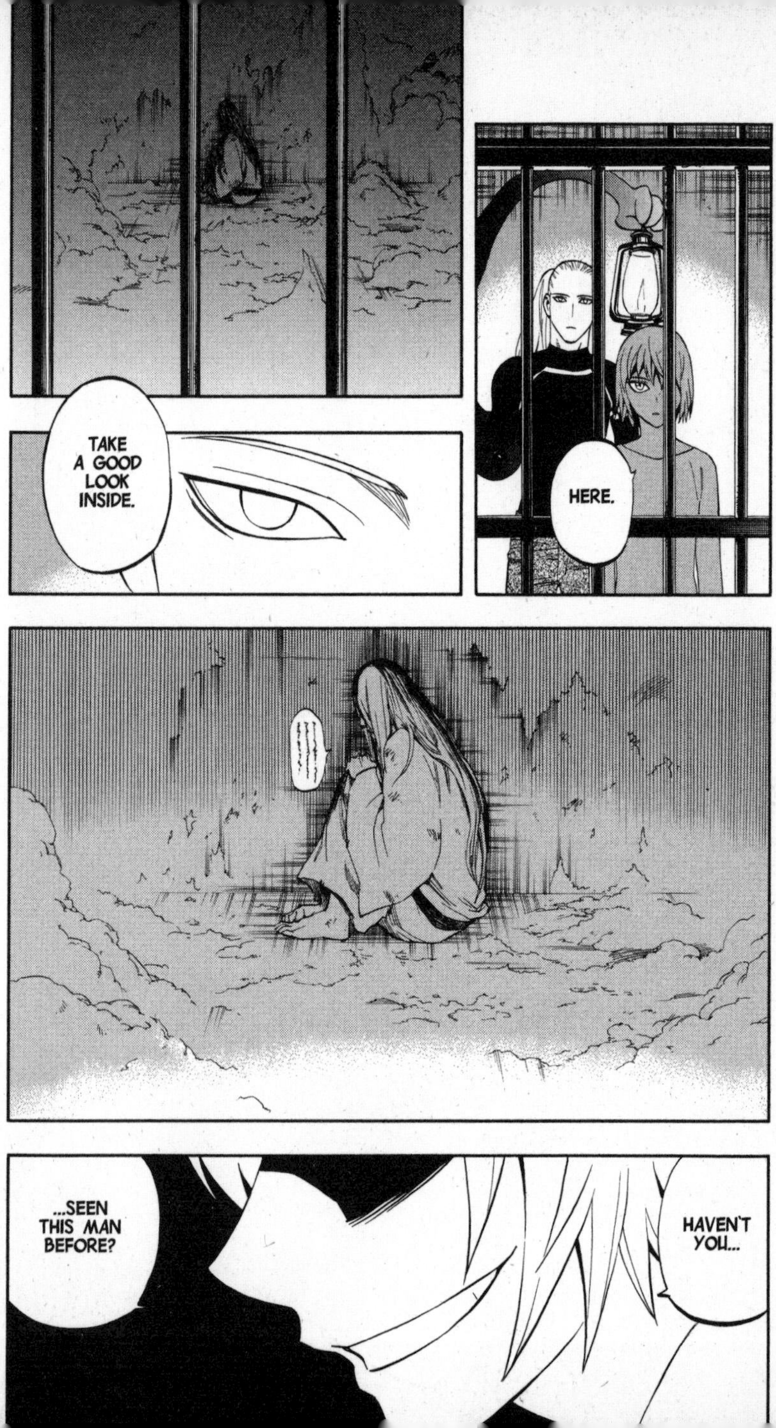
HERE.
TAKE A GOOD LOOK INSIDE.
HAVEN'T YOU...
...SEEN THIS MAN BEFORE?

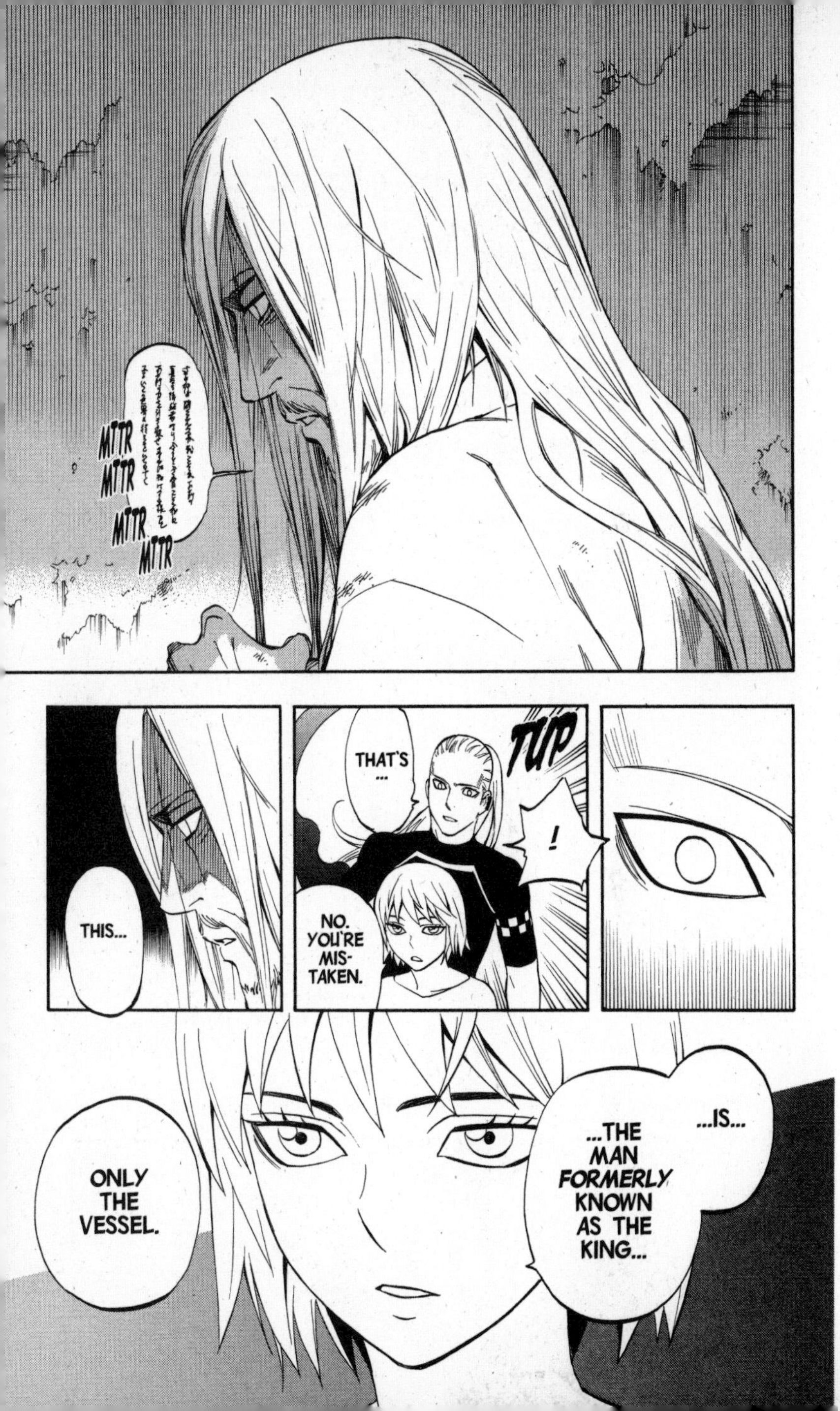
MITR
MITR
MITR
MITR
TUP
THAT'S...
!
NO. YOU'RE MIS-TAKEN.
THIS...
...IS...
...THE MAN FORMERLY KNOWN AS THE KING...
ONLY THE VESSEL.

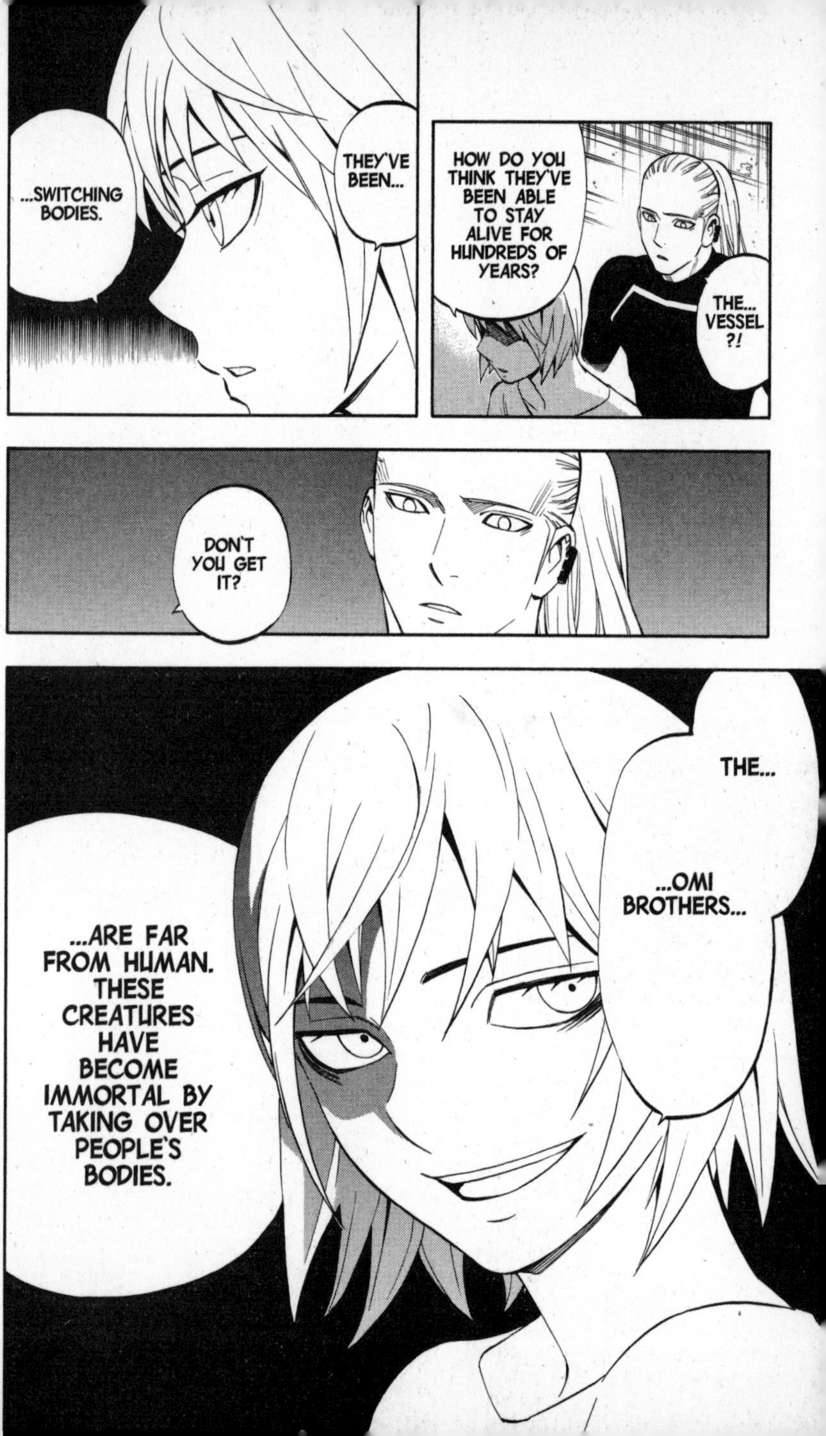
THE... VESSEL ?!
HOW DO YOU THINK THEY'VE BEEN ABLE TO STAY ALIVE FOR HUNDREDS OF YEARS?
THEY'VE BEEN...
...SWITCHING BODIES.
DON'T YOU GET IT?
THE...
...OMI BROTHERS...
...ARE FAR FROM HUMAN. THESE CREATURES HAVE BECOME IMMORTAL BY TAKING OVER PEOPLE'S BODIES.

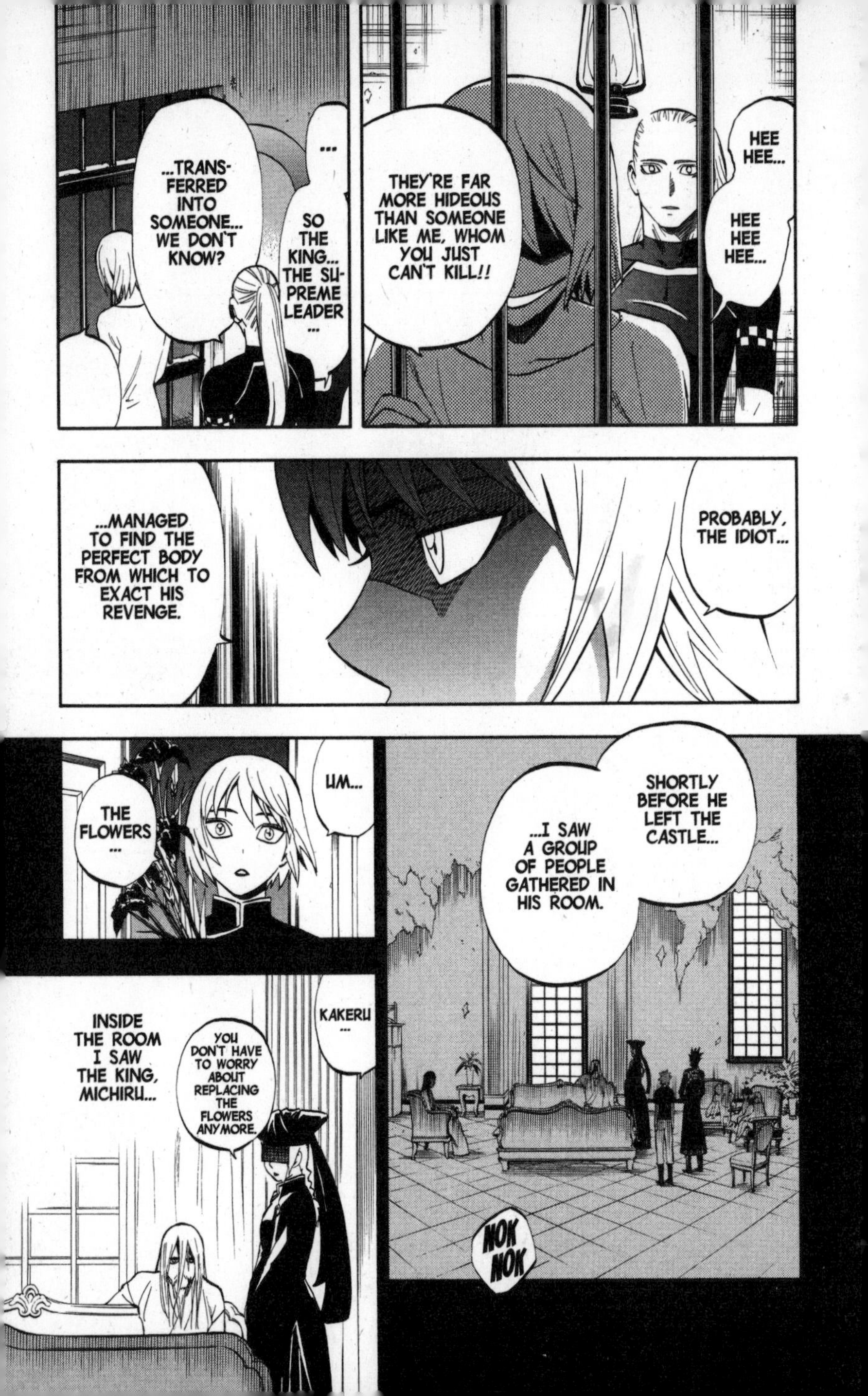
HEE HEE...
HEE HEE HEE...
THEY'RE FAR MORE HIDEOUS THAN SOMEONE LIKE ME, WHOM YOU JUST CAN'T KILL!!
...
SO THE KING... THE SUPREME LEADER...
...TRANSFERRED INTO SOMEONE... WE DON'T KNOW?
PROBABLY, THE IDIOT...
...MANAGED TO FIND THE PERFECT BODY FROM WHICH TO EXACT HIS REVENGE.
SHORTLY BEFORE HE LEFT THE CASTLE...
...I SAW A GROUP OF PEOPLE GATHERED IN HIS ROOM.
NOK NOK
UM...
THE FLOWERS...
KAKERU...
YOU DON'T HAVE TO WORRY ABOUT REPLACING THE FLOWERS ANYMORE.
INSIDE THE ROOM I SAW THE KING, MICHIRU...

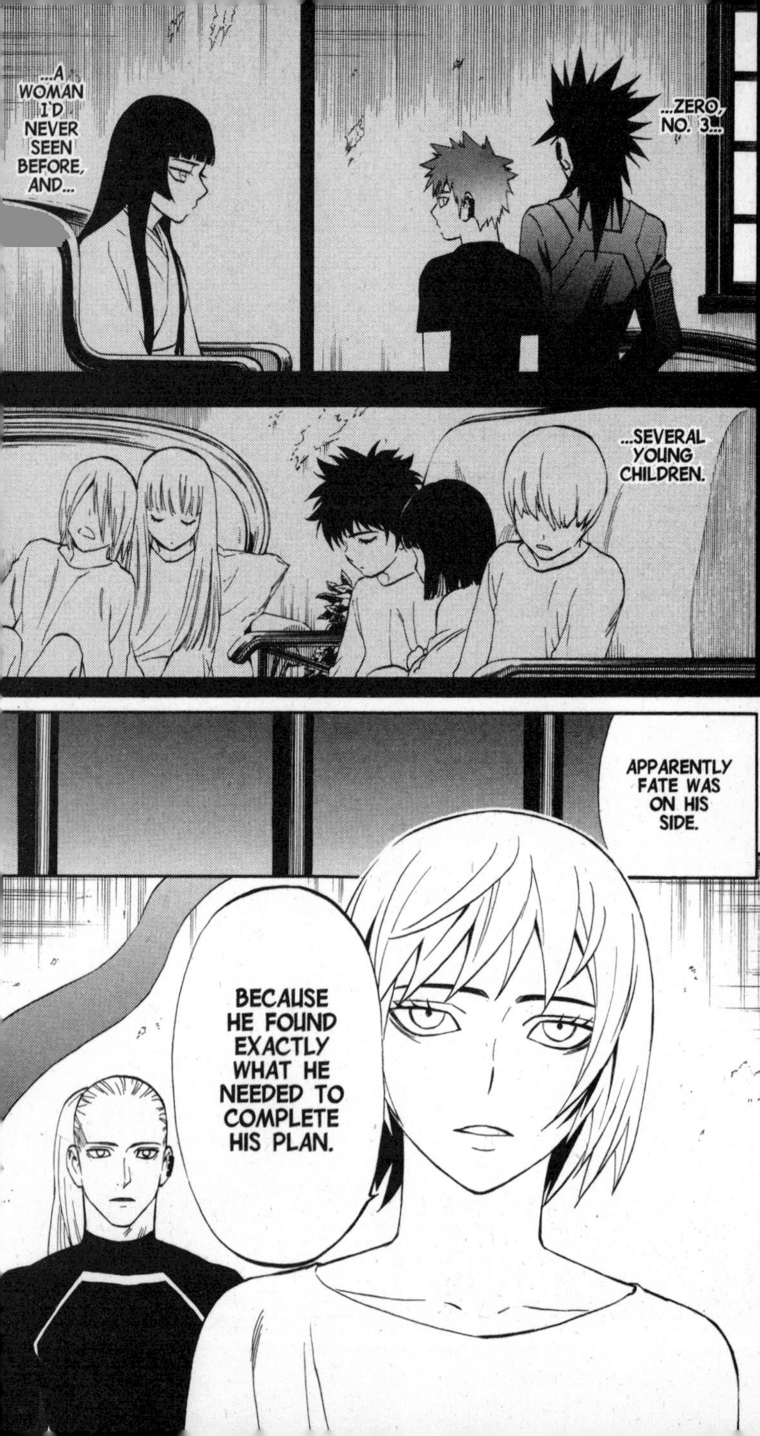
...ZERO, NO. 3...
...A WOMAN I'D NEVER SEEN BEFORE, AND...
...SEVERAL YOUNG CHILDREN.
APPARENTLY FATE WAS ON HIS SIDE.
BECAUSE HE FOUND EXACTLY WHAT HE NEEDED TO COMPLETE HIS PLAN.

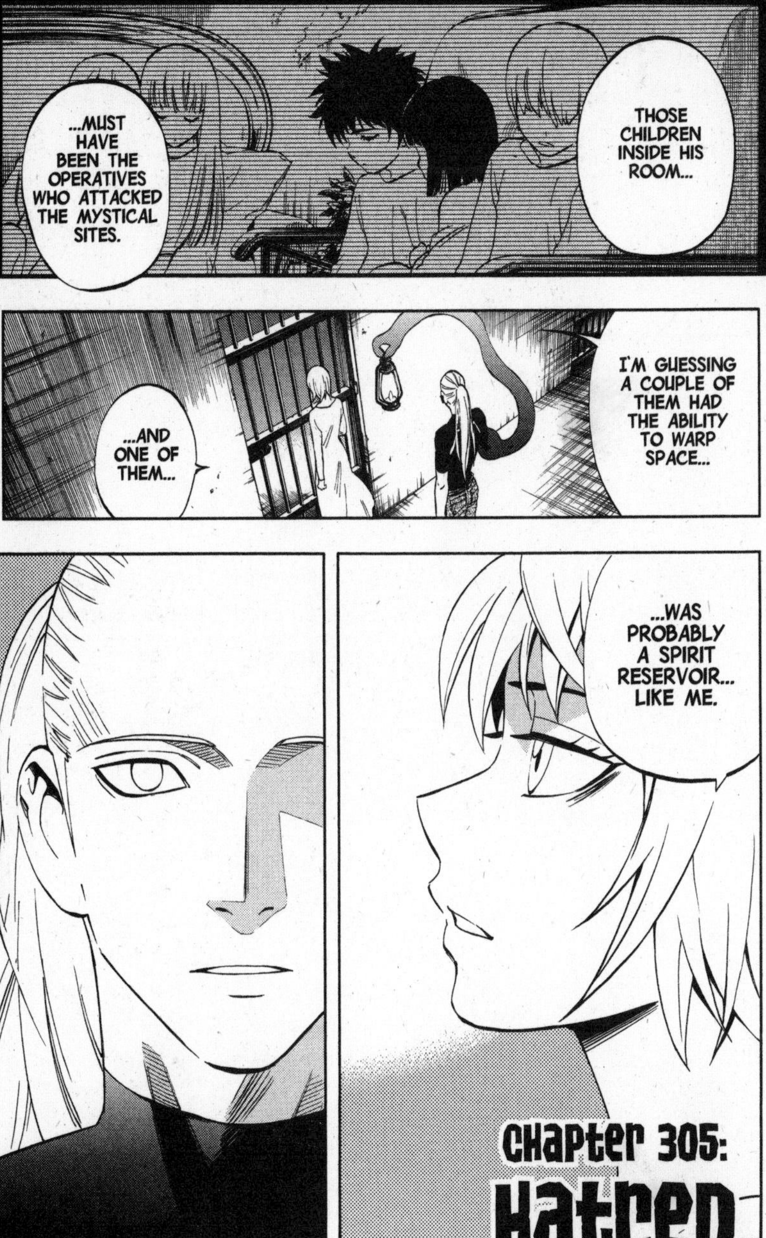
THOSE CHILDREN INSIDE HIS ROOM...
...MUST HAVE BEEN THE OPERATIVES WHO ATTACKED THE MYSTICAL SITES.
I'M GUESSING A COUPLE OF THEM HAD THE ABILITY TO WARP SPACE...
...AND ONE OF THEM...
...WAS PROBABLY A SPIRIT RESERVOIR... LIKE ME.
Chapter 305:
Hatred

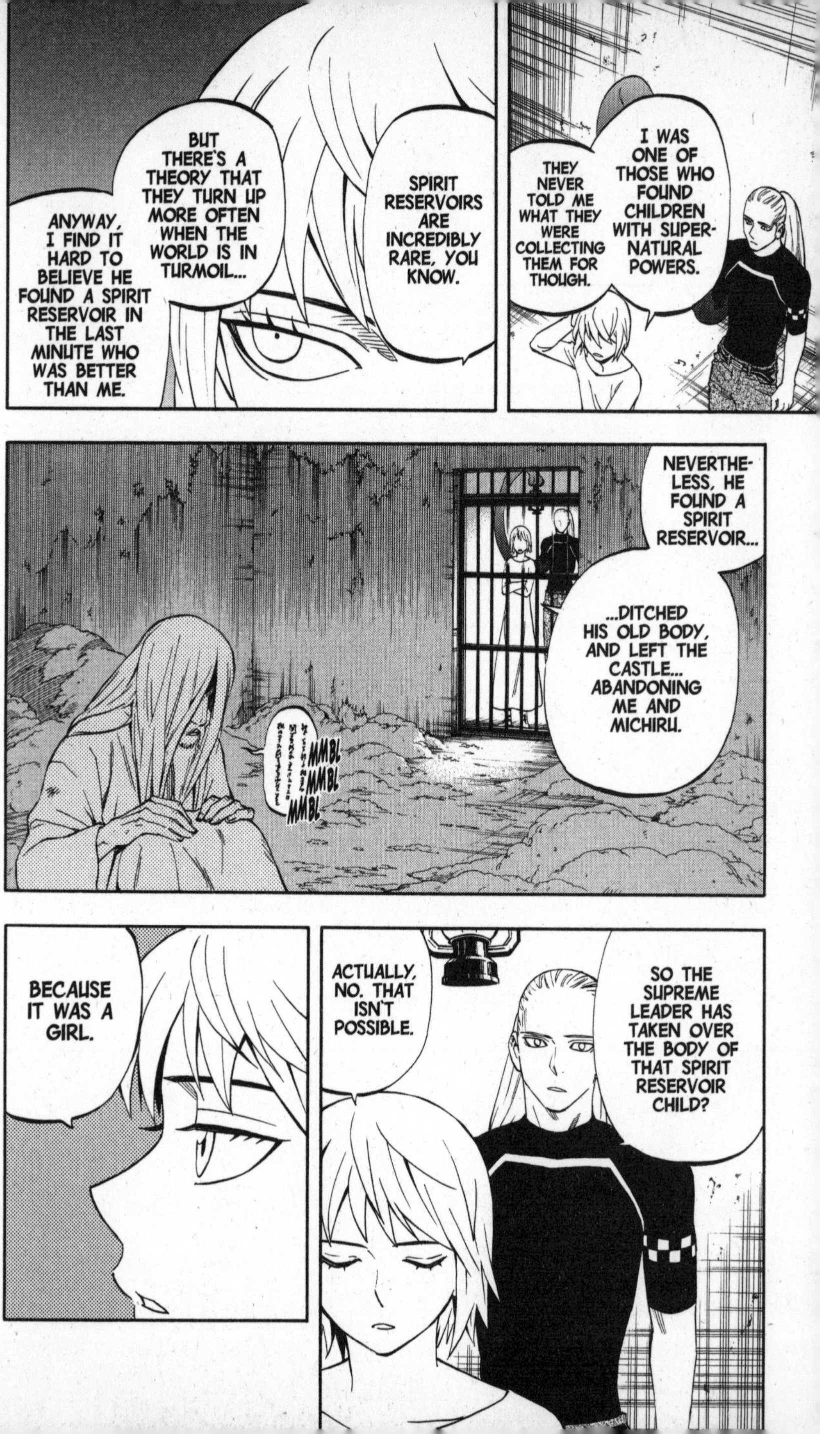
I WAS ONE OF THOSE WHO FOUND CHILDREN WITH SUPER-NATURAL POWERS.
THEY NEVER TOLD ME WHAT THEY WERE COLLECTING THEM FOR THOUGH.
SPIRIT RESERVOIRS ARE INCREDIBLY RARE, YOU KNOW.
BUT THERE'S A THEORY THAT THEY TURN UP MORE OFTEN WHEN THE WORLD IS IN TURMOIL...
ANYWAY, I FIND IT HARD TO BELIEVE HE FOUND A SPIRIT RESERVOIR IN THE LAST MINUTE WHO WAS BETTER THAN ME.
NEVERTHE-LESS, HE FOUND A SPIRIT RESERVOIR...
...DITCHED HIS OLD BODY, AND LEFT THE CASTLE... ABANDONING ME AND MICHIRU.
MMBL MMBL MMBL
SO THE SUPREME LEADER HAS TAKEN OVER THE BODY OF THAT SPIRIT RESERVOIR CHILD?
ACTUALLY, NO. THAT ISN'T POSSIBLE.
BECAUSE IT WAS A GIRL.

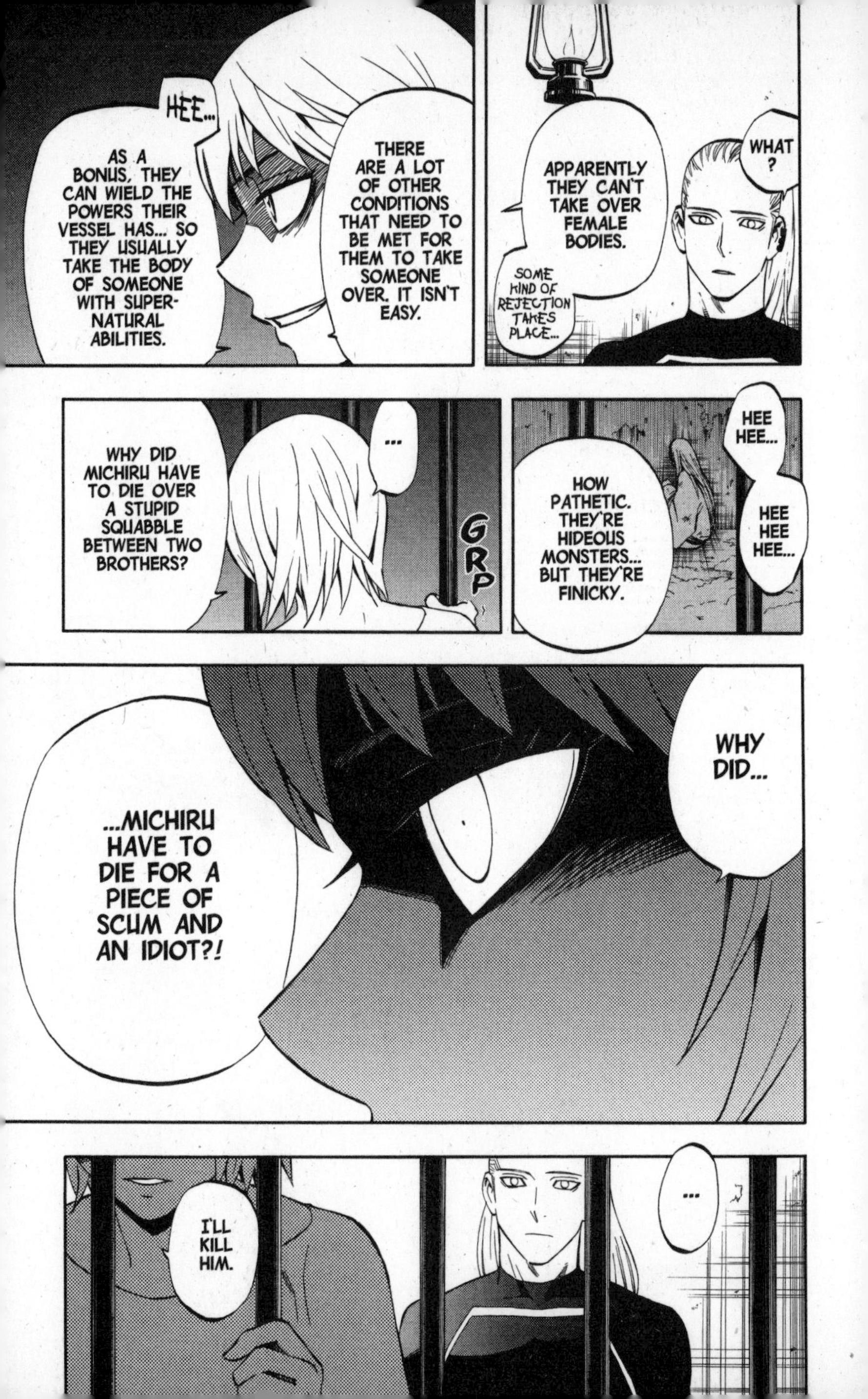
WHAT?
APPARENTLY THEY CAN'T TAKE OVER FEMALE BODIES.
SOME KIND OF REJECTION TAKES PLACE...
HEE...
THERE ARE A LOT OF OTHER CONDITIONS THAT NEED TO BE MET FOR THEM TO TAKE SOMEONE OVER. IT ISN'T EASY.
AS A BONUS, THEY CAN WIELD THE POWERS THEIR VESSEL HAS... SO THEY USUALLY TAKE THE BODY OF SOMEONE WITH SUPER-NATURAL ABILITIES.
HEE HEE...
HEE HEE HEE...
HOW PATHETIC. THEY'RE HIDEOUS MONSTERS... BUT THEY'RE FINICKY.
...
GRP
WHY DID MICHIRU HAVE TO DIE OVER A STUPID SQUABBLE BETWEEN TWO BROTHERS?
WHY DID...
...MICHIRU HAVE TO DIE FOR A PIECE OF SCUM AND AN IDIOT?!
...
I'LL KILL HIM.

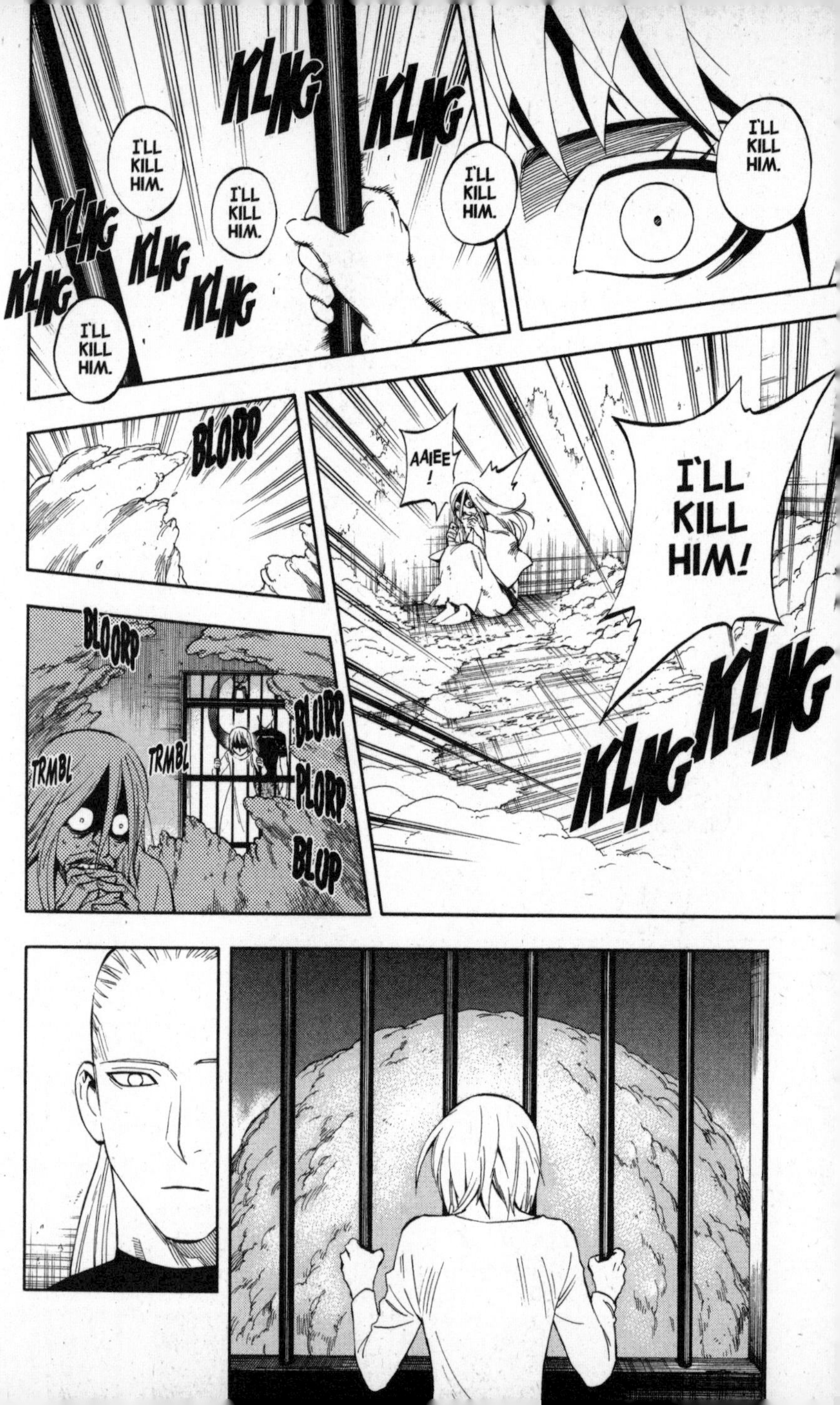
I'LL KILL HIM.
I'LL KILL HIM.
KLNG
KLNG
I'LL KILL HIM.
KLNG
KLNG
KLNG
KLNG
I'LL KILL HIM.
I'LL KILL HIM!
KLNG
KLNG
AAIEE!
BLORP
BLOORP
BLURP
PLORP
BLUP
TRMBL
TRMBL

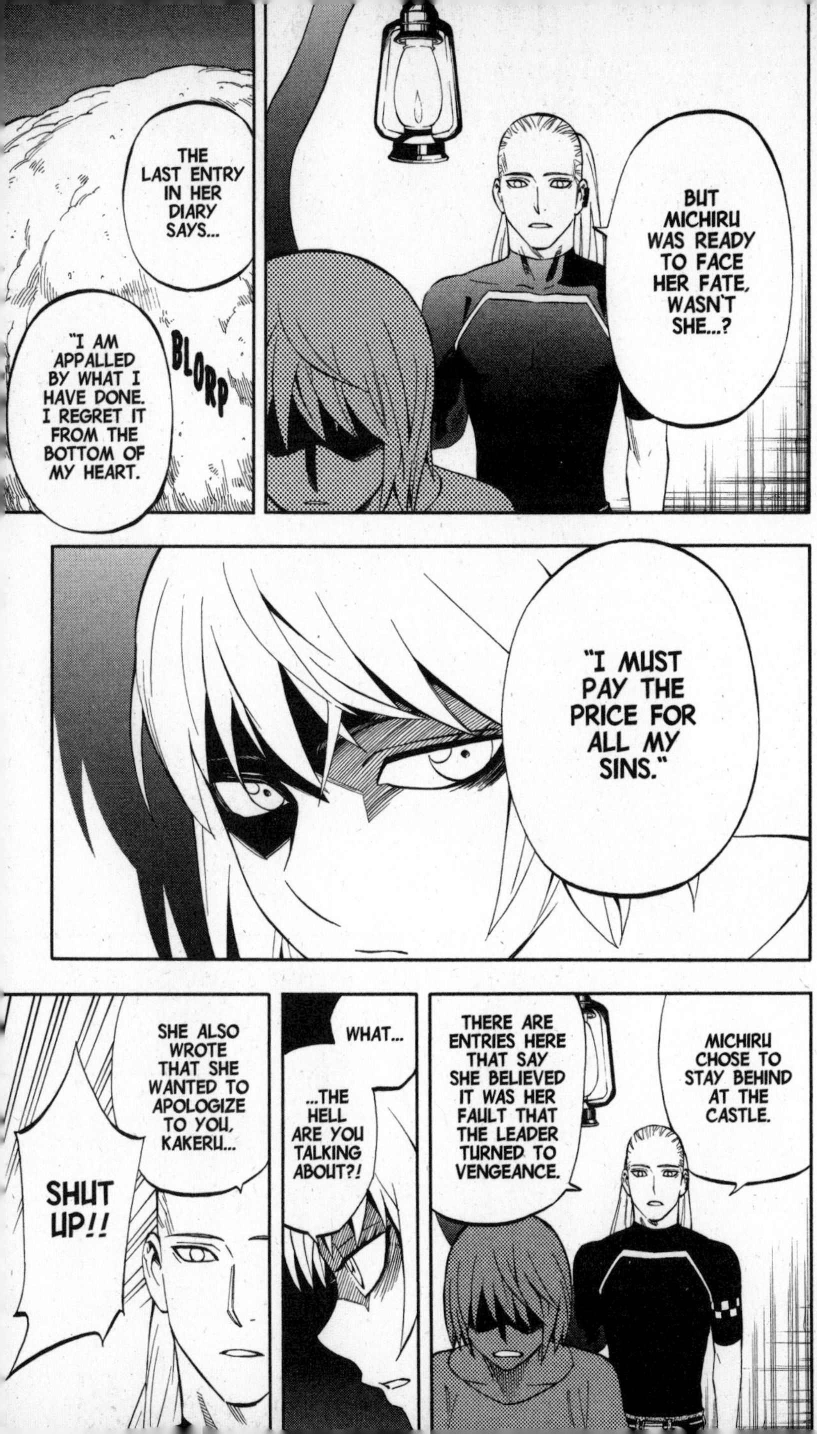
BUT MICHIRU WAS READY TO FACE HER FATE, WASN'T SHE...?
THE LAST ENTRY IN HER DIARY SAYS...
"I AM APPALLED BY WHAT I HAVE DONE. I REGRET IT FROM THE BOTTOM OF MY HEART.
BLORP
"I MUST PAY THE PRICE FOR ALL MY SINS."
MICHIRU CHOSE TO STAY BEHIND AT THE CASTLE.
THERE ARE ENTRIES HERE THAT SAY SHE BELIEVED IT WAS HER FAULT THAT THE LEADER TURNED TO VENGEANCE.
WHAT...
...THE HELL ARE YOU TALKING ABOUT?!
SHE ALSO WROTE THAT SHE WANTED TO APOLOGIZE TO YOU, KAKERU...
SHUT UP!!

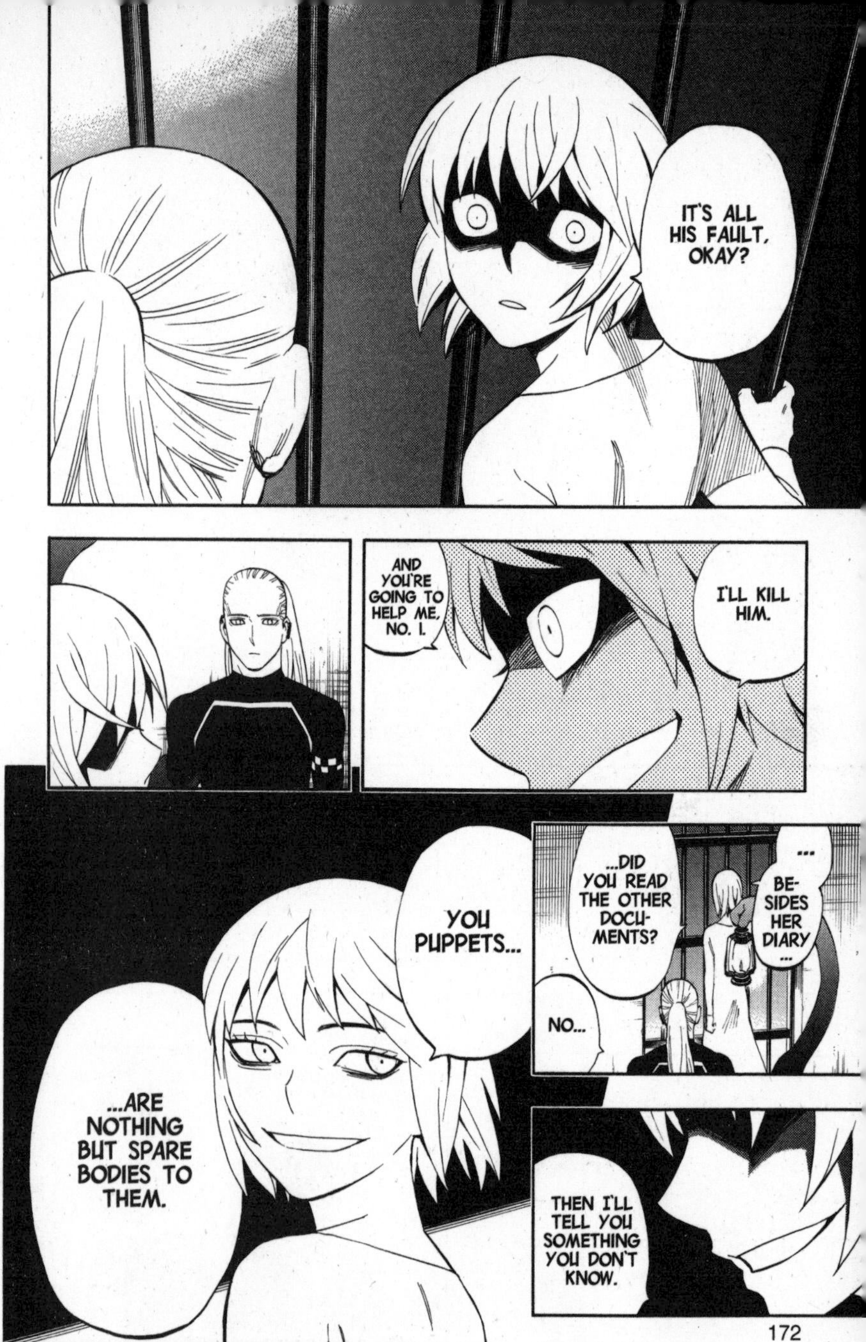
IT'S ALL HIS FAULT, OKAY?
I'LL KILL HIM.
AND YOU'RE GOING TO HELP ME, NO. 1.
...
BE-SIDES HER DIARY ...
...DID YOU READ THE OTHER DOCU-MENTS?
NO...
THEN I'LL TELL YOU SOMETHING YOU DON'T KNOW.
YOU PUPPETS...
...ARE NOTHING BUT SPARE BODIES TO THEM.

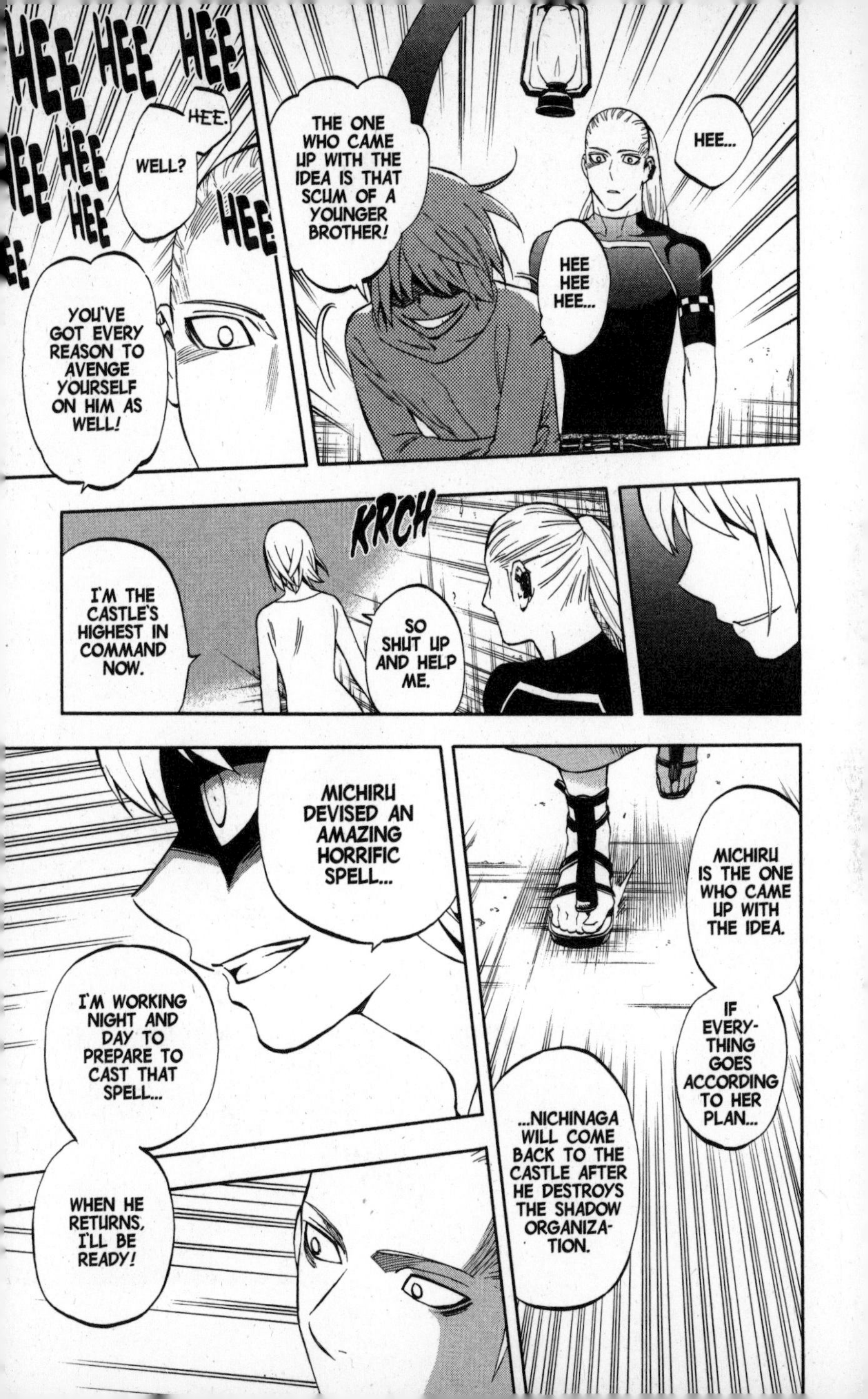
HEE...
THE ONE WHO CAME UP WITH THE IDEA IS THAT SCUM OF A YOUNGER BROTHER!
HEE HEE HEE...
HEE HEE HEE HEE HEE HEE HEE HEE
HEE.
WELL?
YOU'VE GOT EVERY REASON TO AVENGE YOURSELF ON HIM AS WELL!
KRCH
I'M THE CASTLE'S HIGHEST IN COMMAND NOW.
SO SHUT UP AND HELP ME.
MICHIRU IS THE ONE WHO CAME UP WITH THE IDEA.
IF EVERY-THING GOES ACCORDING TO HER PLAN...
...NICHINAGA WILL COME BACK TO THE CASTLE AFTER HE DESTROYS THE SHADOW ORGANIZA-TION.
MICHIRU DEVISED AN AMAZING HORRIFIC SPELL...
I'M WORKING NIGHT AND DAY TO PREPARE TO CAST THAT SPELL...
WHEN HE RETURNS, I'LL BE READY!

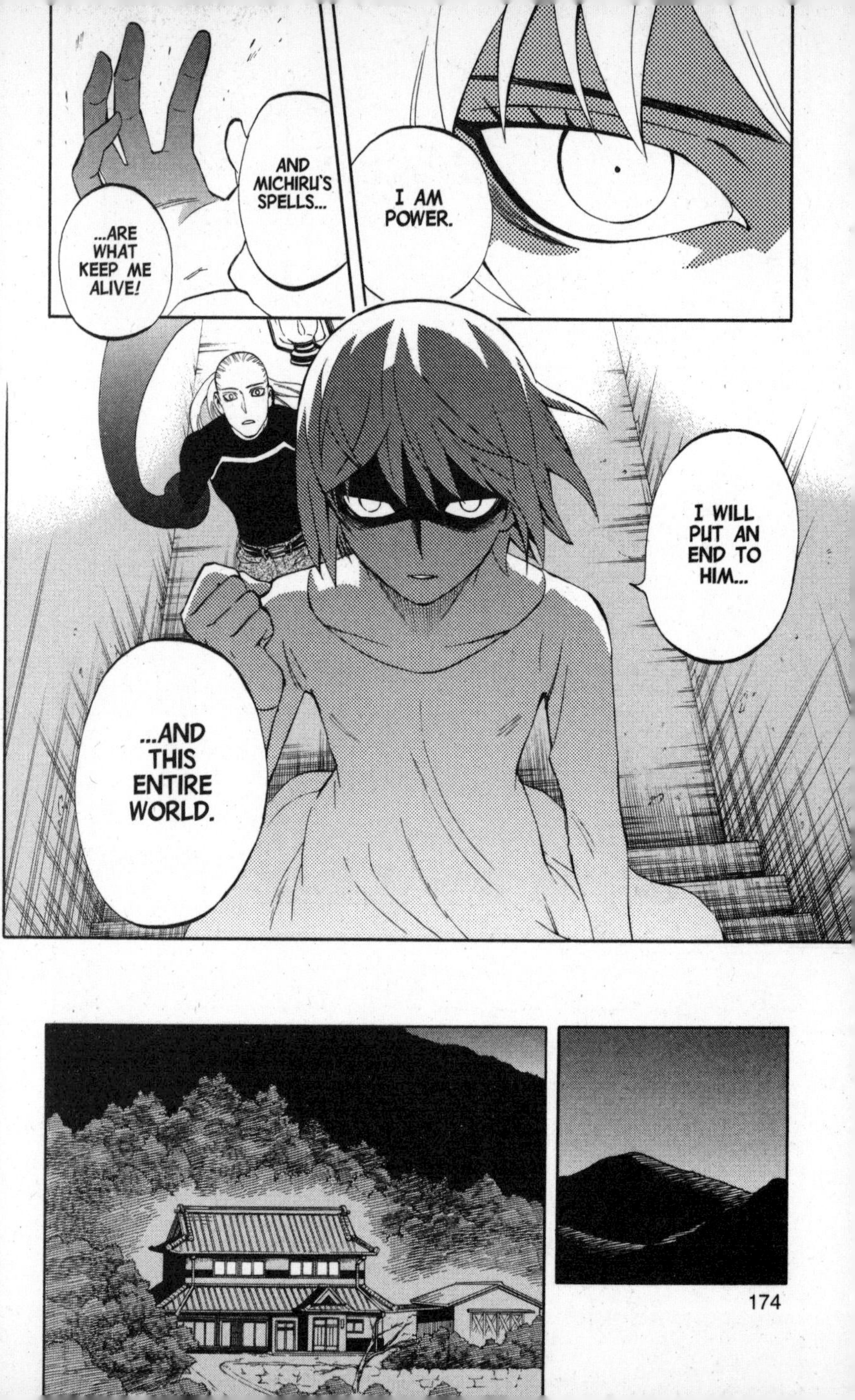
I AM POWER.
AND MICHIRU'S SPELLS...
...ARE WHAT KEEP ME ALIVE!
I WILL PUT AN END TO HIM...
...AND THIS ENTIRE WORLD.

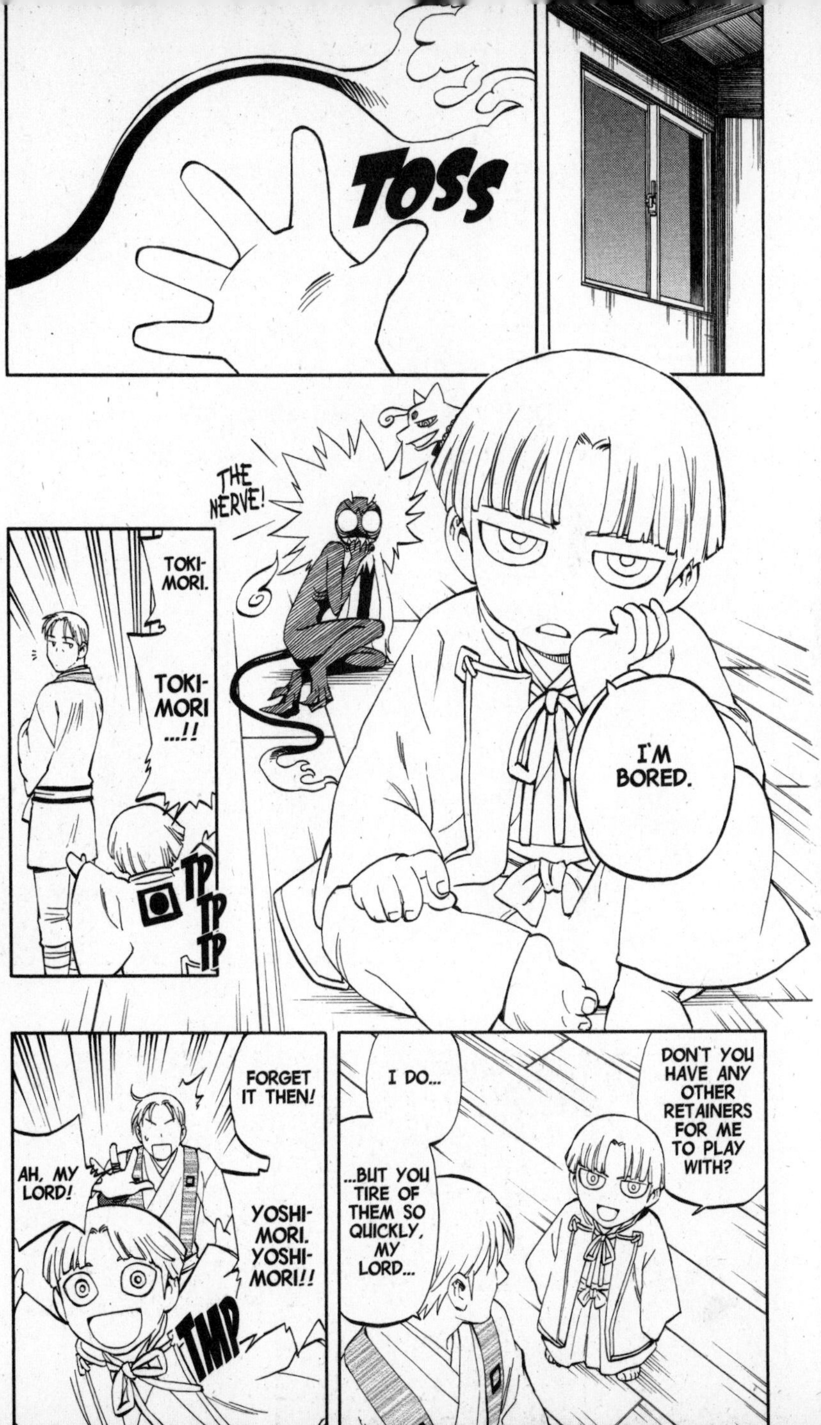
TOSS
THE NERVE!
I'M BORED.
TOKI-MORI.
TOKI-MORI...!!
TP TP TP
DON'T YOU HAVE ANY OTHER RETAINERS FOR ME TO PLAY WITH?
I DO...
...BUT YOU TIRE OF THEM SO QUICKLY, MY LORD...
FORGET IT THEN!
AH, MY LORD!
YOSHI-MORI. YOSHI-MORI!!
TMP

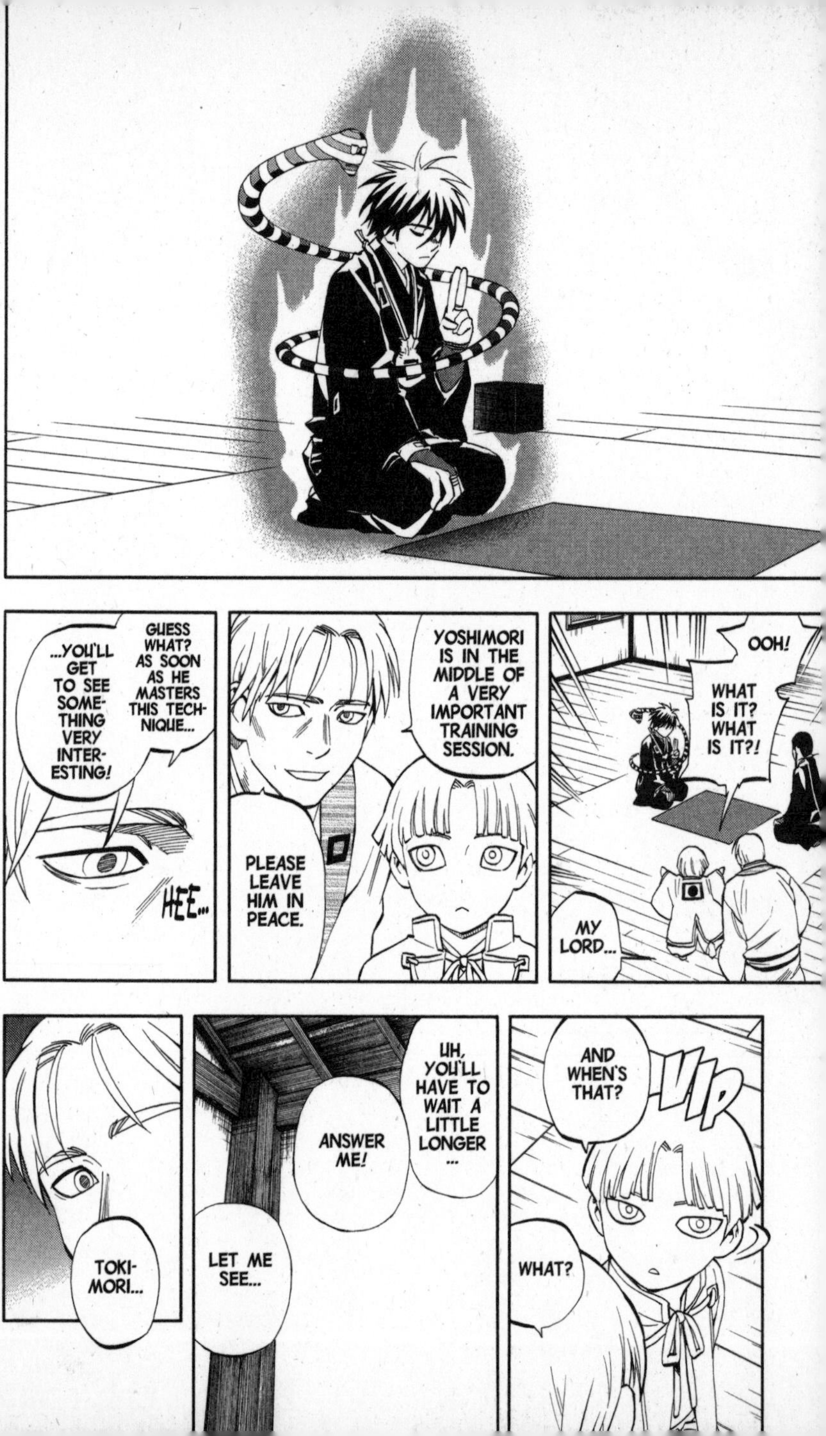
OOH!
WHAT IS IT? WHAT IS IT?!
MY LORD...
YOSHIMORI IS IN THE MIDDLE OF A VERY IMPORTANT TRAINING SESSION.
PLEASE LEAVE HIM IN PEACE.
GUESS WHAT? AS SOON AS HE MASTERS THIS TECHNIQUE...
...YOU'LL GET TO SEE SOMETHING VERY INTERESTING!
HEE...
AND WHEN'S THAT?
VIP
WHAT?
UH, YOU'LL HAVE TO WAIT A LITTLE LONGER...
ANSWER ME!
LET ME SEE...
TOKIMORI...

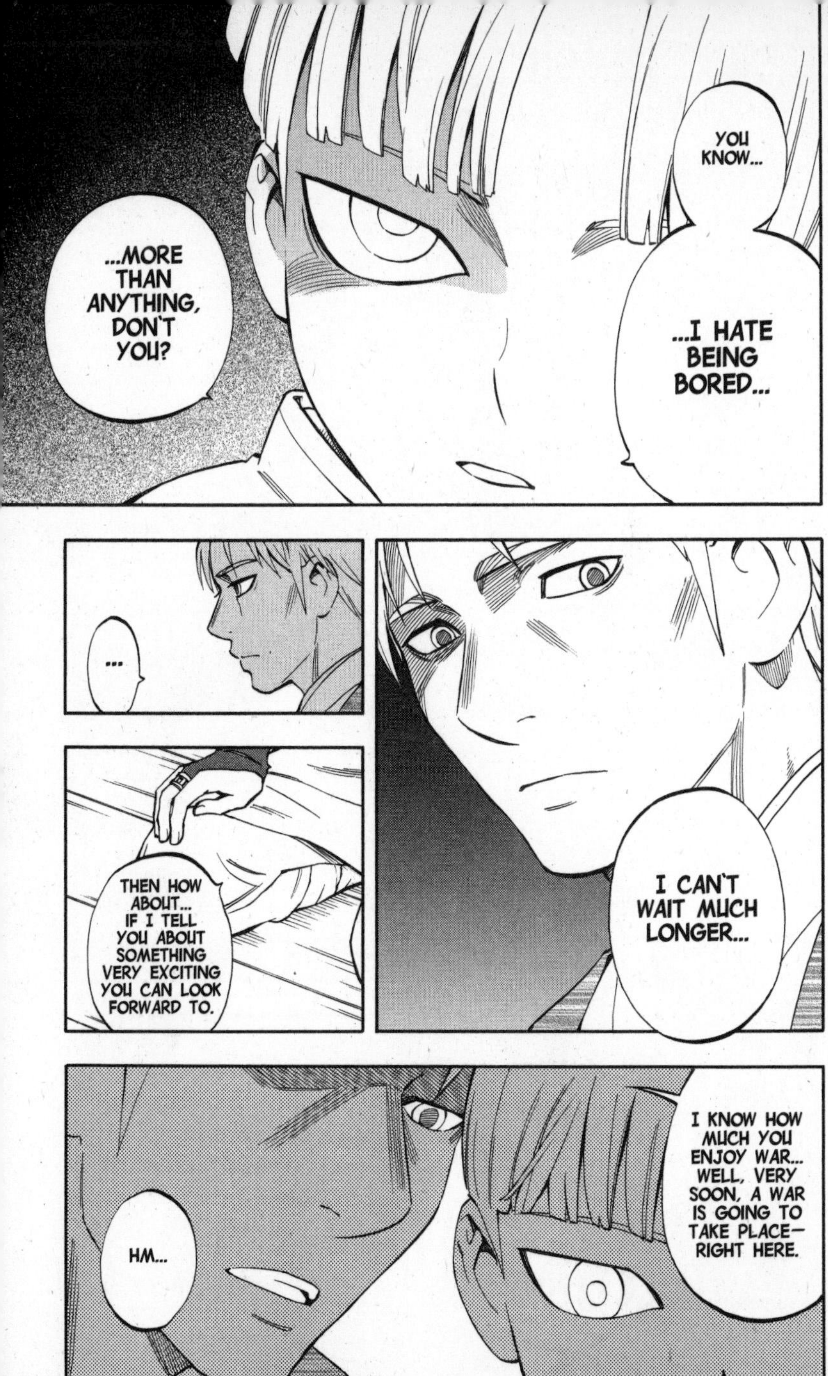
YOU KNOW...
...I HATE BEING BORED...
...MORE THAN ANYTHING, DON'T YOU?
I CAN'T WAIT MUCH LONGER...
...
THEN HOW ABOUT... IF I TELL YOU ABOUT SOMETHING VERY EXCITING YOU CAN LOOK FORWARD TO.
I KNOW HOW MUCH YOU ENJOY WAR... WELL, VERY SOON, A WAR IS GOING TO TAKE PLACE—RIGHT HERE.
HM...

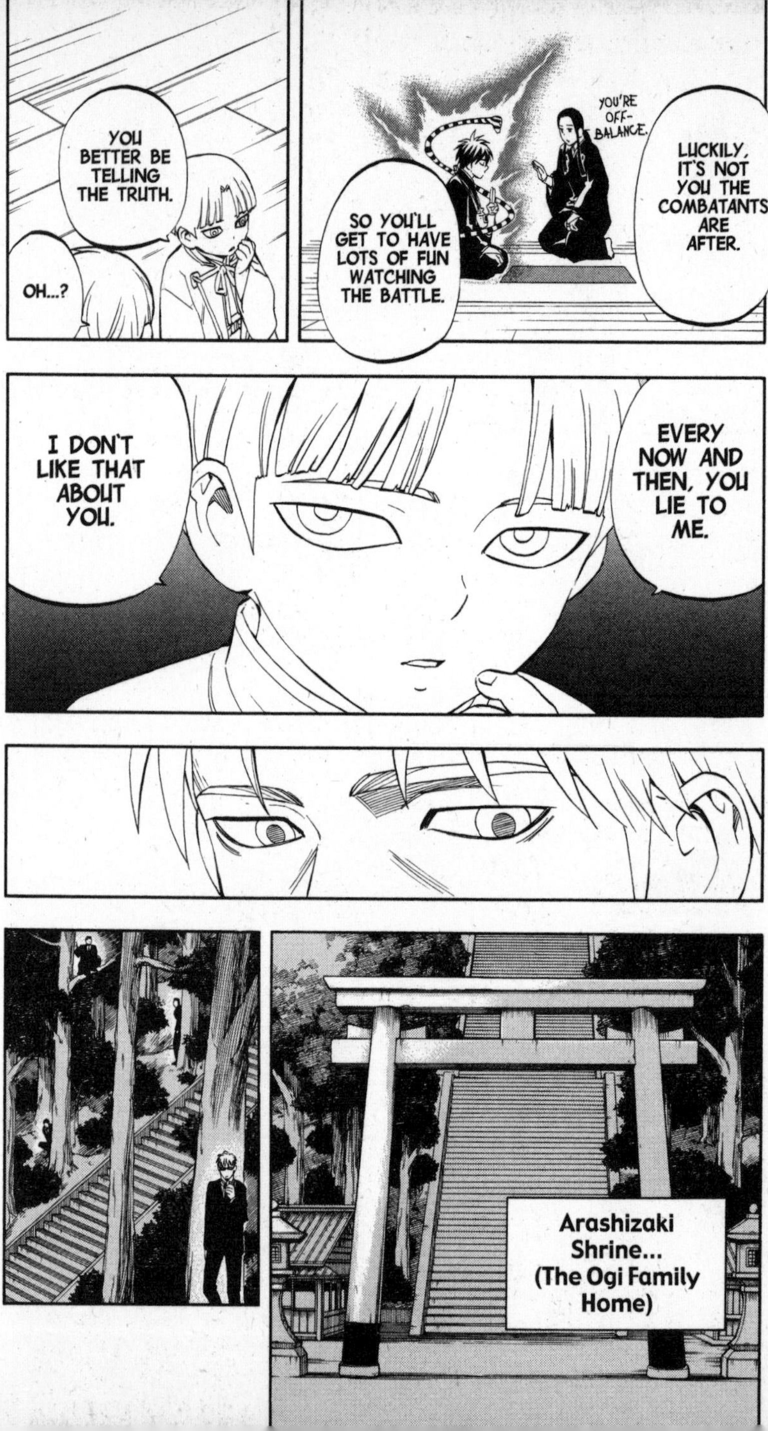
YOU'RE OFF-BALANCE.
LUCKILY, IT'S NOT YOU THE COMBATANTS ARE AFTER.
SO YOU'LL GET TO HAVE LOTS OF FUN WATCHING THE BATTLE.
YOU BETTER BE TELLING THE TRUTH.
OH...?
EVERY NOW AND THEN, YOU LIE TO ME.
I DON'T LIKE THAT ABOUT YOU.
Arashizaki Shrine... (The Ogi Family Home)

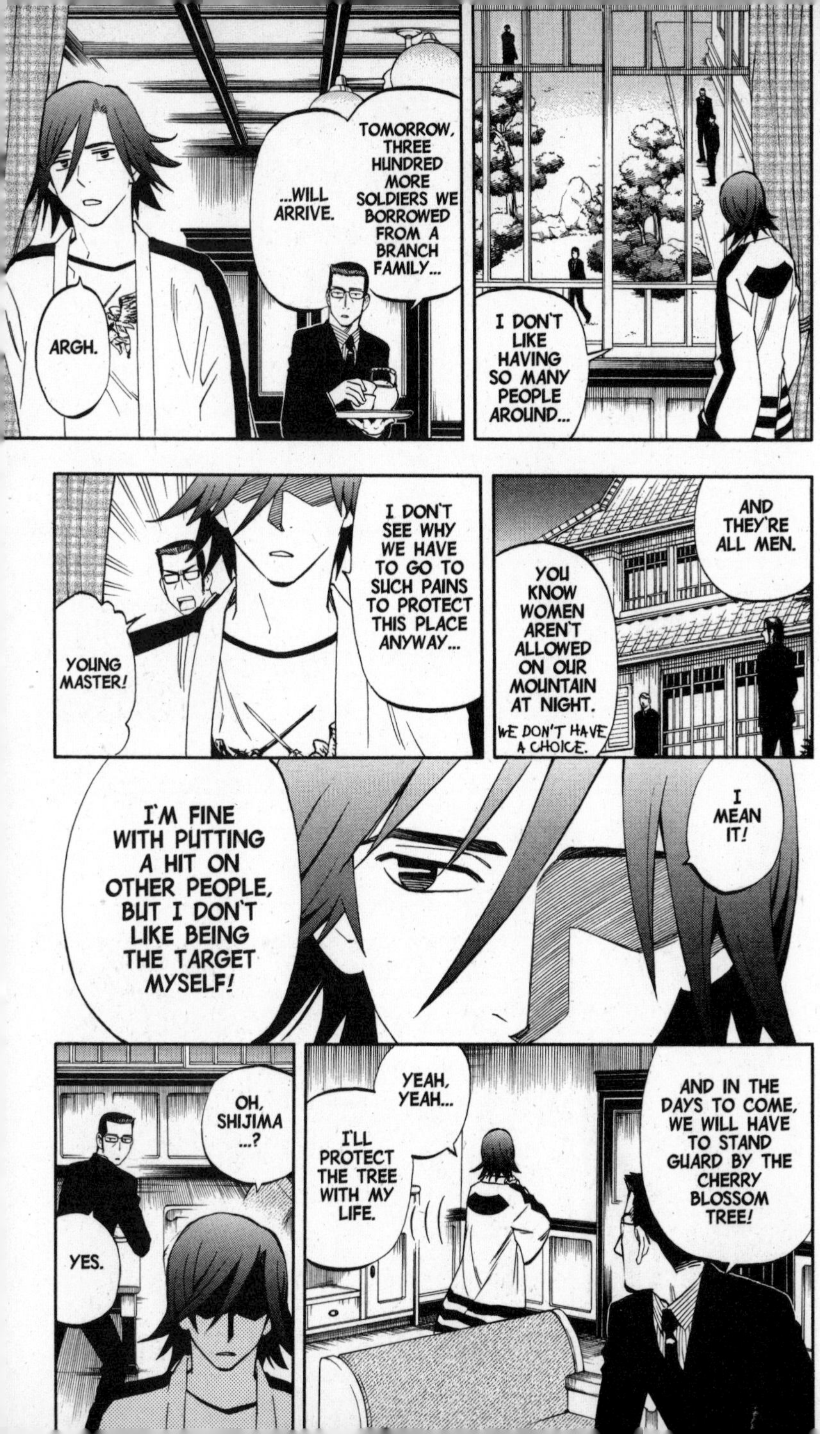
I DON'T LIKE HAVING SO MANY PEOPLE AROUND...
TOMORROW, THREE HUNDRED MORE SOLDIERS WE BORROWED FROM A BRANCH FAMILY...
...WILL ARRIVE.
ARGH.
AND THEY'RE ALL MEN.
YOU KNOW WOMEN AREN'T ALLOWED ON OUR MOUNTAIN AT NIGHT.
WE DON'T HAVE A CHOICE.
I DON'T SEE WHY WE HAVE TO GO TO SUCH PAINS TO PROTECT THIS PLACE ANYWAY...
YOUNG MASTER!
I'M FINE WITH PUTTING A HIT ON OTHER PEOPLE, BUT I DON'T LIKE BEING THE TARGET MYSELF!
I MEAN IT!
AND IN THE DAYS TO COME, WE WILL HAVE TO STAND GUARD BY THE CHERRY BLOSSOM TREE!
YEAH, YEAH...
I'LL PROTECT THE TREE WITH MY LIFE.
OH, SHIJIMA ...?
YES.

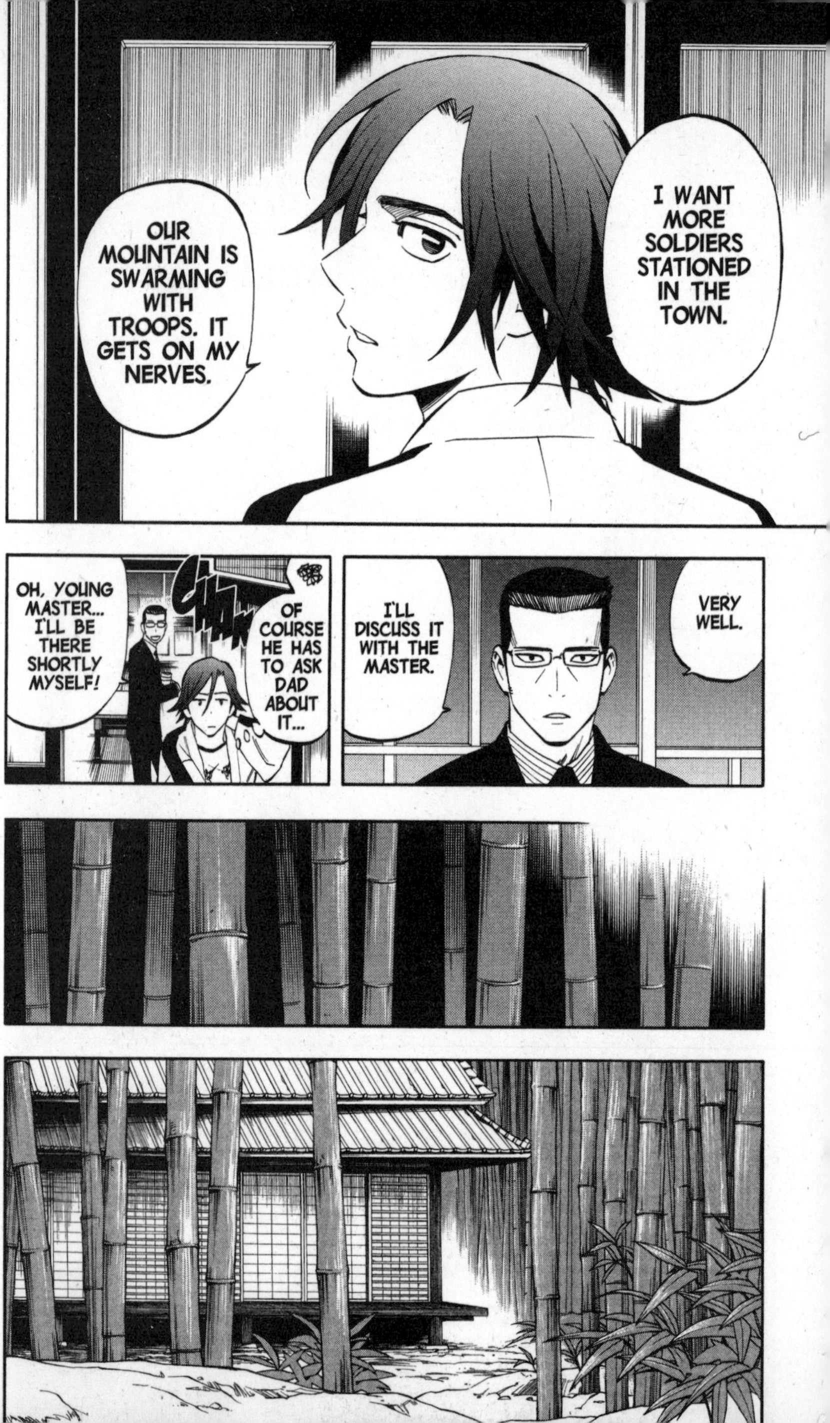
I WANT MORE SOLDIERS STATIONED IN THE TOWN.
OUR MOUNTAIN IS SWARMING WITH TROOPS. IT GETS ON MY NERVES.
VERY WELL.
I'LL DISCUSS IT WITH THE MASTER.
OF COURSE HE HAS TO ASK DAD ABOUT IT...
OH, YOUNG MASTER... I'LL BE THERE SHORTLY MYSELF!

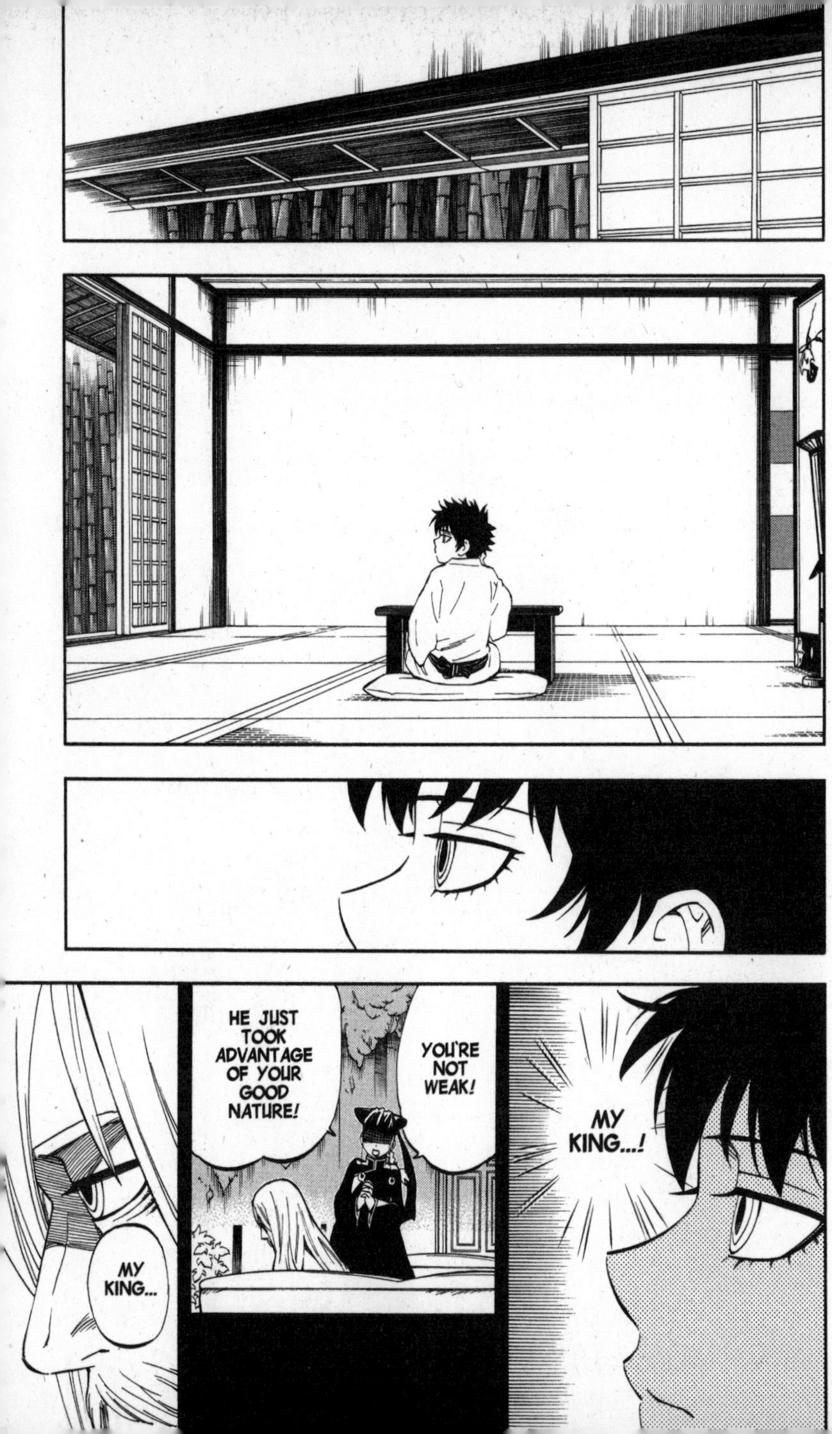
MY KING...!
YOU'RE NOT WEAK!
HE JUST TOOK ADVANTAGE OF YOUR GOOD NATURE!
MY KING...

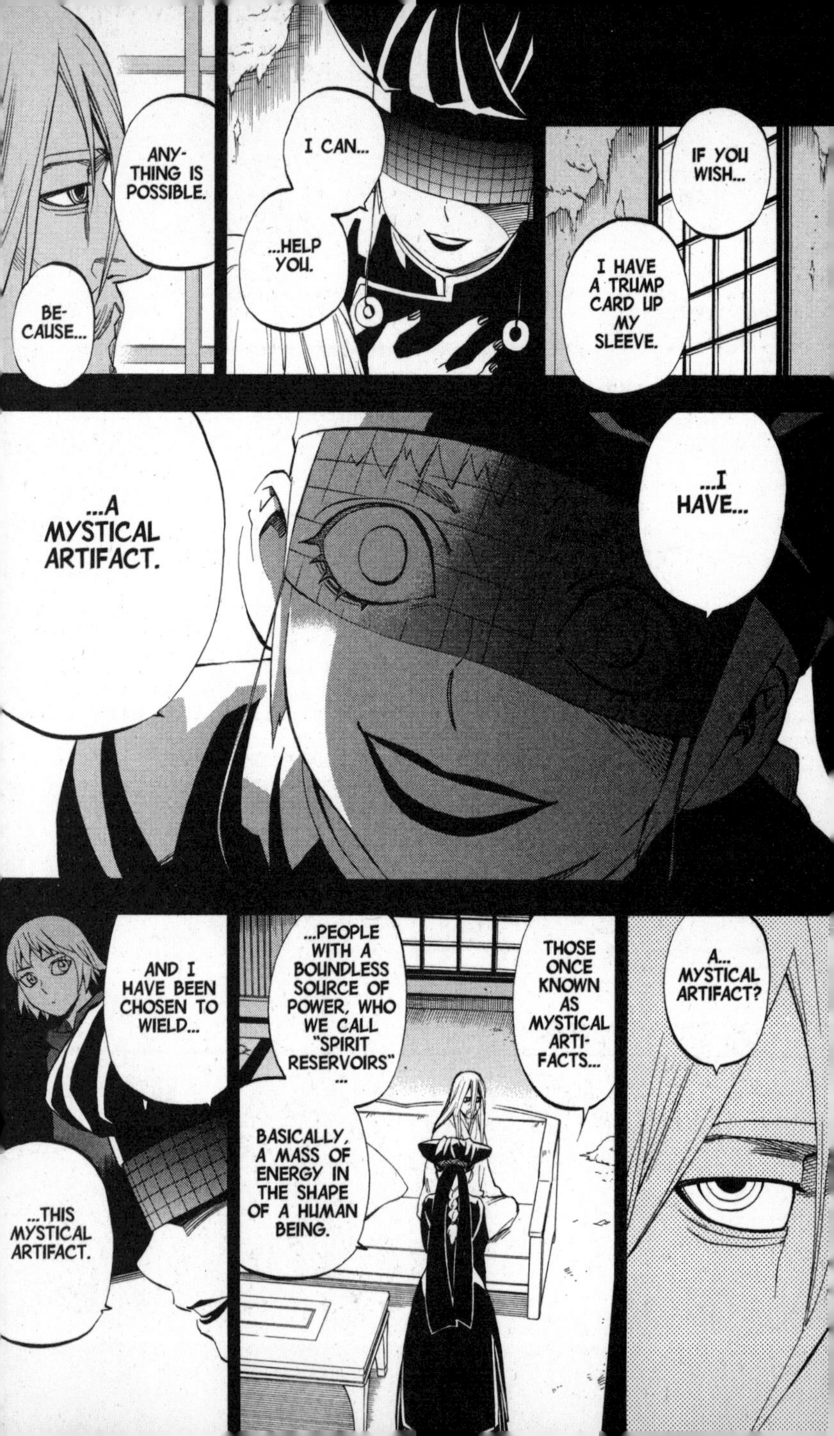
IF YOU WISH...
I HAVE A TRUMP CARD UP MY SLEEVE.
I CAN...
...HELP YOU.
ANY-THING IS POSSIBLE.
BE-CAUSE...
...I HAVE...
...A MYSTICAL ARTIFACT.
A... MYSTICAL ARTIFACT?
THOSE ONCE KNOWN AS MYSTICAL ARTI-FACTS...
...PEOPLE WITH A BOUNDLESS SOURCE OF POWER, WHO WE CALL "SPIRIT RESERVOIRS"...
BASICALLY, A MASS OF ENERGY IN THE SHAPE OF A HUMAN BEING.
AND I HAVE BEEN CHOSEN TO WIELD...
...THIS MYSTICAL ARTIFACT.

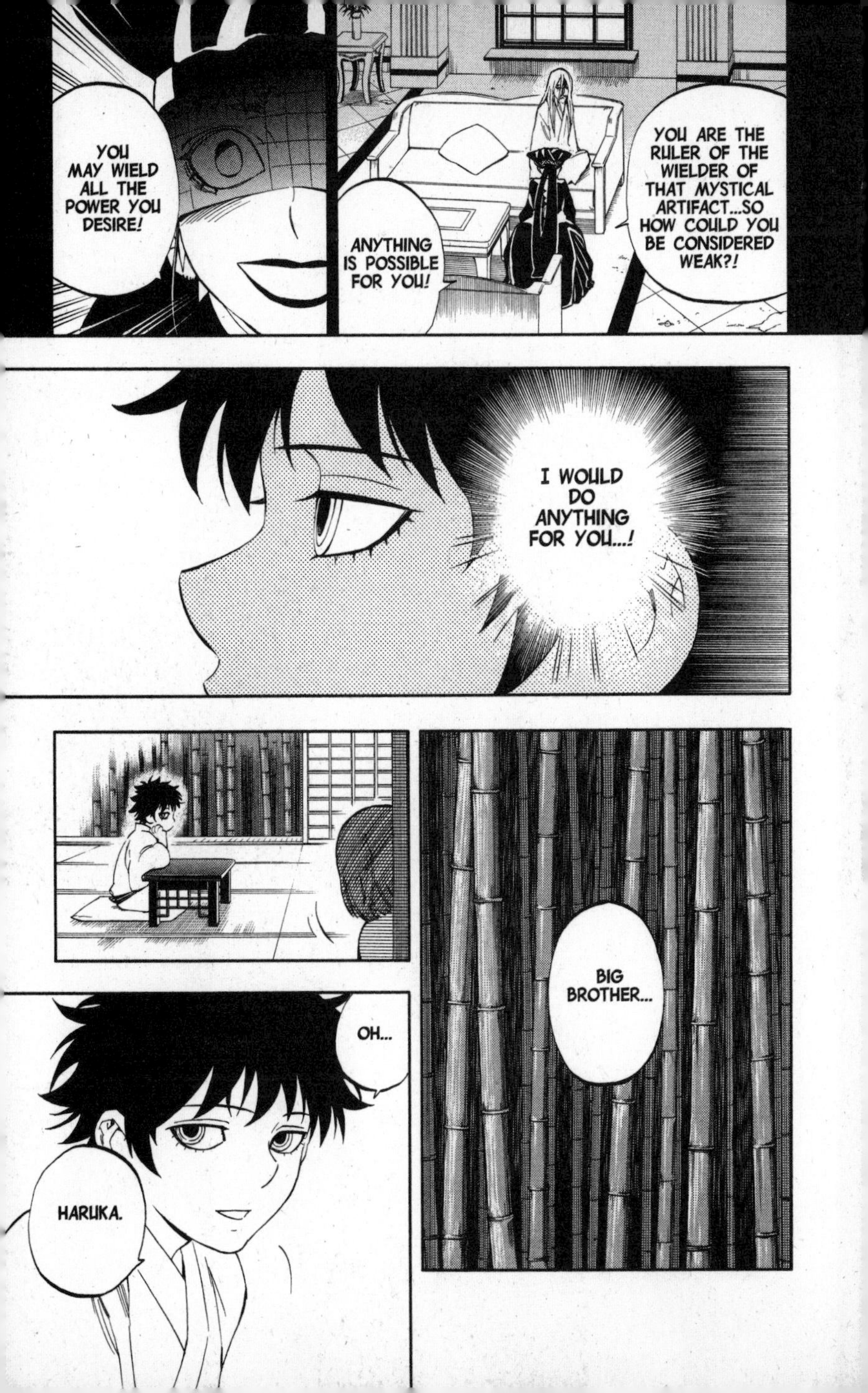
YOU ARE THE RULER OF THE WIELDER OF THAT MYSTICAL ARTIFACT...SO HOW COULD YOU BE CONSIDERED WEAK?!
ANYTHING IS POSSIBLE FOR YOU!
YOU MAY WIELD ALL THE POWER YOU DESIRE!
I WOULD DO ANYTHING FOR YOU...!
BIG BROTHER...
OH...
HARUKA.

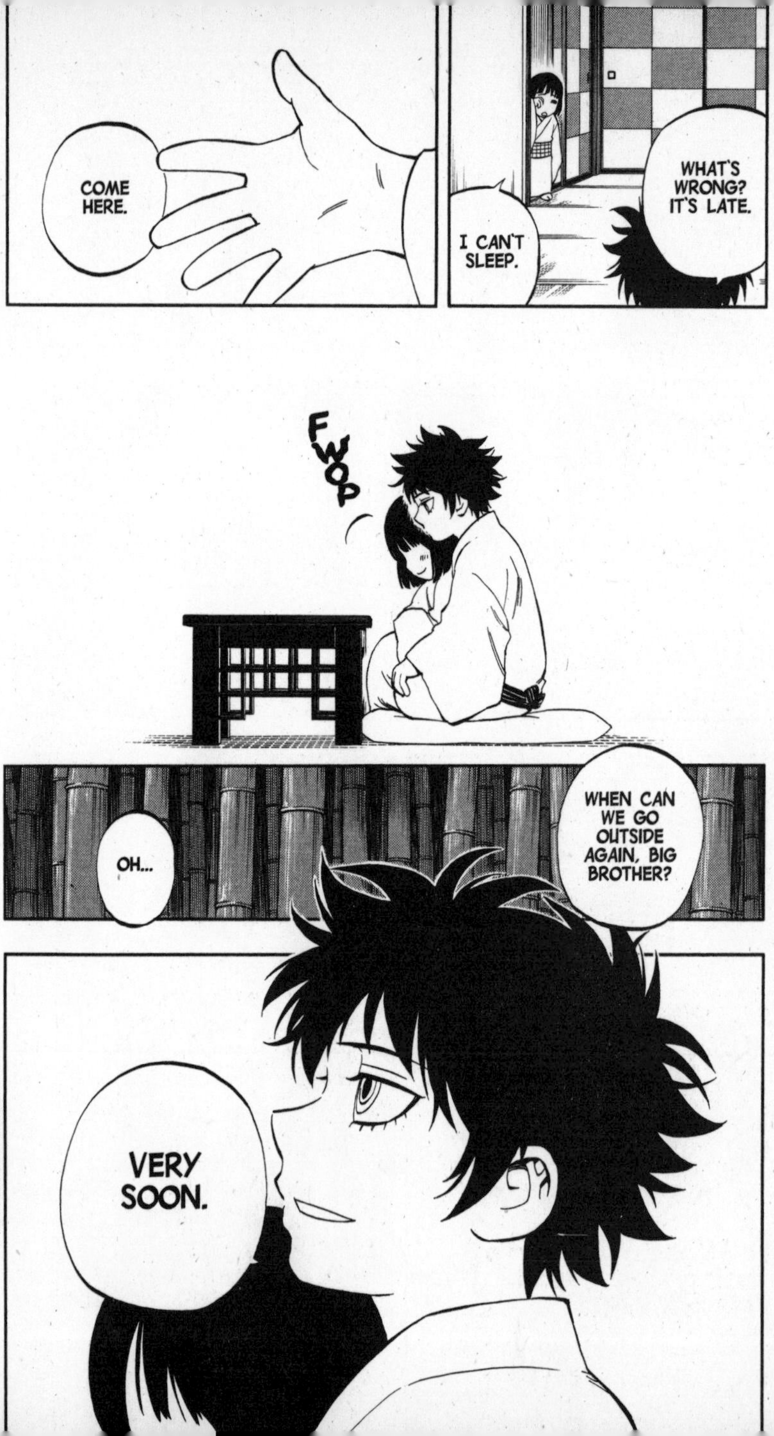
WHAT'S WRONG? IT'S LATE.
I CAN'T SLEEP.
COME HERE.
FWOP
WHEN CAN WE GO OUTSIDE AGAIN, BIG BROTHER?
OH...
VERY SOON.

TO BE CONTINUED...

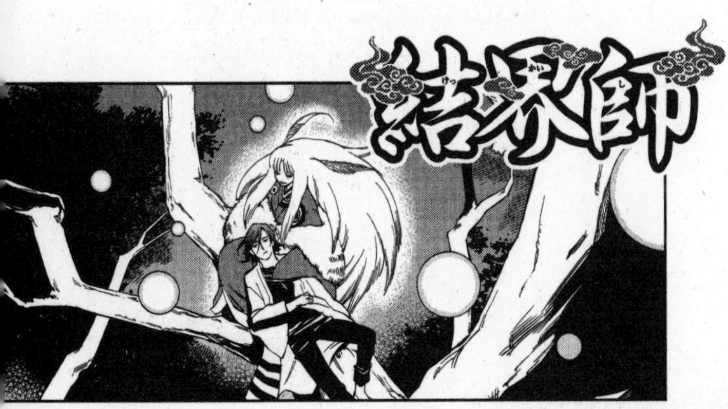
結界師

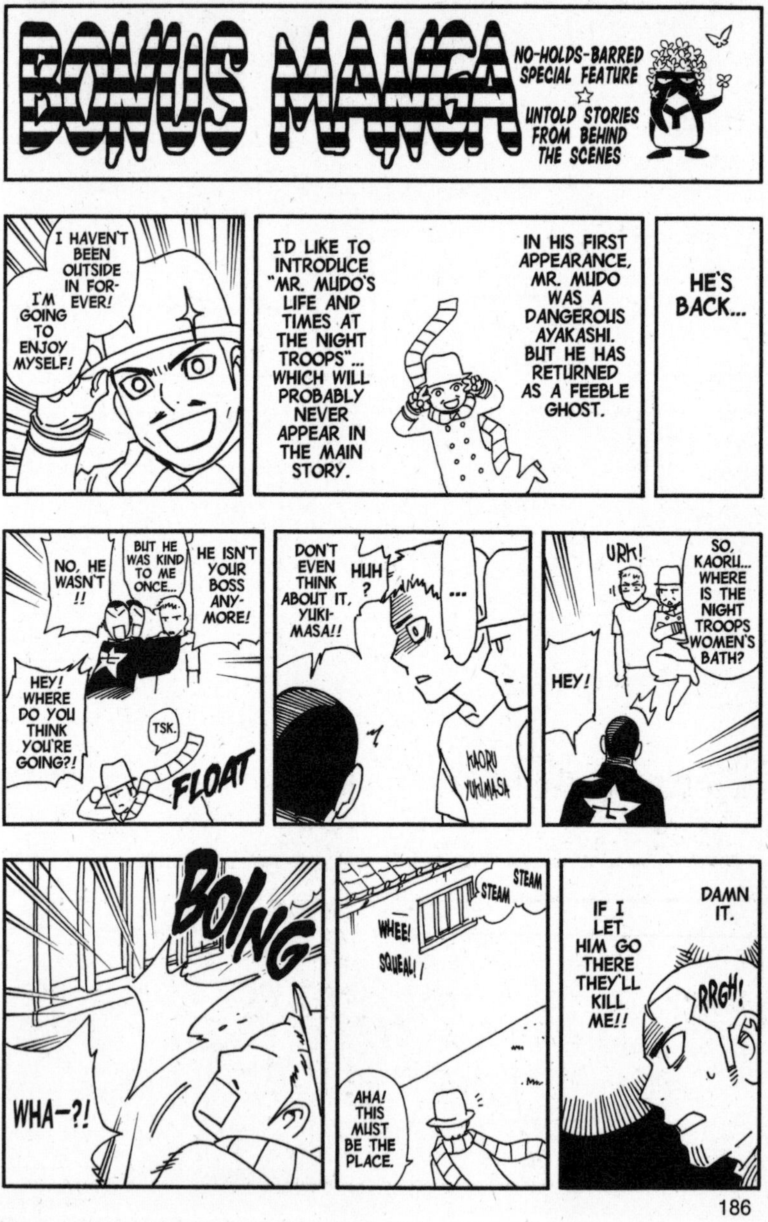
BONUS MANGA
NO-HOLDS-BARRED SPECIAL FEATURE ☆ UNTOLD STORIES FROM BEHIND THE SCENES
HE'S BACK...
IN HIS FIRST APPEARANCE, MR. MUDO WAS A DANGEROUS AYAKASHI. BUT HE HAS RETURNED AS A FEEBLE GHOST.
I'D LIKE TO INTRODUCE "MR. MUDO'S LIFE AND TIMES AT THE NIGHT TROOPS"... WHICH WILL PROBABLY NEVER APPEAR IN THE MAIN STORY.
I HAVEN'T BEEN OUTSIDE IN FOREVER! I'M GOING TO ENJOY MYSELF!
SO, KAORU... WHERE IS THE NIGHT TROOPS WOMEN'S BATH?
URK!
HEY!
HUH?
DON'T EVEN THINK ABOUT IT, YUKIMASA!!
...
KAORU YUKIMASA
HE ISN'T YOUR BOSS ANYMORE!
BUT HE WAS KIND TO ME ONCE...
NO, HE WASN'T!!
HEY! WHERE DO YOU THINK YOU'RE GOING?!
TSK.
FLOAT
DAMN IT.
IF I LET HIM GO THERE THEY'LL KILL ME!!
RRGH!
STEAM
STEAM
WHEE!
SQUEAL!
AHA! THIS MUST BE THE PLACE.
BOING
WHA-?!

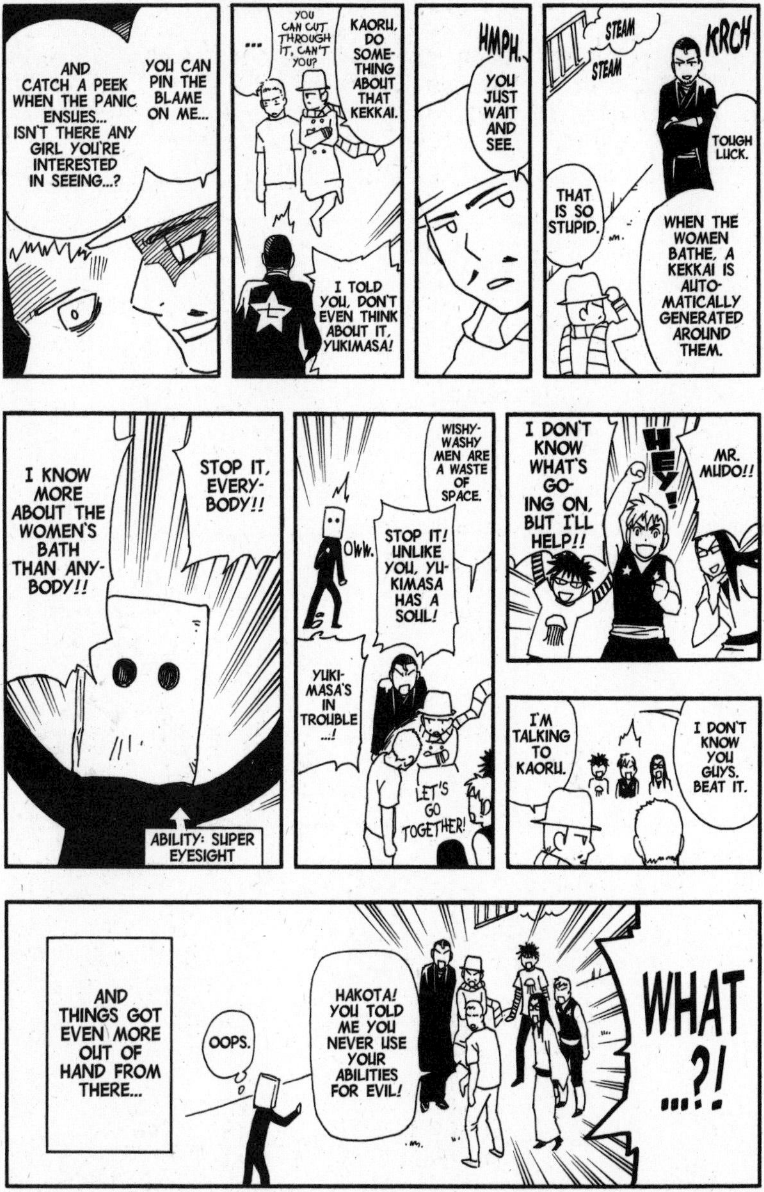
KRCH
STEAM
STEAM
TOUGH LUCK.
WHEN THE WOMEN BATHE, A KEKKAI IS AUTOMATICALLY GENERATED AROUND THEM.
THAT IS SO STUPID.
HMPH.
YOU JUST WAIT AND SEE.
KAORU, DO SOMETHING ABOUT THAT KEKKAI.
YOU CAN CUT THROUGH IT, CAN'T YOU?
...
I TOLD YOU, DON'T EVEN THINK ABOUT IT, YUKIMASA!
YOU CAN PIN THE BLAME ON ME...
AND CATCH A PEEK WHEN THE PANIC ENSUES... ISN'T THERE ANY GIRL YOU'RE INTERESTED IN SEEING...?
MR. MUDO!!
HEY!
I DON'T KNOW WHAT'S GOING ON, BUT I'LL HELP!!
I DON'T KNOW YOU GUYS. BEAT IT.
I'M TALKING TO KAORU.
WISHY-WASHY MEN ARE A WASTE OF SPACE.
STOP IT! UNLIKE YOU, YUKIMASA HAS A SOUL!
OWW.
YUKIMASA'S IN TROUBLE...!
LET'S GO TOGETHER!
STOP IT, EVERYBODY!!
I KNOW MORE ABOUT THE WOMEN'S BATH THAN ANYBODY!!
ABILITY: SUPER EYESIGHT
WHAT...?!
HAKOTA! YOU TOLD ME YOU NEVER USE YOUR ABILITIES FOR EVIL!
OOPS.
AND THINGS GOT EVEN MORE OUT OF HAND FROM THERE...

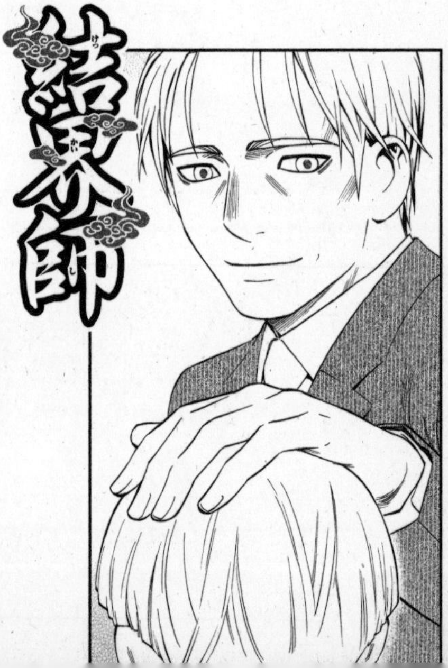
結界師

SO MANY SHAPES...!

MESSAGE FROM YELLOW TANABE

This time, I bought some small cacti on a whim.
The cactus shapes are really interesting.
They're all so geometrical.
I got so many of them, I haven't even given
them names yet.

KEKKAISHI

VOLUME 31

SHONEN SUNDAY EDITION

STORY AND ART BY YELLOW TANABE

Translation/Yuko Sawada
Touch-up Art & Lettering/Stephen Dutro
Cover Design & Graphic Layout/Ronnie Casson
Editor/Annette Roman

Printed in the U.S.A.

Published by VIZ Media, LLC
P.O. Box 77010
San Francisco, CA 94107

10 9 8 7 6 5 4 3 2 1
First printing, April 2012

www.viz.com

RATED T FOR TEEN

PARENTAL ADVISORY
KEKKAISHI is rated T for Teen and is recommended for ages 13 and up. It contains fantasy violence.
ratings.viz.com

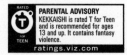

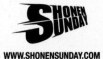

WWW.SHONENSUNDAY.COM

結界師
KEKKAISHI
»SET ONE«
EPISODES 1-13

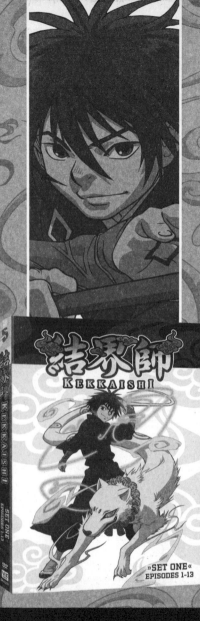

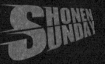